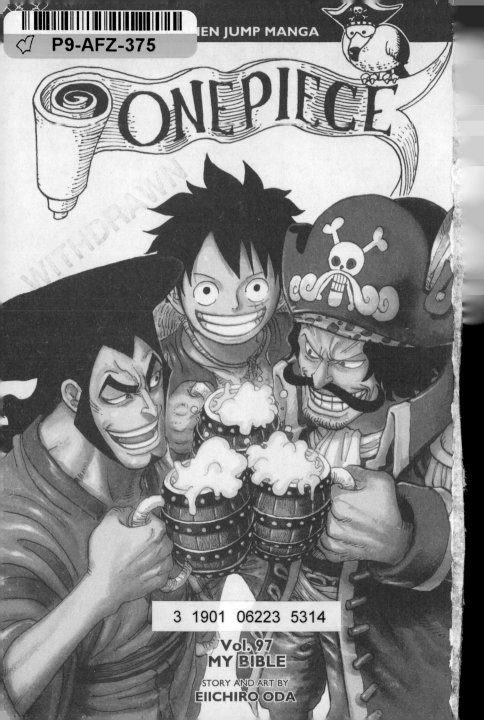

SHONEN JUMP MANGA

ONE PIECE

Vol. 97
MY BIBLE

STORY AND ART BY
EIICHIRO ODA

The Straw Hat Crew

Chopperemon [Ninja]
Tony Tony Chopper

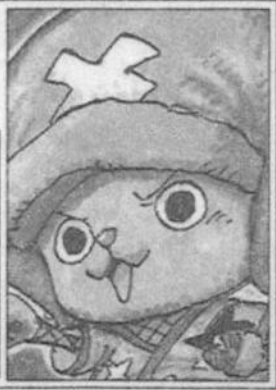

Studied powerful medicines in the Birdie Kingdom as he waited to rejoin the crew.

Ship's Doctor, Bounty: 100 berries

Luffytaro [Ronin]
Monkey D. Luffy

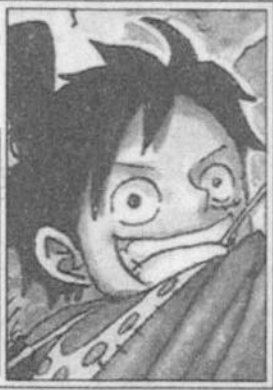

A young man dreaming of being the Pirate King. After two years of training he rejoins his friends in search of the New World!

Captain, Bounty: 1.5 billion berries

Orobi [Geisha]
Nico Robin

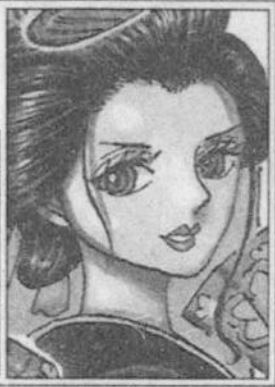

Spent time on the island of Baltigo with Dragon, Luffy's father and leader of the Revolutionary Army.

Archeologist, Bounty: 130 million berries

Zolojuro [Ronin]
Roronoa Zolo

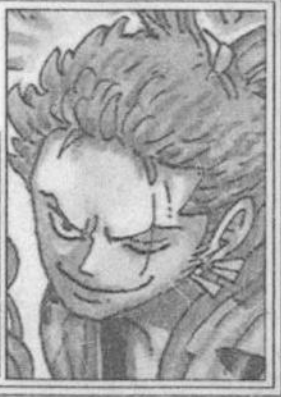

Swallowed his pride on Gloom Island and trained under Mihawk before rejoining Luffy.

Fighter, Bounty: 320 million berries

Franosuke [Carpenter]
Franky

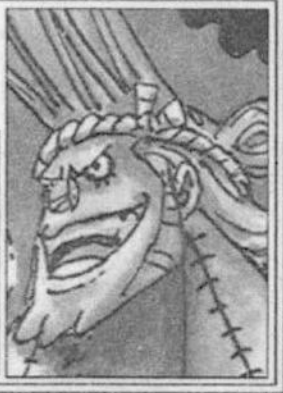

Upgraded himself into "Armored Franky" in the Future Land, Baldimore.

Shipwright, Bounty: 94 million berries

Onami [Kunoichi]
Nami

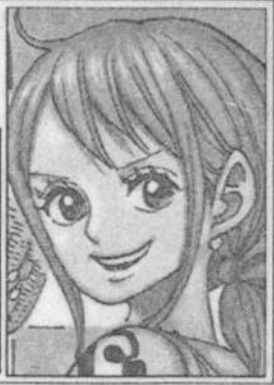

Learned about the climates of the New World on Weatheria, a Sky Island that studies the atmosphere.

Navigator, Bounty: 66 million berries

Bonekichi [Ghost]
Brook

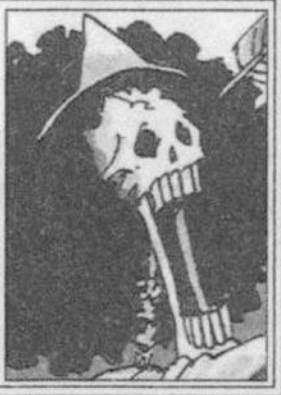

Originally captured by Long-Arm bandits for a freak show, he is now the mega-star "Soul King" Brook.

Musician, Bounty: 83 million berries

Usohachi [Toad Oil Salesman]
Usopp

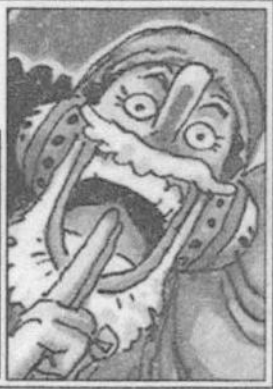

Received Heraclesun's lessons on the Bowin Islands in his quest to be the "king of the snipers."

Sniper, Bounty: 200 million berries

Shanks

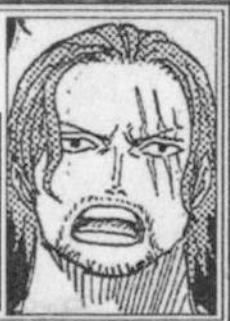

One of the Four Emperors. Waits for Luffy in the "New World," the second half of the Grand Line.

Captain of the Red-Haired Pirates

Sangoro [Soba Cook]
Sanji

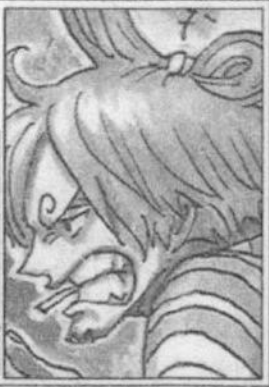

Honed his skills fighting with the masters of Newcomer Kenpo in the Kamabakka Kingdom.

Cook, Bounty: 330 million berries

The story of ONE PIECE 1»97

Land of Wano (Kozuki Clan)

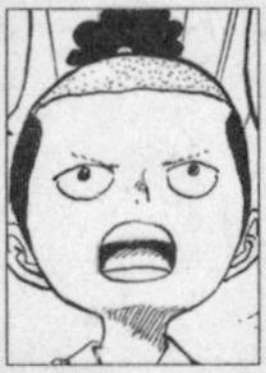

Kozuki Momonosuke

Daimyo (Heir) to Kuri in Wano

Akazaya Nine

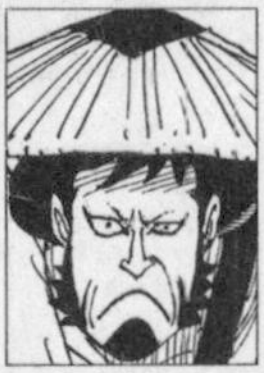

Foxfire Kin'emon

Samurai of Wano

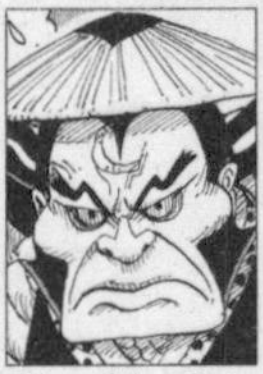

Raizo of the Mist

Ninja of Wano

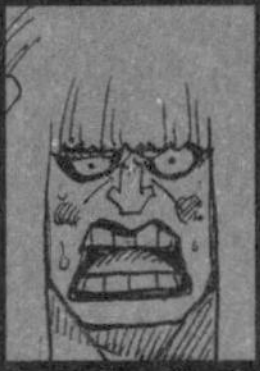

Evening Shower Kanjuro

Samurai of Wano

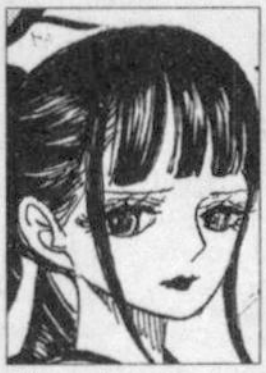

Kikunojo

Samurai of Wano

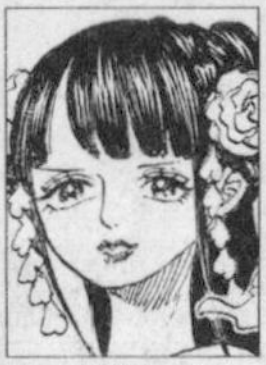

Kozuki Hiyori

Momonosuke's Little Sister

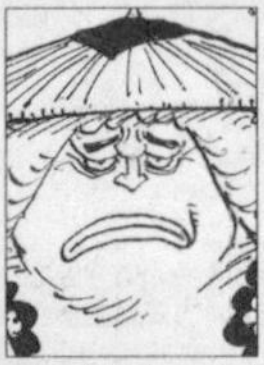

Ashura Doji (Shutenmaru)

Chief, Atamayama Thieves Brigade

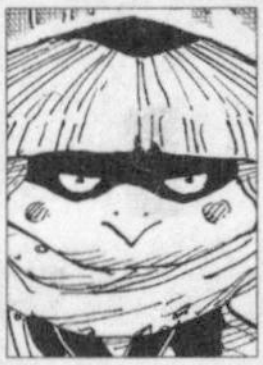

Kawamatsu

Samurai of Wano

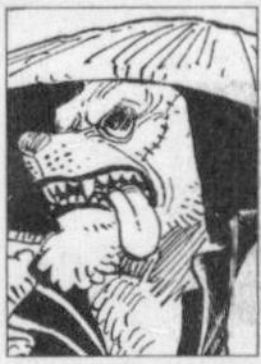

Duke Dogstorm

King of the Day, Mokomo

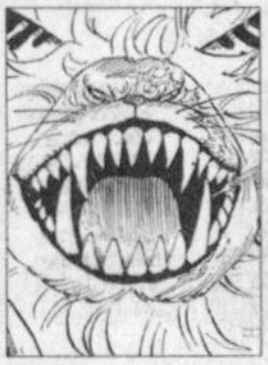

Cat Viper

King of the Night, Mokomo

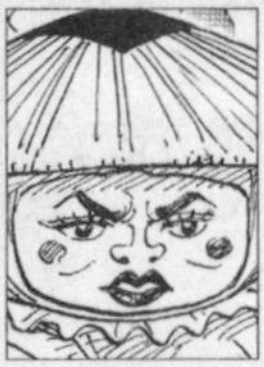

Shinobu

Veteran Kunoichi

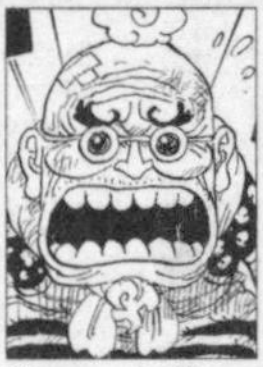

Hyogoro the Flower

Senior Yakuza Boss

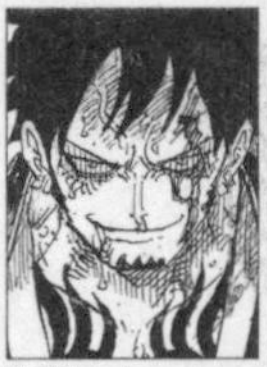

Trafalgar Law

Captain, Heart Pirates

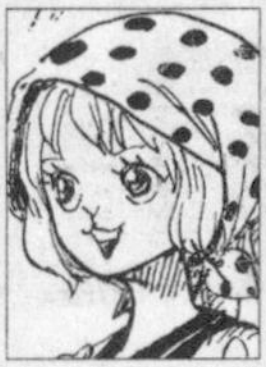

Carrot (Bunny Mink)

Battlebeast Tribe, Kingsbird

Kozuki Oden

Sailed around the world with Roger. But when he returned to Wano, he was killed by Orochi's trap.

Heir to the Shogunate of Wano

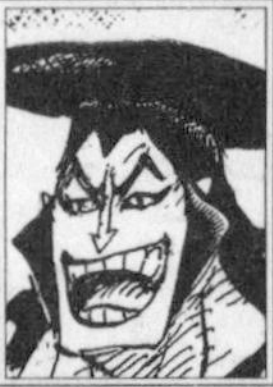

Kid Pirates

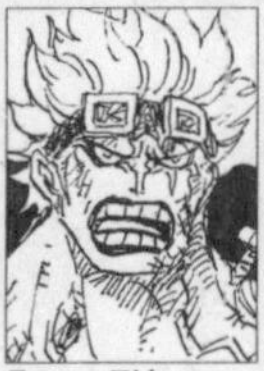

Eustass Kid

Captain, Kid Pirates

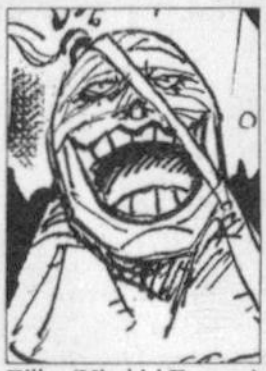

Killer (Hitokiri Kamazo)

Fighter, Kid Pirates

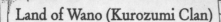

Land of Wano (Kurozumi Clan)

Kurozumi Orochi

The ruler of Wano, using Kaido's help. He cunningly schemed to overthrow his archenemy, the Kozuki Clan.

Shogun of Wano

Fukurokuju

Leader, Orochi Oniwabanshu

Orochi Oniwabanshu

Shogun of Wano's Private Ninja Squad

Napping Kyoshiro

Money Changer for the Kurozumi Clan

Kurozumi Kanjuro

Orochi's Spy

Big Mom Pirates

Big Mom
(Emperor of the Sea)

One of the Four Emperors. Uses the Soul-Soul Fruit that extracts life span from others.

Captain, Big Mom Pirates

no-show because of Orochi's schemes...

Twenty years ago, Orochi and Kaido set a trap that cost Kozuki Oden his life. In order to avenge his death, the Akazaya rush into battle rather than waiting for the Straw Hats to arrive. But they were shocked by what they learned next!! Kanjuro, whom they believed was their companion, was actually a spy for Orochi!! The rest of the samurai are stunned, but then Luffy appears at last...

Animal Kingdom Pirates

Kaido, King of the Beasts
(Emperor of the Sea)

A pirate known as the "strongest creature alive." Despite numerous tortures and death sentences, none have been able to kill him.

Captain, Animal Kingdom Pirates

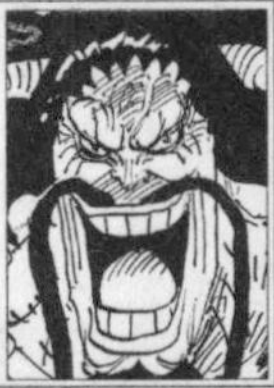

Lead Performers

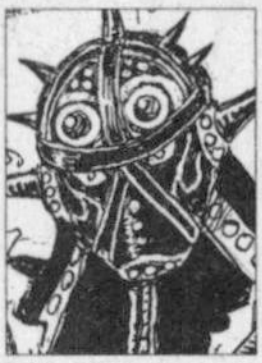
King the Wildfire

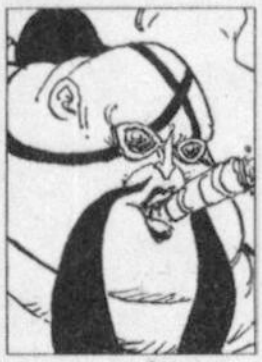
Queen the Plague

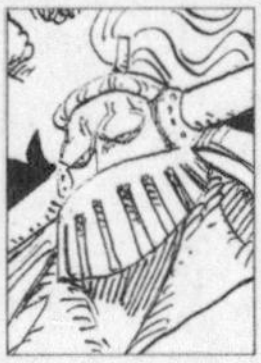
Jack the Drought

Tobi Roppo

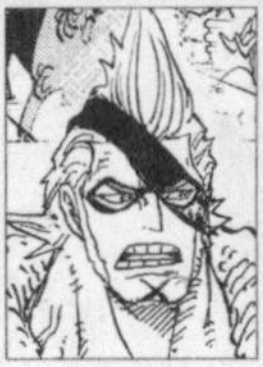
X. (Diez) Drake

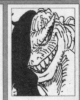

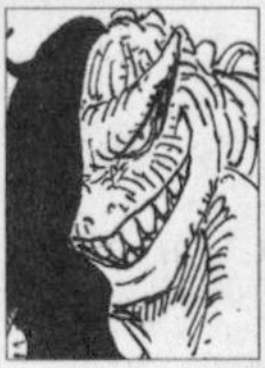
Page One

Headliners

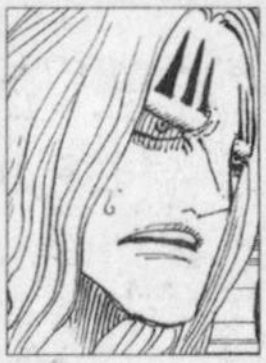
Basil Hawkins

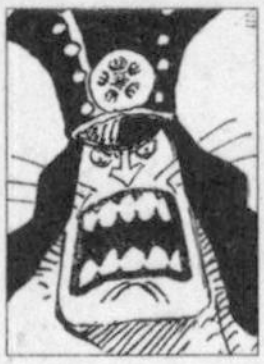
Holdem

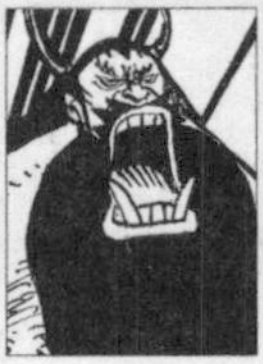
Babanuki

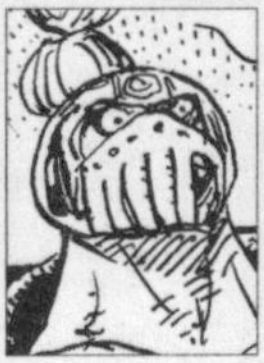
Daifugo

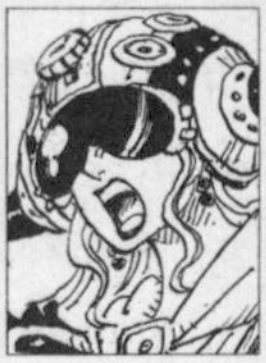
Solitaire

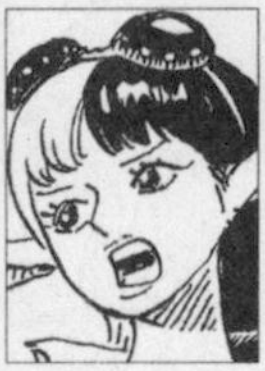
Speed

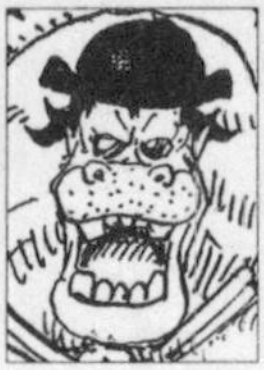
Dobon

Story

After two years of hard training, the Straw Hat pirates are back together, first at the Sabaody Archipelago and then through Fish-Man Island to their next stage: the New World!!

Luffy and crew disembark on Wano for the purpose of defeating Kaido, one of the Four Emperors. They begin to recruit allies for a raid in two weeks' time. But Kaido's side finds out, and the plan is in peril. With great effort, the alliance rebounds and gathers members to await the day of the raid. But on the big day, the Straw Hats are a

WANO

ONE PIECE

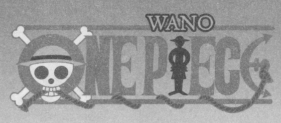

Vol. 97
MY BIBLE

CONTENTS

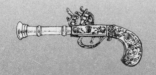

Chapter 975:
KIN'EMON'S CLEVER TRICK

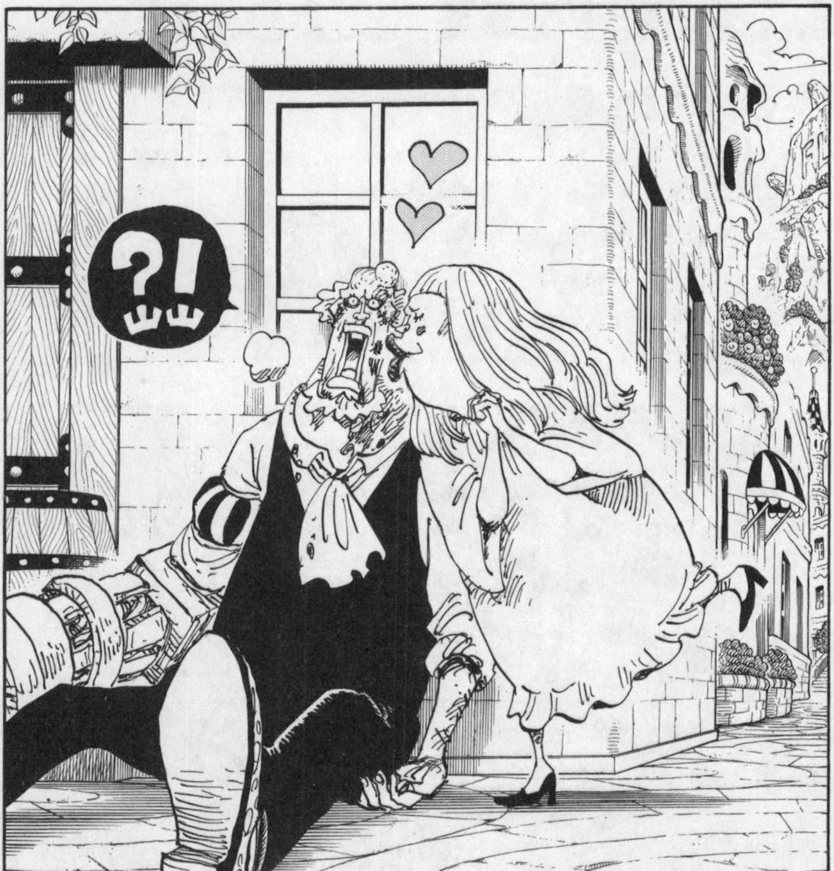
?!

GANG BEGE'S OH MY FAMILY
VOL. 23: "THANK YOU, WHOEVER YOU ARE ♡"

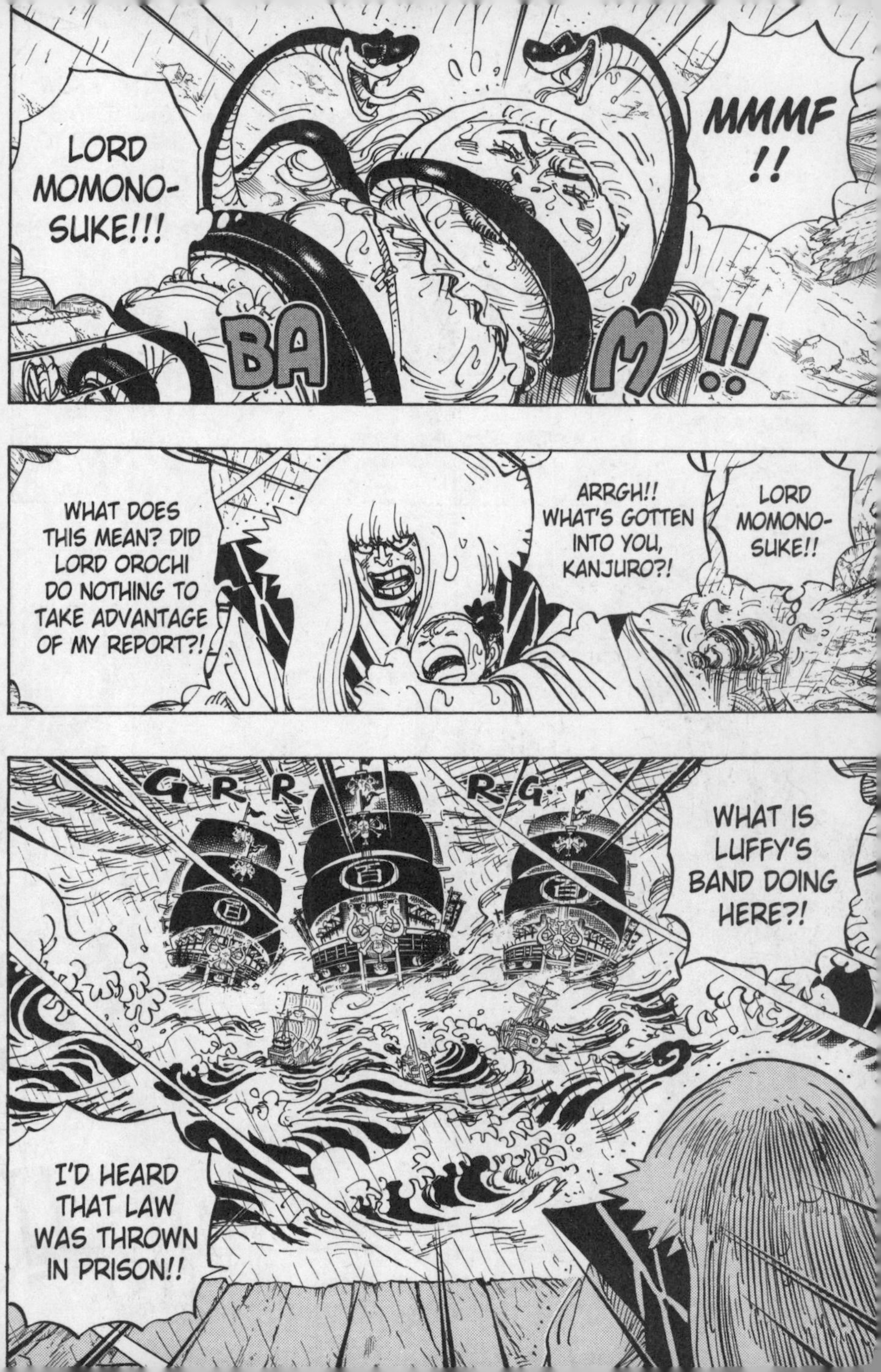
MMMF !!
LORD MOMONO-SUKE!!!
BAM!!
LORD MOMONO-SUKE!!
ARRGH!! WHAT'S GOTTEN INTO YOU, KANJURO?!
WHAT DOES THIS MEAN? DID LORD OROCHI DO NOTHING TO TAKE ADVANTAGE OF MY REPORT?!
GRRRG
WHAT IS LUFFY'S BAND DOING HERE?!
I'D HEARD THAT LAW WAS THROWN IN PRISON!!

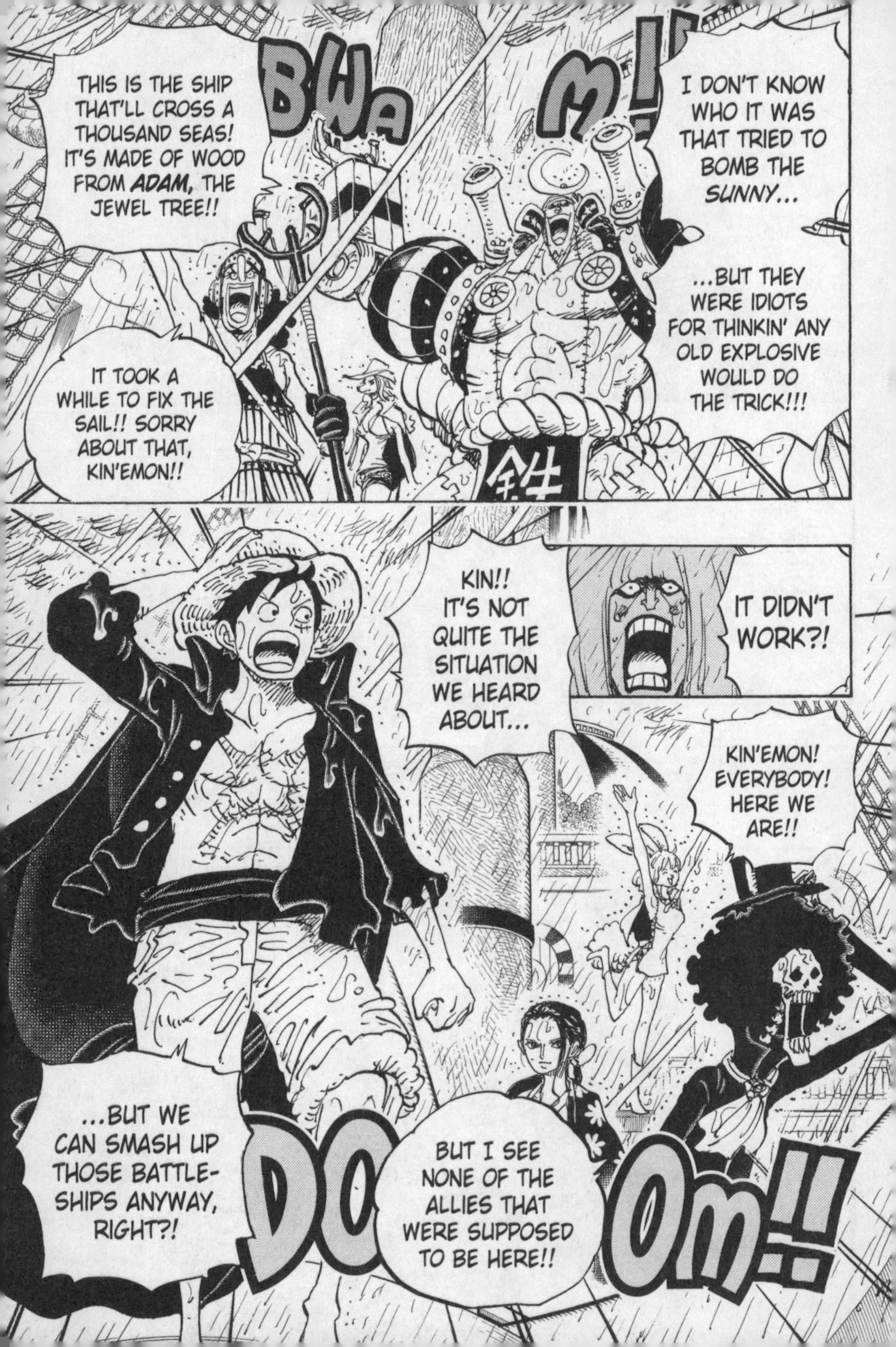
I DON'T KNOW WHO IT WAS THAT TRIED TO BOMB THE *SUNNY*...
BWAM!!
THIS IS THE SHIP THAT'LL CROSS A THOUSAND SEAS! IT'S MADE OF WOOD FROM *ADAM*, THE JEWEL TREE!!
...BUT THEY WERE IDIOTS FOR THINKIN' ANY OLD EXPLOSIVE WOULD DO THE TRICK!!!
IT TOOK A WHILE TO FIX THE SAIL!! SORRY ABOUT THAT, KIN'EMON!!
IT DIDN'T WORK?!
KIN'EMON! EVERYBODY! HERE WE ARE!!
KIN!! IT'S NOT QUITE THE SITUATION WE HEARD ABOUT...
BUT I SEE NONE OF THE ALLIES THAT WERE SUPPOSED TO BE HERE!!
DOOM!!
...BUT WE CAN SMASH UP THOSE BATTLE-SHIPS ANYWAY, RIGHT?!

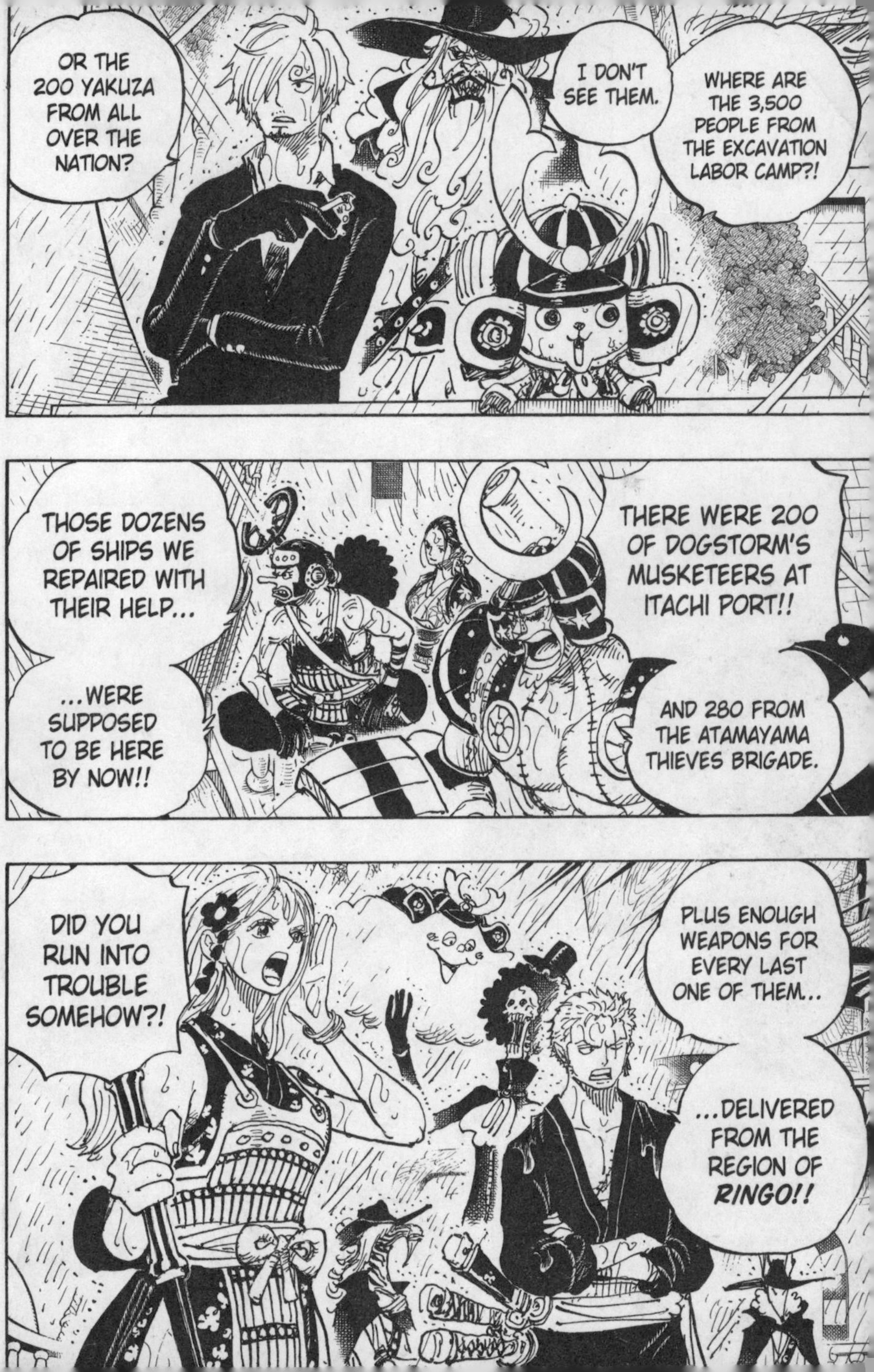

WHERE ARE THE 3,500 PEOPLE FROM THE EXCAVATION LABOR CAMP?!
I DON'T SEE THEM.
OR THE 200 YAKUZA FROM ALL OVER THE NATION?
THERE WERE 200 OF DOGSTORM'S MUSKETEERS AT ITACHI PORT!!
AND 280 FROM THE ATAMAYAMA THIEVES BRIGADE.
THOSE DOZENS OF SHIPS WE REPAIRED WITH THEIR HELP...
...WERE SUPPOSED TO BE HERE BY NOW!!
PLUS ENOUGH WEAPONS FOR EVERY LAST ONE OF THEM...
...DELIVERED FROM THE REGION OF *RINGO!!*
DID YOU RUN INTO TROUBLE SOMEHOW?!

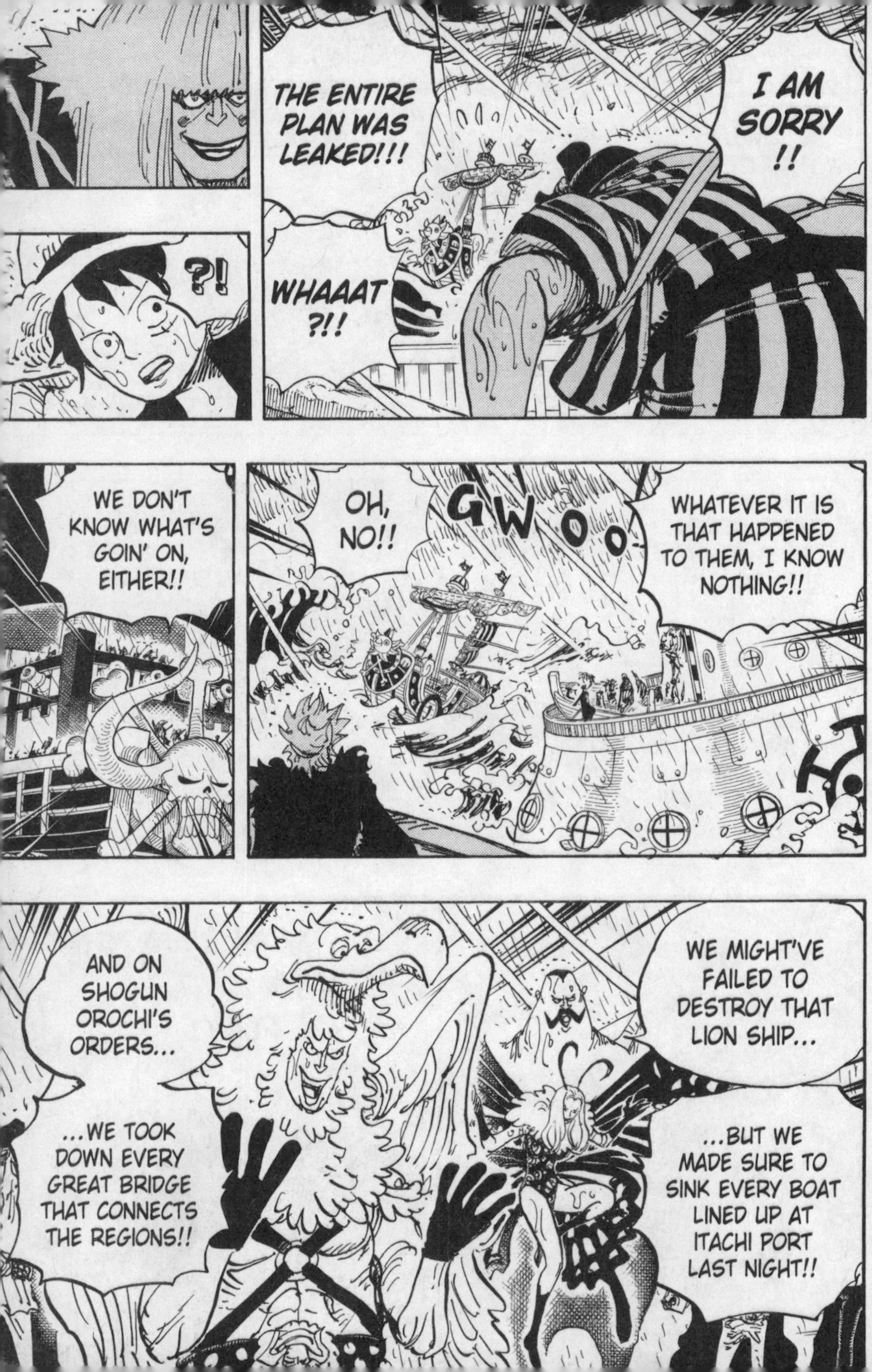
I AM SORRY!!
THE ENTIRE PLAN WAS LEAKED!!!
WHAAAT?!!
?!
WHATEVER IT IS THAT HAPPENED TO THEM, I KNOW NOTHING!!
GWOO
OH, NO!!
WE DON'T KNOW WHAT'S GOIN' ON, EITHER!!
WE MIGHT'VE FAILED TO DESTROY THAT LION SHIP...
...BUT WE MADE SURE TO SINK EVERY BOAT LINED UP AT ITACHI PORT LAST NIGHT!!
AND ON SHOGUN OROCHI'S ORDERS...
...WE TOOK DOWN EVERY GREAT BRIDGE THAT CONNECTS THE REGIONS!!

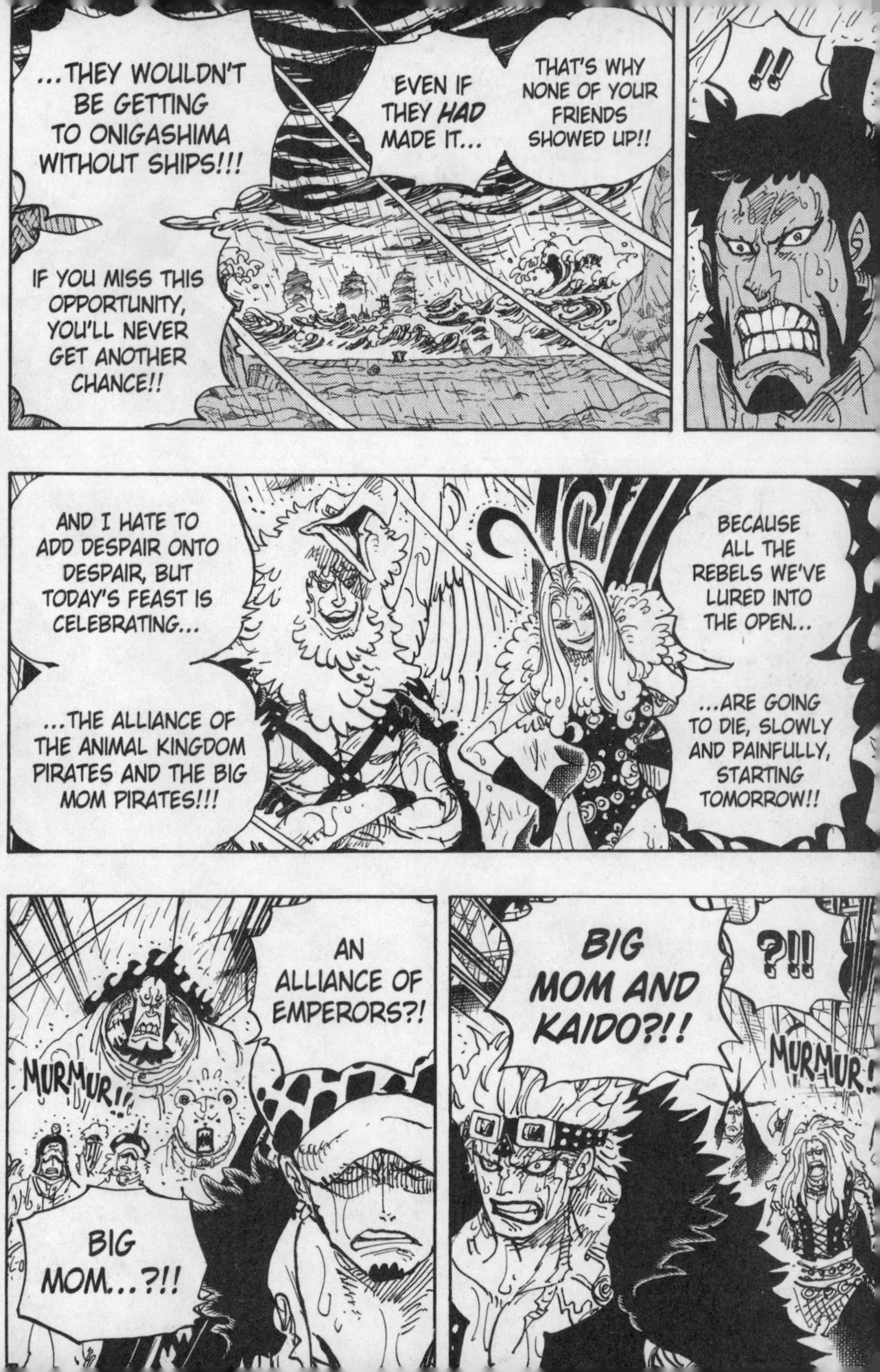
!!
THAT'S WHY NONE OF YOUR FRIENDS SHOWED UP!!
EVEN IF THEY *HAD* MADE IT...
...THEY WOULDN'T BE GETTING TO ONIGASHIMA WITHOUT SHIPS!!!
IF YOU MISS THIS OPPORTUNITY, YOU'LL NEVER GET ANOTHER CHANCE!!
BECAUSE ALL THE REBELS WE'VE LURED INTO THE OPEN...
...ARE GOING TO DIE, SLOWLY AND PAINFULLY, STARTING TOMORROW!!
AND I HATE TO ADD DESPAIR ONTO DESPAIR, BUT TODAY'S FEAST IS CELEBRATING...
...THE ALLIANCE OF THE ANIMAL KINGDOM PIRATES AND THE BIG MOM PIRATES!!!
?!!
BIG MOM AND KAIDO?!!
MURMUR
AN ALLIANCE OF EMPERORS?!
MURMUR!!
BIG MOM...?!!

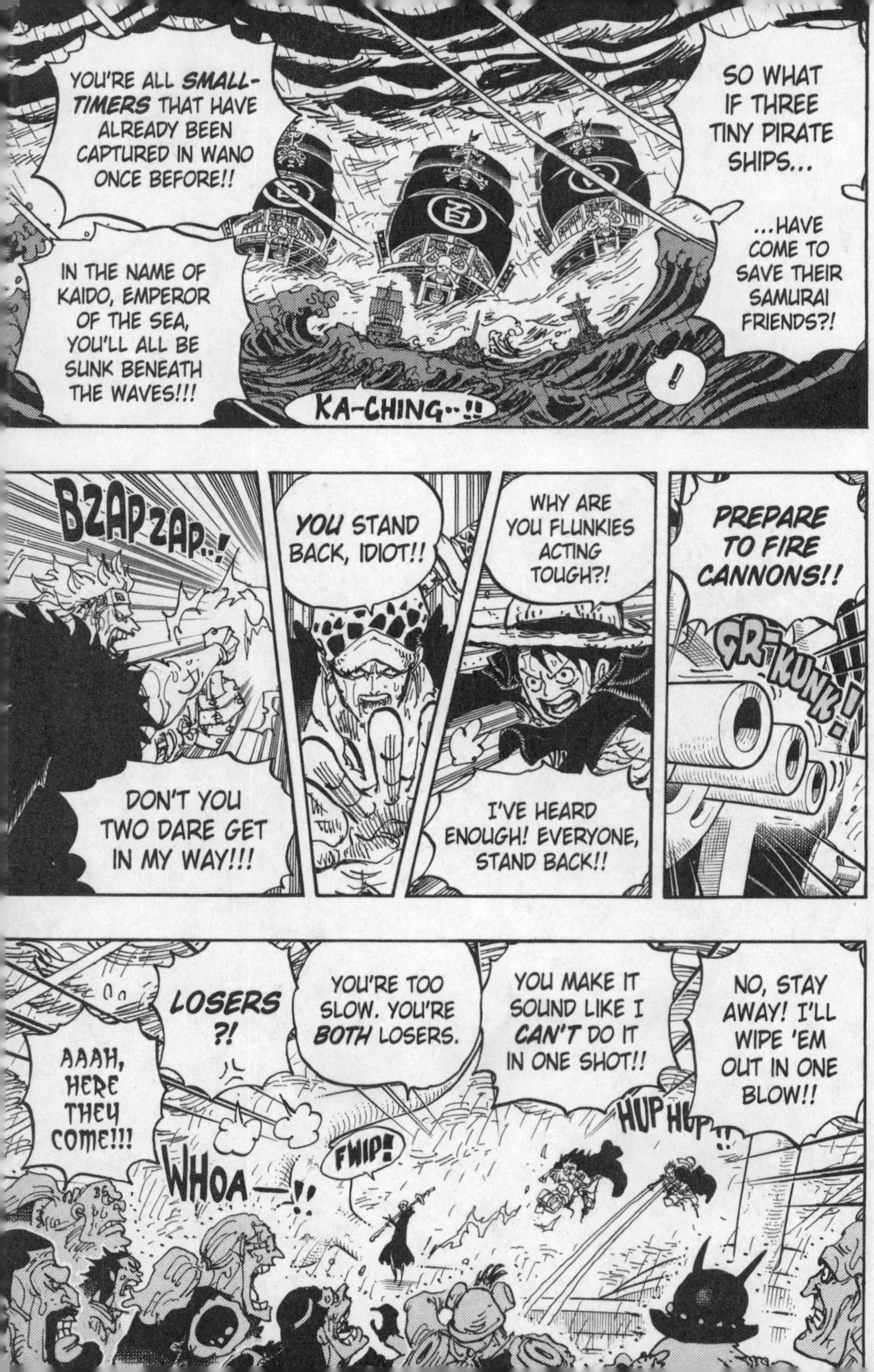
SO WHAT IF THREE TINY PIRATE SHIPS...
...HAVE COME TO SAVE THEIR SAMURAI FRIENDS?!
YOU'RE ALL *SMALL-TIMERS* THAT HAVE ALREADY BEEN CAPTURED IN WANO ONCE BEFORE!!
!
IN THE NAME OF KAIDO, EMPEROR OF THE SEA, YOU'LL ALL BE SUNK BENEATH THE WAVES!!!
KA-CHING..!!
PREPARE TO FIRE CANNONS!!
GR-KUNK!
WHY ARE YOU FLUNKIES ACTING TOUGH?!
I'VE HEARD ENOUGH! EVERYONE, STAND BACK!!
YOU STAND BACK, IDIOT!!
BZAP ZAP..!
DON'T YOU TWO DARE GET IN MY WAY!!!
NO, STAY AWAY! I'LL WIPE 'EM OUT IN ONE BLOW!!
YOU MAKE IT SOUND LIKE I *CAN'T* DO IT IN ONE SHOT!!
HUP HUP!!
YOU'RE TOO SLOW. YOU'RE *BOTH* LOSERS.
LOSERS ?!
FWIP!
AAAH, HERE THEY COME!!!
WHOA—!!

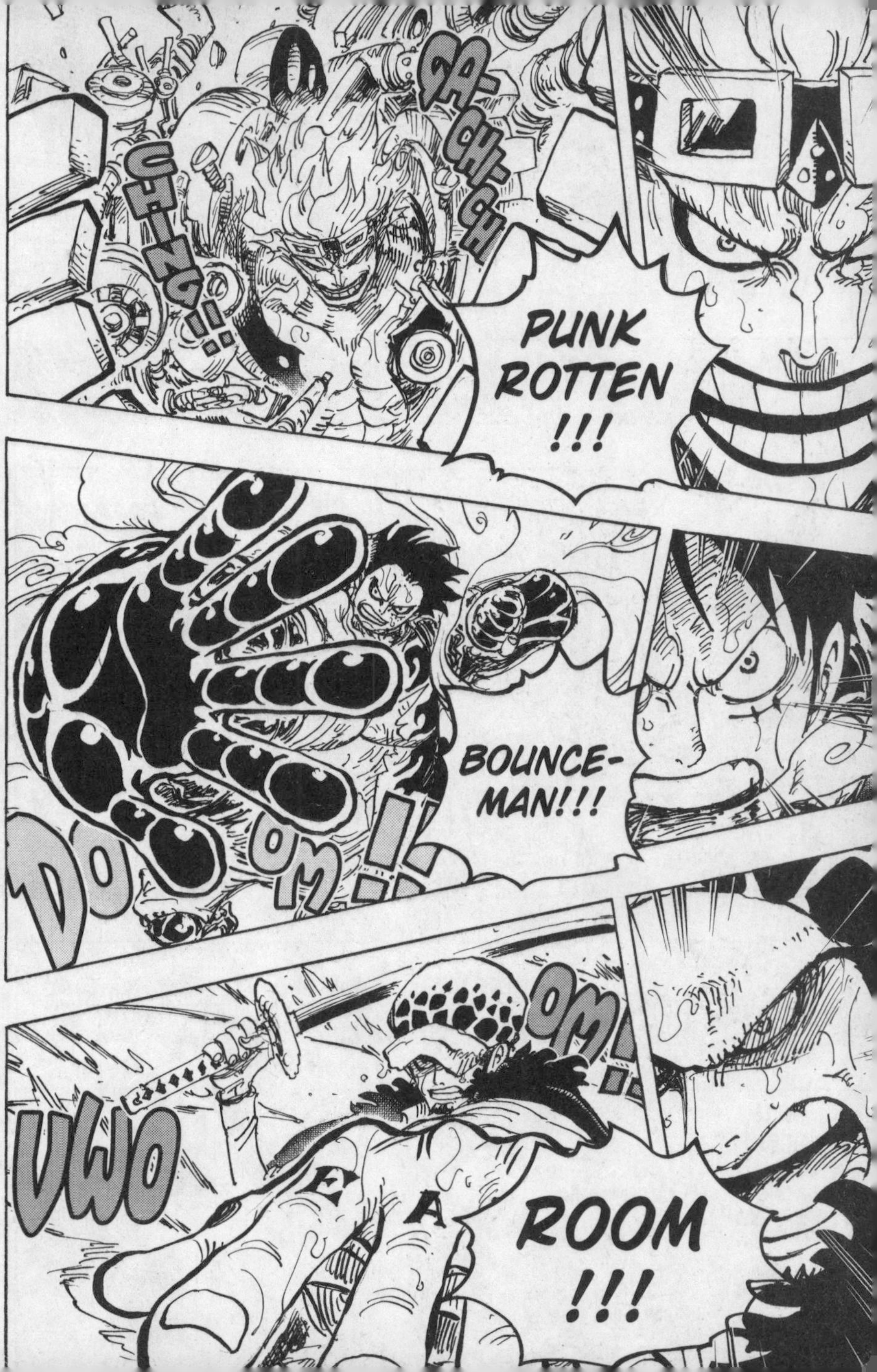
PUNK ROTTEN !!!
GA-CHI-CHI
CHING!!
BOUNCE-MAN!!!
DOOM!!
ROOM !!!
OM!!
UWO
EA

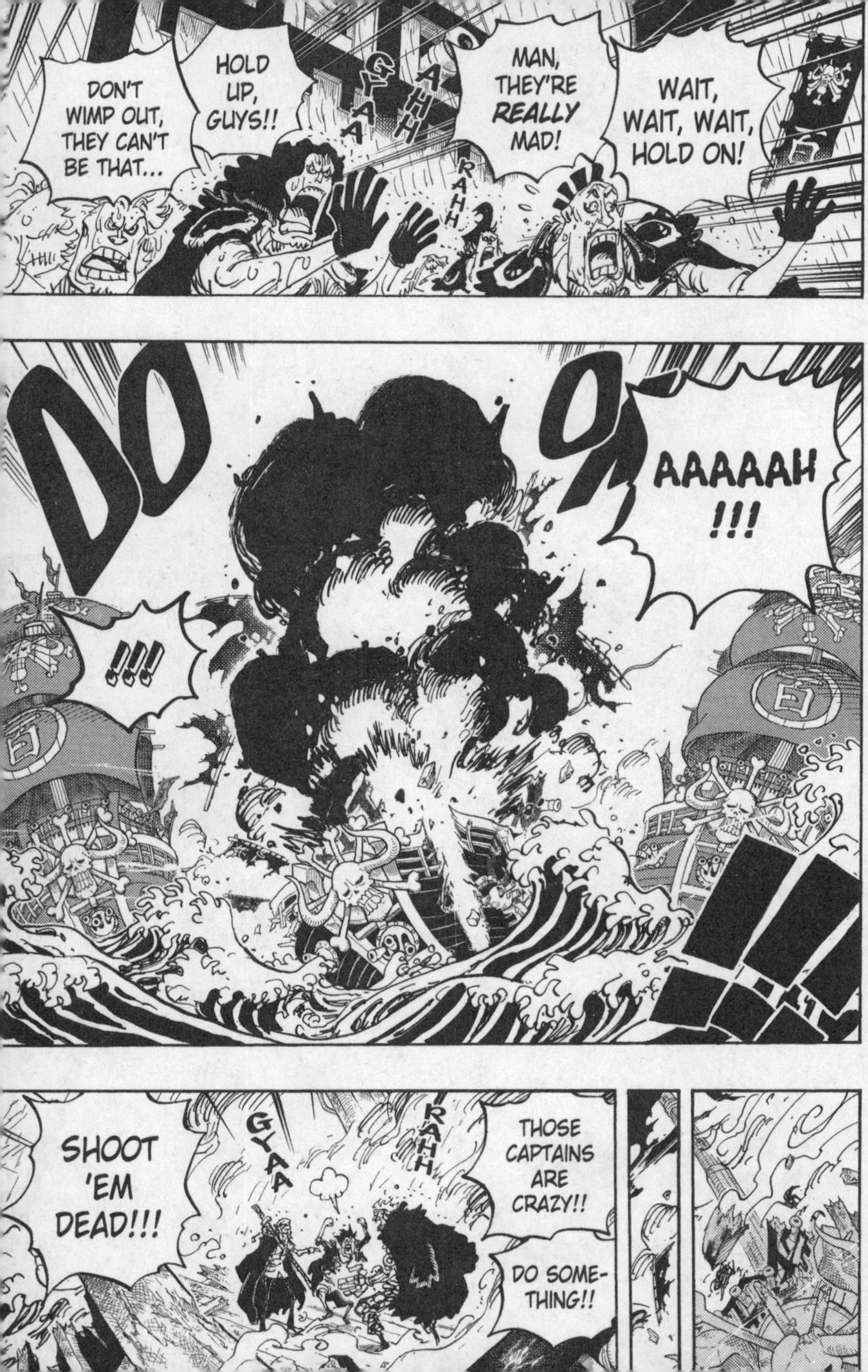
WAIT, WAIT, WAIT, HOLD ON!
MAN, THEY'RE *REALLY* MAD!
RAHH
AHH
GYAA
HOLD UP, GUYS!!
DON'T WIMP OUT, THEY CAN'T BE THAT...
AAAAAH !!!
DO
O
!!
!!!
THOSE CAPTAINS ARE CRAZY!!
DO SOME-THING!!
RAHH
GYAA
SHOOT 'EM DEAD!!!

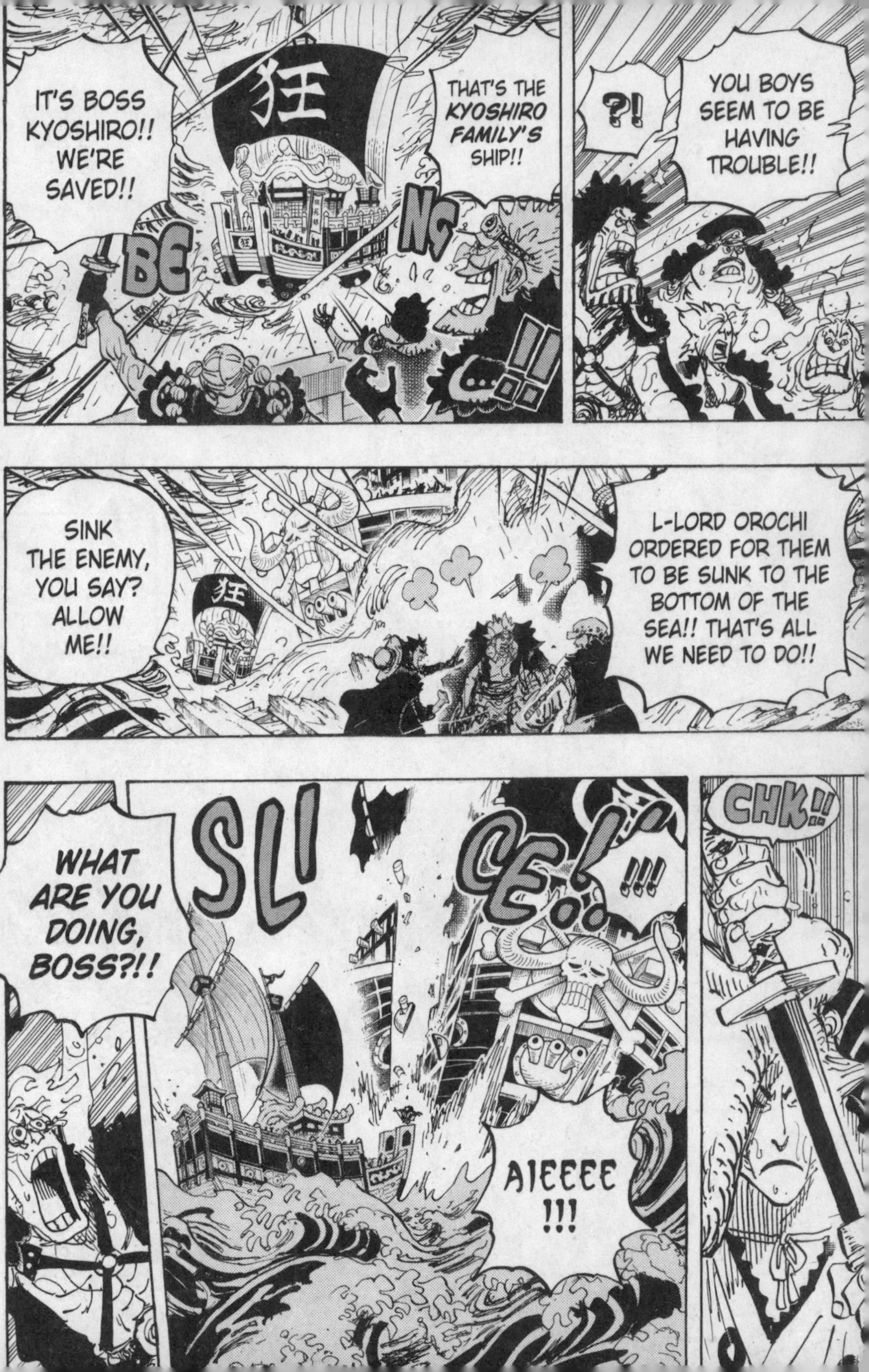
YOU BOYS SEEM TO BE HAVING TROUBLE!!
?!
THAT'S THE KYOSHIRO FAMILY'S SHIP!!
IT'S BOSS KYOSHIRO!! WE'RE SAVED!!
BENG
!!
L-LORD OROCHI ORDERED FOR THEM TO BE SUNK TO THE BOTTOM OF THE SEA!! THAT'S ALL WE NEED TO DO!!
SINK THE ENEMY, YOU SAY? ALLOW ME!!
CHK!!
SLICE!!!
AIEEEE!!!
WHAT ARE YOU DOING, BOSS?!!

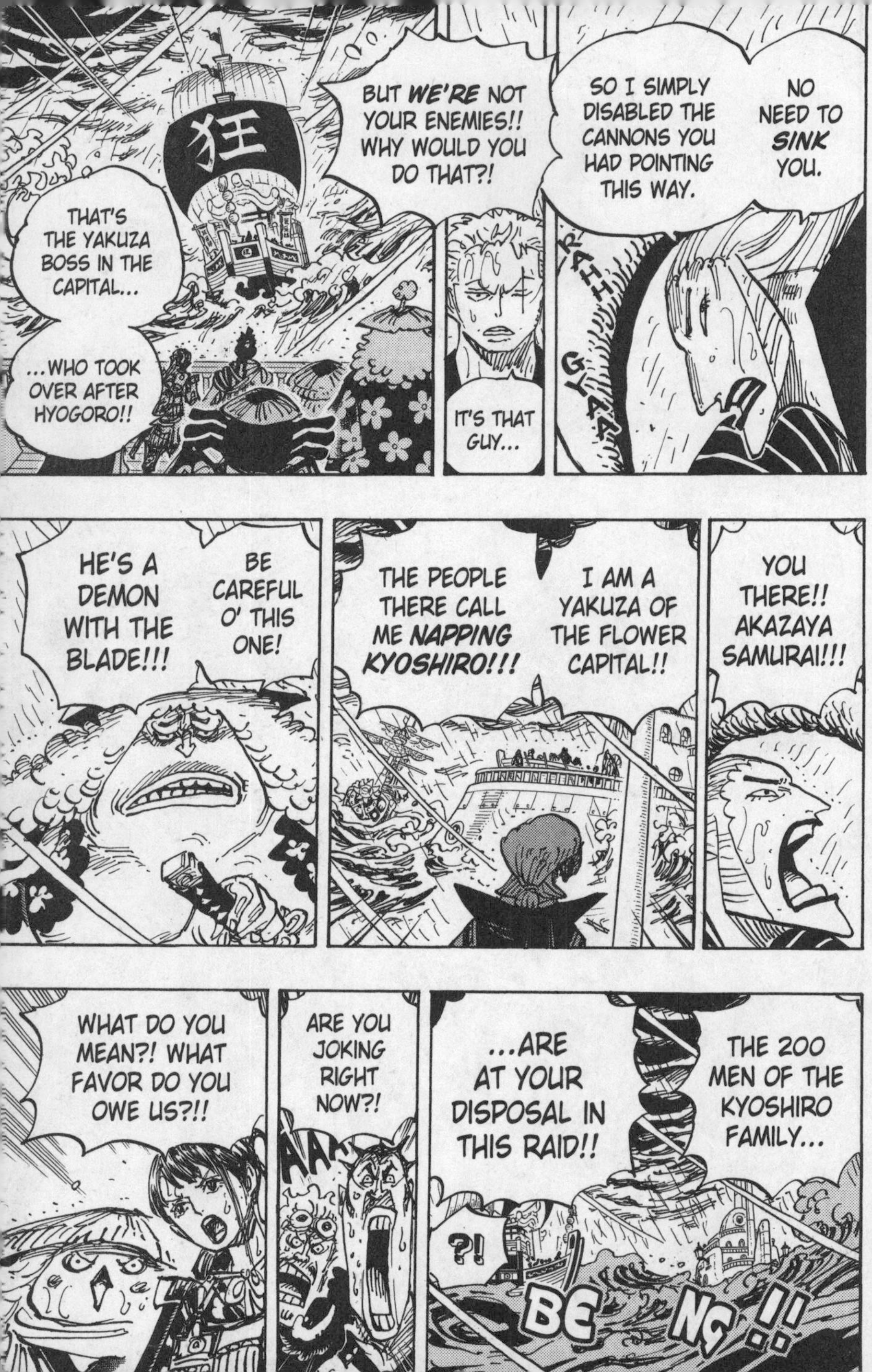
NO NEED TO SINK YOU.
SO I SIMPLY DISABLED THE CANNONS YOU HAD POINTING THIS WAY.
IT'S THAT GUY...
BUT WE'RE NOT YOUR ENEMIES!! WHY WOULD YOU DO THAT?!
THAT'S THE YAKUZA BOSS IN THE CAPITAL...
...WHO TOOK OVER AFTER HYOGORO!!
YOU THERE!! AKAZAYA SAMURAI!!!!
I AM A YAKUZA OF THE FLOWER CAPITAL!!
THE PEOPLE THERE CALL ME NAPPING KYOSHIRO!!!
BE CAREFUL O' THIS ONE!
HE'S A DEMON WITH THE BLADE!!!
THE 200 MEN OF THE KYOSHIRO FAMILY...
...ARE AT YOUR DISPOSAL IN THIS RAID!!
?!
BENG!!
ARE YOU JOKING RIGHT NOW?!
WHAT DO YOU MEAN?! WHAT FAVOR DO YOU OWE US?!!

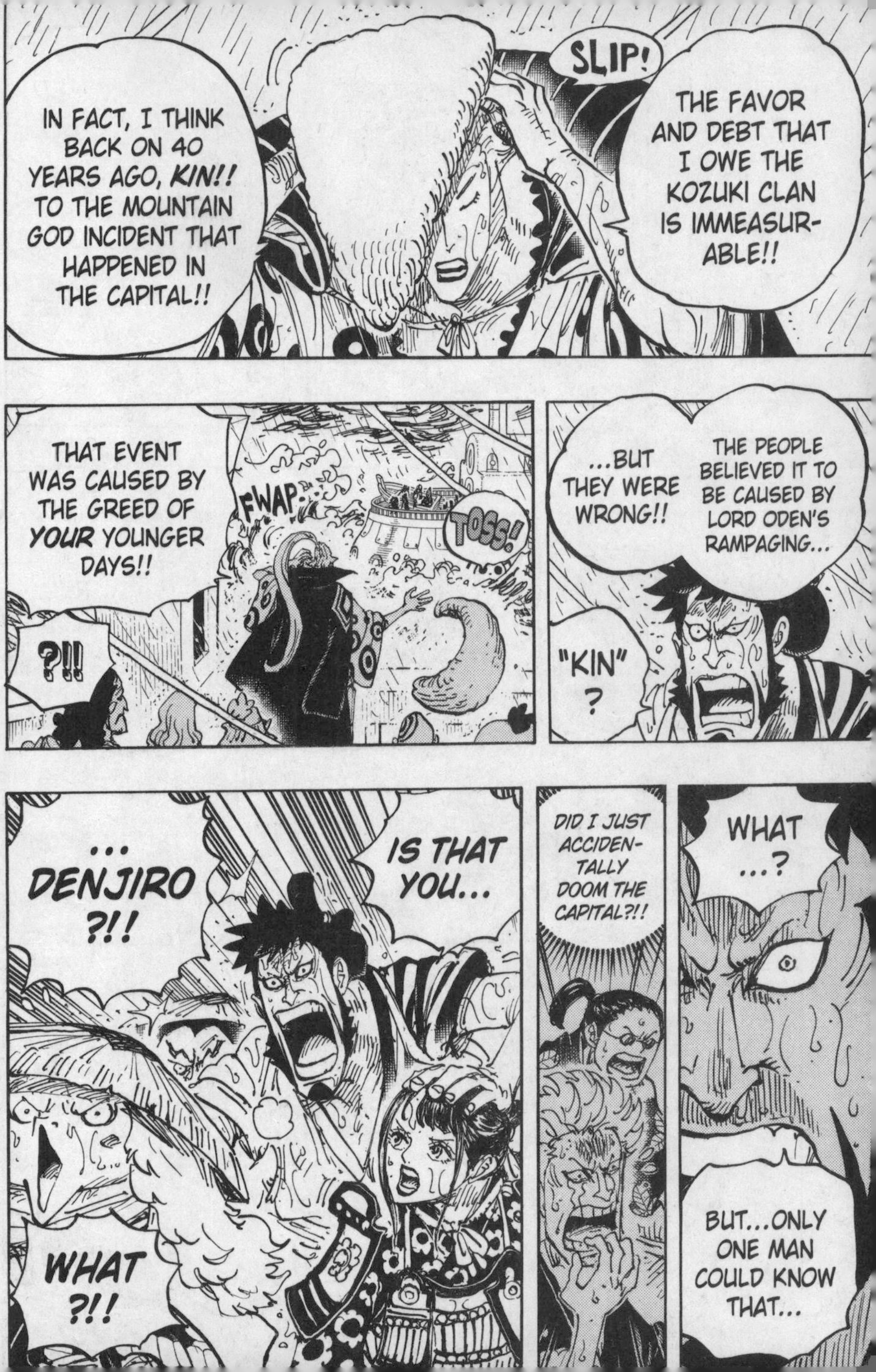
SLIP!
THE FAVOR AND DEBT THAT I OWE THE KOZUKI CLAN IS IMMEASUR-ABLE!!
IN FACT, I THINK BACK ON 40 YEARS AGO, KIN!! TO THE MOUNTAIN GOD INCIDENT THAT HAPPENED IN THE CAPITAL!!
THE PEOPLE BELIEVED IT TO BE CAUSED BY LORD ODEN'S RAMPAGING...
...BUT THEY WERE WRONG!!
"KIN" ?
THAT EVENT WAS CAUSED BY THE GREED OF YOUR YOUNGER DAYS!!
FWAP
TOSS!
?!!
WHAT ...?
BUT...ONLY ONE MAN COULD KNOW THAT...
DID I JUST ACCIDEN-TALLY DOOM THE CAPITAL?!!
IS THAT YOU...
... DENJIRO ?!!
WHAT ?!!

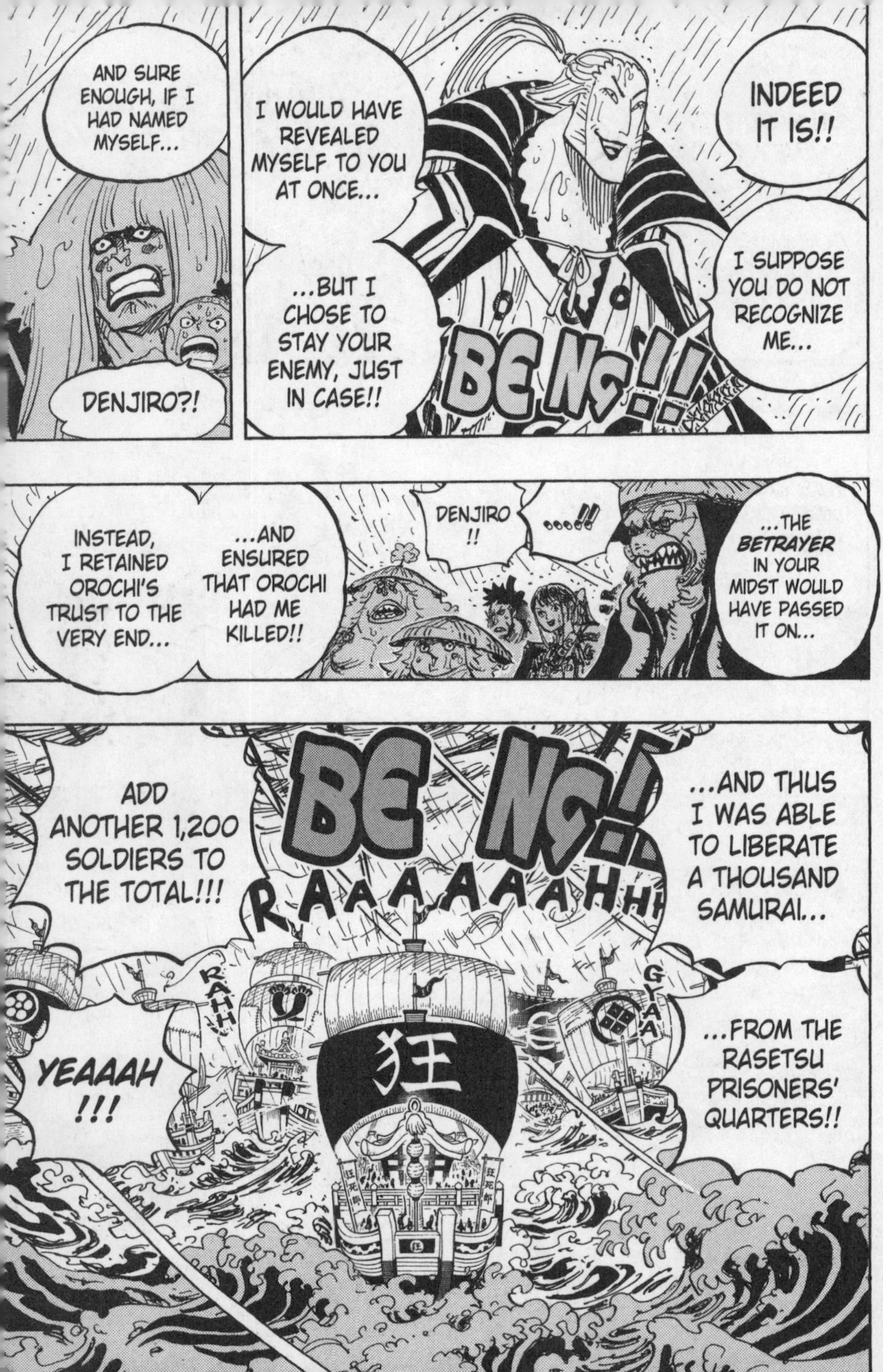
INDEED IT IS!!
I SUPPOSE YOU DO NOT RECOGNIZE ME...
I WOULD HAVE REVEALED MYSELF TO YOU AT ONCE...
...BUT I CHOSE TO STAY YOUR ENEMY, JUST IN CASE!!
BE NG!!
AND SURE ENOUGH, IF I HAD NAMED MYSELF...
DENJIRO?!
...THE BETRAYER IN YOUR MIDST WOULD HAVE PASSED IT ON...
....!!
DENJIRO !!
INSTEAD, I RETAINED OROCHI'S TRUST TO THE VERY END...
...AND ENSURED THAT OROCHI HAD ME KILLED!!
...AND THUS I WAS ABLE TO LIBERATE A THOUSAND SAMURAI...
BE NG!
ADD ANOTHER 1,200 SOLDIERS TO THE TOTAL!!!
RAAAAAAHH
GYAA
狂
RAHH
...FROM THE RASETSU PRISONERS' QUARTERS!!
YEAAAH !!!

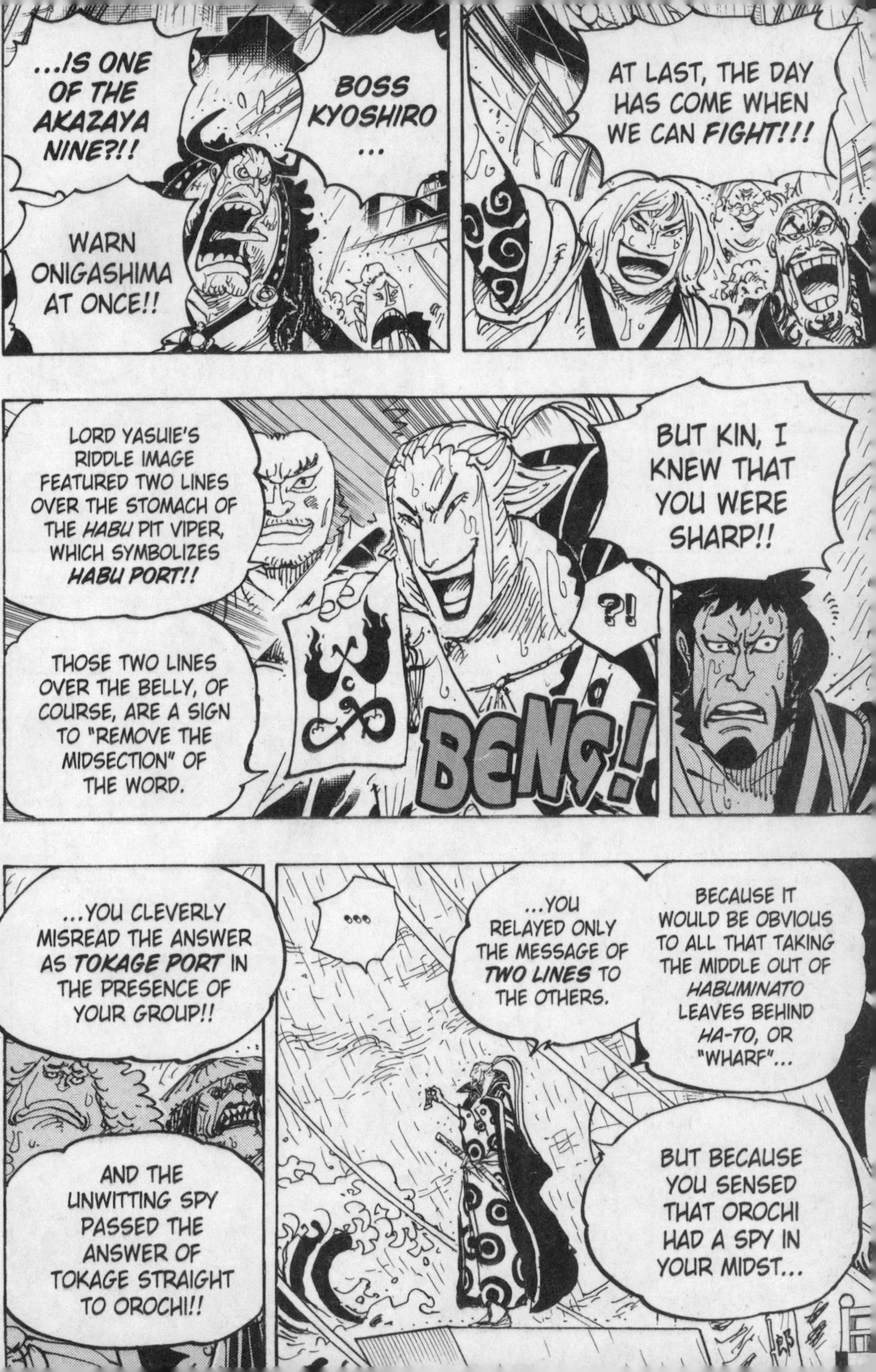
AT LAST, THE DAY HAS COME WHEN WE CAN FIGHT!!!
BOSS KYOSHIRO ...
...IS ONE OF THE AKAZAYA NINE?!!
WARN ONIGASHIMA AT ONCE!!
BUT KIN, I KNEW THAT YOU WERE SHARP!!
?!
LORD YASUIE'S RIDDLE IMAGE FEATURED TWO LINES OVER THE STOMACH OF THE HABU PIT VIPER, WHICH SYMBOLIZES HABU PORT!!
THOSE TWO LINES OVER THE BELLY, OF COURSE, ARE A SIGN TO "REMOVE THE MIDSECTION" OF THE WORD.
BENG!
...
BECAUSE IT WOULD BE OBVIOUS TO ALL THAT TAKING THE MIDDLE OUT OF HABUMINATO LEAVES BEHIND HA-TO, OR "WHARF"...
BUT BECAUSE YOU SENSED THAT OROCHI HAD A SPY IN YOUR MIDST...
...YOU RELAYED ONLY THE MESSAGE OF TWO LINES TO THE OTHERS.
...YOU CLEVERLY MISREAD THE ANSWER AS TOKAGE PORT IN THE PRESENCE OF YOUR GROUP!!
AND THE UNWITTING SPY PASSED THE ANSWER OF TOKAGE STRAIGHT TO OROCHI!!

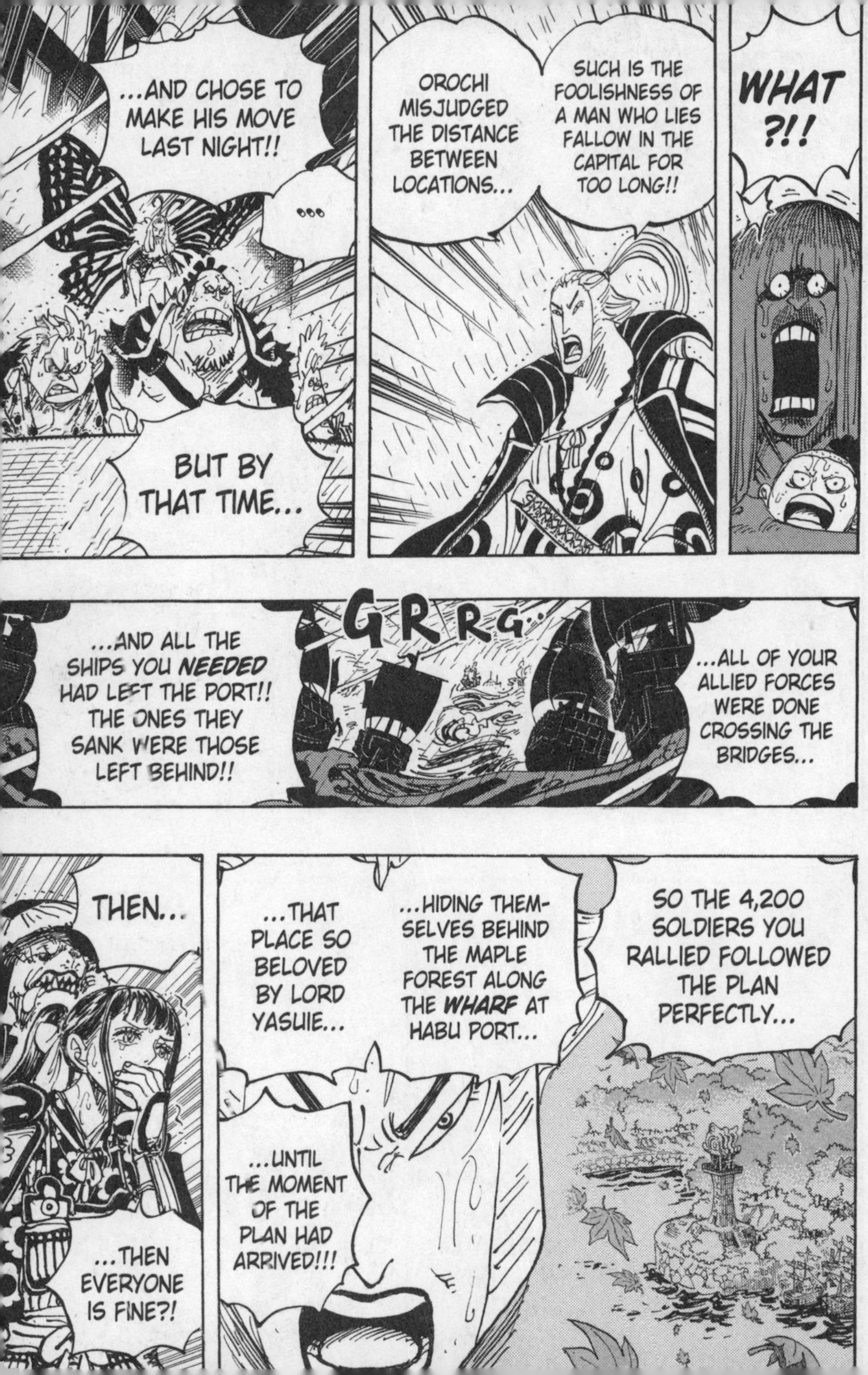
WHAT ?!!
SUCH IS THE FOOLISHNESS OF A MAN WHO LIES FALLOW IN THE CAPITAL FOR TOO LONG!!
OROCHI MISJUDGED THE DISTANCE BETWEEN LOCATIONS...
...AND CHOSE TO MAKE HIS MOVE LAST NIGHT!!
...
BUT BY THAT TIME...
...ALL OF YOUR ALLIED FORCES WERE DONE CROSSING THE BRIDGES...
GRRG
...AND ALL THE SHIPS YOU NEEDED HAD LEFT THE PORT!! THE ONES THEY SANK WERE THOSE LEFT BEHIND!!
SO THE 4,200 SOLDIERS YOU RALLIED FOLLOWED THE PLAN PERFECTLY...
...HIDING THEMSELVES BEHIND THE MAPLE FOREST ALONG THE WHARF AT HABU PORT...
...THAT PLACE SO BELOVED BY LORD YASUIE...
...UNTIL THE MOMENT OF THE PLAN HAD ARRIVED!!!
THEN...
...THEN EVERYONE IS FINE?!

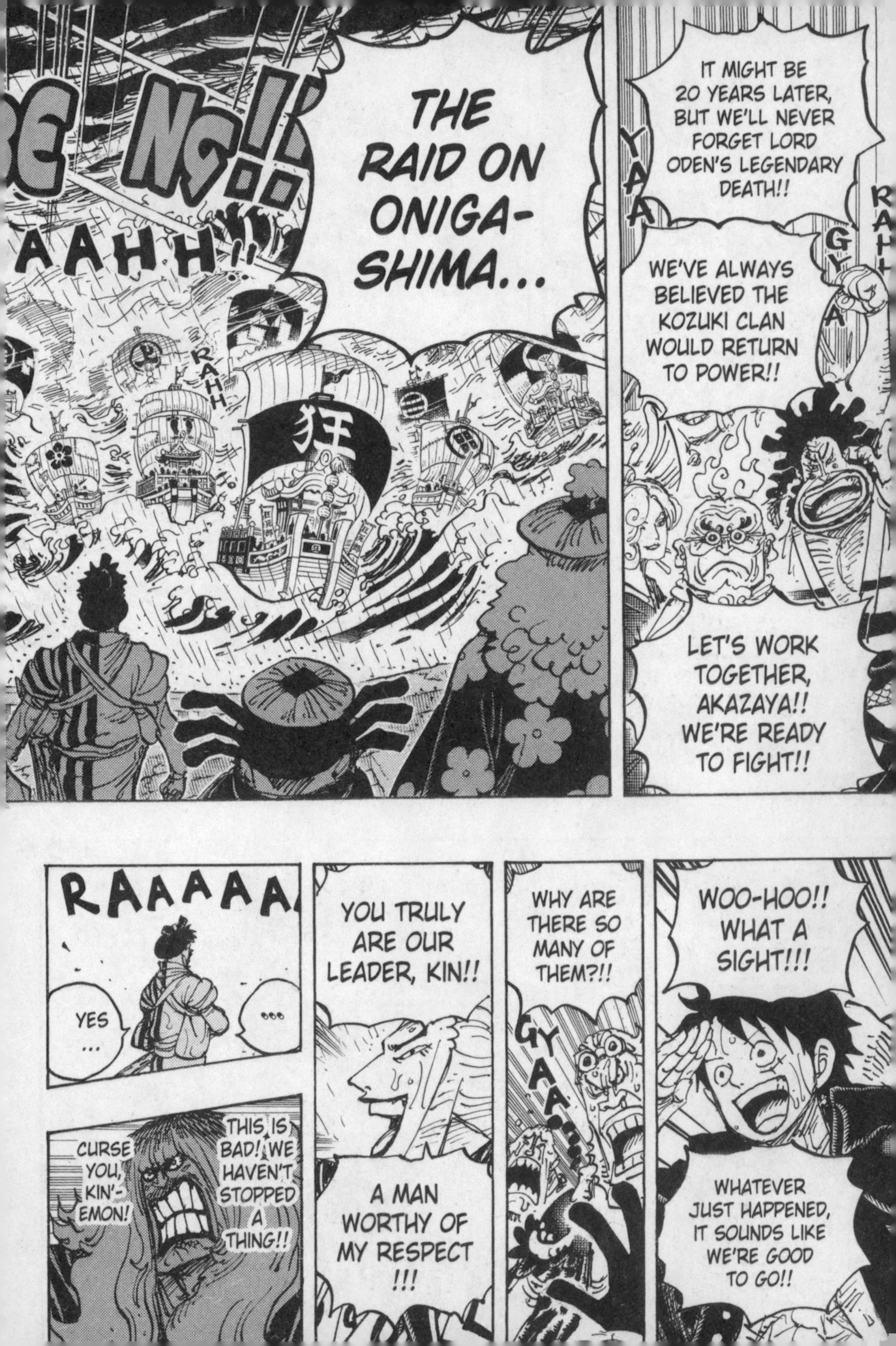
IT MIGHT BE 20 YEARS LATER, BUT WE'LL NEVER FORGET LORD ODEN'S LEGENDARY DEATH!!
YAA
GYA
WE'VE ALWAYS BELIEVED THE KOZUKI CLAN WOULD RETURN TO POWER!!
LET'S WORK TOGETHER, AKAZAYA!! WE'RE READY TO FIGHT!!
AAHH!!
THE RAID ON ONIGA-SHIMA...
RAHH
WOO-HOO!! WHAT A SIGHT!!!
WHATEVER JUST HAPPENED, IT SOUNDS LIKE WE'RE GOOD TO GO!!
WHY ARE THERE SO MANY OF THEM?!!
GYAA
YOU TRULY ARE OUR LEADER, KIN!!
A MAN WORTHY OF MY RESPECT!!!
RAAAAA
...
YES...
THIS IS BAD! WE HAVEN'T STOPPED A THING!!
CURSE YOU, KIN'EMON!

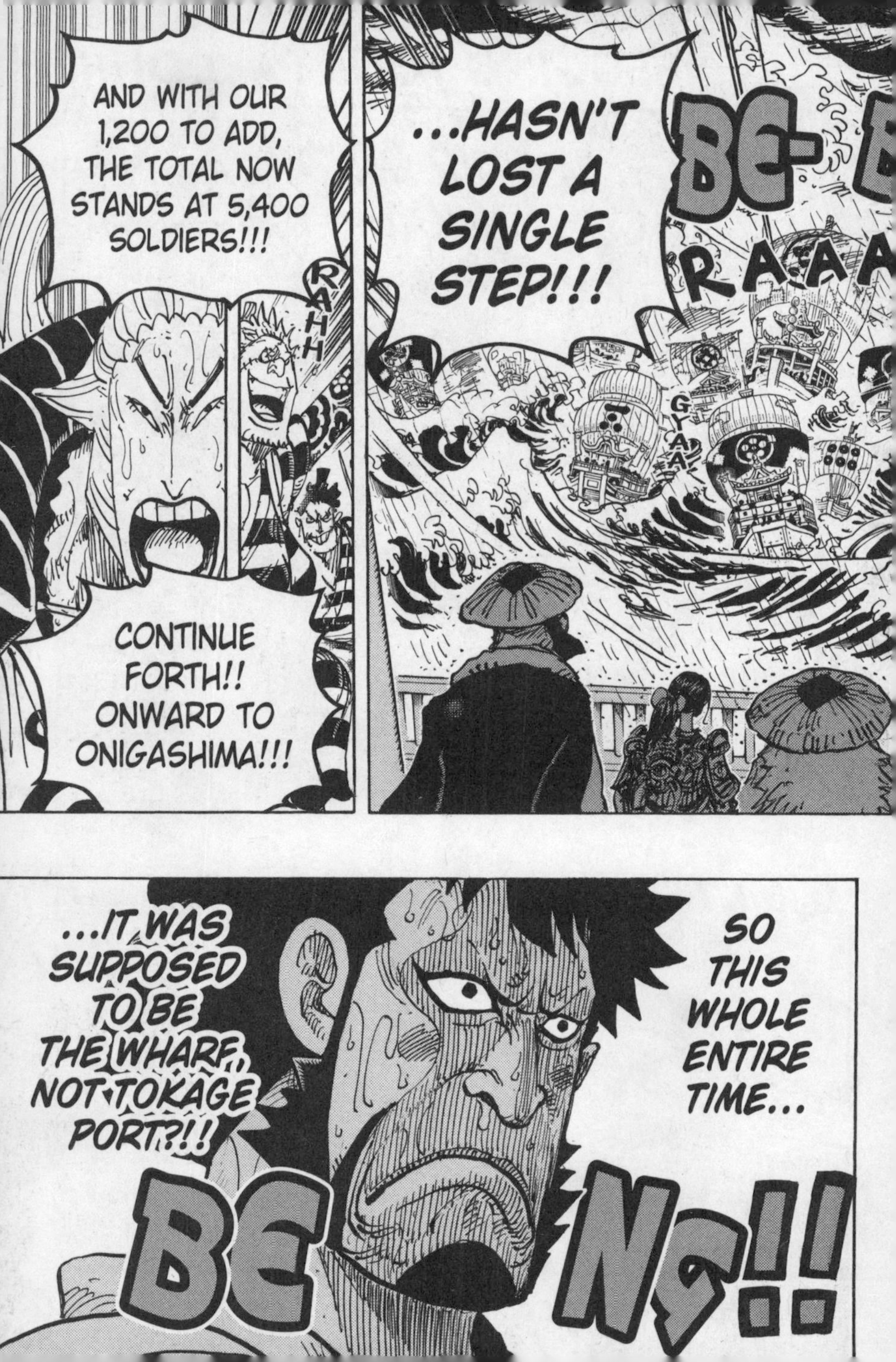
...HASN'T LOST A SINGLE STEP!!!
BE-B
RAAA
GYAA
AND WITH OUR 1,200 TO ADD, THE TOTAL NOW STANDS AT 5,400 SOLDIERS!!!
RAHH
CONTINUE FORTH!! ONWARD TO ONIGASHIMA!!!
SO THIS WHOLE ENTIRE TIME...
...IT WAS SUPPOSED TO BE THE WHARF, NOT TOKAGE PORT?!!
BENG!!

BEGGING YOUR PARDON!!!

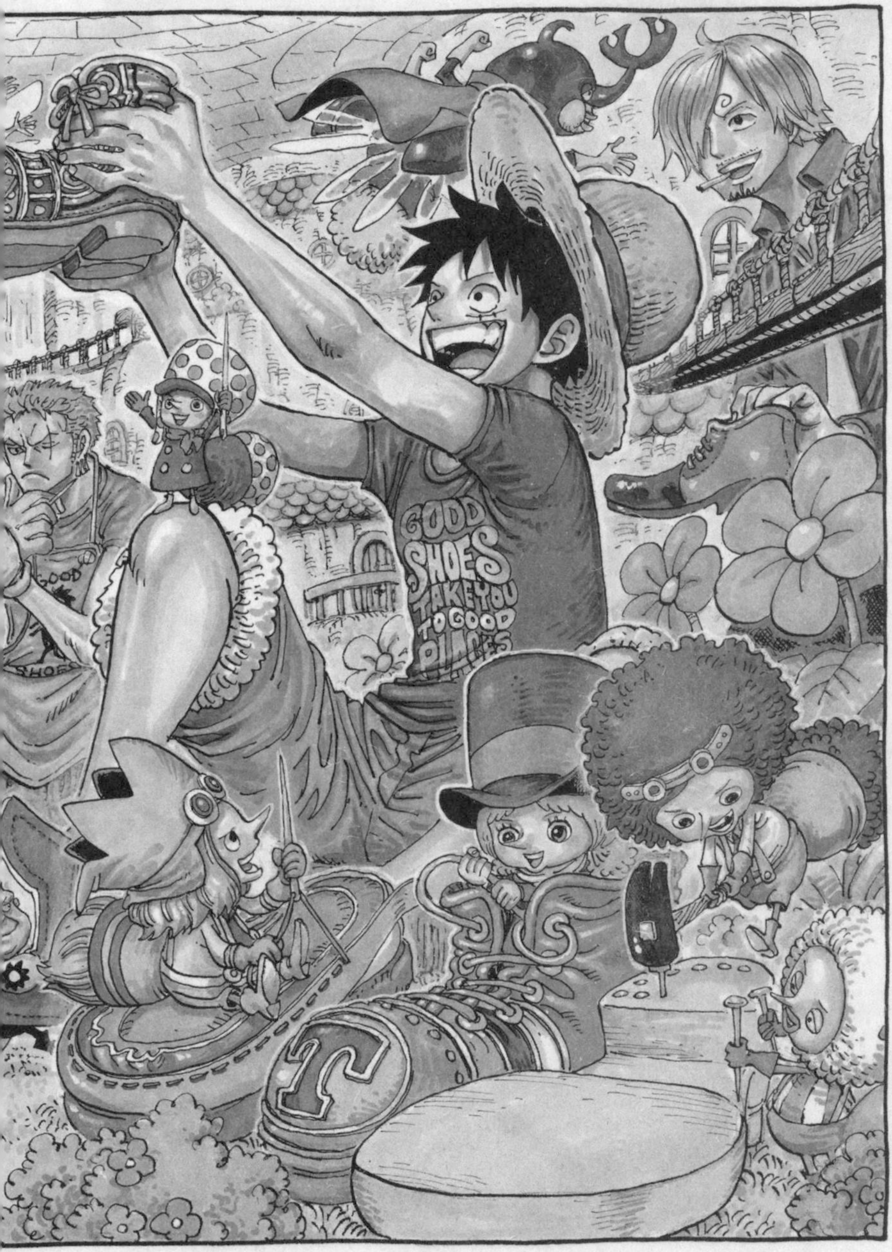
GOOD
SHOES
TAKE YOU
TO GOOD
PLACES

THE STRAW HAT CREW MAKE SHOES" BY HONEYLICKER

Chapter 976:

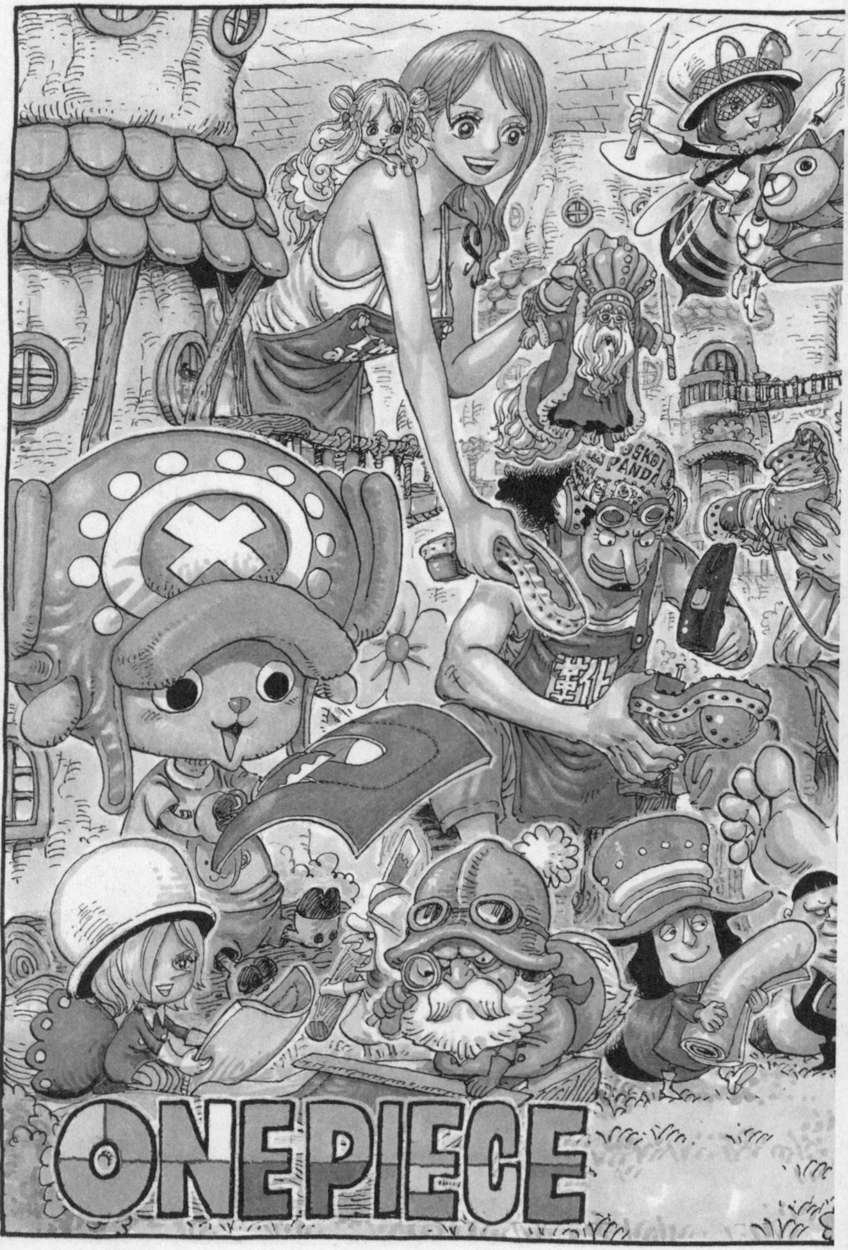
ONEPIECE

REQUEST: "THE TONTATTAS HELPING

vol.97
ONE PIECE

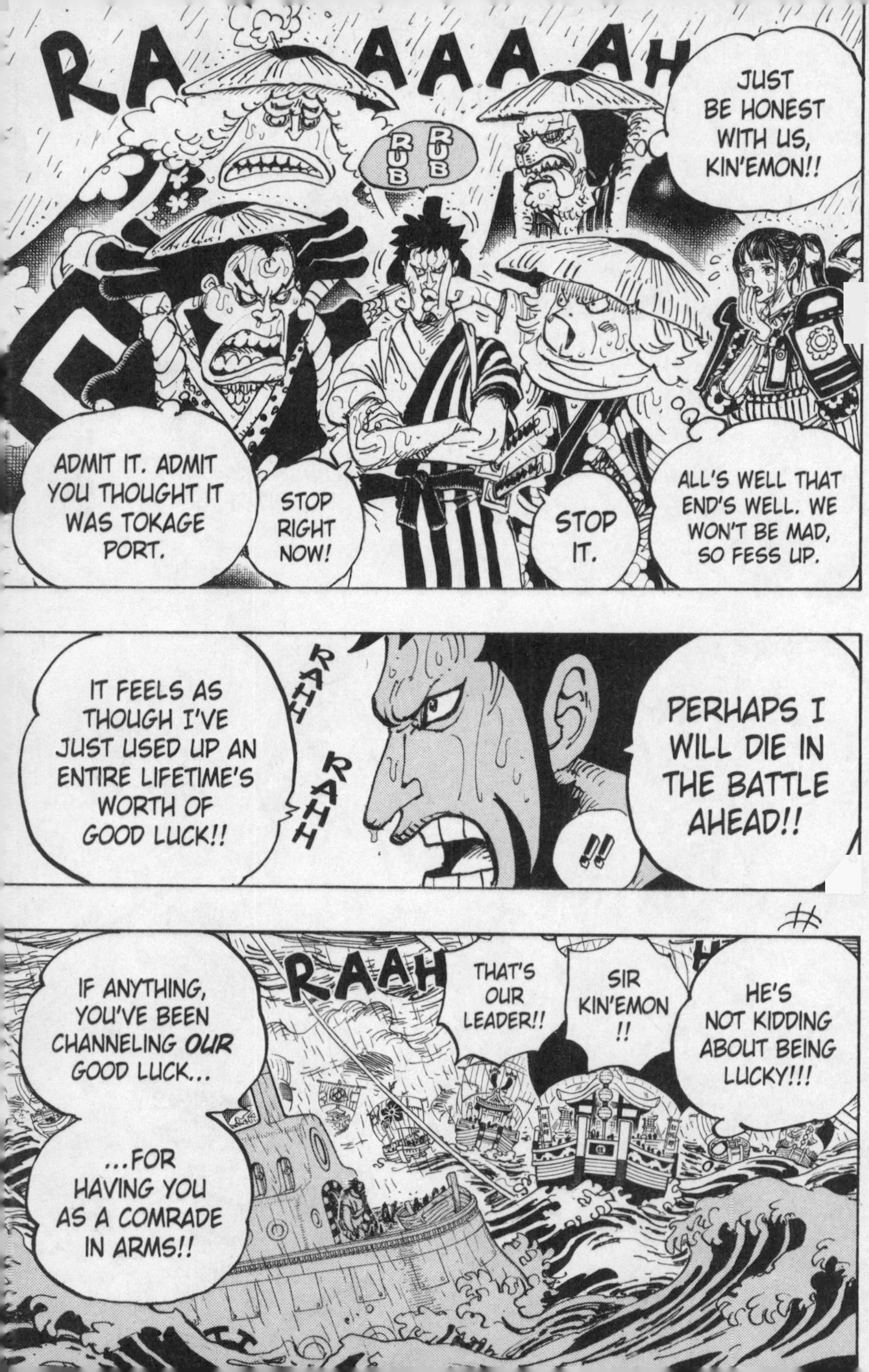
RAAAAAH
JUST BE HONEST WITH US, KIN'EMON!!
RUB RUB
ALL'S WELL THAT END'S WELL. WE WON'T BE MAD, SO FESS UP.
STOP IT.
STOP RIGHT NOW!
ADMIT IT. ADMIT YOU THOUGHT IT WAS TOKAGE PORT.
PERHAPS I WILL DIE IN THE BATTLE AHEAD!!
!!
RAHH
RAHH
IT FEELS AS THOUGH I'VE JUST USED UP AN ENTIRE LIFETIME'S WORTH OF GOOD LUCK!!
HE'S NOT KIDDING ABOUT BEING LUCKY!!!
SIR KIN'EMON !!
THAT'S OUR LEADER!!
RAAH
IF ANYTHING, YOU'VE BEEN CHANNELING *OUR* GOOD LUCK...
...FOR HAVING YOU AS A COMRADE IN ARMS!!

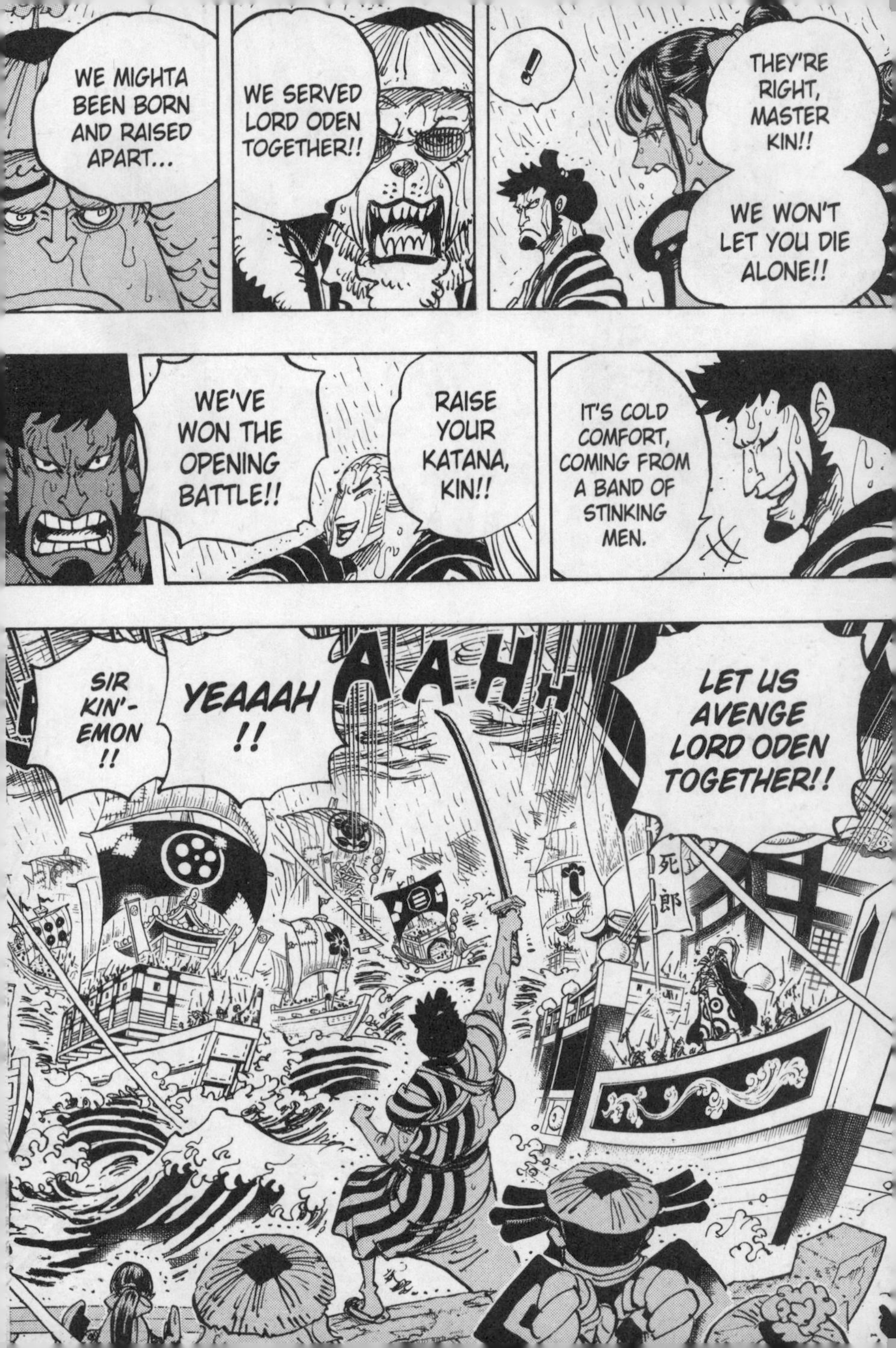
THEY'RE RIGHT, MASTER KIN!!
!
WE WON'T LET YOU DIE ALONE!!
WE SERVED LORD ODEN TOGETHER!!
WE MIGHTA BEEN BORN AND RAISED APART...
IT'S COLD COMFORT, COMING FROM A BAND OF STINKING MEN.
RAISE YOUR KATANA, KIN!!
WE'VE WON THE OPENING BATTLE!!
LET US AVENGE LORD ODEN TOGETHER!!
死郎
AAHH
YEAAAH !!
SIR KIN'-EMON !!

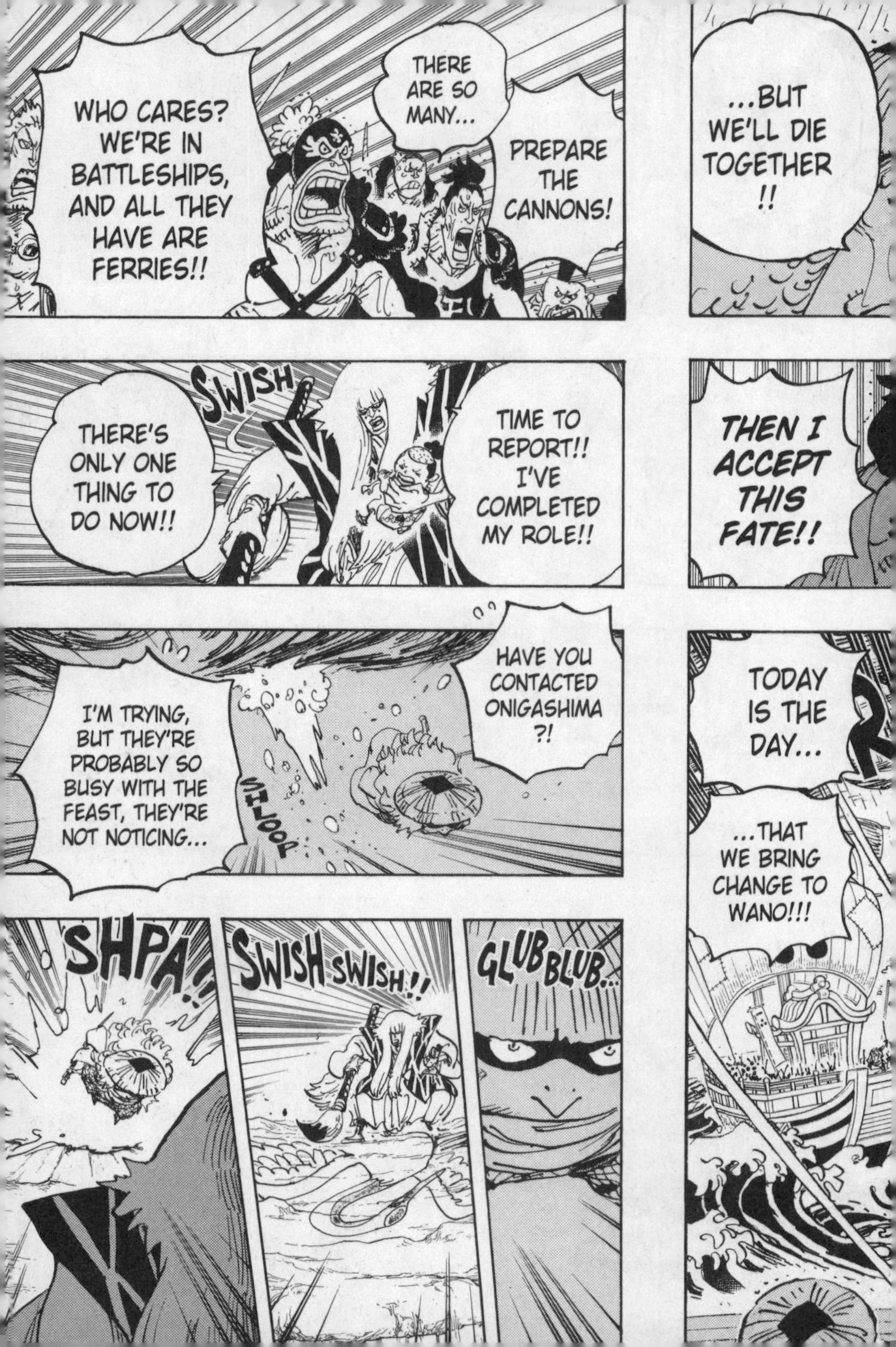

...BUT WE'LL DIE TOGETHER!!
THERE ARE SO MANY...
PREPARE THE CANNONS!
WHO CARES? WE'RE IN BATTLESHIPS, AND ALL THEY HAVE ARE FERRIES!!
THEN I ACCEPT THIS FATE!!
TIME TO REPORT!! I'VE COMPLETED MY ROLE!!
SWISH
THERE'S ONLY ONE THING TO DO NOW!!
TODAY IS THE DAY...
...THAT WE BRING CHANGE TO WANO!!!
HAVE YOU CONTACTED ONIGASHIMA?!
SHLOOP
I'M TRYING, BUT THEY'RE PROBABLY SO BUSY WITH THE FEAST, THEY'RE NOT NOTICING...
GLUB BLUB...
SWISH SWISH!!
SHPA!!

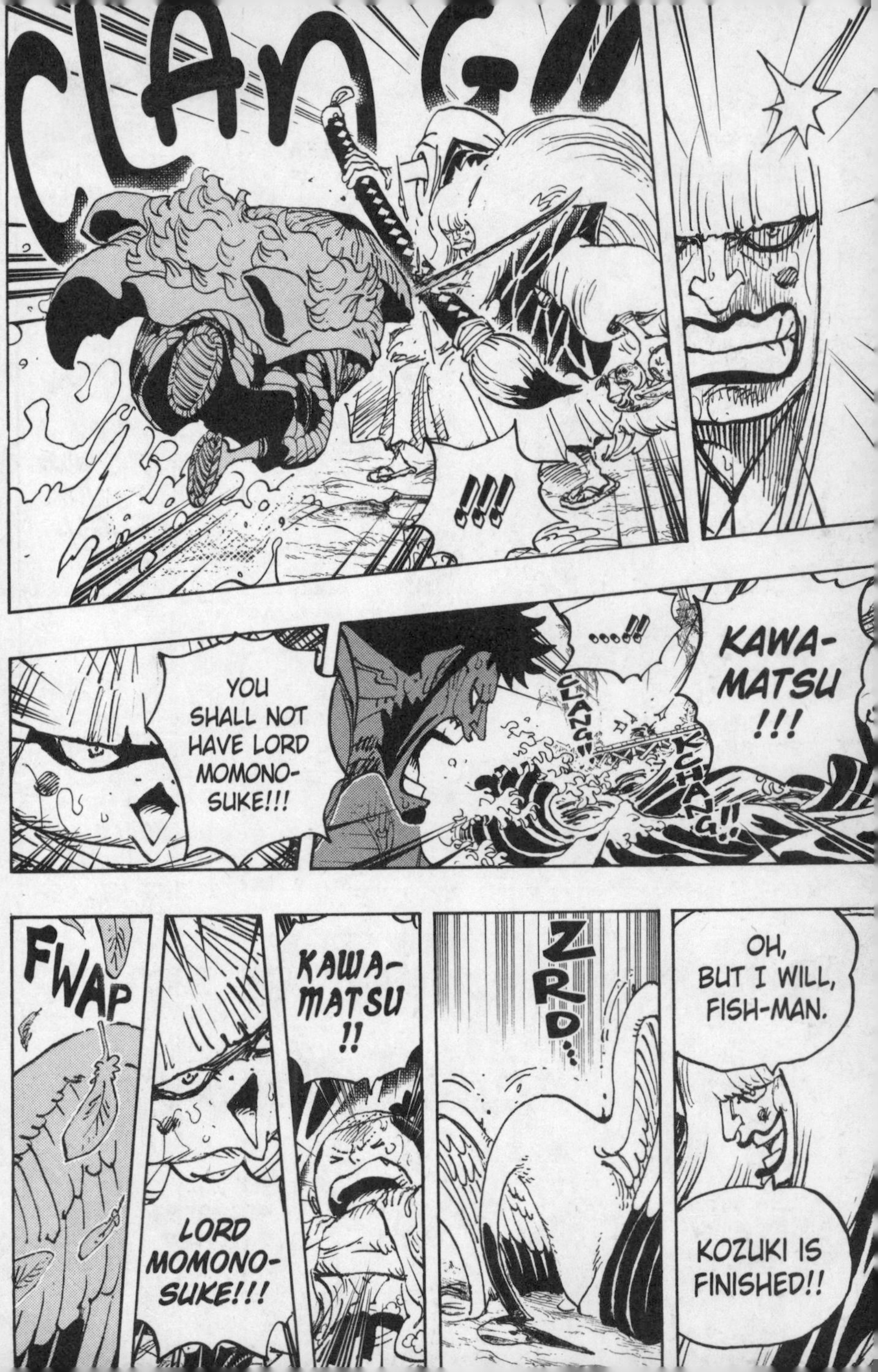
CLANG!!
!!!
KAWA-MATSU!!!
...!!
CLANG!!
KCHANG!!
YOU SHALL NOT HAVE LORD MOMONO-SUKE!!!
OH, BUT I WILL, FISH-MAN.
KOZUKI IS FINISHED!!
ZRD...
KAWA-MATSU!!
LORD MOMONO-SUKE!!!
FWAP

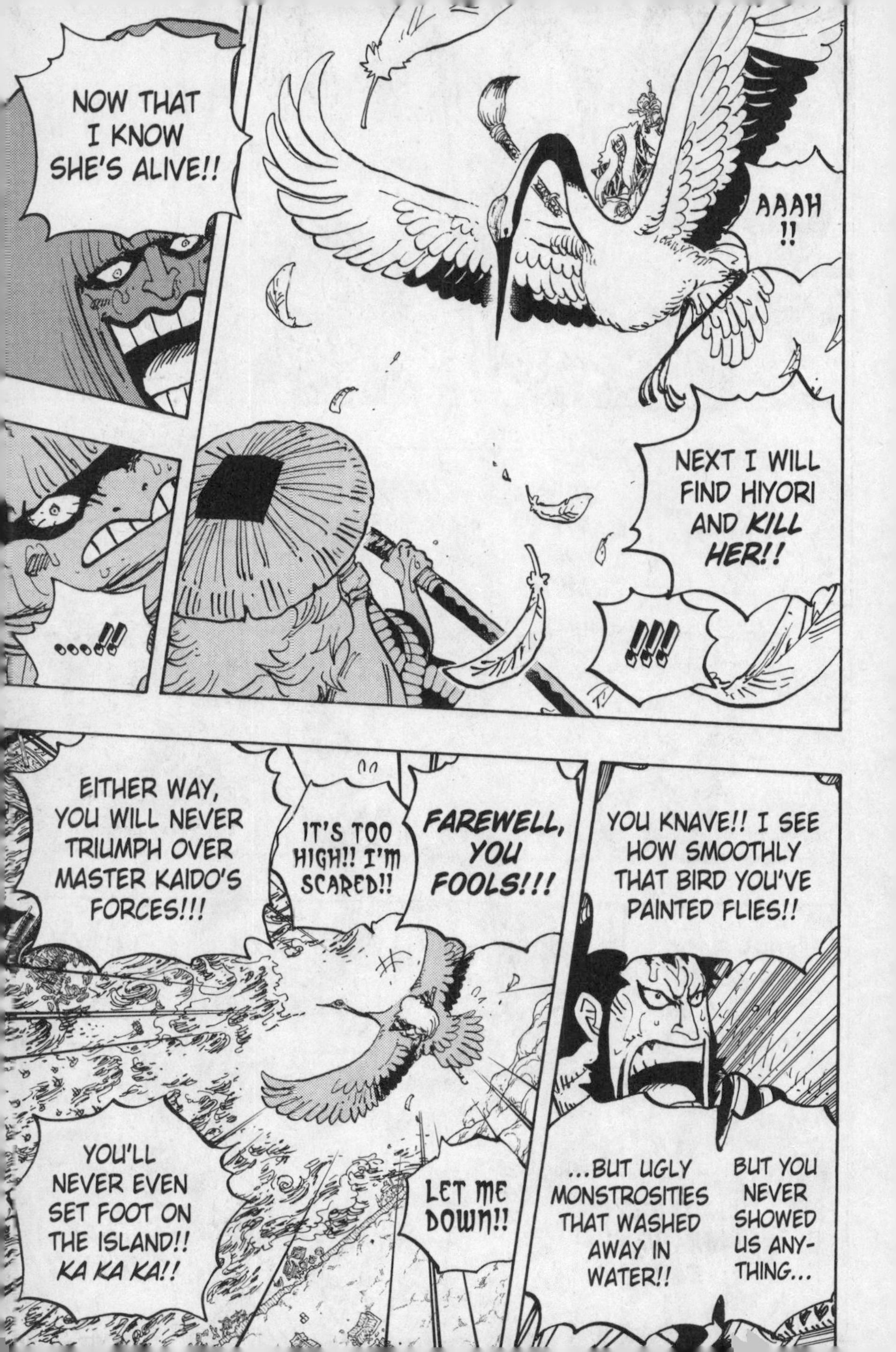
AAAH !!
NOW THAT I KNOW SHE'S ALIVE!!
NEXT I WILL FIND HIYORI AND *KILL HER!!*
!!!
....!!
YOU KNAVE!! I SEE HOW SMOOTHLY THAT BIRD YOU'VE PAINTED FLIES!!
BUT YOU NEVER SHOWED US ANY-THING...
...BUT UGLY MONSTROSITIES THAT WASHED AWAY IN WATER!!
FAREWELL, YOU FOOLS!!!
IT'S TOO HIGH!! I'M SCARED!!
EITHER WAY, YOU WILL NEVER TRIUMPH OVER MASTER KAIDO'S FORCES!!!
LET ME DOWN!!
YOU'LL NEVER EVEN SET FOOT ON THE ISLAND!! *KA KA KA!!*

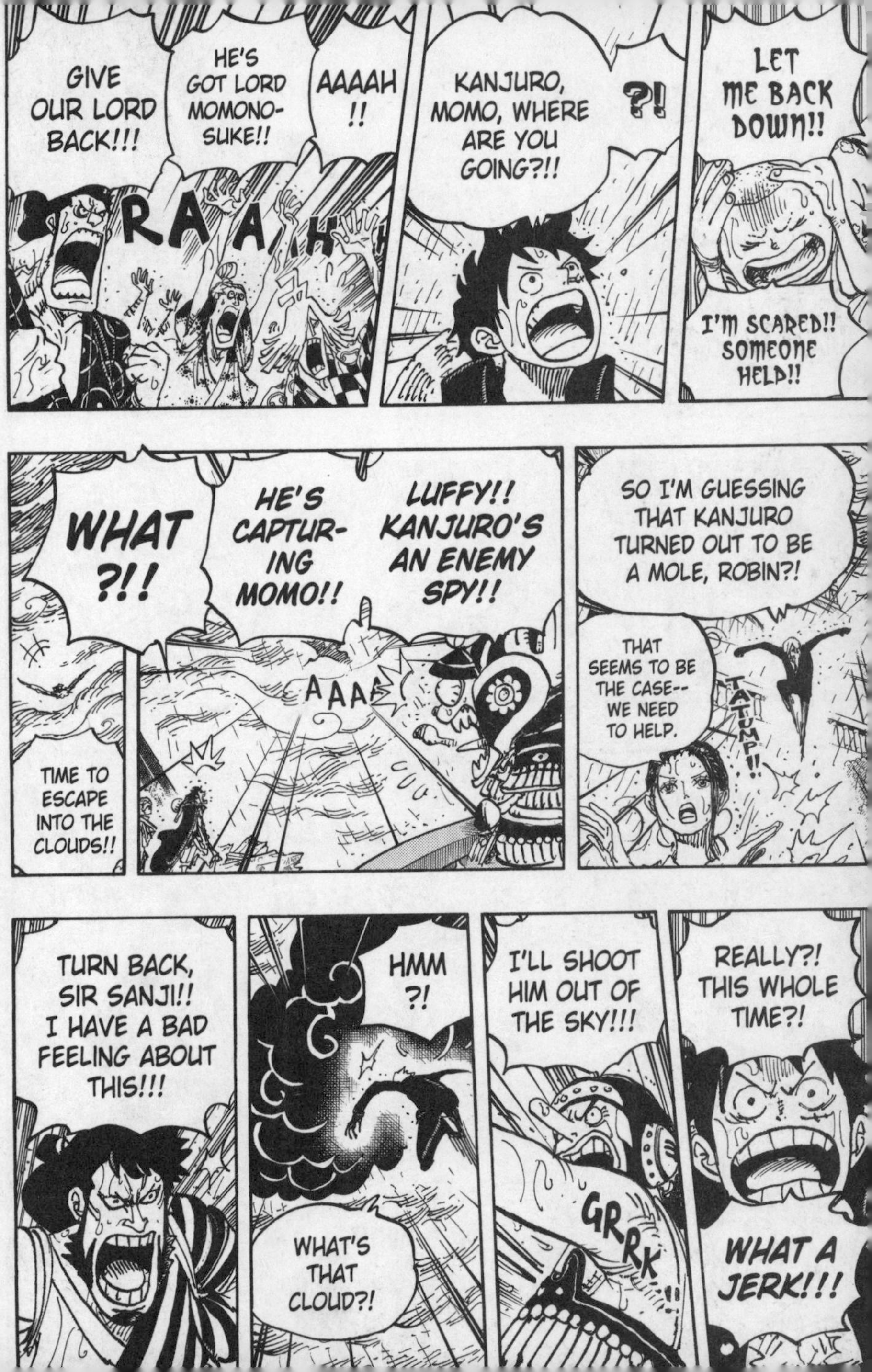
LET ME BACK DOWN!!
I'M SCARED!! SOMEONE HELP!!
?!
KANJURO, MOMO, WHERE ARE YOU GOING?!!
AAAAH !!
HE'S GOT LORD MOMONO-SUKE!!
GIVE OUR LORD BACK!!!
RAAAH
SO I'M GUESSING THAT KANJURO TURNED OUT TO BE A MOLE, ROBIN?!
THAT SEEMS TO BE THE CASE-- WE NEED TO HELP.
TATUMP!!
LUFFY!! KANJURO'S AN ENEMY SPY!!
HE'S CAPTUR-ING MOMO!!
WHAT ?!!
AAAA
TIME TO ESCAPE INTO THE CLOUDS!!
REALLY?! THIS WHOLE TIME?!
WHAT A JERK!!!
I'LL SHOOT HIM OUT OF THE SKY!!!
GRRK!!
HMM ?!
WHAT'S THAT CLOUD?!
TURN BACK, SIR SANJI!! I HAVE A BAD FEELING ABOUT THIS!!!

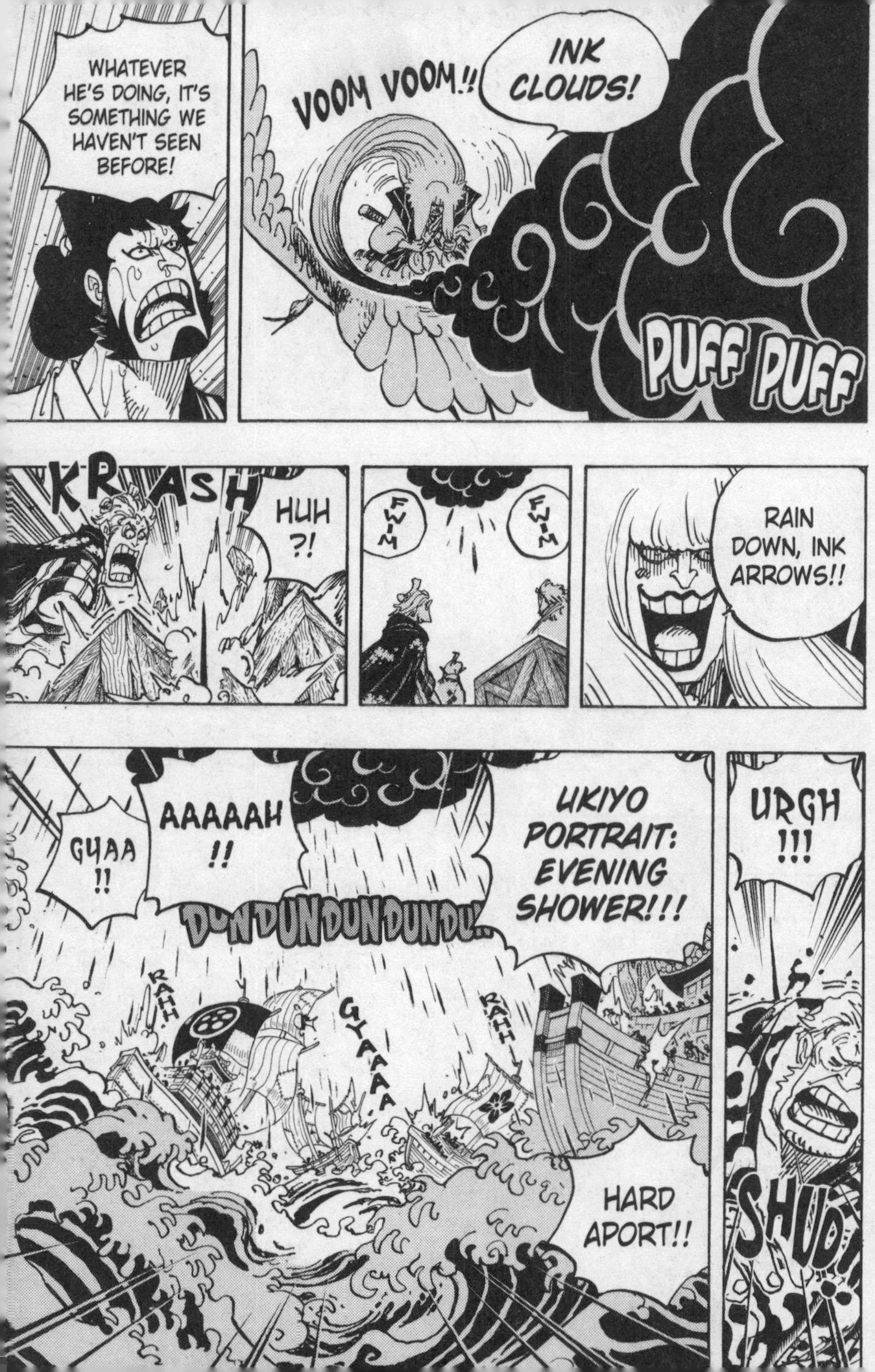
INK CLOUDS!
VOOM VOOM!!
PUFF PUFF
WHATEVER HE'S DOING, IT'S SOMETHING WE HAVEN'T SEEN BEFORE!
RAIN DOWN, INK ARROWS!!
FWIM
FWIM
KRASH
HUH ?!
URGH !!!
SHUD
UKIYO PORTRAIT: EVENING SHOWER!!!
AAAAAH !!
GYAA !!
DUN DUN DUN DUN DU...
RAHH
GYAAAA
RAHH
HARD APORT!!

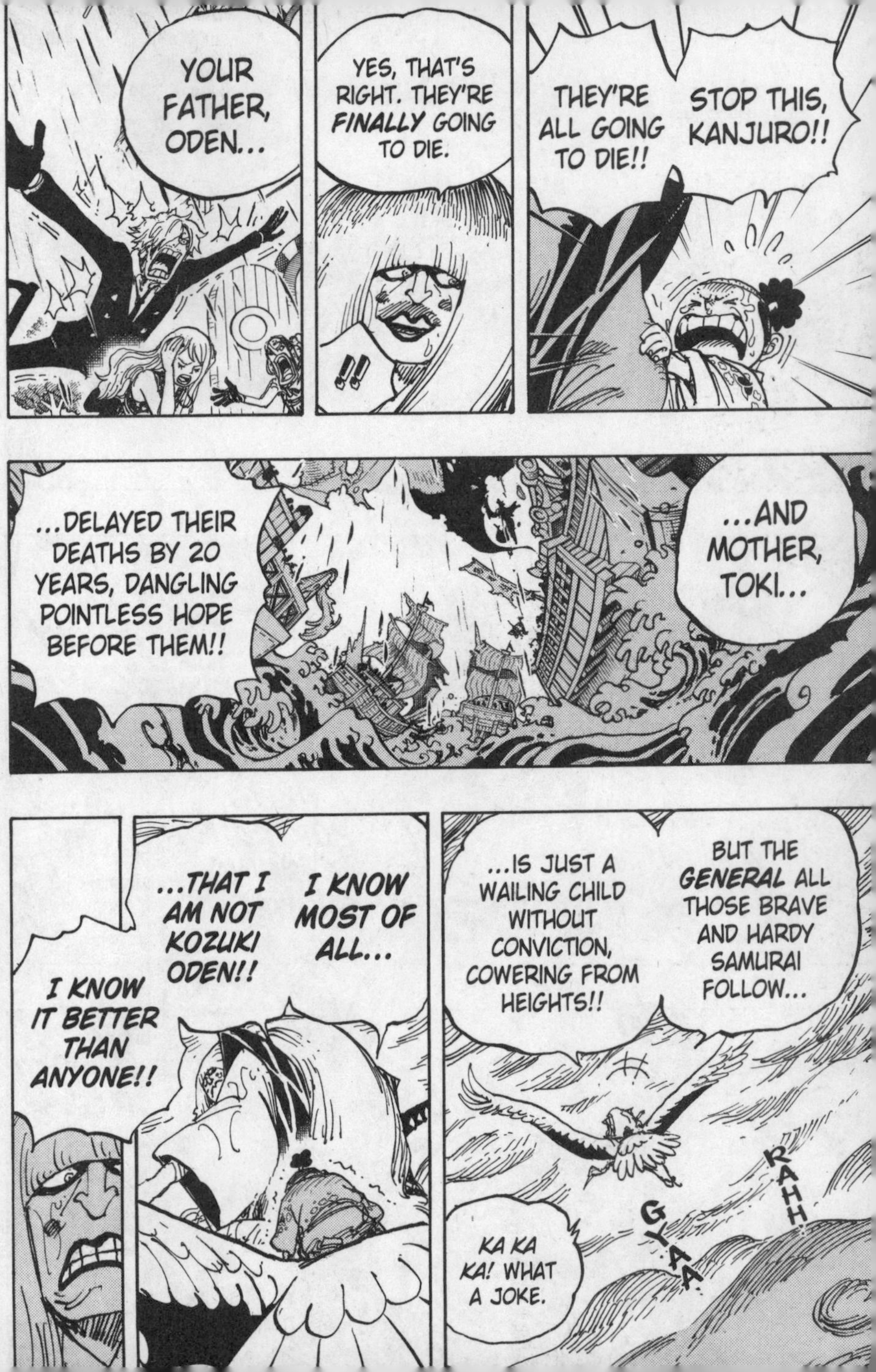
STOP THIS, KANJURO!!
THEY'RE ALL GOING TO DIE!!
YES, THAT'S RIGHT. THEY'RE *FINALLY* GOING TO DIE.
!!
YOUR FATHER, ODEN...
...AND MOTHER, TOKI...
...DELAYED THEIR DEATHS BY 20 YEARS, DANGLING POINTLESS HOPE BEFORE THEM!!
BUT THE *GENERAL* ALL THOSE BRAVE AND HARDY SAMURAI FOLLOW...
...IS JUST A WAILING CHILD WITHOUT CONVICTION, COWERING FROM HEIGHTS!!
RAHH!
GYAA
KA KA KA! WHAT A JOKE.
I KNOW MOST OF ALL...
...THAT I AM NOT KOZUKI ODEN!!
I KNOW IT BETTER THAN ANYONE!!

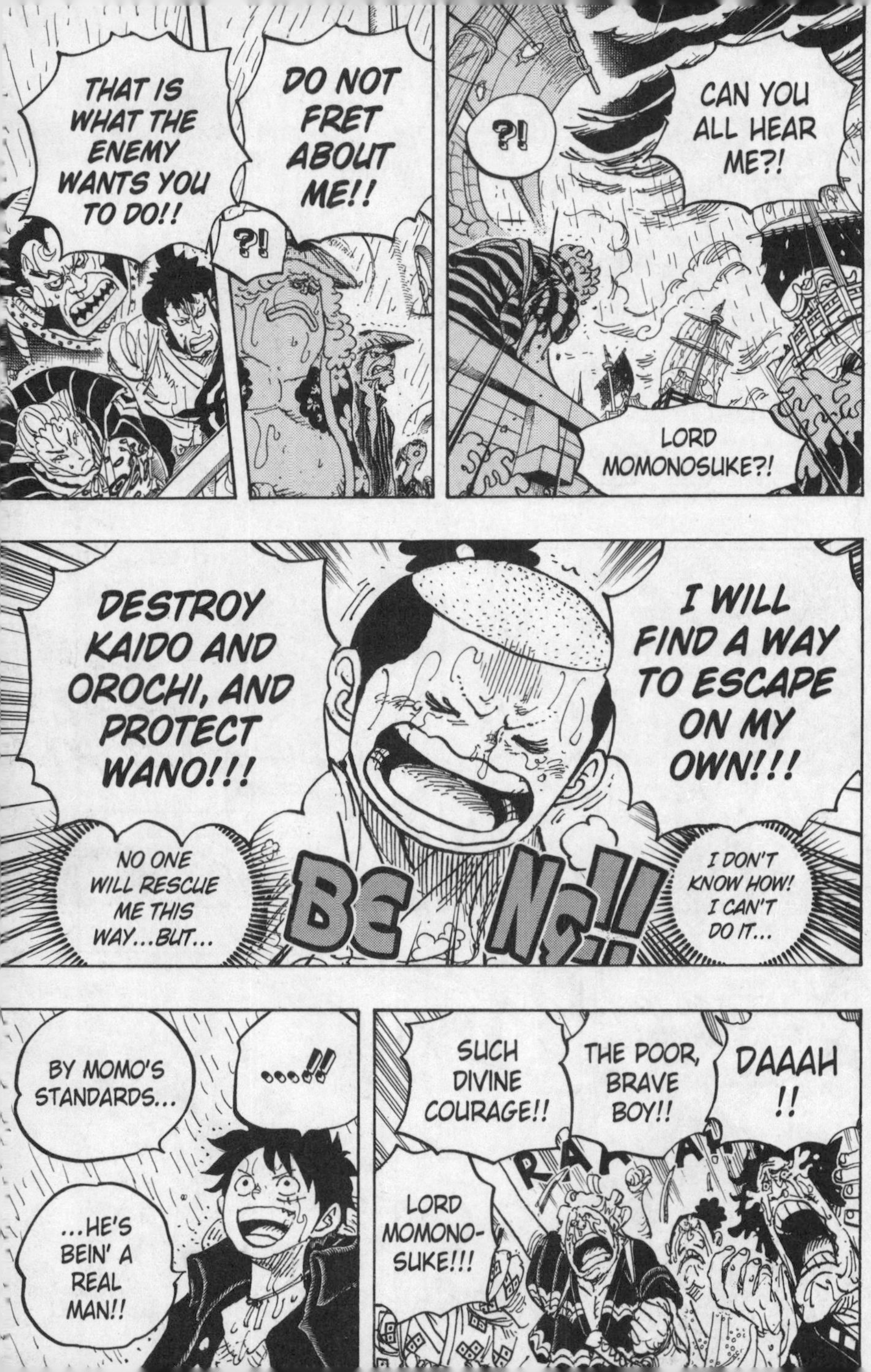
CAN YOU ALL HEAR ME?!
?!
LORD MOMONOSUKE?!
DO NOT FRET ABOUT ME!!
?!
THAT IS WHAT THE ENEMY WANTS YOU TO DO!!
I WILL FIND A WAY TO ESCAPE ON MY OWN!!!
DESTROY KAIDO AND OROCHI, AND PROTECT WANO!!!
I DON'T KNOW HOW! I CAN'T DO IT...
BE NG!!
NO ONE WILL RESCUE ME THIS WAY...BUT...
DAAAH !!
THE POOR, BRAVE BOY!!
SUCH DIVINE COURAGE!!
LORD MOMONO-SUKE!!!
....!!
BY MOMO'S STANDARDS...
...HE'S BEIN' A REAL MAN!!

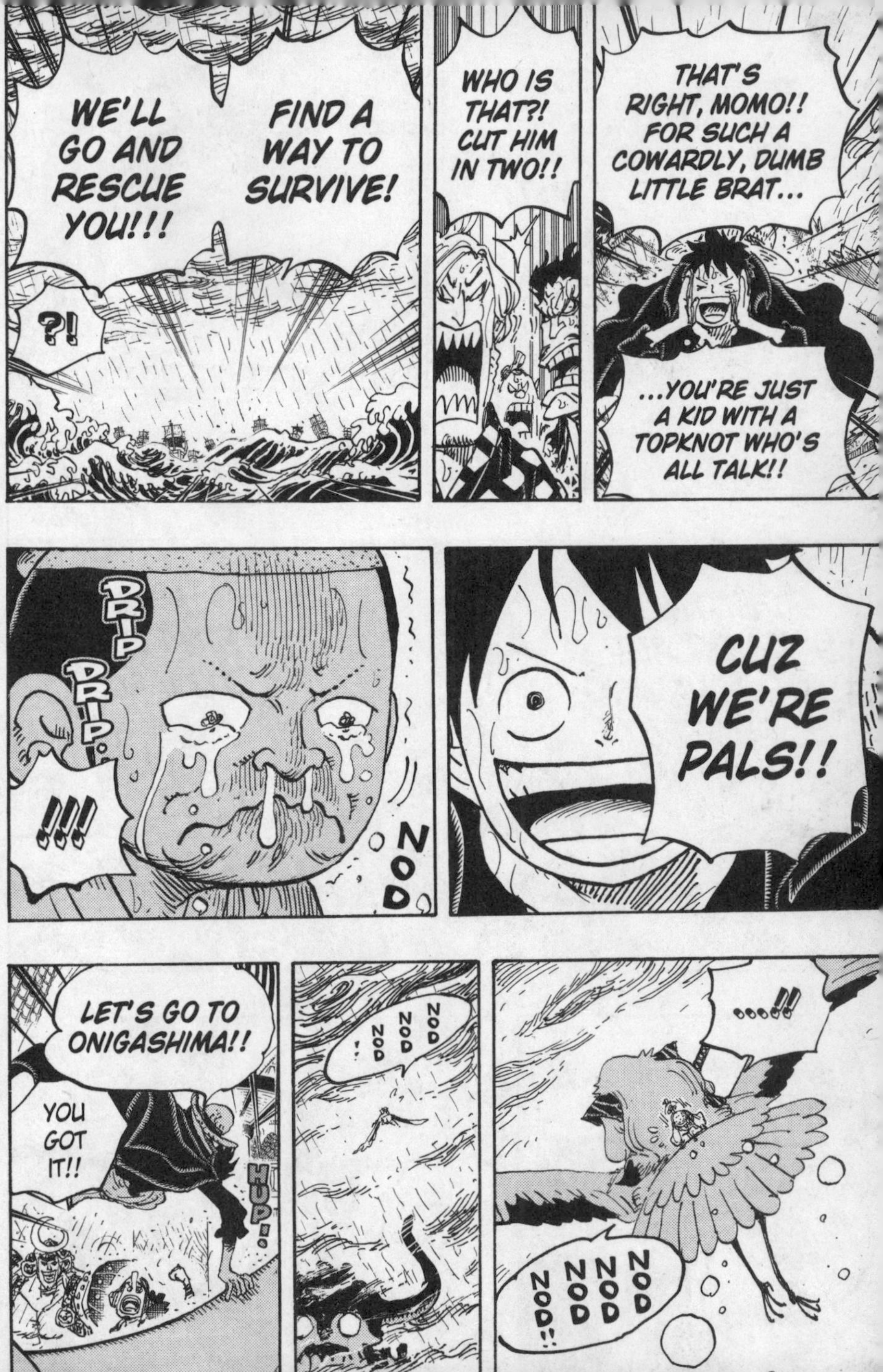
THAT'S RIGHT, MOMO!! FOR SUCH A COWARDLY, DUMB LITTLE BRAT...
...YOU'RE JUST A KID WITH A TOPKNOT WHO'S ALL TALK!!
WHO IS THAT?! CUT HIM IN TWO!!
FIND A WAY TO SURVIVE!
WE'LL GO AND RESCUE YOU!!!
?!
CUZ WE'RE PALS!!
NOD
DRIP DRIP DRIP
!!!
...!!
NOD NOD NOD NOD!!
NOD NOD NOD !
LET'S GO TO ONIGASHIMA!!
YOU GOT IT!!
HUP!

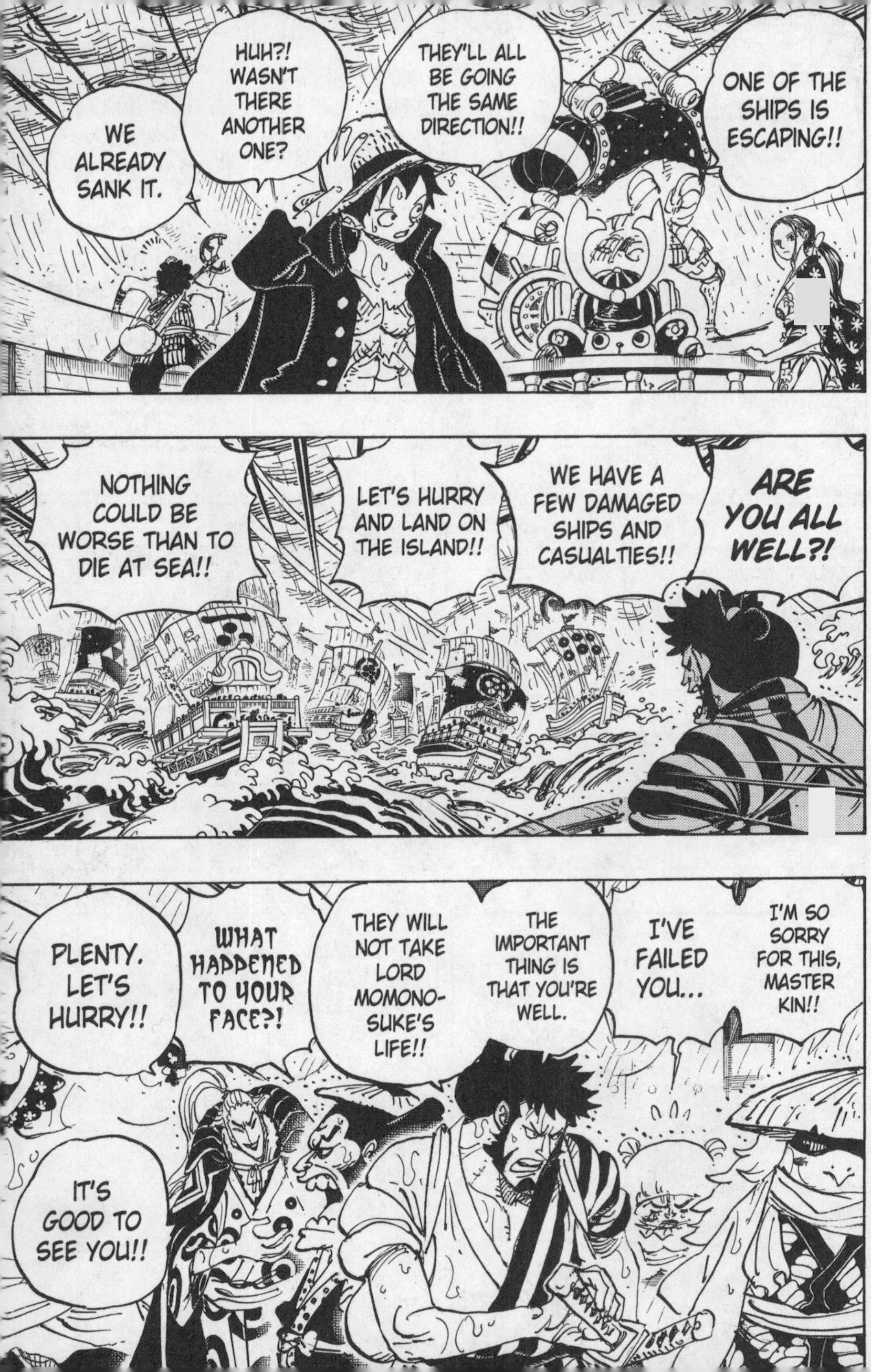
ONE OF THE SHIPS IS ESCAPING!!
THEY'LL ALL BE GOING THE SAME DIRECTION!!
HUH?! WASN'T THERE ANOTHER ONE?
WE ALREADY SANK IT.
ARE YOU ALL WELL?!
WE HAVE A FEW DAMAGED SHIPS AND CASUALTIES!!
LET'S HURRY AND LAND ON THE ISLAND!!
NOTHING COULD BE WORSE THAN TO DIE AT SEA!!
I'M SO SORRY FOR THIS, MASTER KIN!!
I'VE FAILED YOU...
THE IMPORTANT THING IS THAT YOU'RE WELL.
THEY WILL NOT TAKE LORD MOMONOSUKE'S LIFE!!
WHAT HAPPENED TO YOUR FACE?!
PLENTY. LET'S HURRY!!
IT'S GOOD TO SEE YOU!!

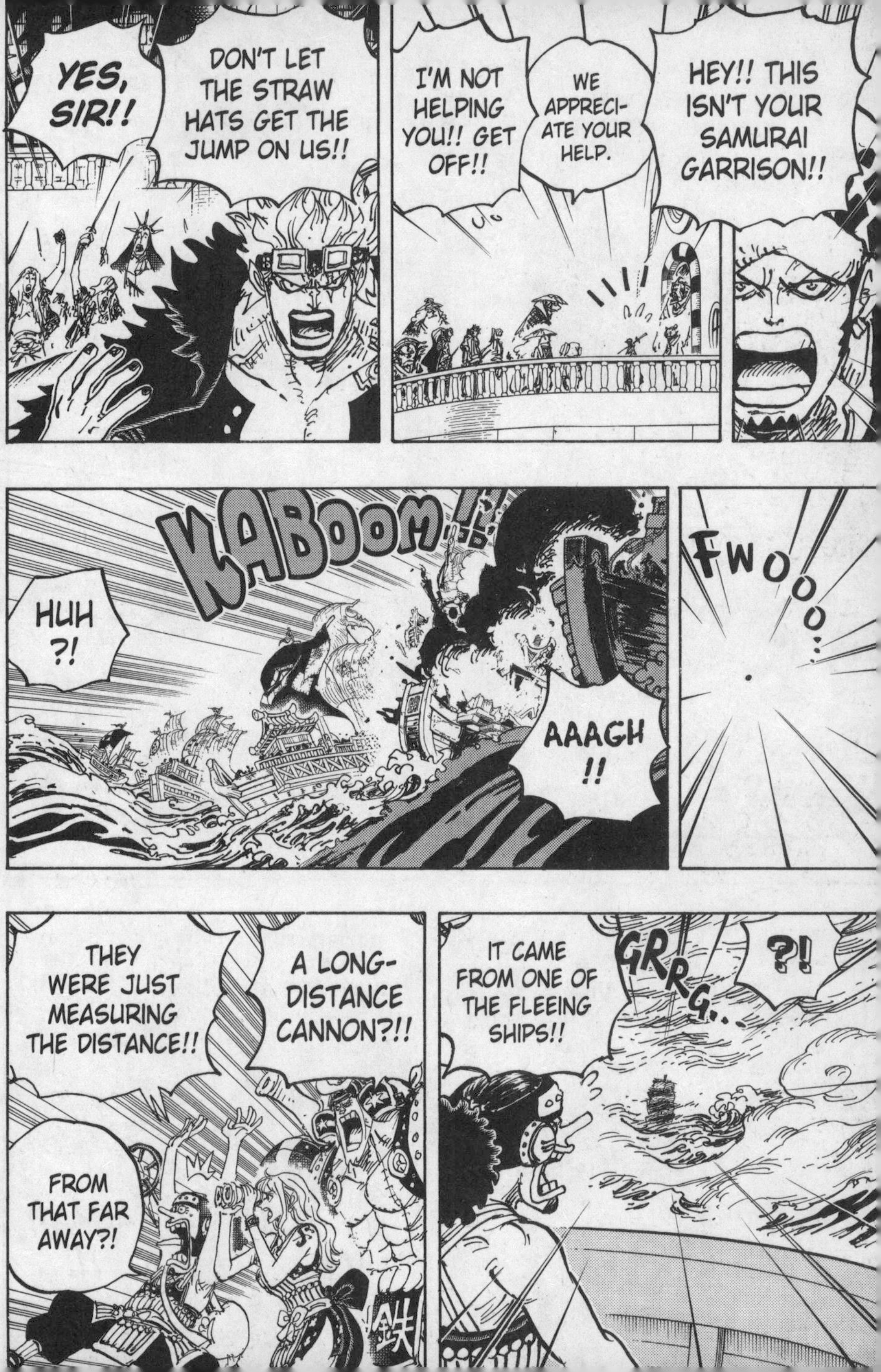
HEY!! THIS ISN'T YOUR SAMURAI GARRISON!!
WE APPRECIATE YOUR HELP.
I'M NOT HELPING YOU!! GET OFF!!
DON'T LET THE STRAW HATS GET THE JUMP ON US!!
YES, SIR!!
FWOOO...
KABOOM!!
AAAGH!!
HUH ?!
?!
GRRRG...
IT CAME FROM ONE OF THE FLEEING SHIPS!!
A LONG-DISTANCE CANNON?!!
THEY WERE JUST MEASURING THE DISTANCE!!
FROM THAT FAR AWAY?!

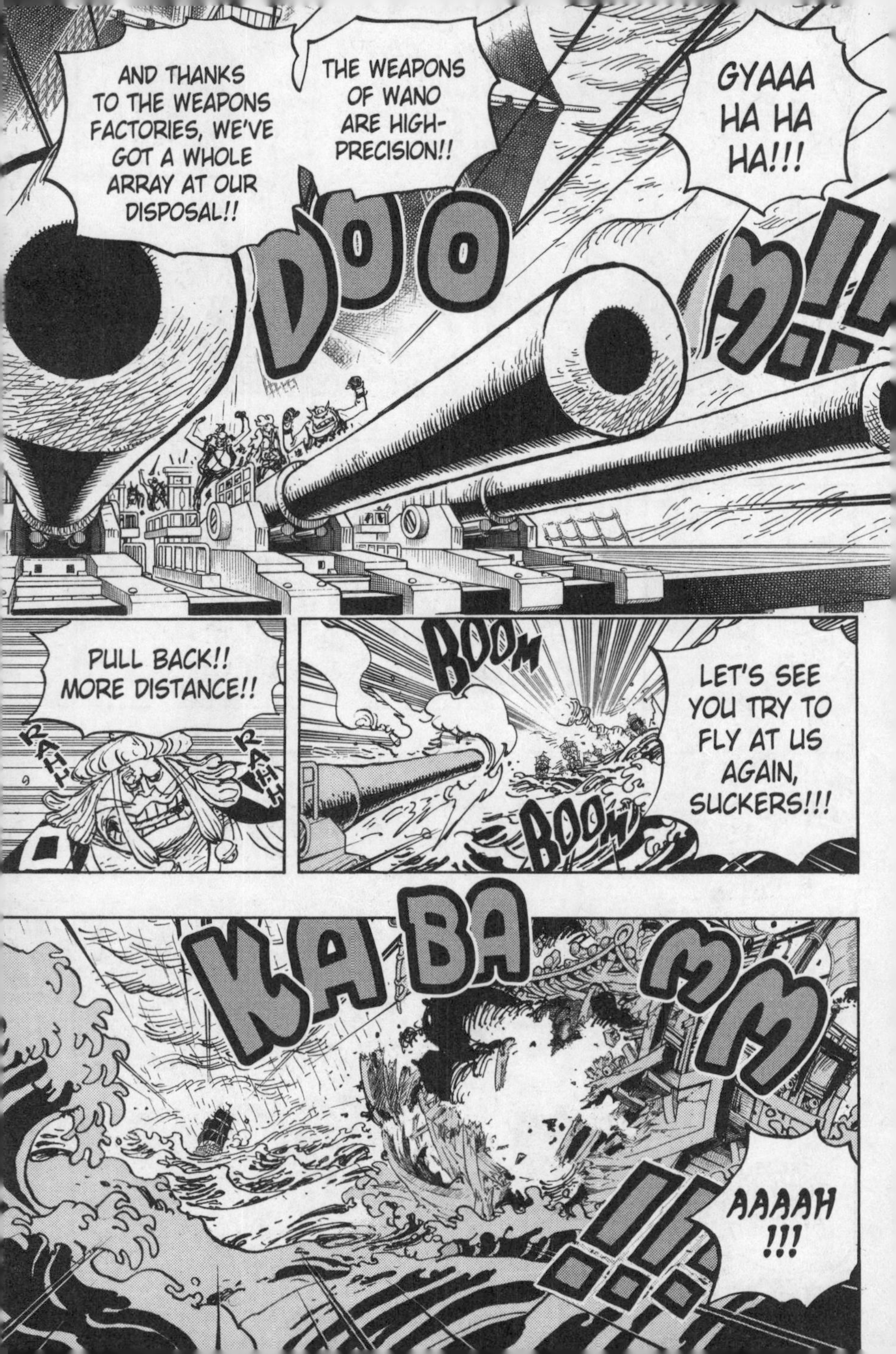
GYAAA HA HA HA!!!
THE WEAPONS OF WANO ARE HIGH-PRECISION!!
AND THANKS TO THE WEAPONS FACTORIES, WE'VE GOT A WHOLE ARRAY AT OUR DISPOSAL!!
DOOOM!!
BOOM
LET'S SEE YOU TRY TO FLY AT US AGAIN, SUCKERS!!!
BOOM
PULL BACK!! MORE DISTANCE!!
RAHH
RAHH
KABAMM!!
AAAAH!!!

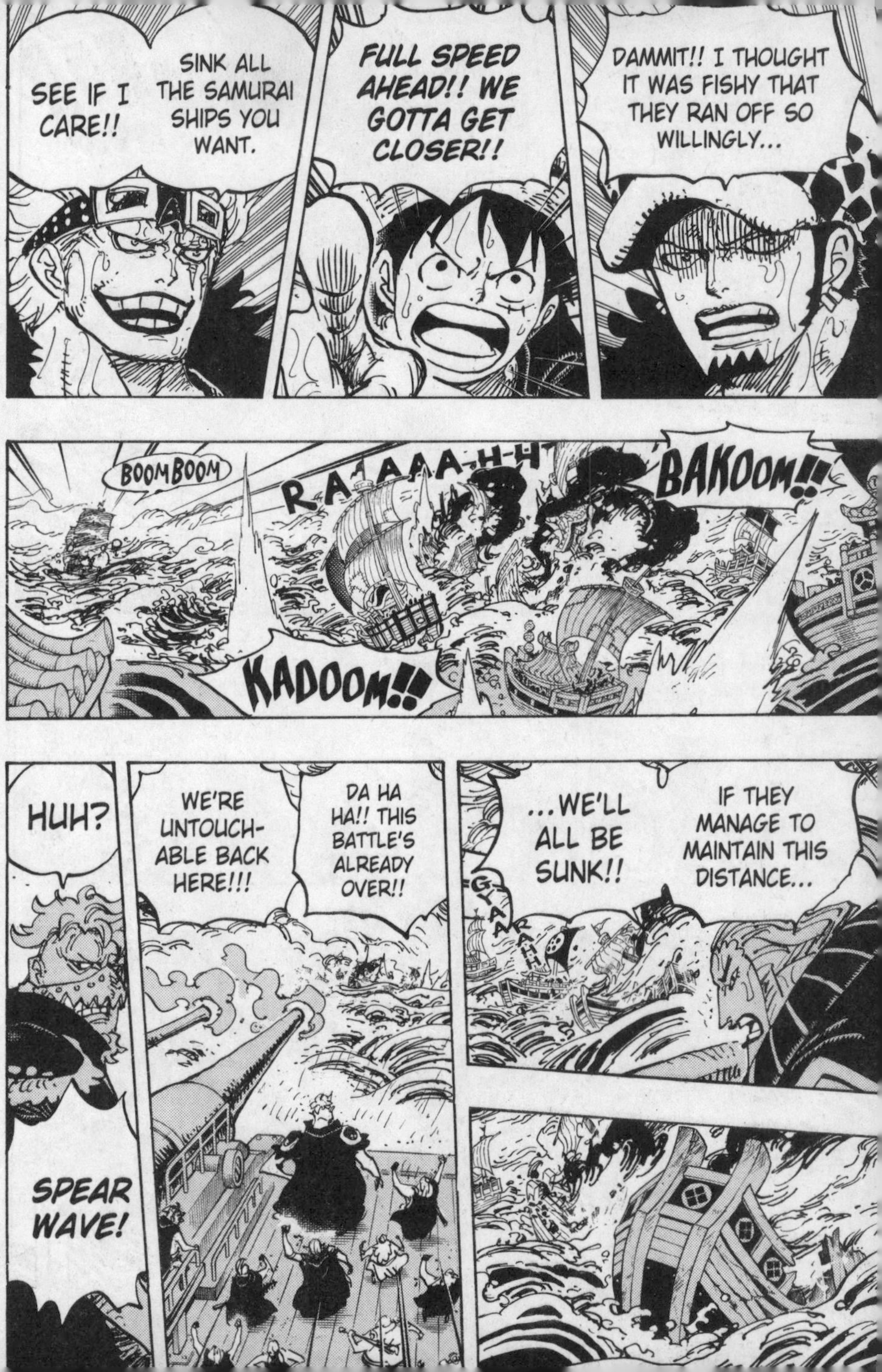
DAMMIT!! I THOUGHT IT WAS FISHY THAT THEY RAN OFF SO WILLINGLY...
FULL SPEED AHEAD!! WE GOTTA GET CLOSER!!
SINK ALL THE SAMURAI SHIPS YOU WANT.
SEE IF I CARE!!
BAKOOM!!
RAAAAA-H-H
BOOMBOOM
KADOOM!!
IF THEY MANAGE TO MAINTAIN THIS DISTANCE...
...WE'LL ALL BE SUNK!!
GYAARAHH
DA HA HA!! THIS BATTLE'S ALREADY OVER!!
WE'RE UNTOUCH-ABLE BACK HERE!!!
HUH?
SPEAR WAVE!

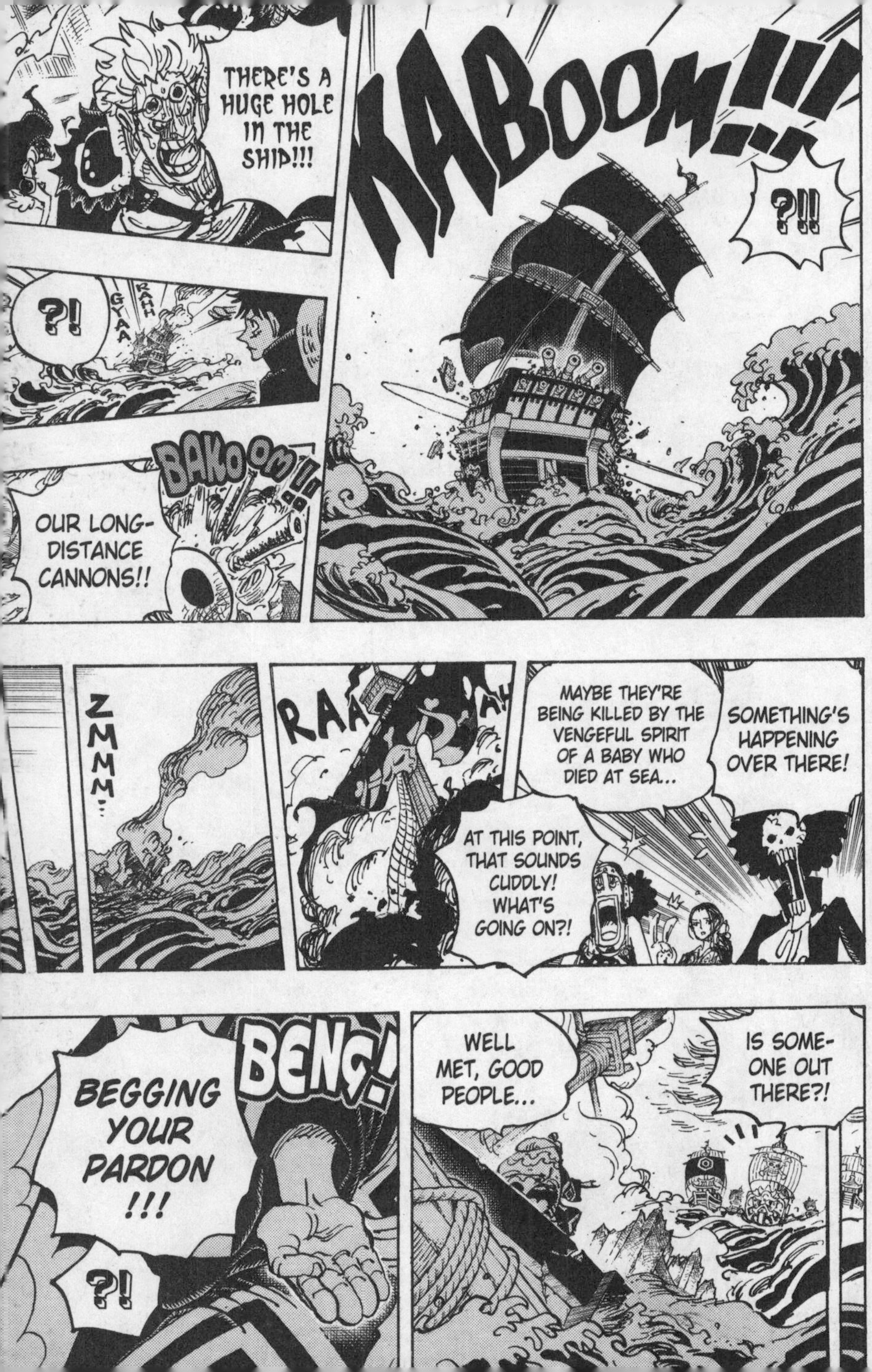
KABOOM!!!
?!!
THERE'S A HUGE HOLE IN THE SHIP!!!
?!
GYAA
RAHH
BAKOOM!!!
OUR LONG-DISTANCE CANNONS!!
SOMETHING'S HAPPENING OVER THERE!
MAYBE THEY'RE BEING KILLED BY THE VENGEFUL SPIRIT OF A BABY WHO DIED AT SEA...
AT THIS POINT, THAT SOUNDS CUDDLY! WHAT'S GOING ON?!
RAA
ZMMM...
IS SOME-ONE OUT THERE?!
WELL MET, GOOD PEOPLE...
BENG!
BEGGING YOUR PARDON!!!
?!

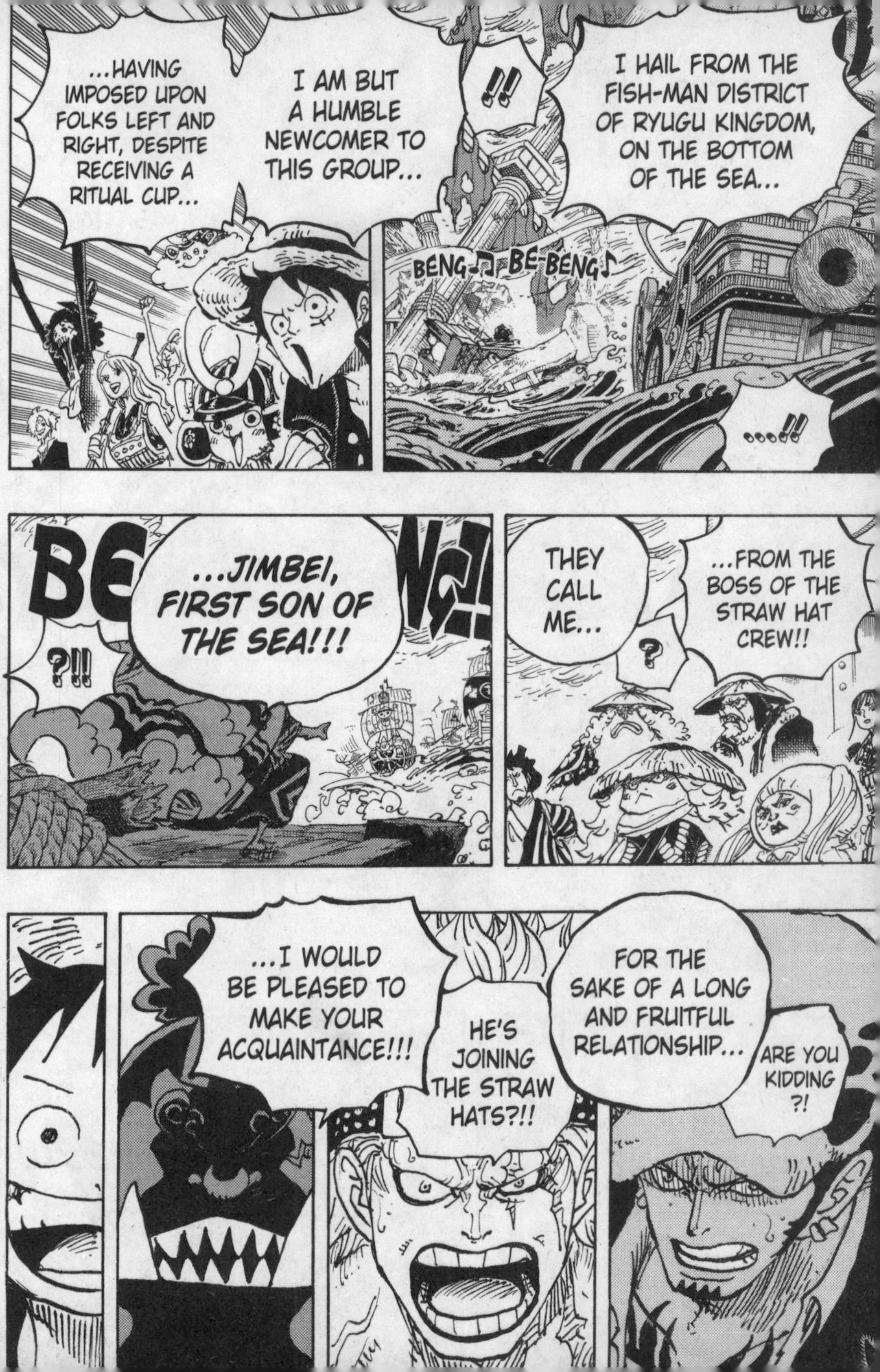
I HAIL FROM THE FISH-MAN DISTRICT OF RYUGU KINGDOM, ON THE BOTTOM OF THE SEA...
!!
BENG♫ BE-BENG♪
....!!
I AM BUT A HUMBLE NEWCOMER TO THIS GROUP...
...HAVING IMPOSED UPON FOLKS LEFT AND RIGHT, DESPITE RECEIVING A RITUAL CUP...
...FROM THE BOSS OF THE STRAW HAT CREW!!
THEY CALL ME...
?
BENG!!
...JIMBEI, FIRST SON OF THE SEA!!!
?!!
FOR THE SAKE OF A LONG AND FRUITFUL RELATIONSHIP...
...I WOULD BE PLEASED TO MAKE YOUR ACQUAINTANCE!!!
ARE YOU KIDDING?!
HE'S JOINING THE STRAW HATS?!!

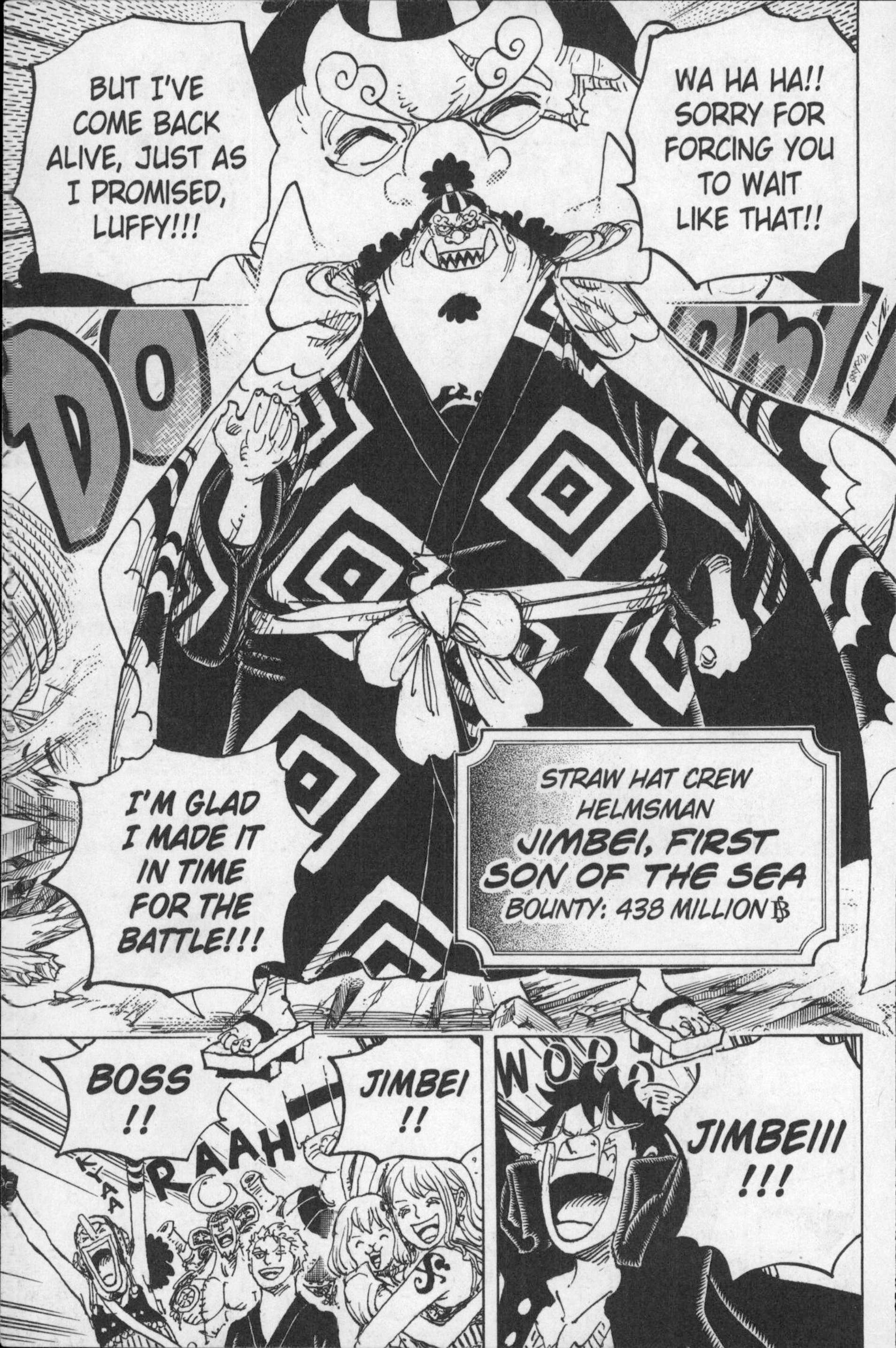
WA HA HA!! SORRY FOR FORCING YOU TO WAIT LIKE THAT!!
BUT I'VE COME BACK ALIVE, JUST AS I PROMISED, LUFFY!!!
DO
STRAW HAT CREW HELMSMAN
JIMBEI, FIRST SON OF THE SEA
BOUNTY: 438 MILLION ฿
I'M GLAD I MADE IT IN TIME FOR THE BATTLE!!!
JIMBEIII !!!
WOO
JIMBEI !!
BOSS !!
RAAH

SBS Question Corner

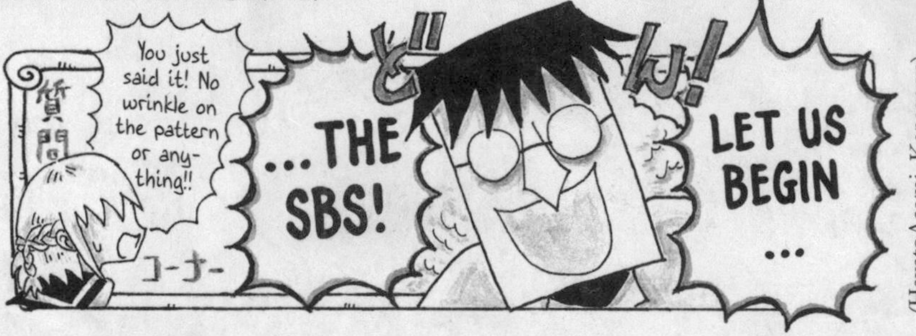
You just said it! No wrinkle on the pattern or anything!!
質問
コーナー
...THE SBS!
どん!
LET US BEGIN ...

(HayatoAsami, Kanagawa)

A: ⬆ What?! Hang on!! You started the SBS without me! You don't have to do this anymore!! That's not even from this manga!! You just drew "Usopp Nakatsugawa" from the *One Piece* spin-off manga *One Piece in Love*!! I mean, look, I love checking it out every week too, but the spin-off can't take over the original series!! Get lost!!

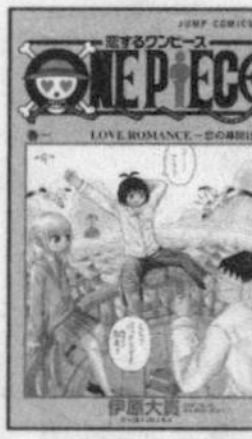
ONE PIECE

Q: Greetings!! I've been a longtime reader, and as a big fan of kappas, I was delighted when Kawamatsu was introduced into the story! I'm writing this letter in the hopes that you'll make Kawamatsu's birthday June 14, which is International Cucumber Day!

--ala

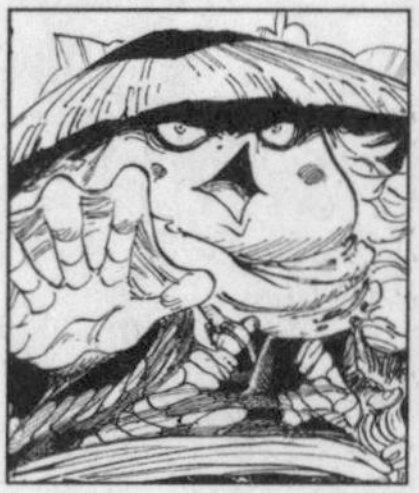

A: Okay, listen... Kawamatsu's cool and all, and I totally get where you're coming from... so if you want to decide the character's birthday for me, **that's cool!!**

Q: Can my birthday be October 11?

--Himawariya

A: **That's cool!!**

Q: The show's staff took responsibiiity for the shrimp tempura on Kyoshiro's head and ate every last bite.

--Takataka

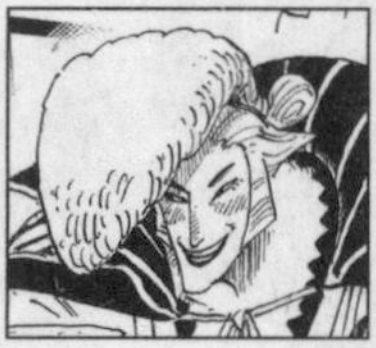

A: Whew... I'm glad to hear it didn't go to waste!

Q: You know that guy in chapter 972 who says, "Man, we look so stupid now"? That's my grandpa. *Shu ho ho ho!*

--The Man Who Loved Fried Rice

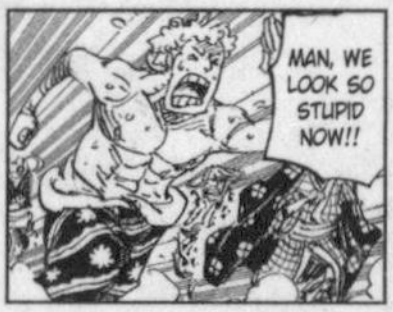
MAN, WE LOOK SO STUPID NOW!!

A: Oh, he is? Well, it's important to be able to admit when you're wrong.

Q: This just in: *One Piece* is as hot as a pot of oden. Back to you in the studio.

--Miito

A: You heard it here, folks. Watch out for burns while in Wano! You know, since it's so wano! (Not actually making a pun)

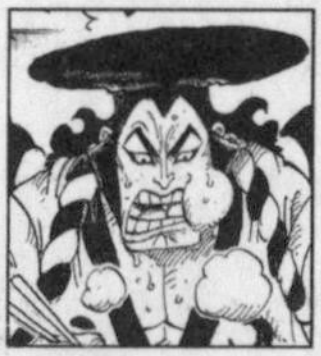

Chapter 977:
THE PARTY'S OFF!!!

**GANG BEGE'S OH MY FAMILY
VOL. 24: "LOLA?! CHIFFON?! THE SISTERS ARE REUNITED!"**

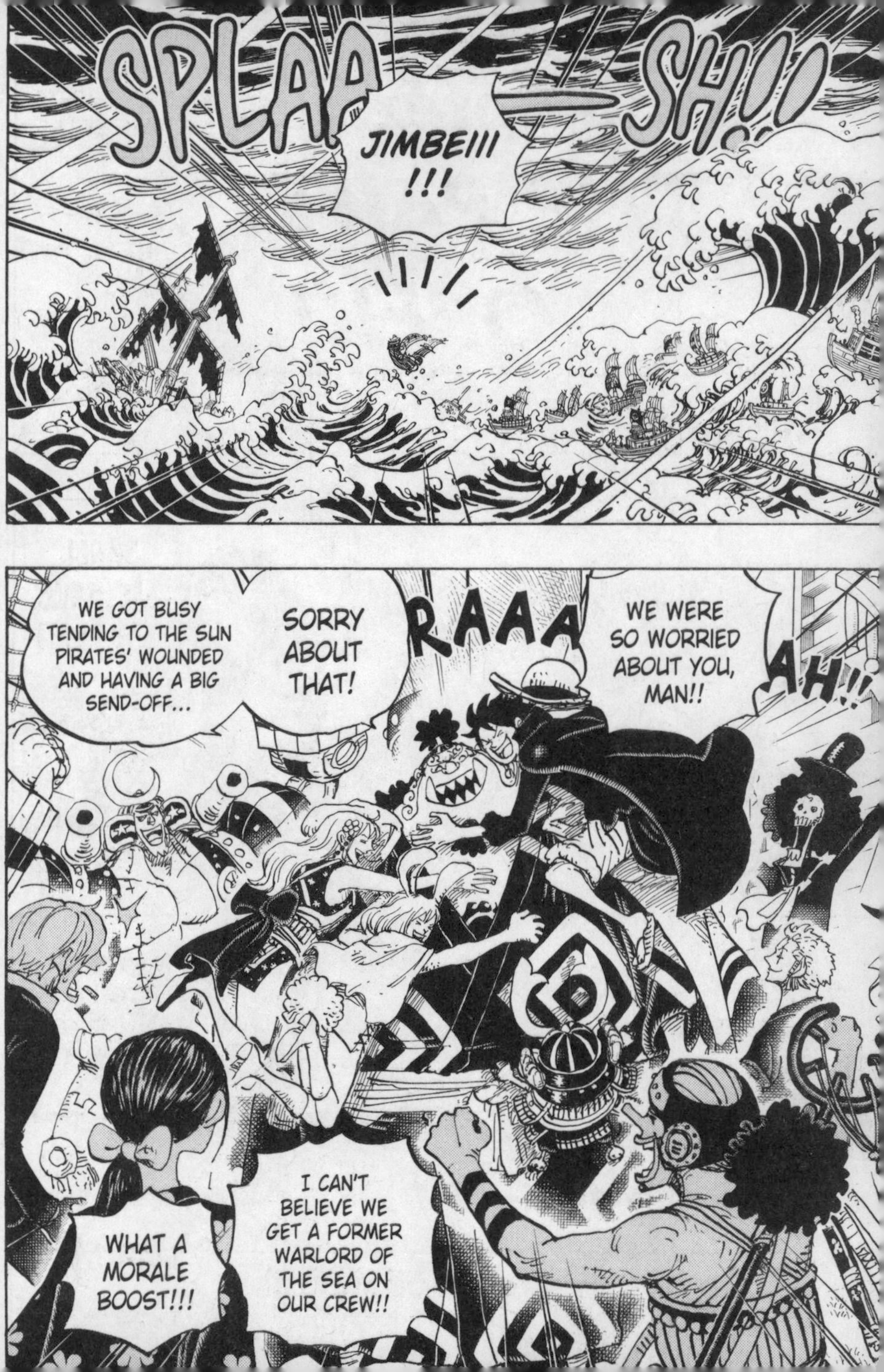
SPLAA—SH!!
JIMBE!!!
!!!
WE WERE SO WORRIED ABOUT YOU, MAN!!
RAAAAH!!
SORRY ABOUT THAT!
WE GOT BUSY TENDING TO THE SUN PIRATES' WOUNDED AND HAVING A BIG SEND-OFF...
I CAN'T BELIEVE WE GET A FORMER WARLORD OF THE SEA ON OUR CREW!!
WHAT A MORALE BOOST!!!

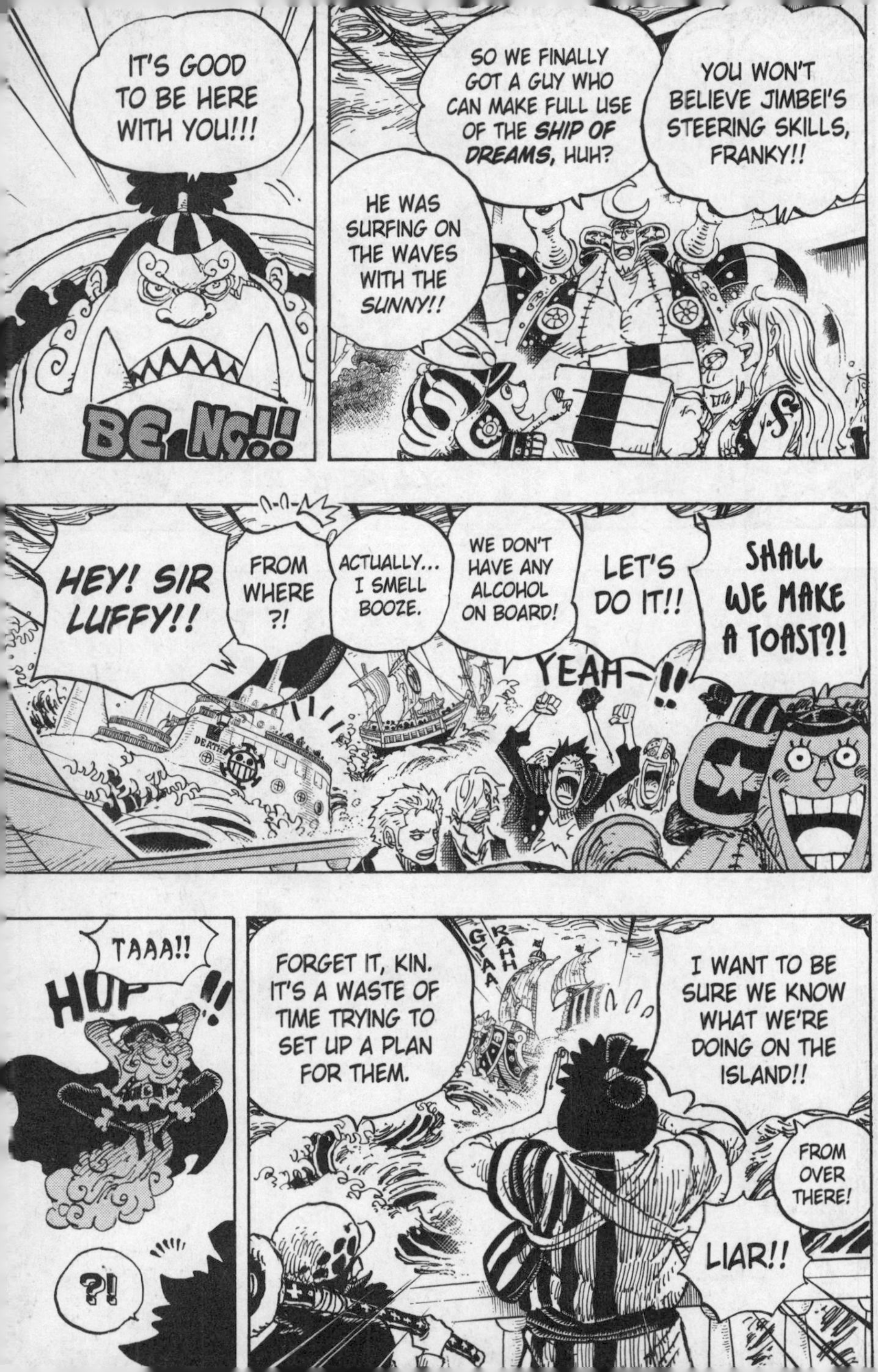
YOU WON'T BELIEVE JIMBEI'S STEERING SKILLS, FRANKY!!
SO WE FINALLY GOT A GUY WHO CAN MAKE FULL USE OF THE *SHIP OF DREAMS*, HUH?
HE WAS SURFING ON THE WAVES WITH THE *SUNNY!!*
IT'S GOOD TO BE HERE WITH YOU!!!
BE NG!!
SHALL WE MAKE A TOAST?!
LET'S DO IT!!
YEAH-!!
WE DON'T HAVE ANY ALCOHOL ON BOARD!
ACTUALLY... I SMELL BOOZE.
FROM WHERE ?!
HEY! SIR LUFFY!!
I WANT TO BE SURE WE KNOW WHAT WE'RE DOING ON THE ISLAND!!
RAHH
GYAA
FORGET IT, KIN. IT'S A WASTE OF TIME TRYING TO SET UP A PLAN FOR THEM.
FROM OVER THERE!
LIAR!!
TAAA!!
HOP !!
?!

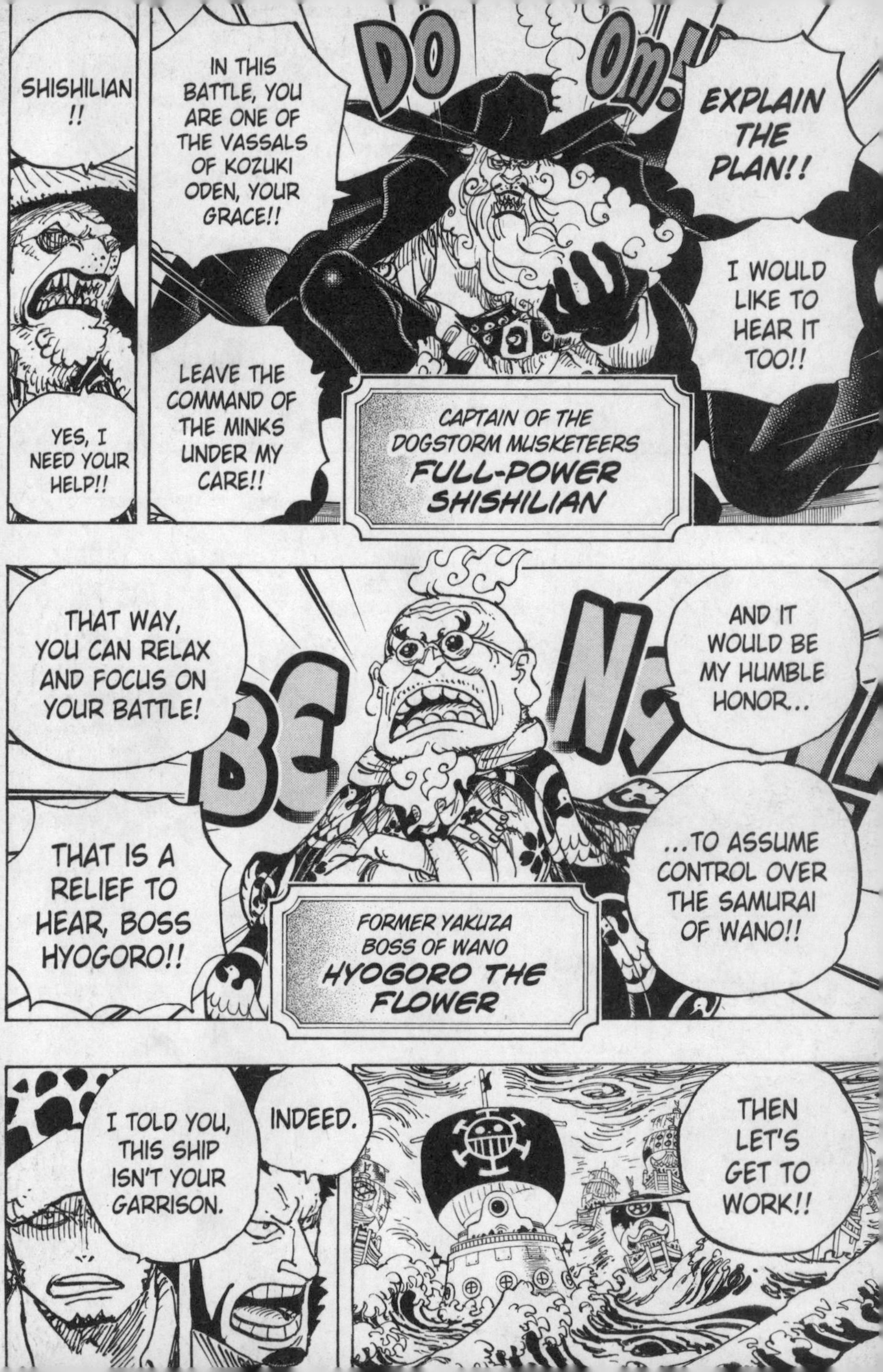
DO
OM!
EXPLAIN THE PLAN!!
I WOULD LIKE TO HEAR IT TOO!!
IN THIS BATTLE, YOU ARE ONE OF THE VASSALS OF KOZUKI ODEN, YOUR GRACE!!
CAPTAIN OF THE DOGSTORM MUSKETEERS FULL-POWER SHISHILIAN
LEAVE THE COMMAND OF THE MINKS UNDER MY CARE!!
SHISHILIAN!!
YES, I NEED YOUR HELP!!
AND IT WOULD BE MY HUMBLE HONOR...
NS
BE
THAT WAY, YOU CAN RELAX AND FOCUS ON YOUR BATTLE!
...TO ASSUME CONTROL OVER THE SAMURAI OF WANO!!
FORMER YAKUZA BOSS OF WANO HYOGORO THE FLOWER
THAT IS A RELIEF TO HEAR, BOSS HYOGORO!!
THEN LET'S GET TO WORK!!
INDEED.
I TOLD YOU, THIS SHIP ISN'T YOUR GARRISON.

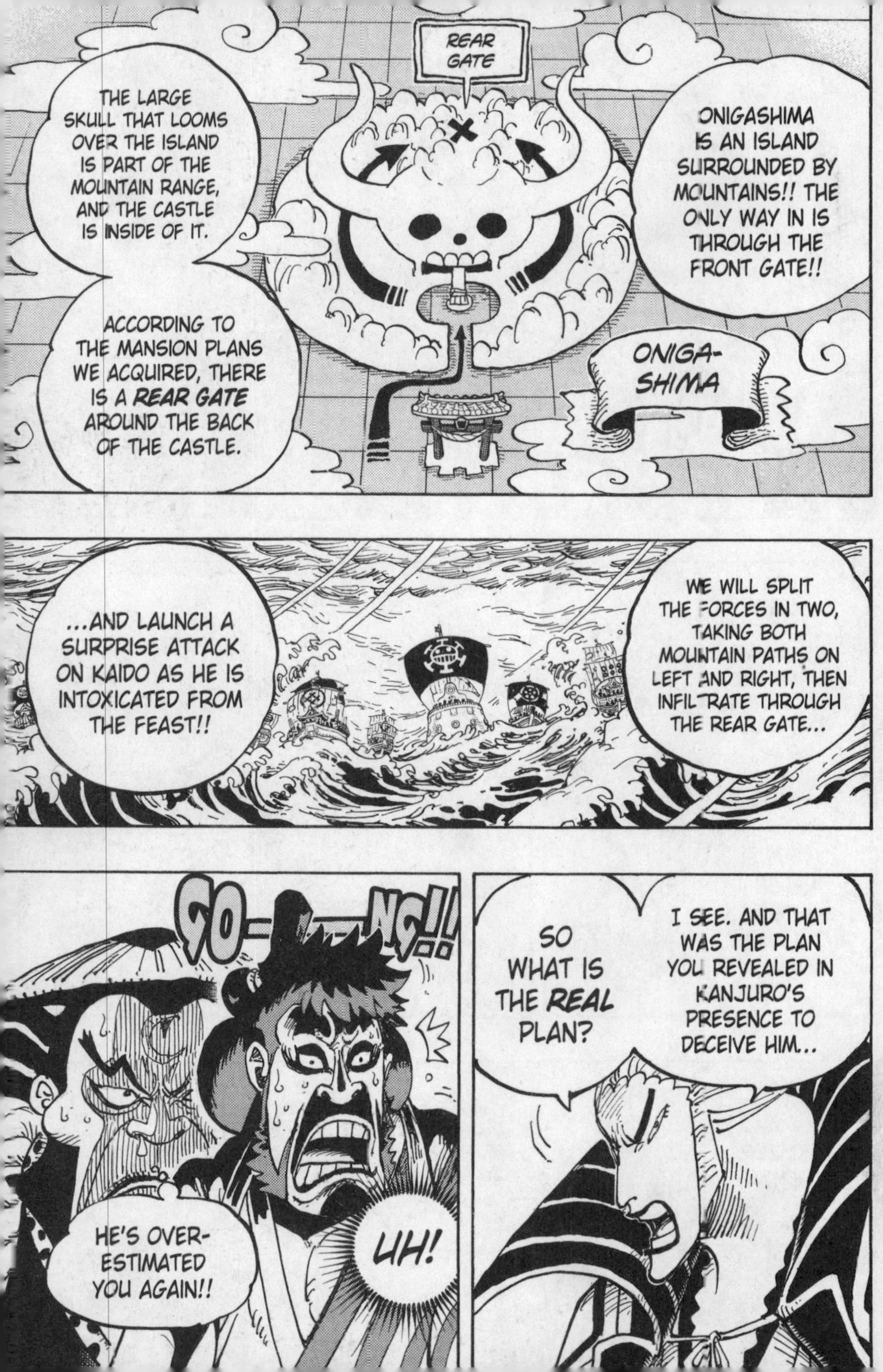
ONIGASHIMA IS AN ISLAND SURROUNDED BY MOUNTAINS!! THE ONLY WAY IN IS THROUGH THE FRONT GATE!!
ONIGA-SHIMA
REAR GATE
THE LARGE SKULL THAT LOOMS OVER THE ISLAND IS PART OF THE MOUNTAIN RANGE, AND THE CASTLE IS INSIDE OF IT.
ACCORDING TO THE MANSION PLANS WE ACQUIRED, THERE IS A *REAR GATE* AROUND THE BACK OF THE CASTLE.
WE WILL SPLIT THE FORCES IN TWO, TAKING BOTH MOUNTAIN PATHS ON LEFT AND RIGHT, THEN INFILTRATE THROUGH THE REAR GATE...
...AND LAUNCH A SURPRISE ATTACK ON KAIDO AS HE IS INTOXICATED FROM THE FEAST!!
I SEE. AND THAT WAS THE PLAN YOU REVEALED IN KANJURO'S PRESENCE TO DECEIVE HIM...
SO WHAT IS THE *REAL* PLAN?
GO- NG!!
UH!
HE'S OVER-ESTIMATED YOU AGAIN!!

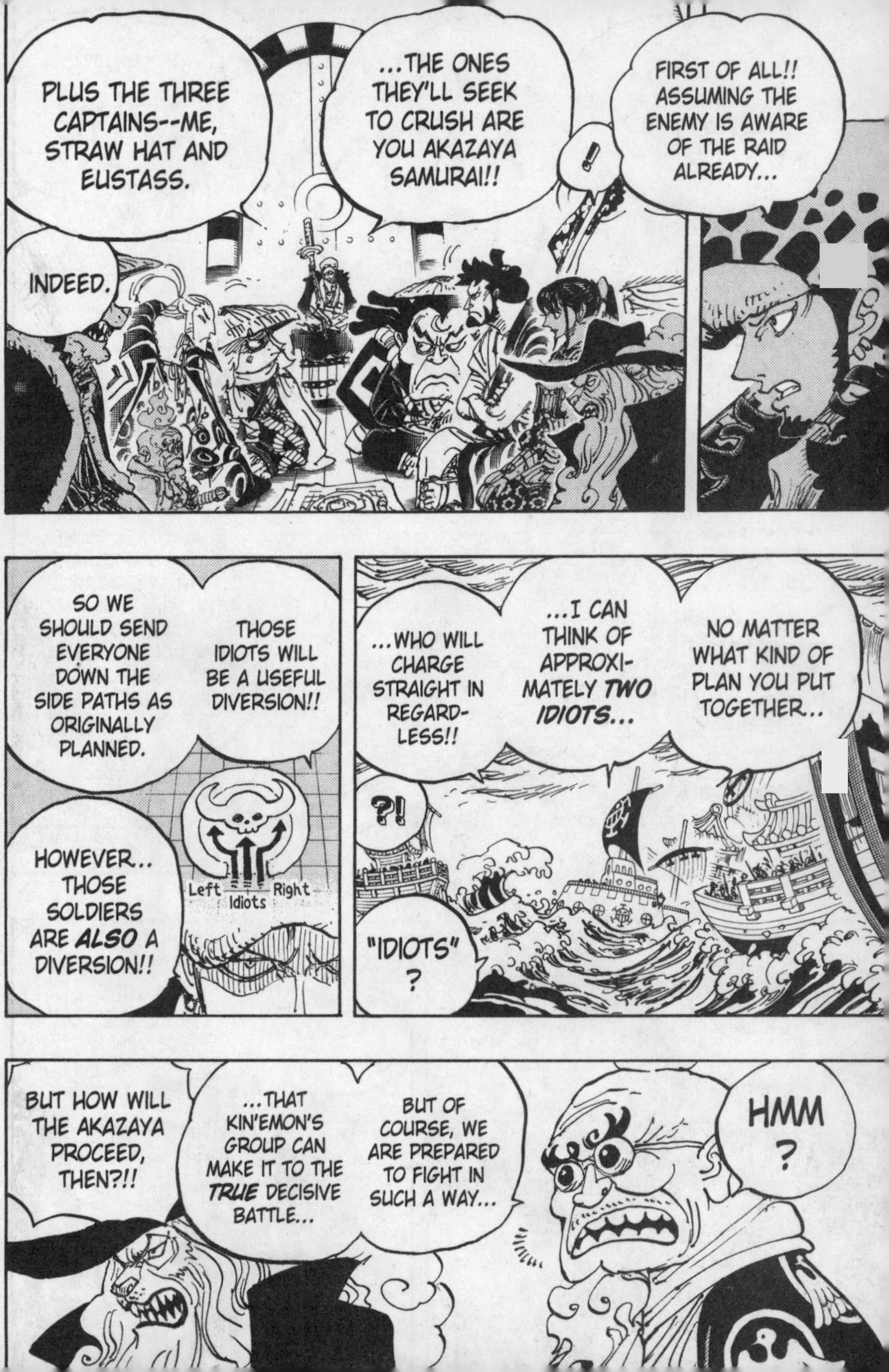
FIRST OF ALL!! ASSUMING THE ENEMY IS AWARE OF THE RAID ALREADY...
!
...THE ONES THEY'LL SEEK TO CRUSH ARE YOU AKAZAYA SAMURAI!!
PLUS THE THREE CAPTAINS--ME, STRAW HAT AND EUSTASS.
INDEED.
NO MATTER WHAT KIND OF PLAN YOU PUT TOGETHER...
...I CAN THINK OF APPROXI-MATELY *TWO IDIOTS*...
...WHO WILL CHARGE STRAIGHT IN REGARD-LESS!!
?!
"IDIOTS"?
THOSE IDIOTS WILL BE A USEFUL DIVERSION!!
SO WE SHOULD SEND EVERYONE DOWN THE SIDE PATHS AS ORIGINALLY PLANNED.
Left
Idiots
Right
HOWEVER... THOSE SOLDIERS ARE *ALSO* A DIVERSION!!
HMM?
BUT OF COURSE, WE ARE PREPARED TO FIGHT IN SUCH A WAY...
...THAT KIN'EMON'S GROUP CAN MAKE IT TO THE *TRUE* DECISIVE BATTLE...
BUT HOW WILL THE AKAZAYA PROCEED, THEN?!!

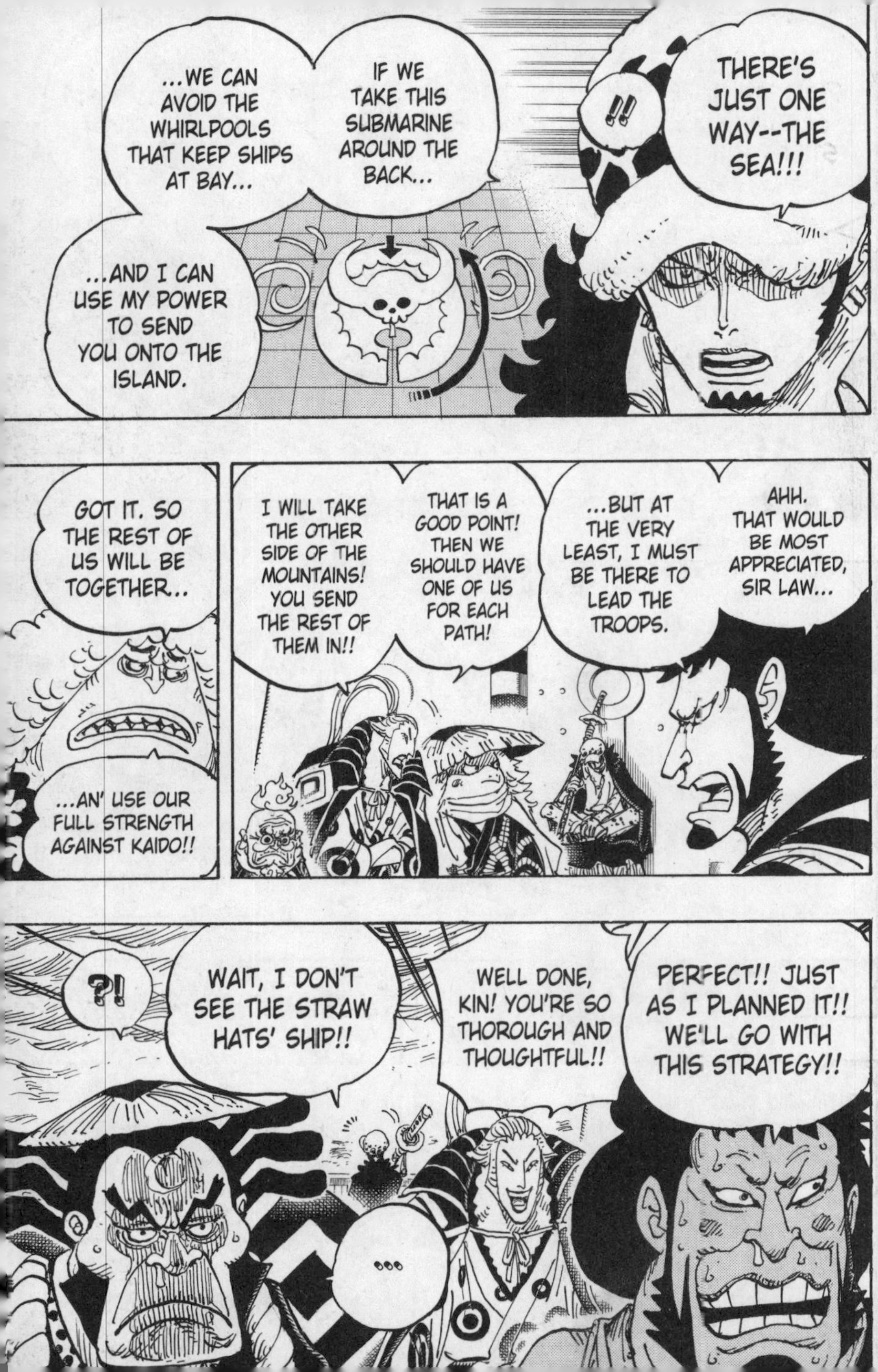
THERE'S JUST ONE WAY--THE SEA!!!
!!
IF WE TAKE THIS SUBMARINE AROUND THE BACK...
...WE CAN AVOID THE WHIRLPOOLS THAT KEEP SHIPS AT BAY...
...AND I CAN USE MY POWER TO SEND YOU ONTO THE ISLAND.
AHH. THAT WOULD BE MOST APPRECIATED, SIR LAW...
...BUT AT THE VERY LEAST, I MUST BE THERE TO LEAD THE TROOPS.
THAT IS A GOOD POINT! THEN WE SHOULD HAVE ONE OF US FOR EACH PATH!
I WILL TAKE THE OTHER SIDE OF THE MOUNTAINS! YOU SEND THE REST OF THEM IN!!
GOT IT. SO THE REST OF US WILL BE TOGETHER...
...AN' USE OUR FULL STRENGTH AGAINST KAIDO!!
PERFECT!! JUST AS I PLANNED IT!! WE'LL GO WITH THIS STRATEGY!!
WELL DONE, KIN! YOU'RE SO THOROUGH AND THOUGHTFUL!!
WAIT, I DON'T SEE THE STRAW HATS' SHIP!!
?!
...

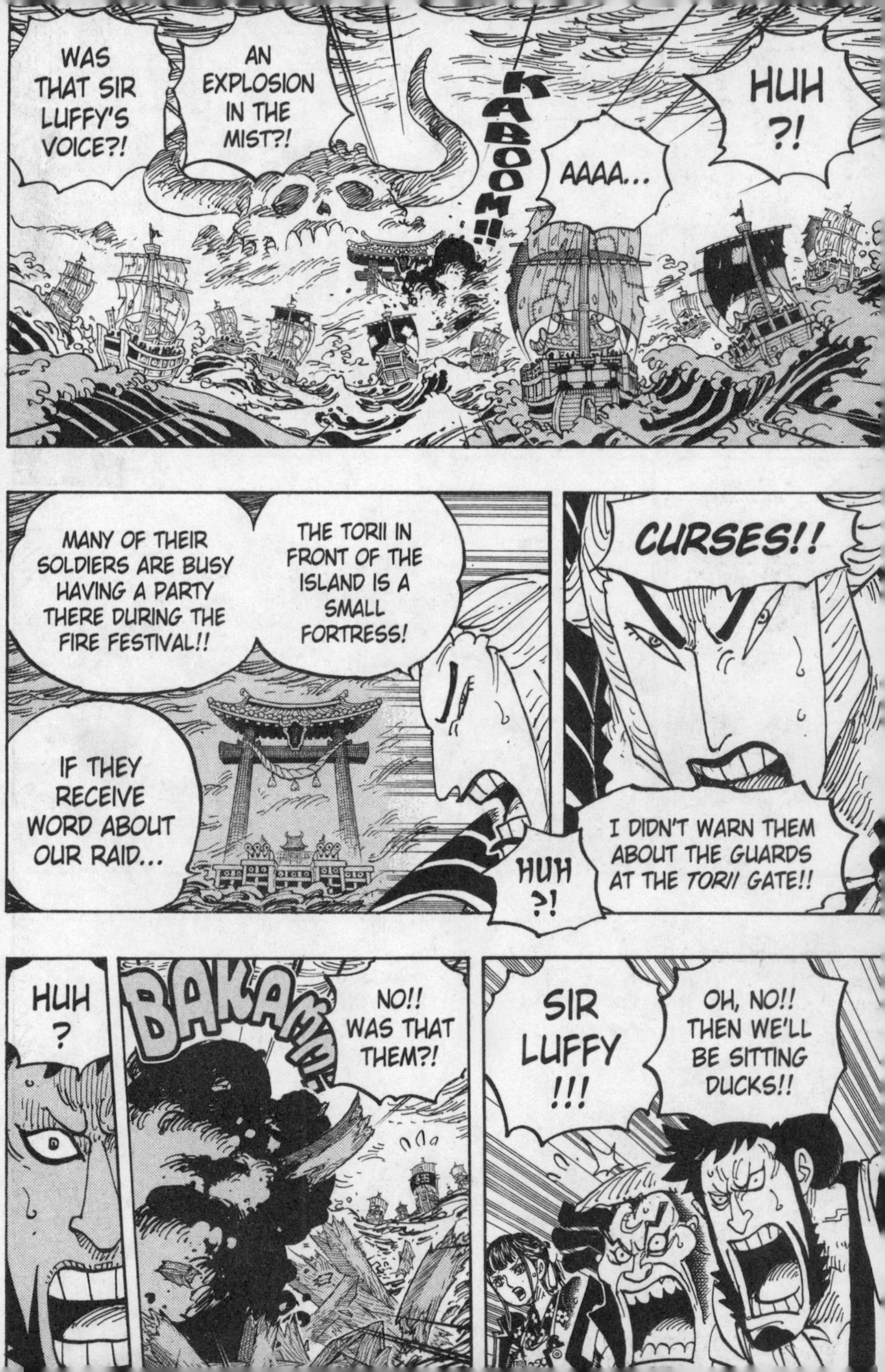
HUH ?!
AAAA...
KABOOM!!
AN EXPLOSION IN THE MIST?!
WAS THAT SIR LUFFY'S VOICE?!
CURSES!!
I DIDN'T WARN THEM ABOUT THE GUARDS AT THE TORII GATE!!
HUH ?!
THE TORII IN FRONT OF THE ISLAND IS A SMALL FORTRESS!
MANY OF THEIR SOLDIERS ARE BUSY HAVING A PARTY THERE DURING THE FIRE FESTIVAL!!
IF THEY RECEIVE WORD ABOUT OUR RAID...
OH, NO!! THEN WE'LL BE SITTING DUCKS!!
SIR LUFFY !!!
NO!! WAS THAT THEM?!
BAKAMM
HUH ?

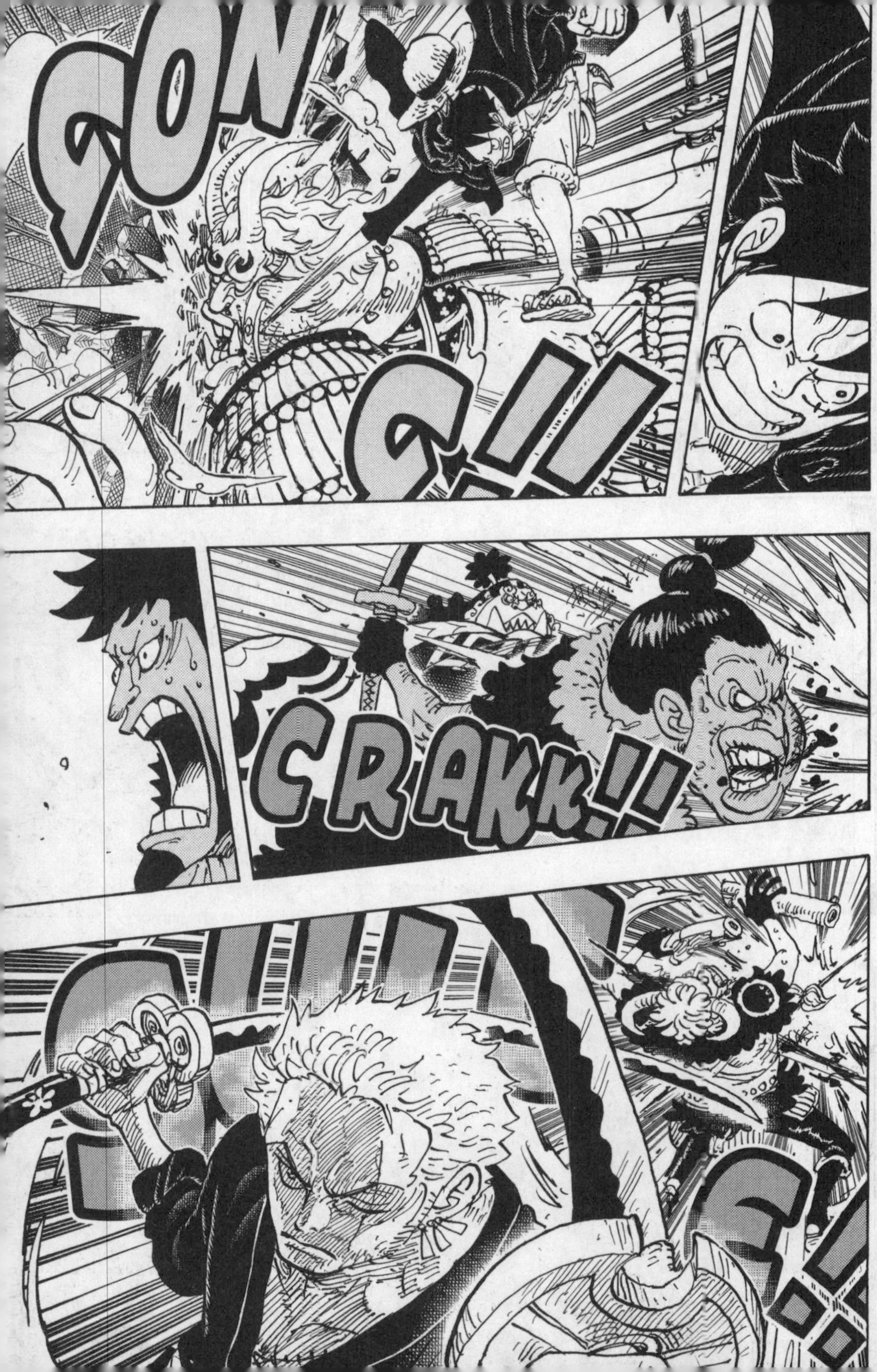
GON
G!!
CRAKK!!
G!!

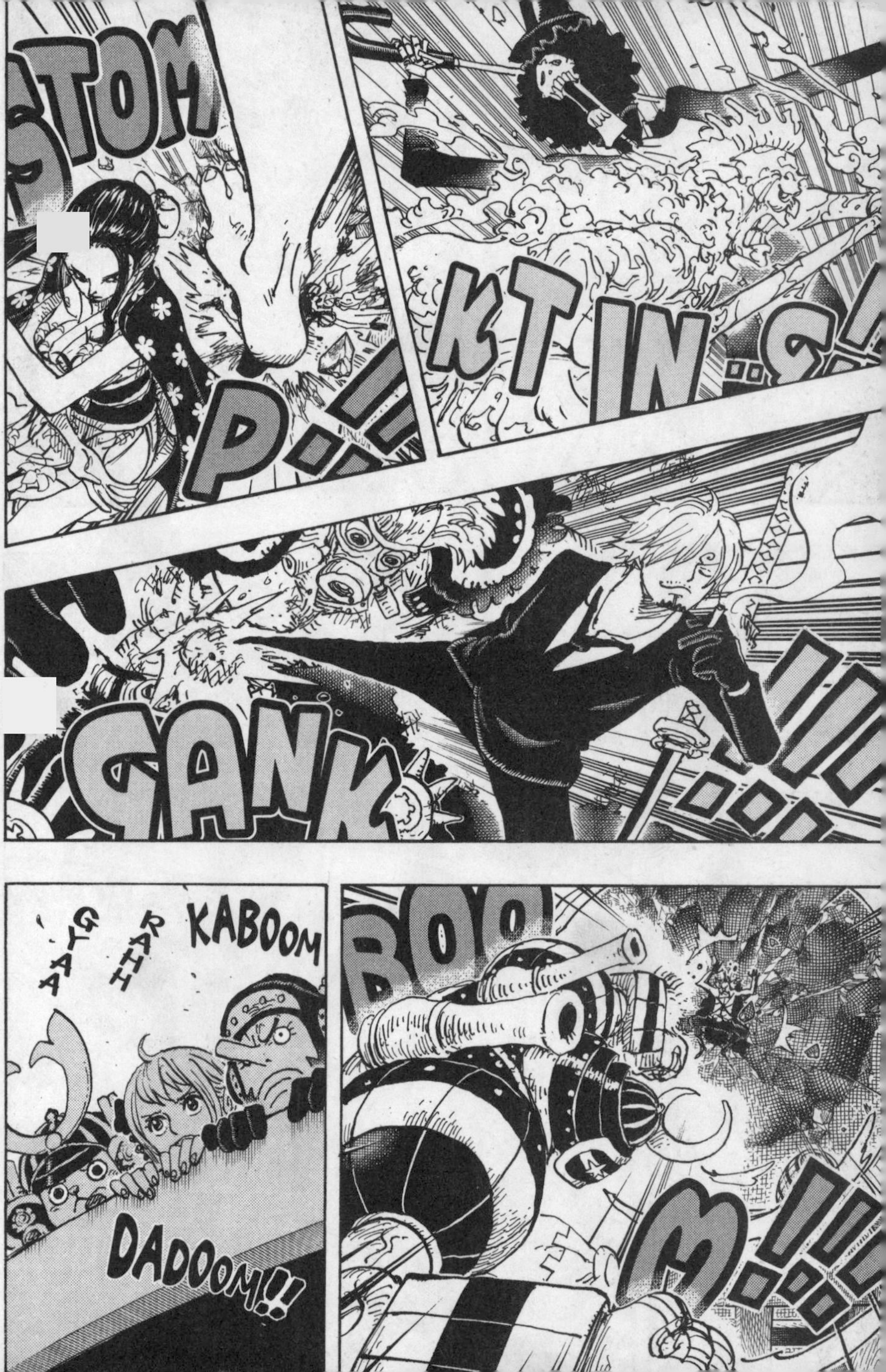
KTIN..G!!
STOM
P..!!
GANK..!!
BOO
M..!!
KABOOM
RAHH
GYAA
DADOOM!!

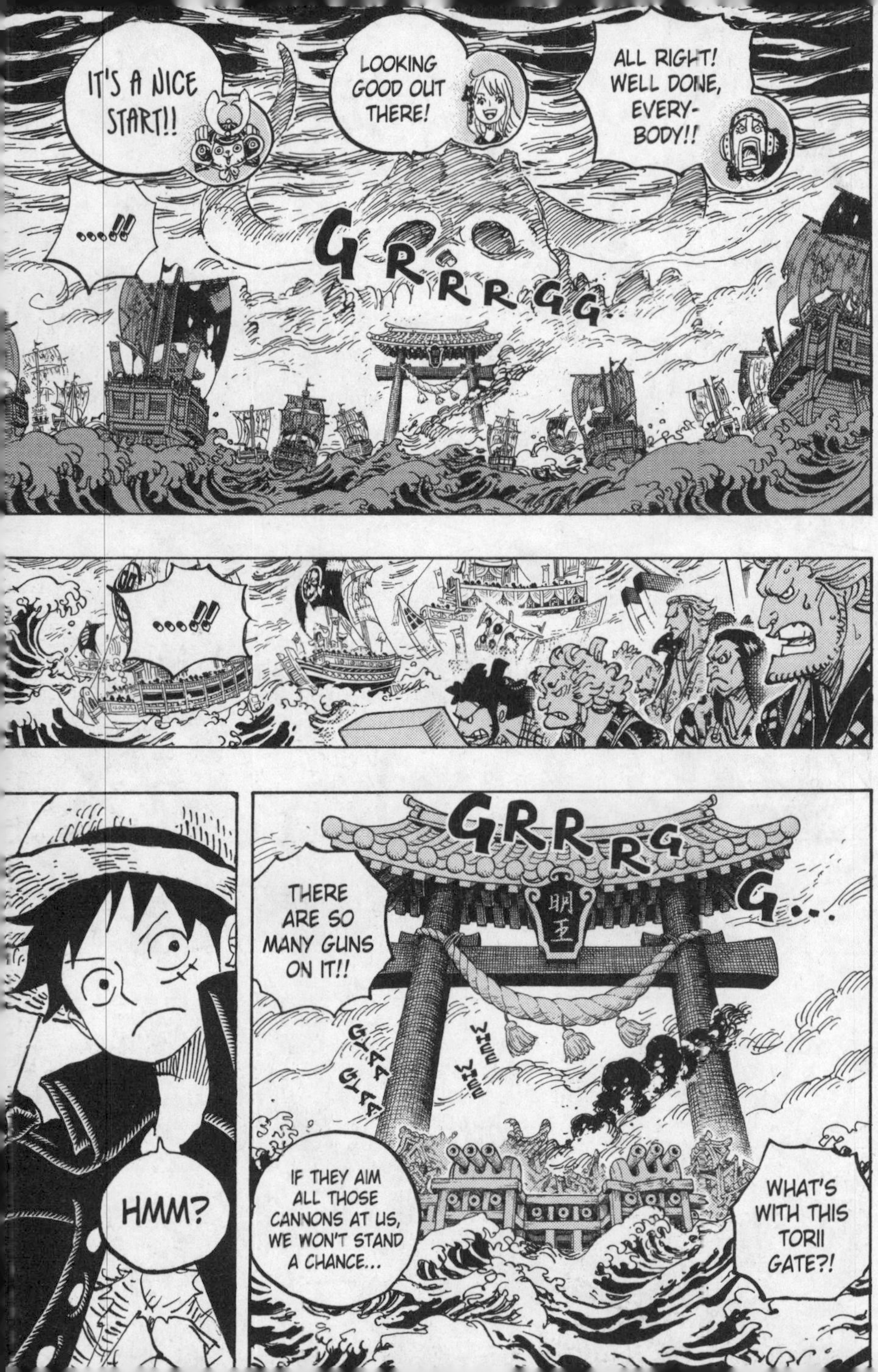
ALL RIGHT! WELL DONE, EVERY-BODY!!
LOOKING GOOD OUT THERE!
IT'S A NICE START!!
...!!
GRRRRGG...
...!!
WHAT'S WITH THIS TORII GATE?!
GRRRRG
G...
THERE ARE SO MANY GUNS ON IT!!
WHEE WHEE
GYAA GYAA
IF THEY AIM ALL THOSE CANNONS AT US, WE WON'T STAND A CHANCE...
HMM?

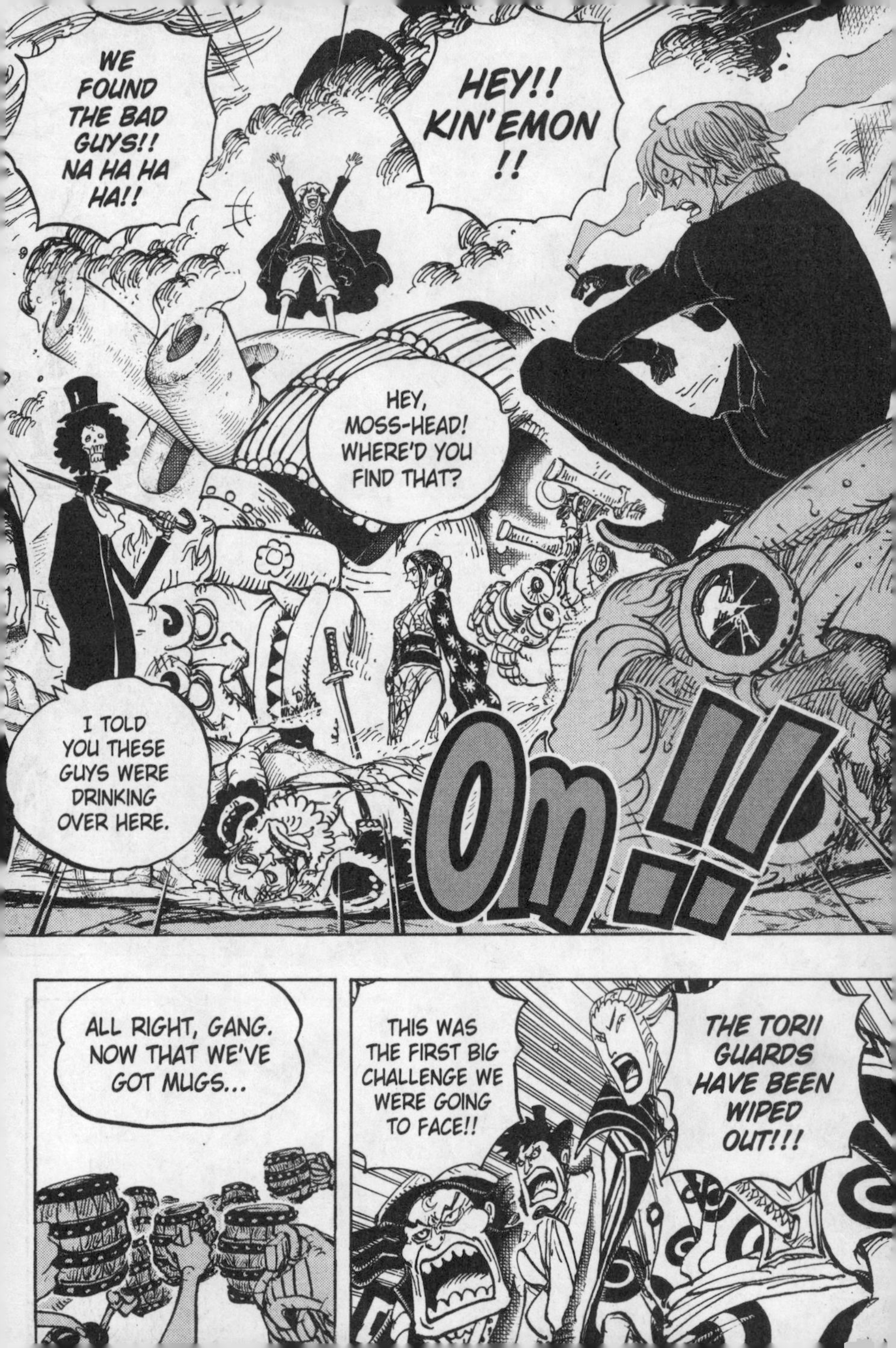
HEY!! KIN'EMON !!
WE FOUND THE BAD GUYS!! NA HA HA HA!!
HEY, MOSS-HEAD! WHERE'D YOU FIND THAT?
Om!!
I TOLD YOU THESE GUYS WERE DRINKING OVER HERE.
THE TORII GUARDS HAVE BEEN WIPED OUT!!!
THIS WAS THE FIRST BIG CHALLENGE WE WERE GOING TO FACE!!
ALL RIGHT, GANG. NOW THAT WE'VE GOT MUGS...

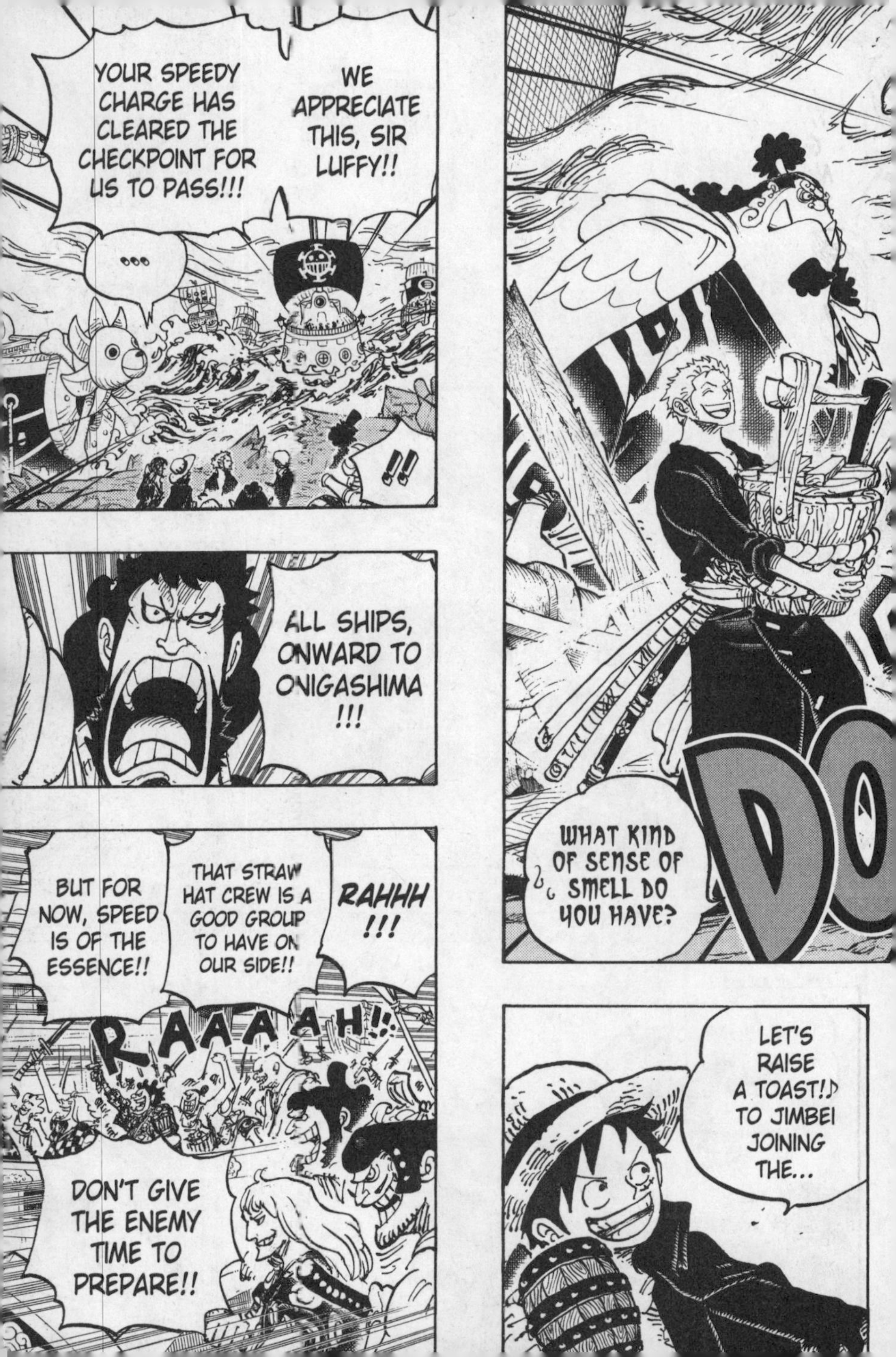

DO
WHAT KIND OF SENSE OF SMELL DO YOU HAVE?
LET'S RAISE A TOAST!♪ TO JIMBEI JOINING THE...
WE APPRECIATE THIS, SIR LUFFY!!
YOUR SPEEDY CHARGE HAS CLEARED THE CHECKPOINT FOR US TO PASS!!!
...
!!
ALL SHIPS, ONWARD TO ONIGASHIMA!!!
RAHHH!!!
THAT STRAW HAT CREW IS A GOOD GROUP TO HAVE ON OUR SIDE!!
BUT FOR NOW, SPEED IS OF THE ESSENCE!!
RAAAAH!!
DON'T GIVE THE ENEMY TIME TO PREPARE!!

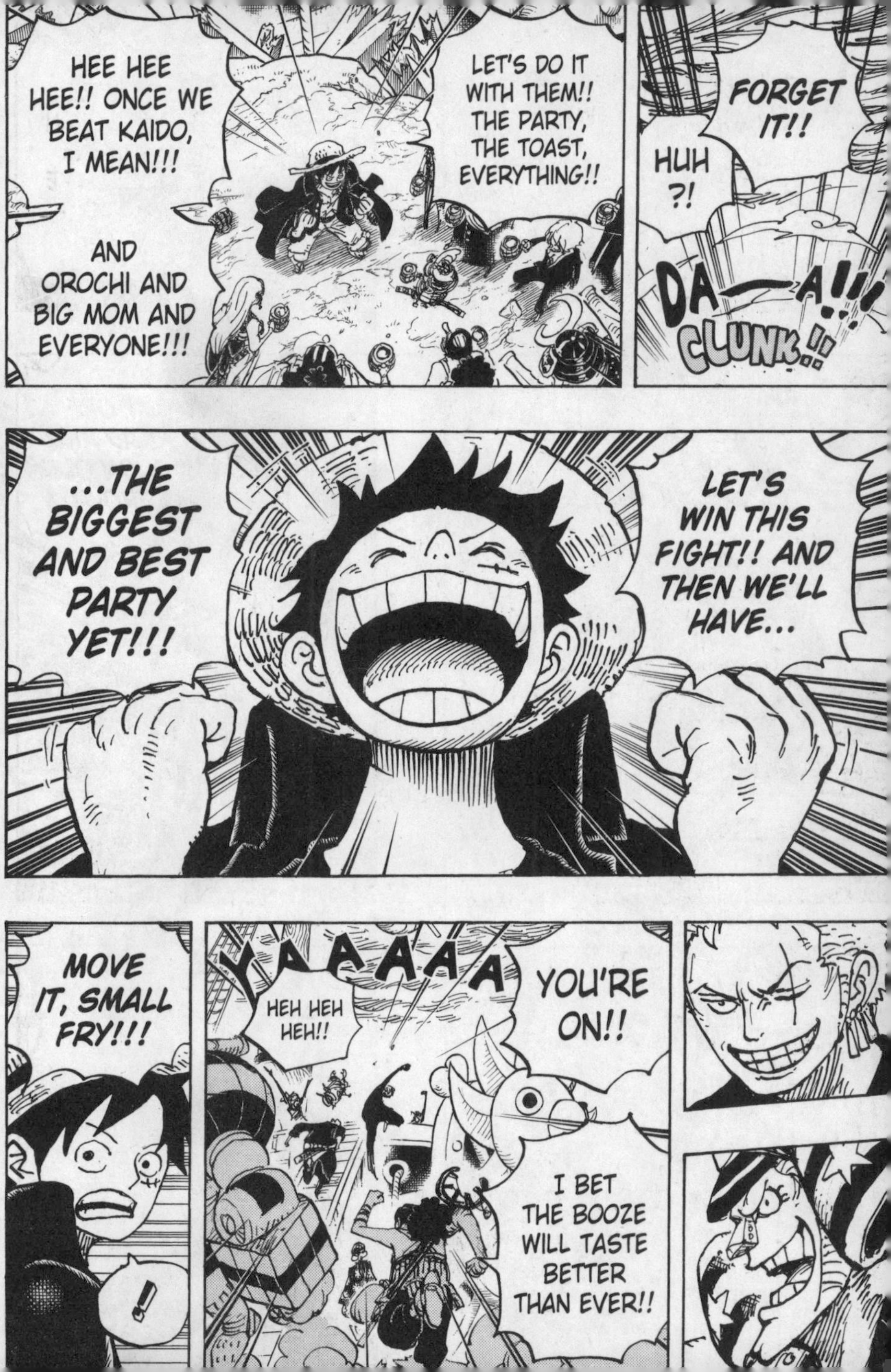
FORGET IT!!
HUH ?!
DA—A!!!
CLUNK!!
LET'S DO IT WITH THEM!! THE PARTY, THE TOAST, EVERYTHING!!
HEE HEE HEE!! ONCE WE BEAT KAIDO, I MEAN!!!
AND OROCHI AND BIG MOM AND EVERYONE!!!
LET'S WIN THIS FIGHT!! AND THEN WE'LL HAVE...
...THE BIGGEST AND BEST PARTY YET!!!
YAAAAA
YOU'RE ON!!
HEH HEH HEH!!
I BET THE BOOZE WILL TASTE BETTER THAN EVER!!
MOVE IT, SMALL FRY!!!
!

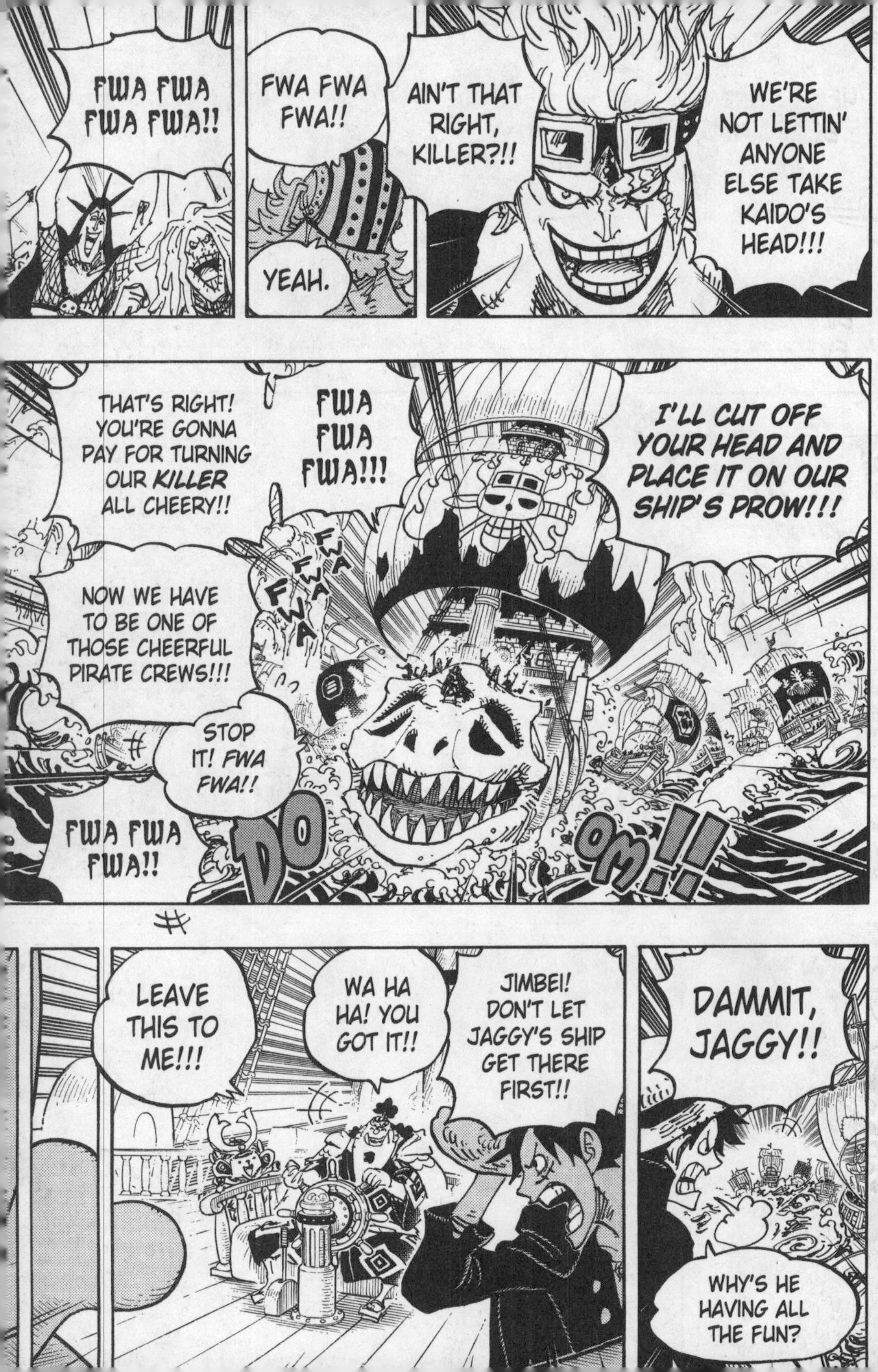
WE'RE NOT LETTIN' ANYONE ELSE TAKE KAIDO'S HEAD!!!
AIN'T THAT RIGHT, KILLER?!!
FWA FWA FWA!!
YEAH.
FWA FWA FWA FWA!!
I'LL CUT OFF YOUR HEAD AND PLACE IT ON OUR SHIP'S PROW!!!
FWA FWA FWA!!!
THAT'S RIGHT! YOU'RE GONNA PAY FOR TURNING OUR KILLER ALL CHEERY!!
FWA FWA FWA FWA
NOW WE HAVE TO BE ONE OF THOSE CHEERFUL PIRATE CREWS!!!
STOP IT! FWA FWA!!
DOOM!!
FWA FWA FWA!!
DAMMIT, JAGGY!!
WHY'S HE HAVING ALL THE FUN?
JIMBEI! DON'T LET JAGGY'S SHIP GET THERE FIRST!!
WA HA HA! YOU GOT IT!!
LEAVE THIS TO ME!!!

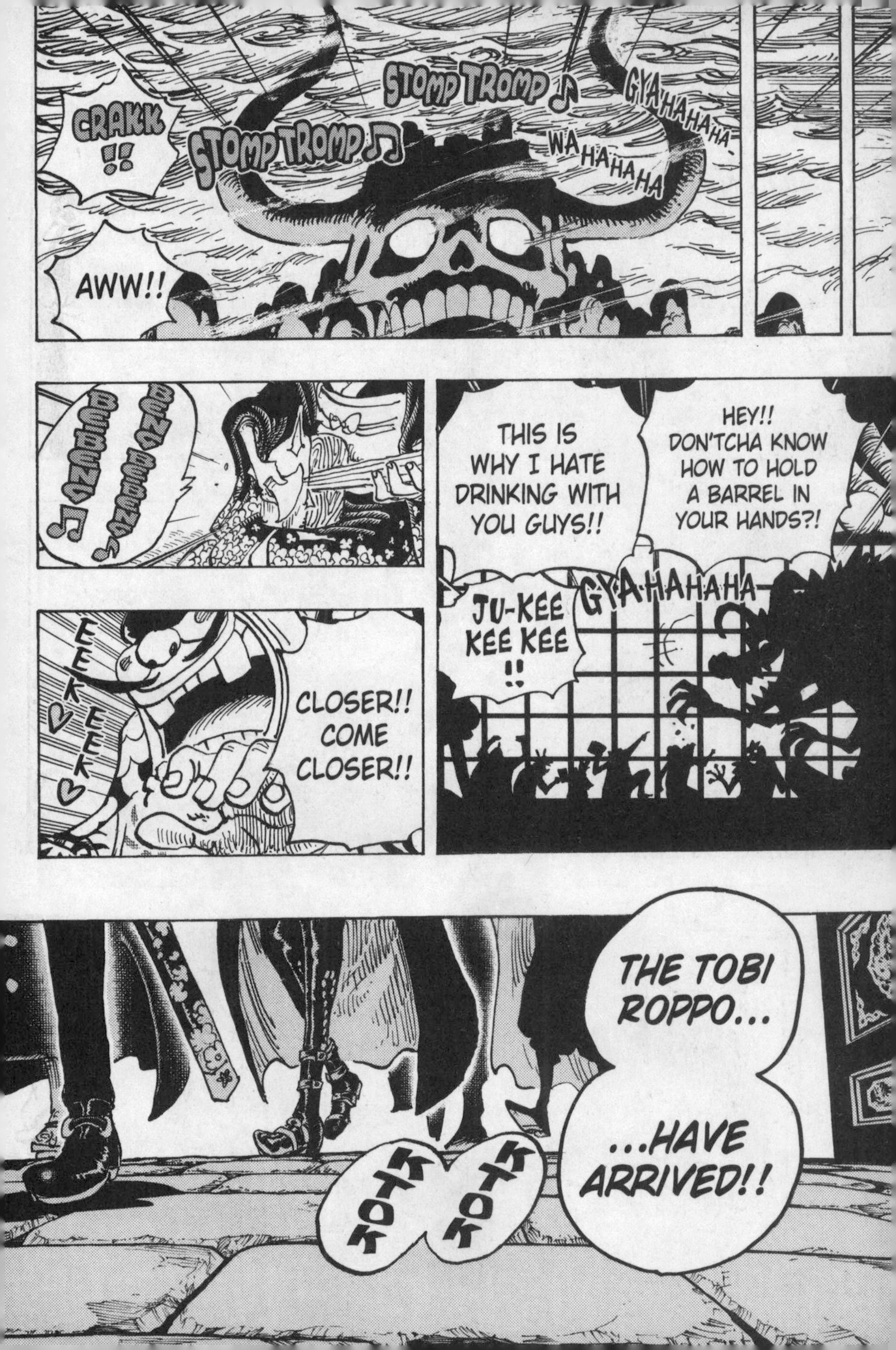
GYAHAHAHA
WAHAHAHAHA
STOMP TROMP ♪
STOMP TROMP ♫
CRAKK!!
AWW!!
HEY!! DON'TCHA KNOW HOW TO HOLD A BARREL IN YOUR HANDS?!
THIS IS WHY I HATE DRINKING WITH YOU GUYS!!
GYAHAHAHA
JU-KEE KEE KEE!!
BENG BEBENG ♪
BEBENG ♫
CLOSER!! COME CLOSER!!
EEK♥
EEK♥
THE TOBI ROPPO...
...HAVE ARRIVED!!
KTOK
KTOK

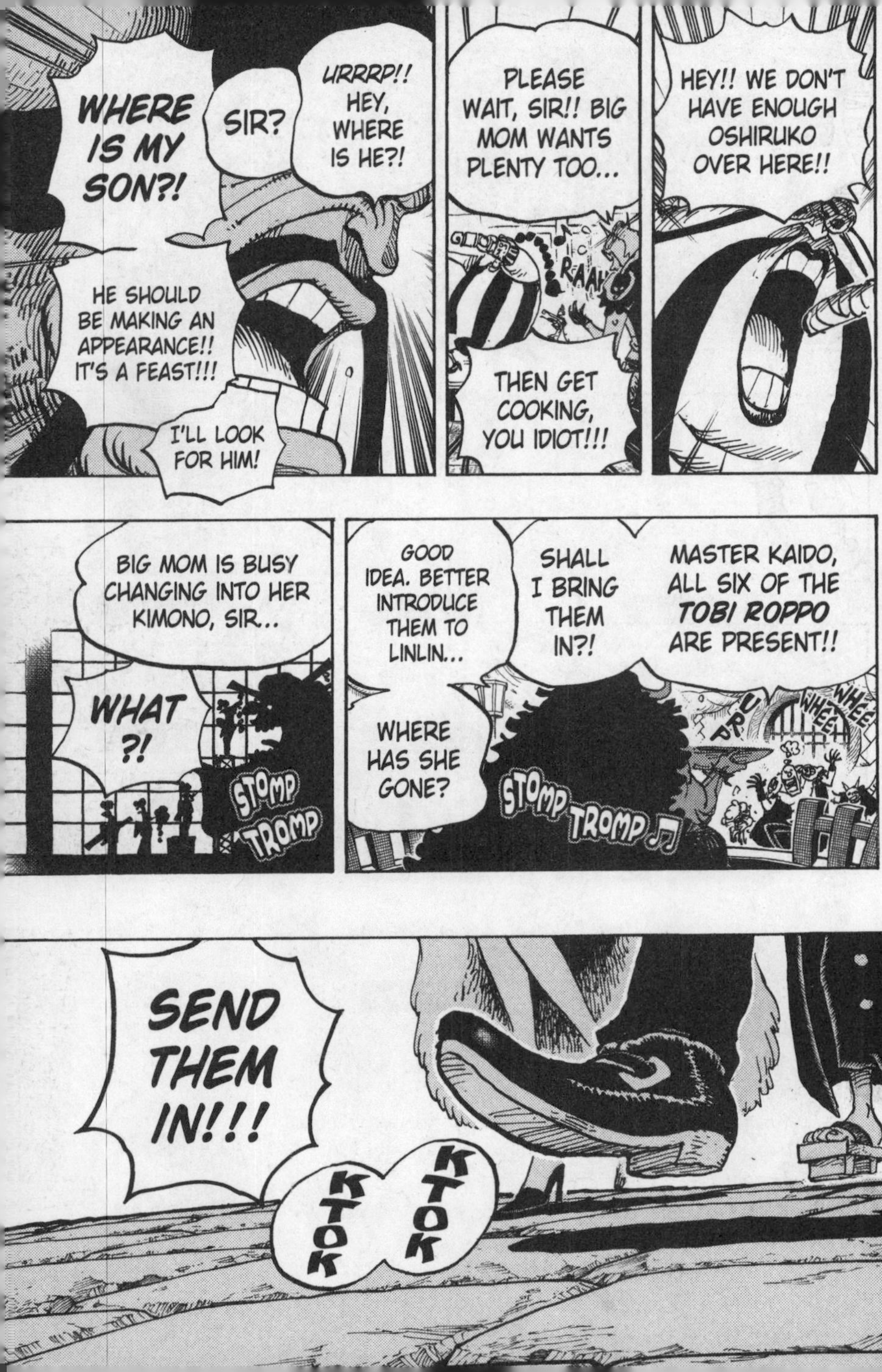
HEY!! WE DON'T HAVE ENOUGH OSHIRUKO OVER HERE!!
PLEASE WAIT, SIR!! BIG MOM WANTS PLENTY TOO...
RAAH
THEN GET COOKING, YOU IDIOT!!!
URRRP!! HEY, WHERE IS HE?!
SIR?
WHERE IS MY SON?!
HE SHOULD BE MAKING AN APPEARANCE!! IT'S A FEAST!!!
I'LL LOOK FOR HIM!
MASTER KAIDO, ALL SIX OF THE TOBI ROPPO ARE PRESENT!!
SHALL I BRING THEM IN?!
GOOD IDEA. BETTER INTRODUCE THEM TO LINLIN...
WHERE HAS SHE GONE?
WHEE WHEE WHEE
URP
STOMP TROMP ♫
BIG MOM IS BUSY CHANGING INTO HER KIMONO, SIR...
WHAT?!
STOMP TROMP
SEND THEM IN!!!
KTOK KTOK
KTOK KTOK

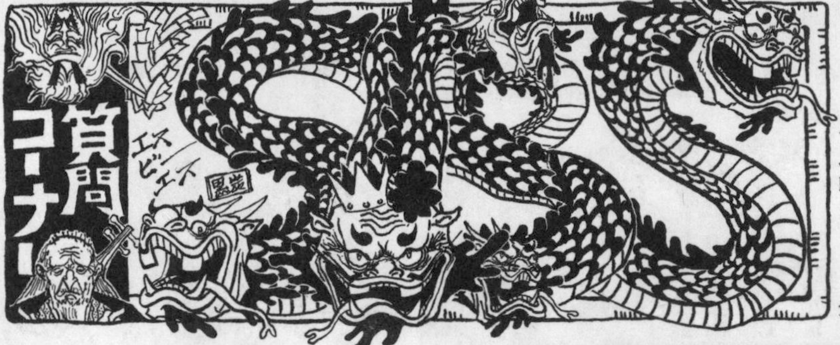

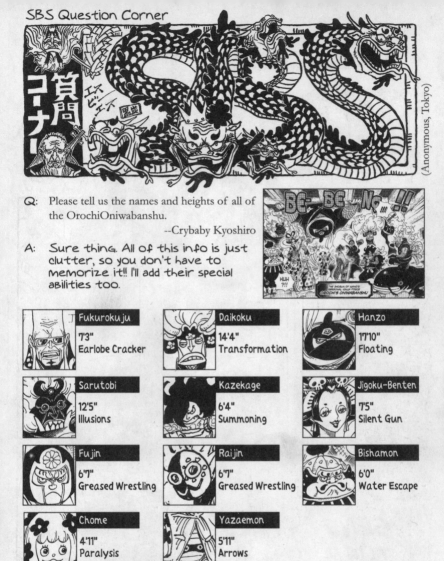

(Anonymous, Tokyo)

Q: Please tell us the names and heights of all of the OrochiOniwabanshu.

--Crybaby Kyoshiro

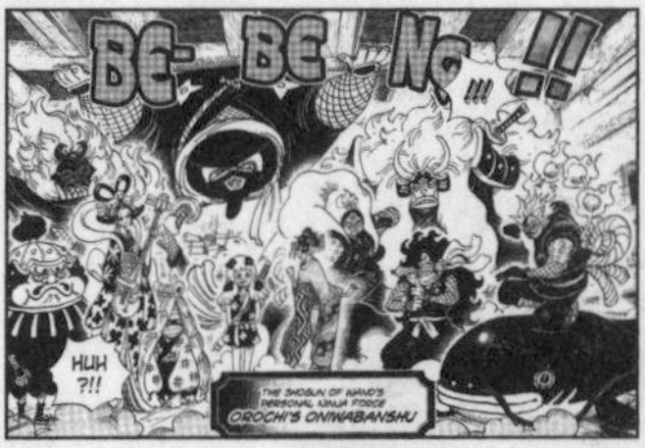

A: Sure thing. All of this info is just clutter, so you don't have to memorize it!! I'll add their special abilities too.

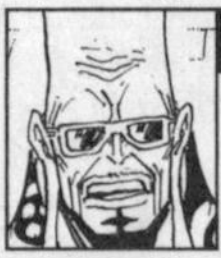
Fukurokuju
7'3"
Earlobe Cracker

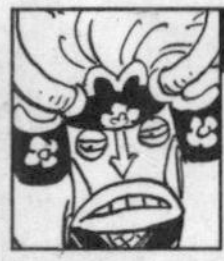
Daikoku
14'4"
Transformation

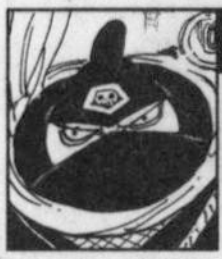
Hanzo
17'10"
Floating

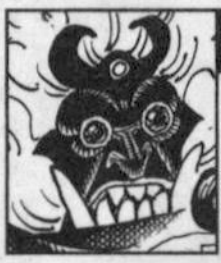
Sarutobi
12'5"
Illusions

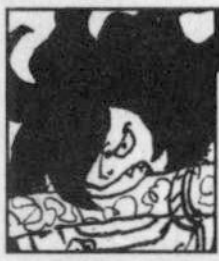
Kazekage
6'4"
Summoning

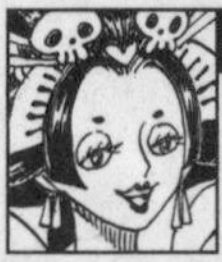
Jigoku-Benten
7'5"
Silent Gun

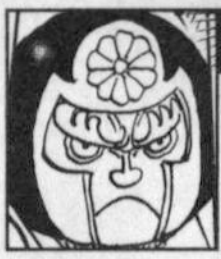
Fujin
6'7"
Greased Wrestling

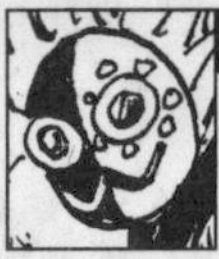
Raijin
6'7"
Greased Wrestling

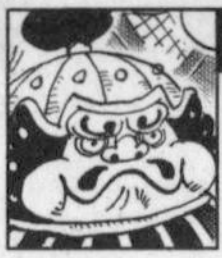
Bishamon
6'0"
Water Escape

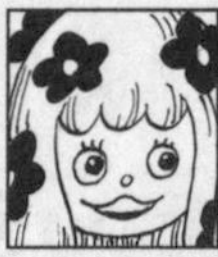
Chome
4'11"
Paralysis

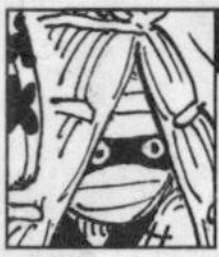
Yazaemon
5'11"
Arrows

Q: Orochi has two honking big teeth in the front. Isn't it hard to eat with those? Can you ask him about that for me?

--Ami

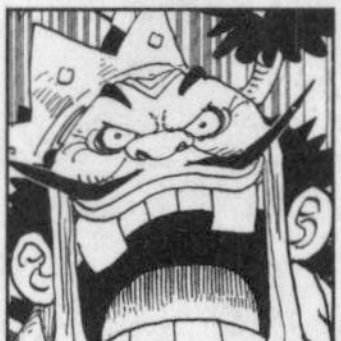

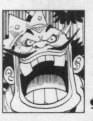

A: Ah, interesting. Let's go find out. What's the deal, Shogun Orochi?!

Orochi: It's not a problem! Munch, munch, chomp!! Yeow!!?

A: Apparently, it's not a problem!

Chapter 978:
INTRODUCING THE TOBI ROPPO

GANG BEGE'S OH MY FAMILY, VOL. 25: "WE'RE GRATEFUL!! THANKS FOR SAVING OUR CAPTAIN!!"

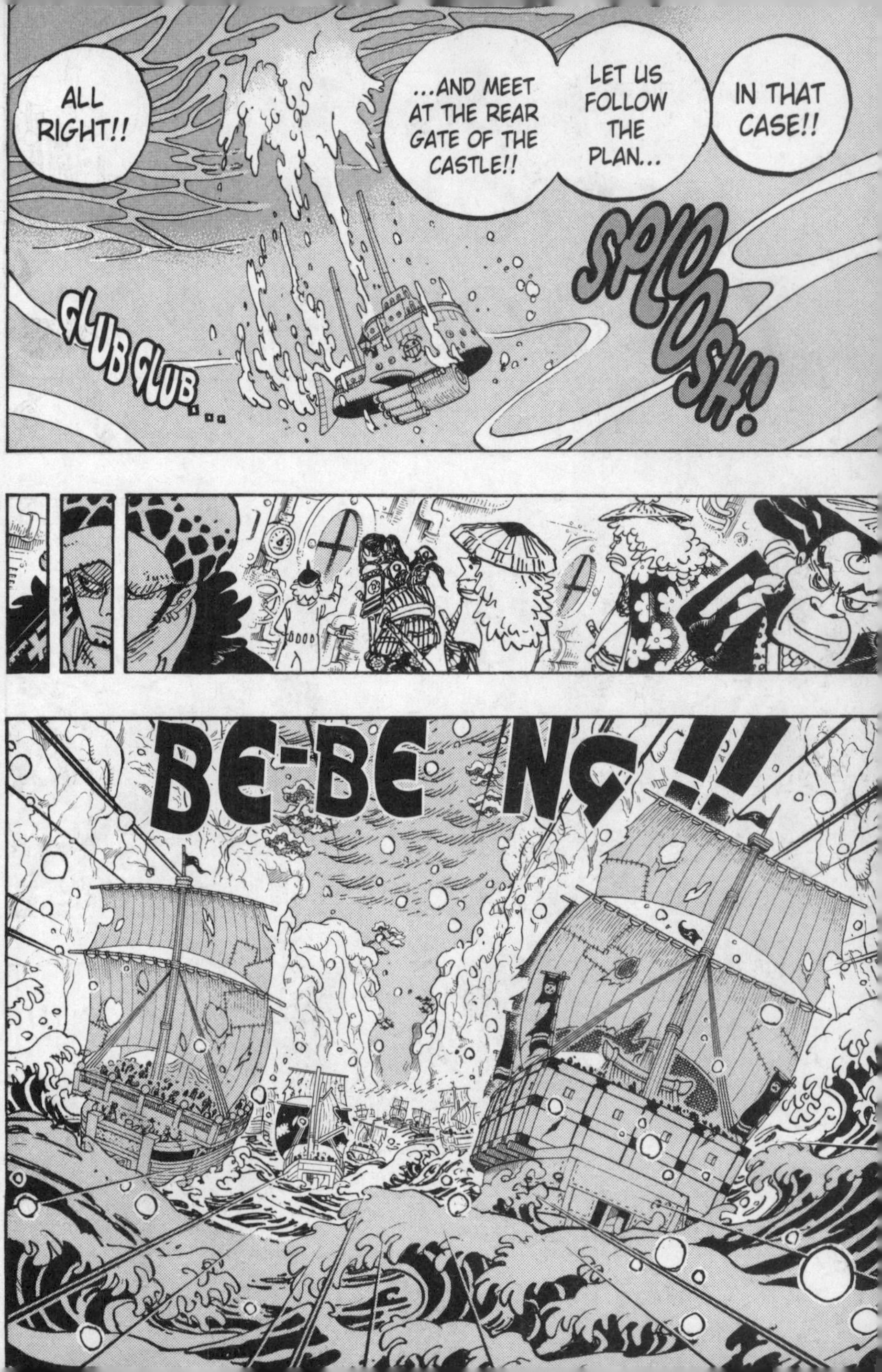
IN THAT CASE!!
LET US FOLLOW THE PLAN...
...AND MEET AT THE REAR GATE OF THE CASTLE!!
ALL RIGHT!!
SPLOOSH!
GLUB GLUB...
BE-BENG!!

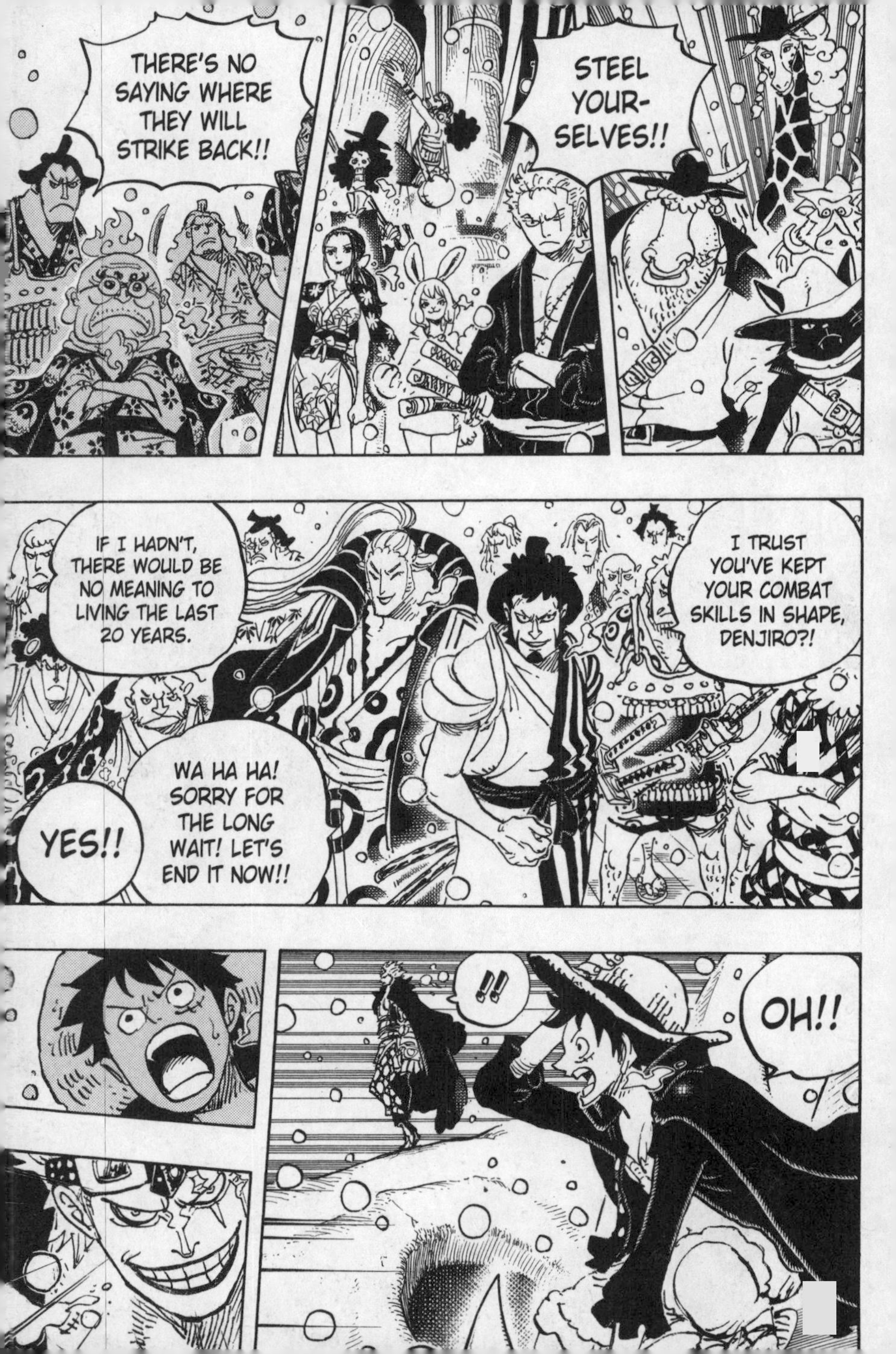
STEEL YOUR-SELVES!!
THERE'S NO SAYING WHERE THEY WILL STRIKE BACK!!
I TRUST YOU'VE KEPT YOUR COMBAT SKILLS IN SHAPE, DENJIRO?!
IF I HADN'T, THERE WOULD BE NO MEANING TO LIVING THE LAST 20 YEARS.
WA HA HA! SORRY FOR THE LONG WAIT! LET'S END IT NOW!!
YES!!
OH!!
!!

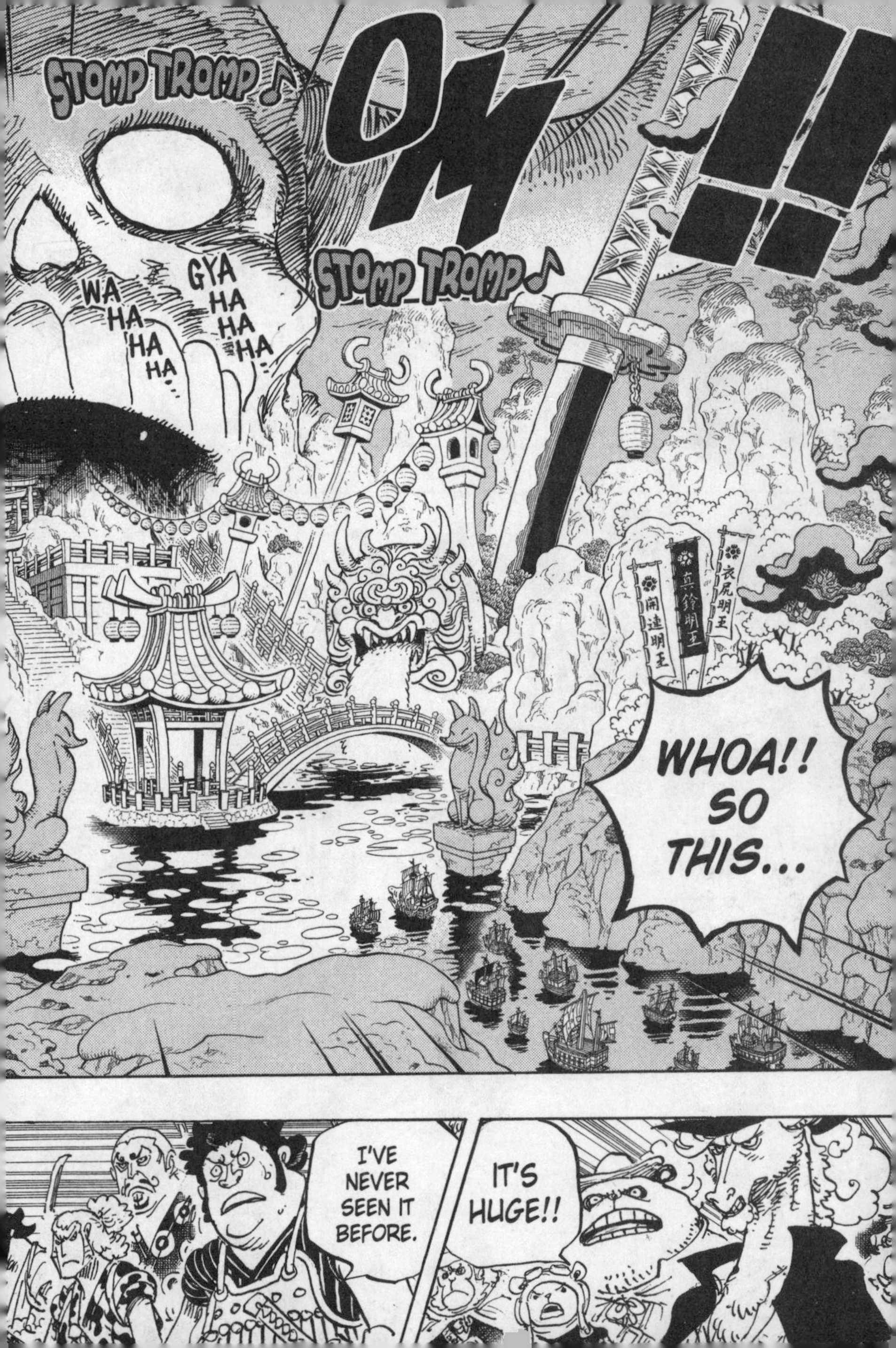
OH!!
STOMP TROMP ♪
STOMP TROMP ♪
GYA HA HA HA HA
WA HA HA HA HA
WHOA!! SO THIS...
IT'S HUGE!!
I'VE NEVER SEEN IT BEFORE.

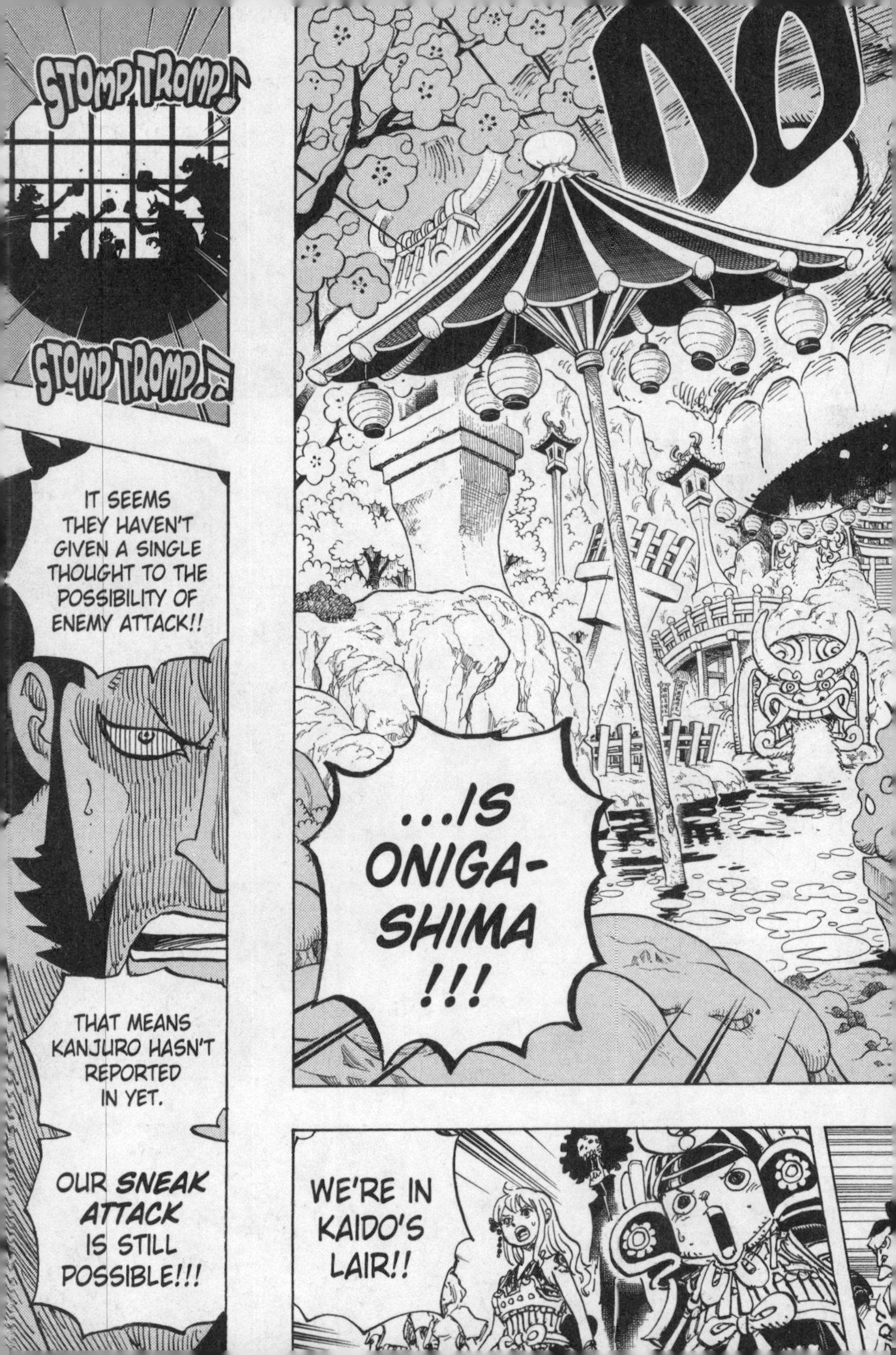
DO
...IS ONIGA-SHIMA!!!
WE'RE IN KAIDO'S LAIR!!
STOMP TROMP♪
STOMP TROMP♪♪
IT SEEMS THEY HAVEN'T GIVEN A SINGLE THOUGHT TO THE POSSIBILITY OF ENEMY ATTACK!!
THAT MEANS KANJURO HASN'T REPORTED IN YET.
OUR SNEAK ATTACK IS STILL POSSIBLE!!!

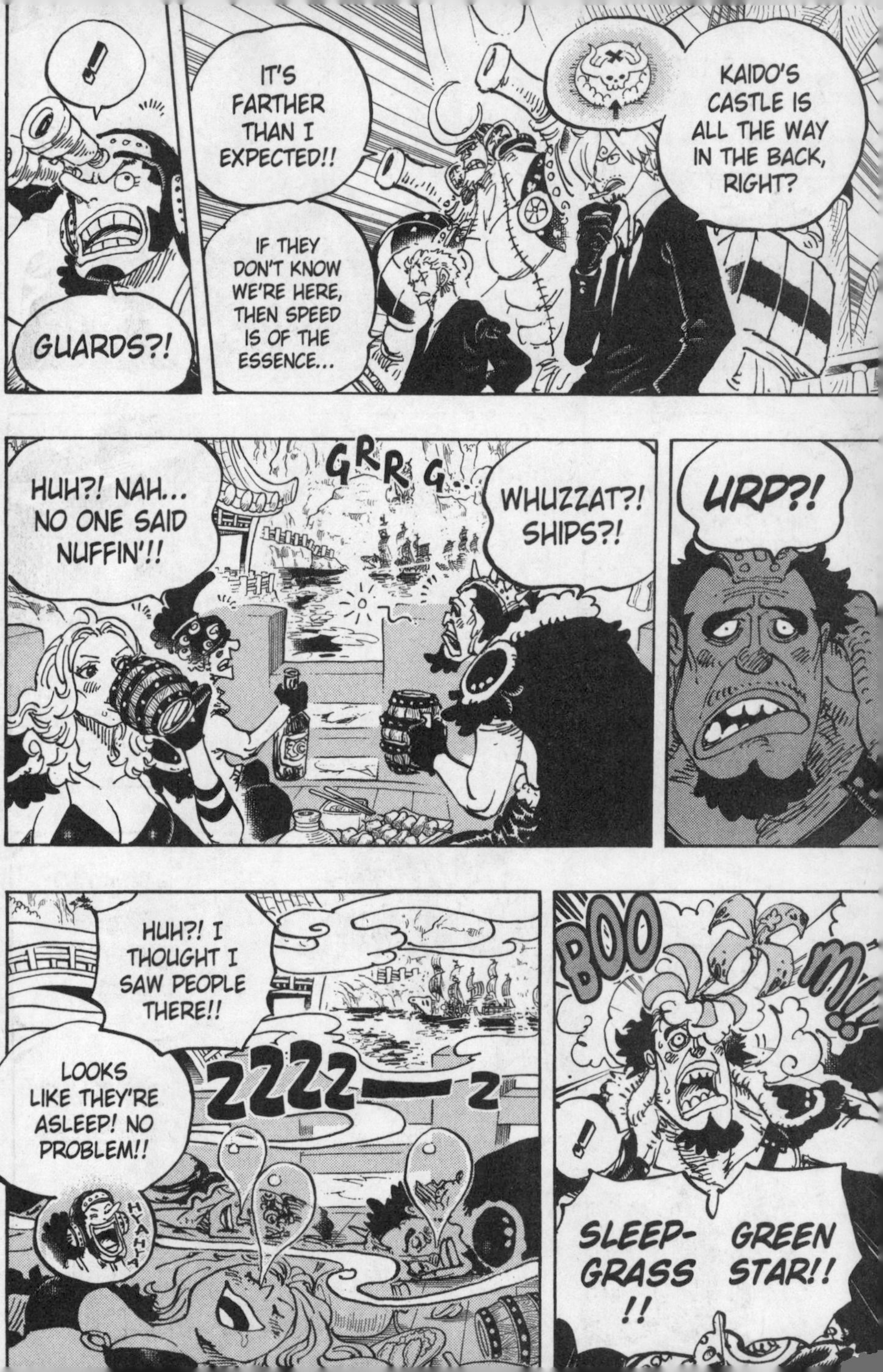
KAIDO'S CASTLE IS ALL THE WAY IN THE BACK, RIGHT?
IT'S FARTHER THAN I EXPECTED!!
IF THEY DON'T KNOW WE'RE HERE, THEN SPEED IS OF THE ESSENCE...
!
GUARDS?!
URP?!
WHUZZAT?! SHIPS?!
GRRG...
HUH?! NAH... NO ONE SAID NUFFIN'!!
BOOM!!
!
GREEN STAR!!
SLEEP-GRASS!!
HUH?! I THOUGHT I SAW PEOPLE THERE!!
ZZZZ—Z
LOOKS LIKE THEY'RE ASLEEP! NO PROBLEM!!

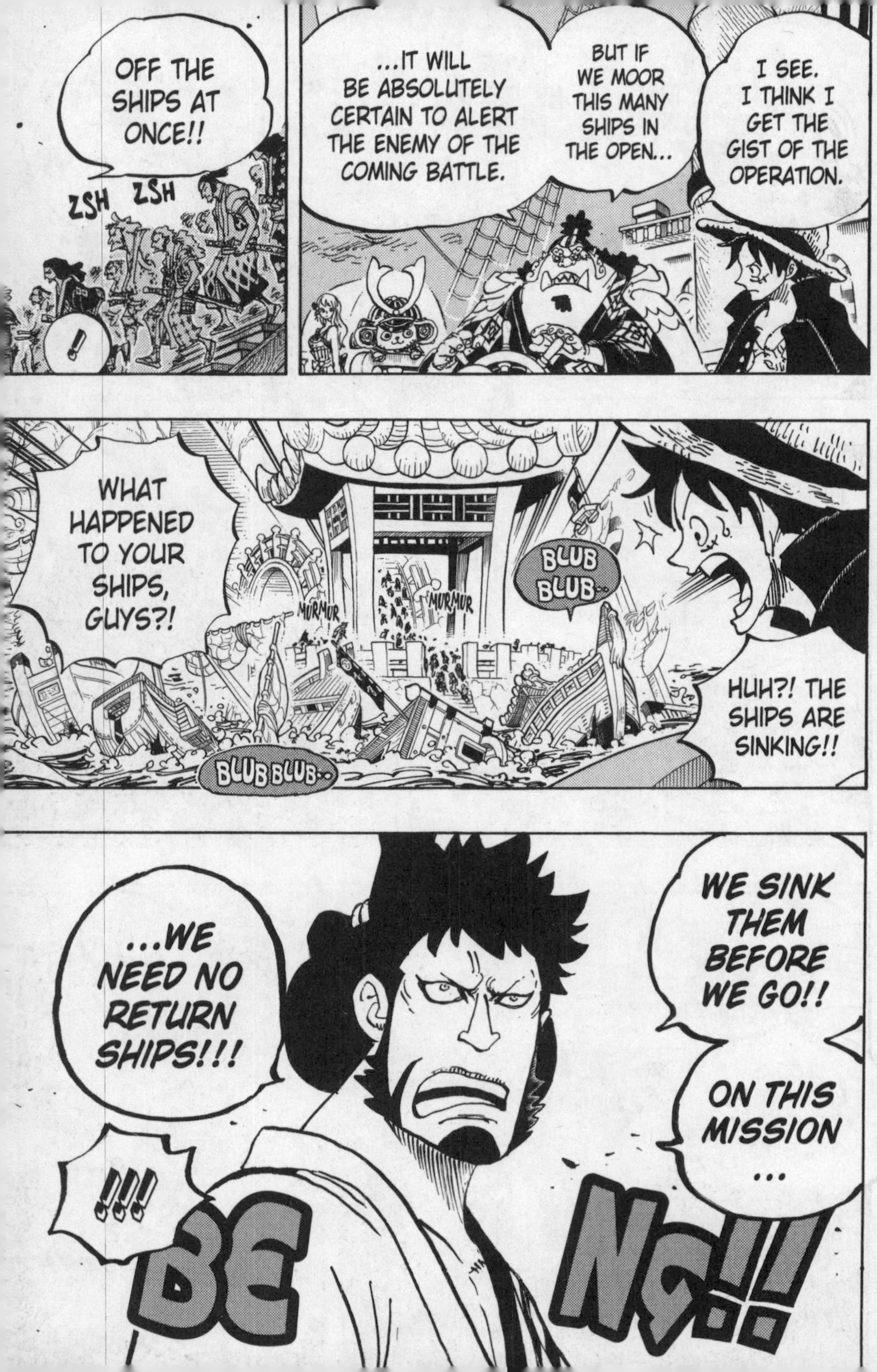
I SEE. I THINK I GET THE GIST OF THE OPERATION.
BUT IF WE MOOR THIS MANY SHIPS IN THE OPEN...
...IT WILL BE ABSOLUTELY CERTAIN TO ALERT THE ENEMY OF THE COMING BATTLE.
OFF THE SHIPS AT ONCE!!
ZSH ZSH
!
HUH?! THE SHIPS ARE SINKING!!
BLUB BLUB
MURMUR
MURMUR
WHAT HAPPENED TO YOUR SHIPS, GUYS?!
BLUB BLUB
WE SINK THEM BEFORE WE GO!!
ON THIS MISSION ...
...WE NEED NO RETURN SHIPS!!!
!!!
BE
NG!!

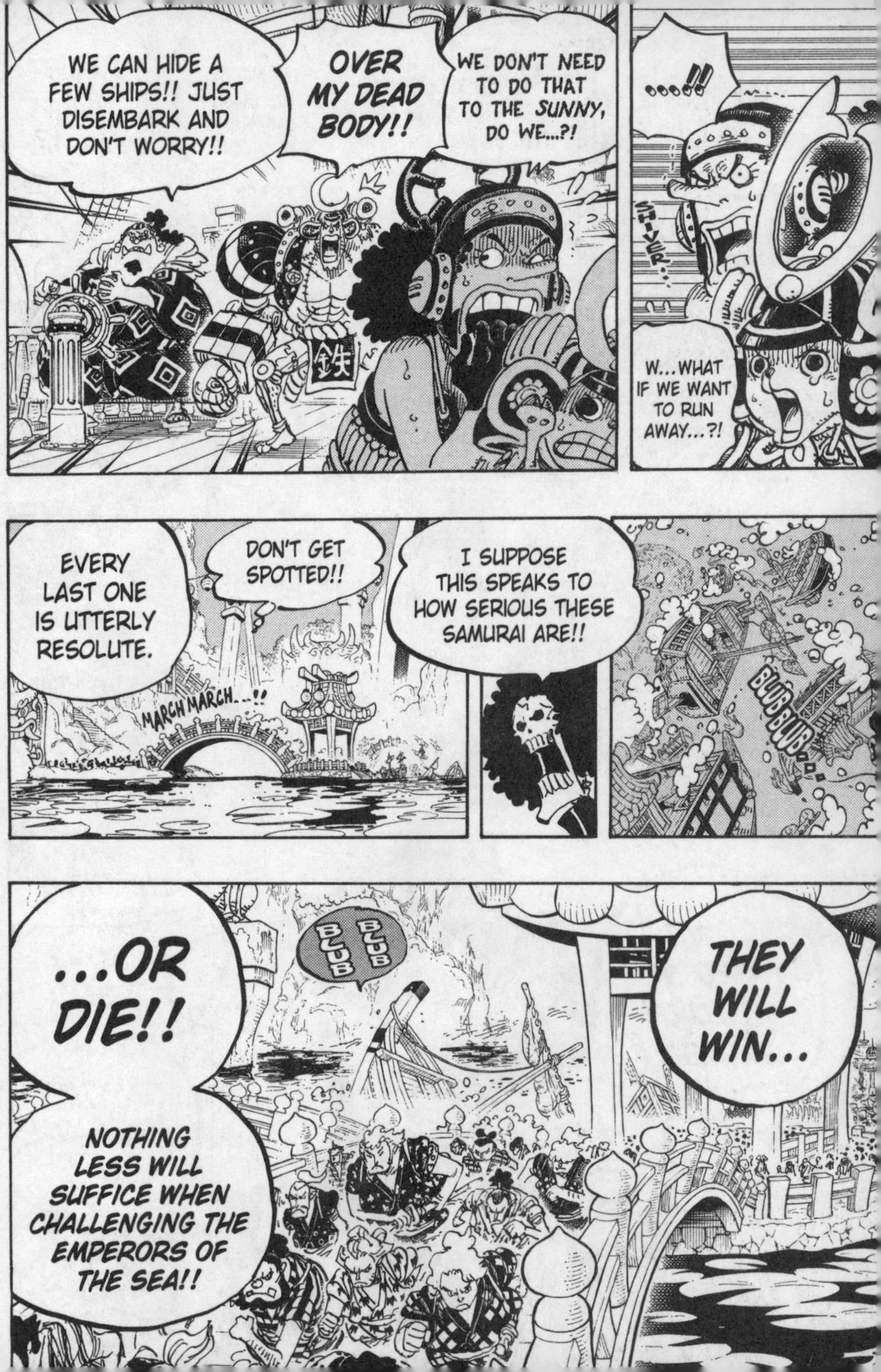
....!!
SHIVER...
W...WHAT IF WE WANT TO RUN AWAY...?!
WE DON'T NEED TO DO THAT TO THE SUNNY, DO WE...?!
OVER MY DEAD BODY!!
WE CAN HIDE A FEW SHIPS!! JUST DISEMBARK AND DON'T WORRY!!
BLUB BLUB...
I SUPPOSE THIS SPEAKS TO HOW SERIOUS THESE SAMURAI ARE!!
DON'T GET SPOTTED!!
EVERY LAST ONE IS UTTERLY RESOLUTE.
MARCH MARCH...!!
THEY WILL WIN...
BLUB BLUB
...OR DIE!!
NOTHING LESS WILL SUFFICE WHEN CHALLENGING THE EMPERORS OF THE SEA!!

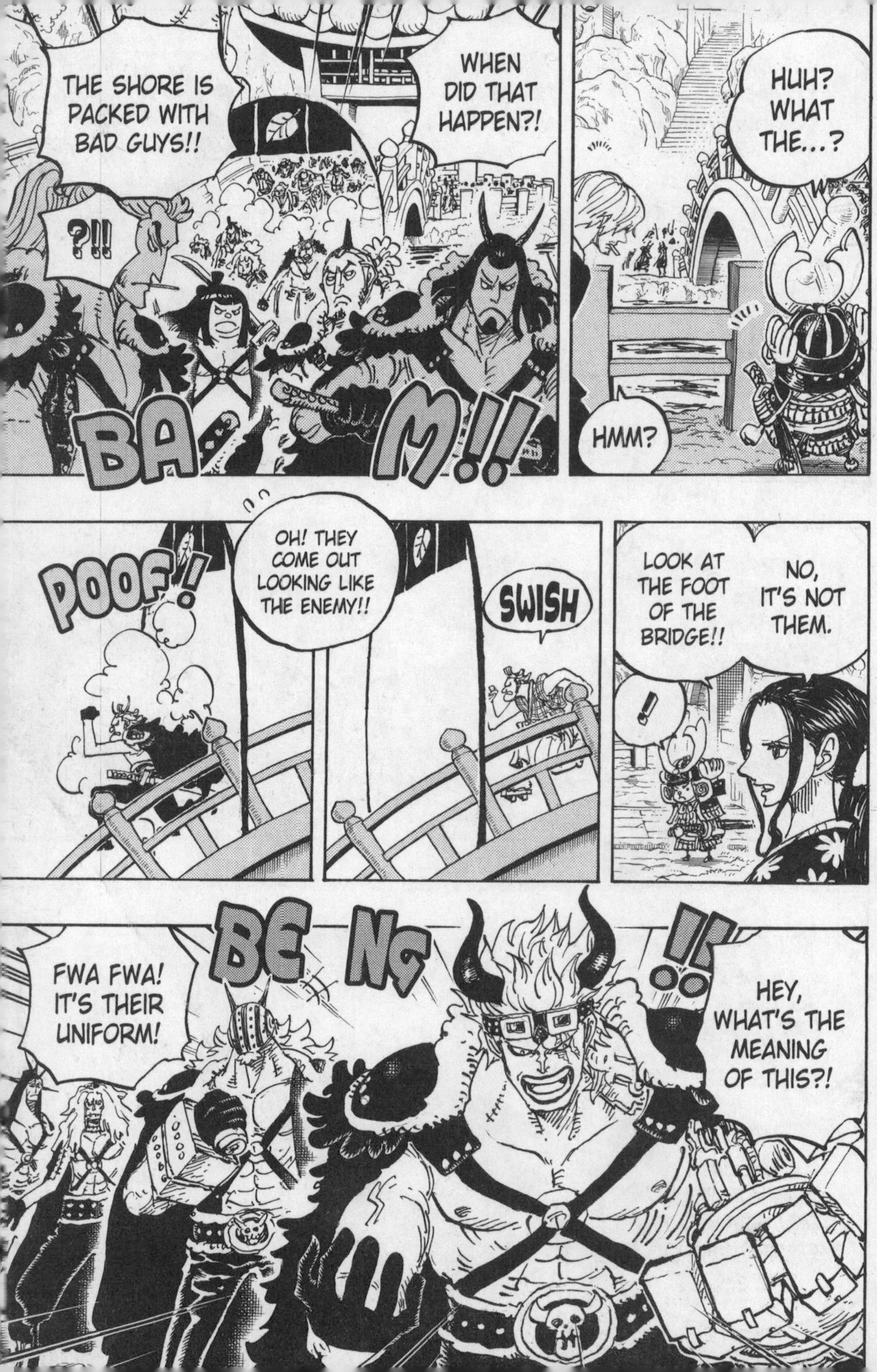
HUH? WHAT THE...?
HMM?
WHEN DID THAT HAPPEN?!
THE SHORE IS PACKED WITH BAD GUYS!!
?!!
BA-M!!
NO, IT'S NOT THEM.
LOOK AT THE FOOT OF THE BRIDGE!!
!
SWISH
OH! THEY COME OUT LOOKING LIKE THE ENEMY!!
POOF!!
HEY, WHAT'S THE MEANING OF THIS?!
BENG!!
FWA FWA! IT'S THEIR UNIFORM!

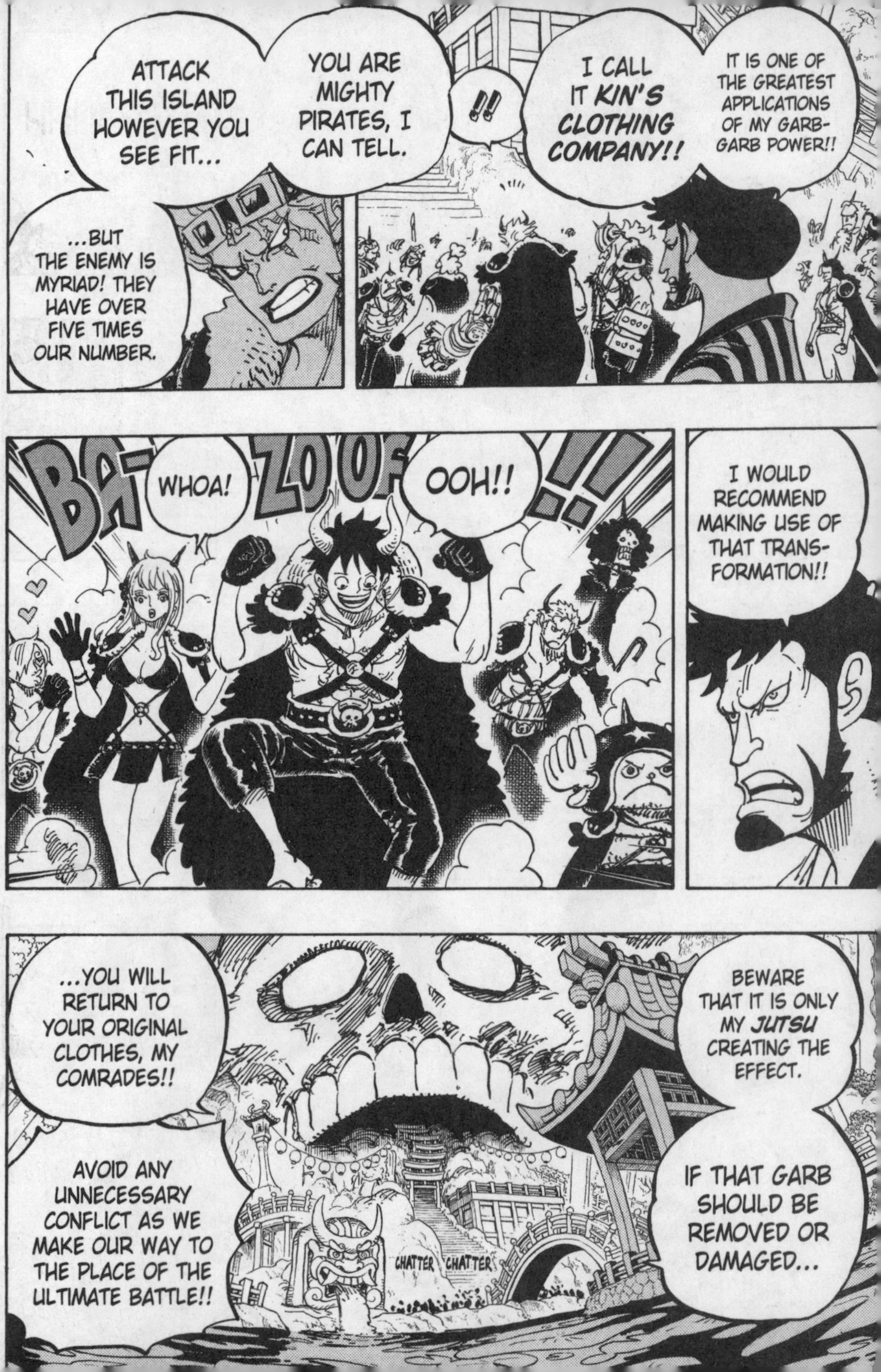

IT IS ONE OF THE GREATEST APPLICATIONS OF MY GARB-GARB POWER!!
I CALL IT *KIN'S CLOTHING COMPANY!!*
!!
YOU ARE MIGHTY PIRATES, I CAN TELL.
ATTACK THIS ISLAND HOWEVER YOU SEE FIT...
...BUT THE ENEMY IS MYRIAD! THEY HAVE OVER FIVE TIMES OUR NUMBER.
I WOULD RECOMMEND MAKING USE OF THAT TRANS-FORMATION!!
BA-ZOOF!!
OOH!!
WHOA!
BEWARE THAT IT IS ONLY MY *JUTSU* CREATING THE EFFECT.
IF THAT GARB SHOULD BE REMOVED OR DAMAGED...
...YOU WILL RETURN TO YOUR ORIGINAL CLOTHES, MY COMRADES!!
AVOID ANY UNNECESSARY CONFLICT AS WE MAKE OUR WAY TO THE PLACE OF THE ULTIMATE BATTLE!!
CHATTER CHATTER

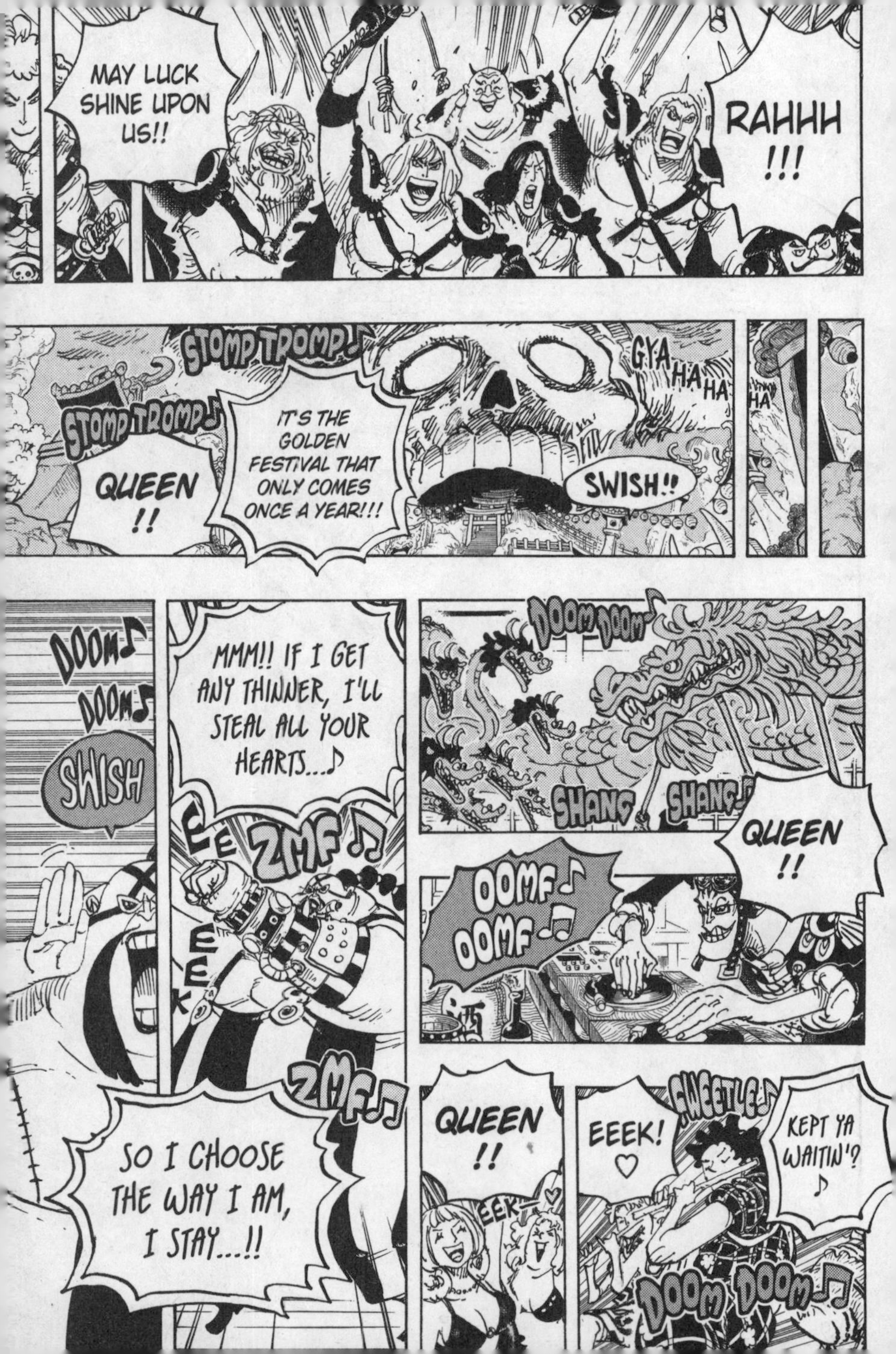
RAHHH!!!
MAY LUCK SHINE UPON US!!
HA
GYA HA HA
SWISH!!
IT'S THE GOLDEN FESTIVAL THAT ONLY COMES ONCE A YEAR!!!
STOMP TROMP♪
STOMP TROMP♪
QUEEN!!
DOOM DOOM♪
SHANG SHANG♪
QUEEN!!
OOMF♪ OOMF♪
MMM!! IF I GET ANY THINNER, I'LL STEAL ALL YOUR HEARTS...♪
ZMF♫
EEEEK
DOOM♪
DOOM♪
SWISH
KEPT YA WAITIN'? ♪
SWEETLE♪
EEEK! ♡
DOOM DOOM♫
QUEEN!!
EEK—♡
ZMF♫
SO I CHOOSE THE WAY I AM, I STAY...!!

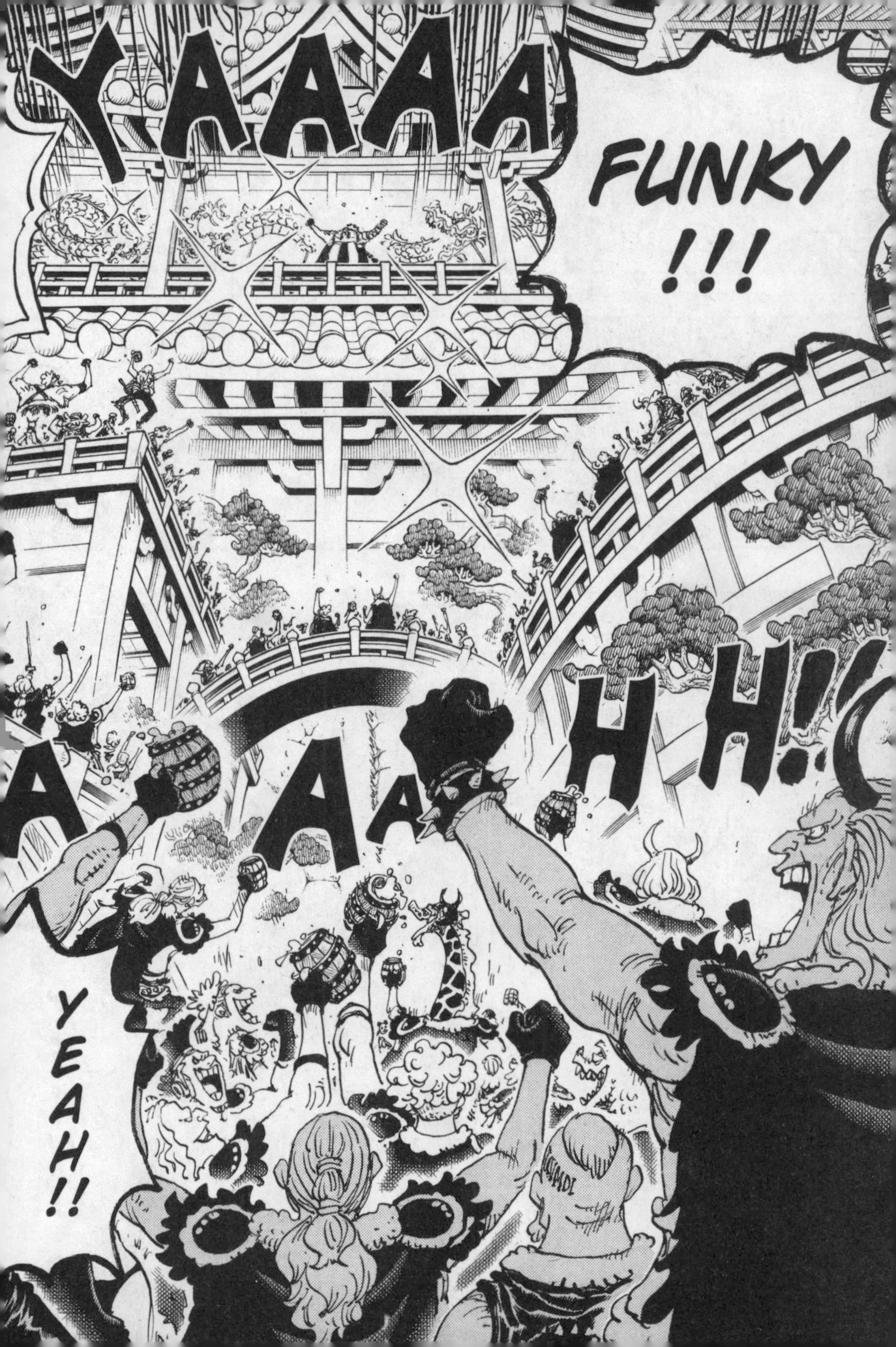
FUNKY!!!
YAAAA
AAAAHH!!
YEAH!!

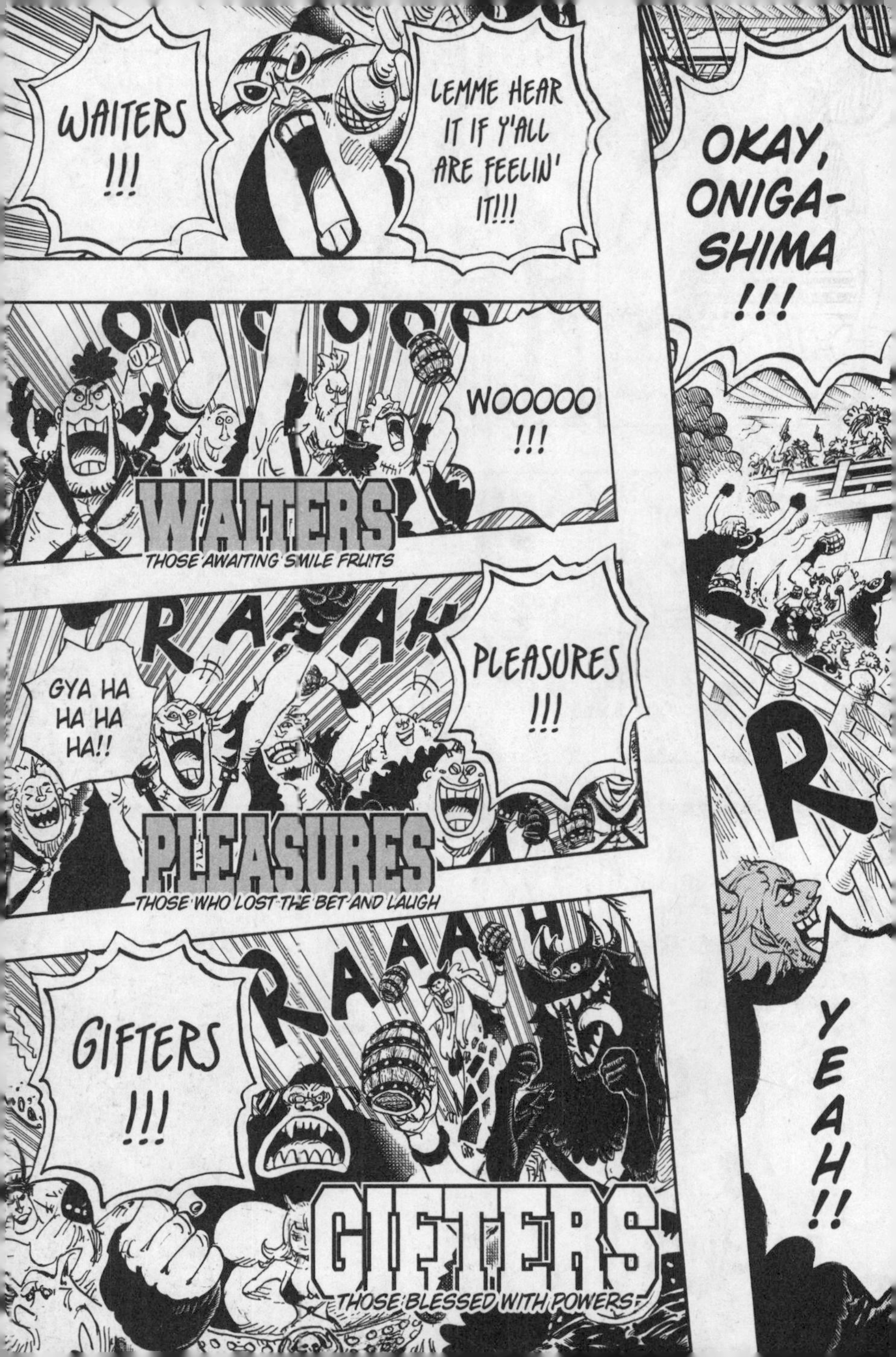
OKAY, ONIGA-SHIMA!!!
R
YEAH!!
LEMME HEAR IT IF Y'ALL ARE FEELIN' IT!!!
WAITERS!!!
WOOOOO!!!
WAITERS
THOSE AWAITING SMILE FRUITS
PLEASURES!!!
RAAAK
GYA HA HA HA HA!!
PLEASURES
THOSE WHO LOST THE BET AND LAUGH
RAAAH
GIFTERS!!!
GIFTERS
THOSE BLESSED WITH POWERS

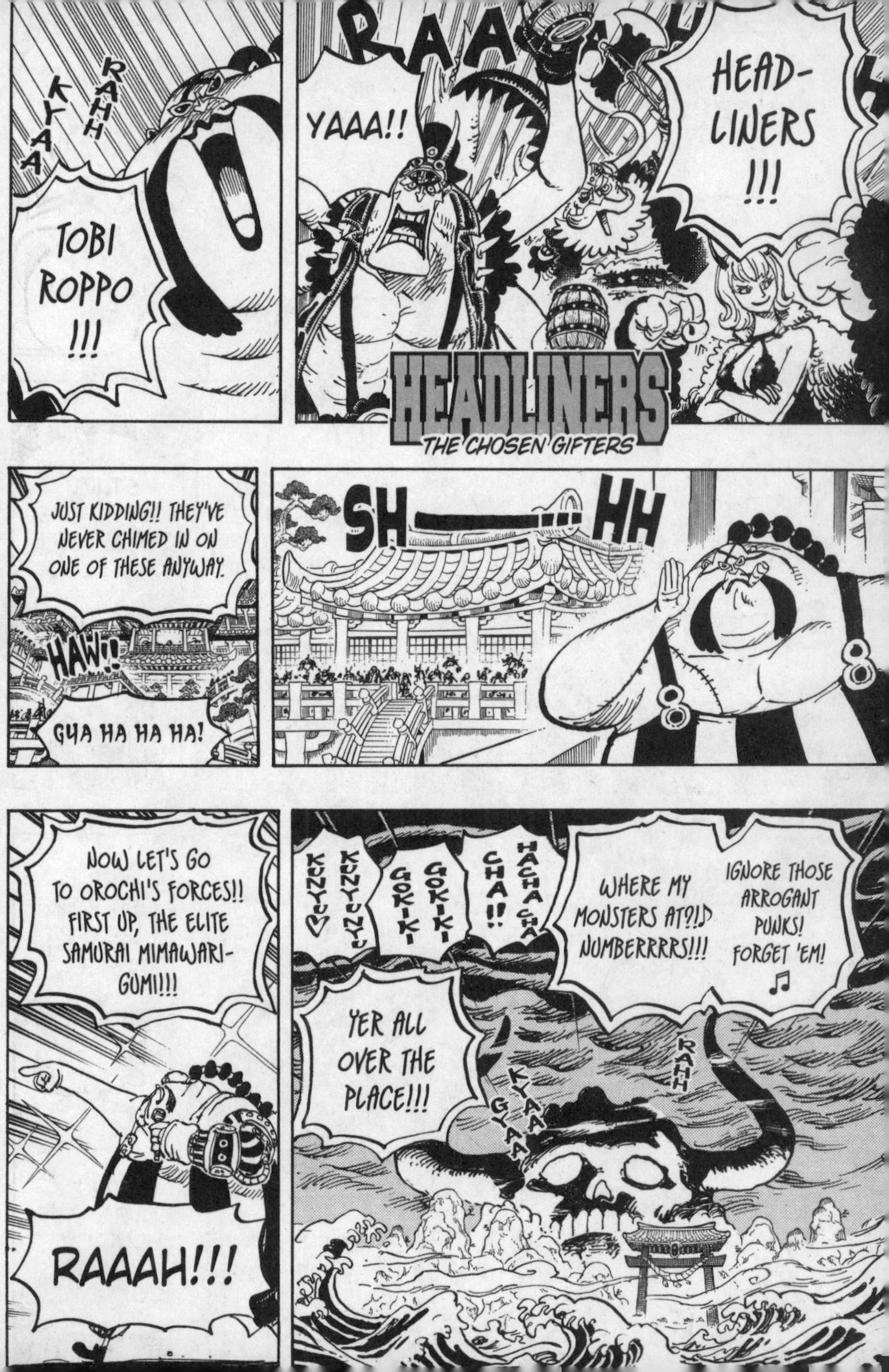
HEAD-LINERS!!!
RAA
YAAA!!
HEADLINERS
THE CHOSEN GIFTERS
RAHH
KYAA
TOBI ROPPO!!!
SH——HH
JUST KIDDING!! THEY'VE NEVER CHIMED IN ON ONE OF THESE ANYWAY.
HAW!!
GUA HA HA HA!
IGNORE THOSE ARROGANT PUNKS! FORGET 'EM! ♫
WHERE MY MONSTERS AT?!♪ NUMBERRRRS!!!
HACHA CHA CHA!!
GOKIKI GOKIKI
KUNYUNYU KUNYU♥
YER ALL OVER THE PLACE!!!
RAHH
KYAA
GYAA
NOW LET'S GO TO OROCHI'S FORCES!! FIRST UP, THE ELITE SAMURAI MIMAWARI-GUMI!!!
RAAAH!!!

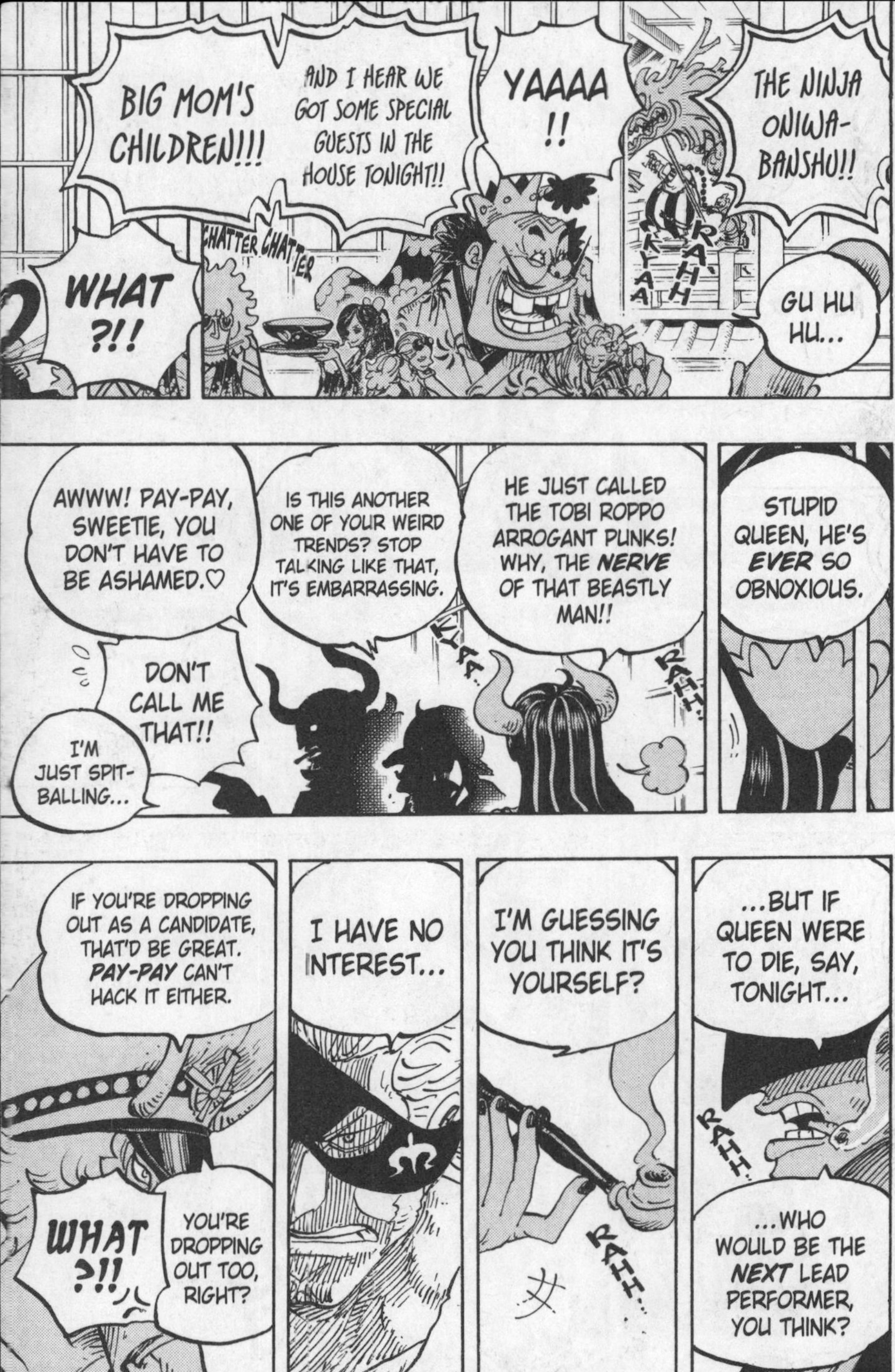
THE NINJA ONIWA-BANSHU!!
YAAAA!!
AND I HEAR WE GOT SOME SPECIAL GUESTS IN THE HOUSE TONIGHT!!
BIG MOM'S CHILDREN!!!
KYAA
RAHH
GU HU HU...
CHATTER CHATTER
WHAT?!!
STUPID QUEEN, HE'S *EVER* SO OBNOXIOUS.
HE JUST CALLED THE TOBI ROPPO ARROGANT PUNKS! WHY, THE *NERVE* OF THAT BEASTLY MAN!!
RAHH
KYAA
IS THIS ANOTHER ONE OF YOUR WEIRD TRENDS? STOP TALKING LIKE THAT, IT'S EMBARRASSING.
AWWW! PAY-PAY, SWEETIE, YOU DON'T HAVE TO BE ASHAMED.♡
DON'T CALL ME THAT!!
I'M JUST SPIT-BALLING...
...BUT IF QUEEN WERE TO DIE, SAY, TONIGHT...
RAHH
...WHO WOULD BE THE *NEXT* LEAD PERFORMER, YOU THINK?
I'M GUESSING YOU THINK IT'S YOURSELF?
RAHH
I HAVE NO INTEREST...
IF YOU'RE DROPPING OUT AS A CANDIDATE, THAT'D BE GREAT. *PAY-PAY* CAN'T HACK IT EITHER.
YOU'RE DROPPING OUT TOO, RIGHT?
WHAT?!!

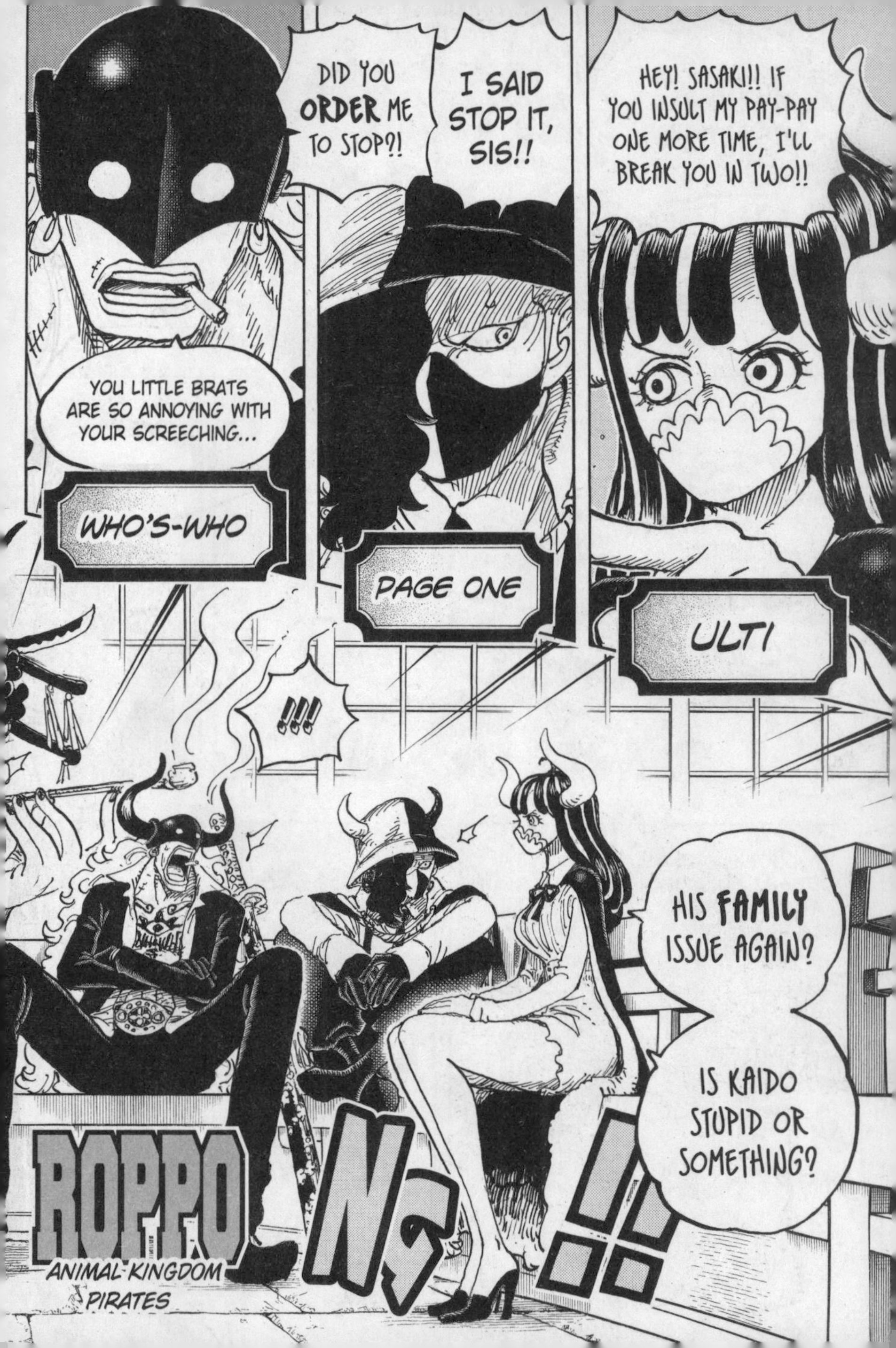
HEY! SASAKI!! IF YOU INSULT MY PAY-PAY ONE MORE TIME, I'LL BREAK YOU IN TWO!!
ULTI
I SAID STOP IT, SIS!!
DID YOU ORDER ME TO STOP?!
PAGE ONE
YOU LITTLE BRATS ARE SO ANNOYING WITH YOUR SCREECHING...
WHO'S-WHO
!!!
HIS FAMILY ISSUE AGAIN?
IS KAIDO STUPID OR SOMETHING?
N?!!
ROPPO
ANIMAL KINGDOM PIRATES

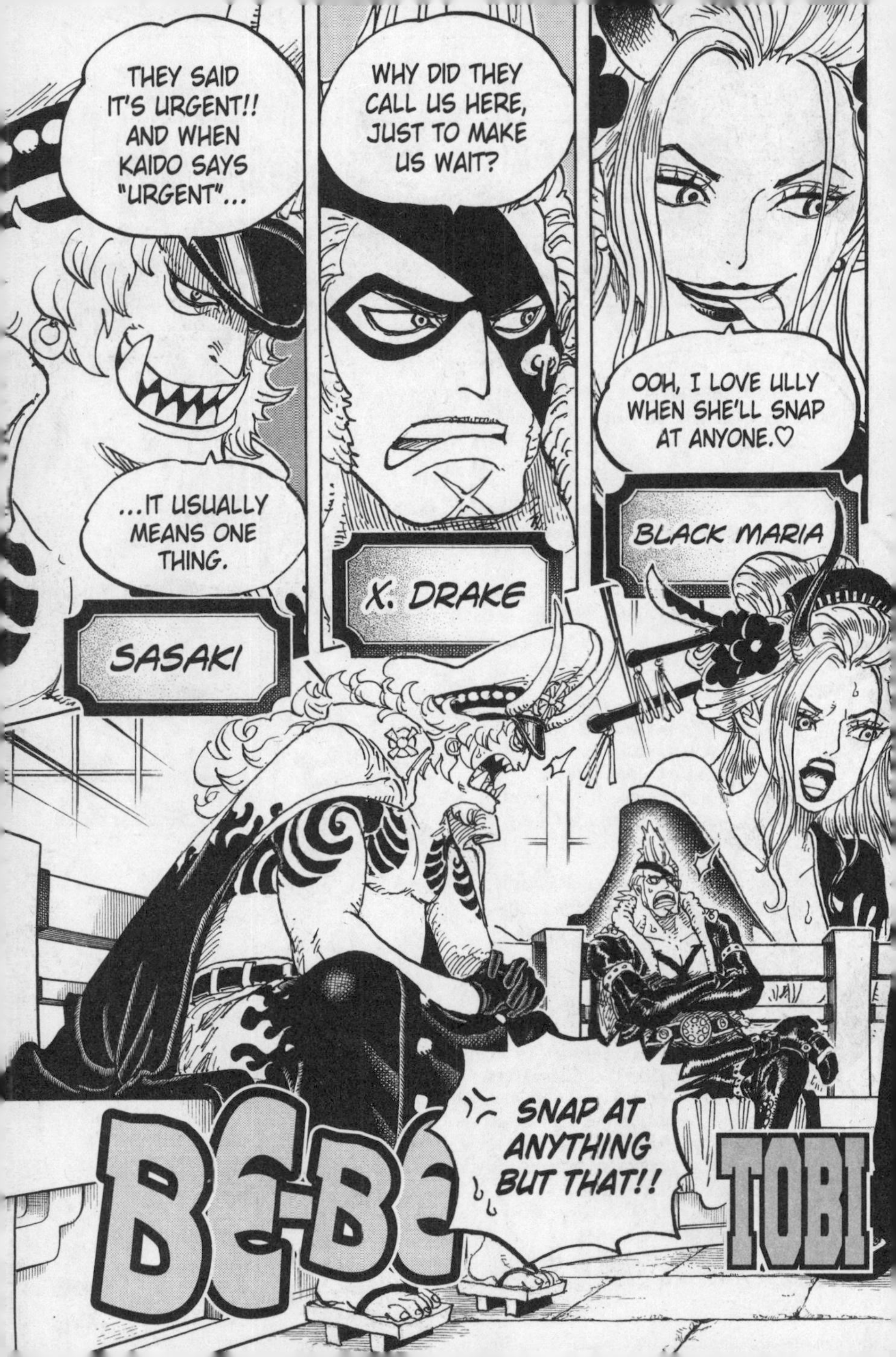

OOH, I LOVE ULLY WHEN SHE'LL SNAP AT ANYONE.♡
BLACK MARIA
WHY DID THEY CALL US HERE, JUST TO MAKE US WAIT?
X. DRAKE
THEY SAID IT'S URGENT!! AND WHEN KAIDO SAYS "URGENT"...
...IT USUALLY MEANS ONE THING.
SASAKI
TOBI
SNAP AT ANYTHING BUT THAT!!
BE-BE

SBS Question Corner

質問コーナー
エス
ビー
エス
MARINE

(I ♡ OP, Ishikawa)

Q: Odacchi!! I have a question. Who has a longer head, Fukurokuju or Vice Admiral Strawberry? I can't get any sleep at night until I learn the answer.

--Kaikai

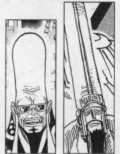

A: I think you can tell by comparing them. The answer is Strawberry. They say his head grows with every sadness he's experienced.

Q: You've been drawing personifications of swords lately, but I'd like to see a human version of Luffy's straw hat now! Thanks for obliging!

--Akimasa

A: Ahh, that's a new wrinkle. But as you know, I'm very good at capturing their spirit. Look, this one even has the scars left by Buggy! ➡

Go ahead and fight, I won't fall off.
Straw

Q: Oda Sensei!! My question is, why is the Kozuki Clan despised in modern Wano? I would have thought that Shinobu cleared his reputation with the public…

--Y.U.

A: Everyone who believes in and follows the Kozuki Clan was purged by Orochi and Kaido. They brainwashed the next generation of children such that everyone in the capital follows Orochi. Basically, it comes down to pressure and brainwashing. These are big things that cause problems in the real world, even today. Scary!

Chapter 979:
FAMILY PROBLEM

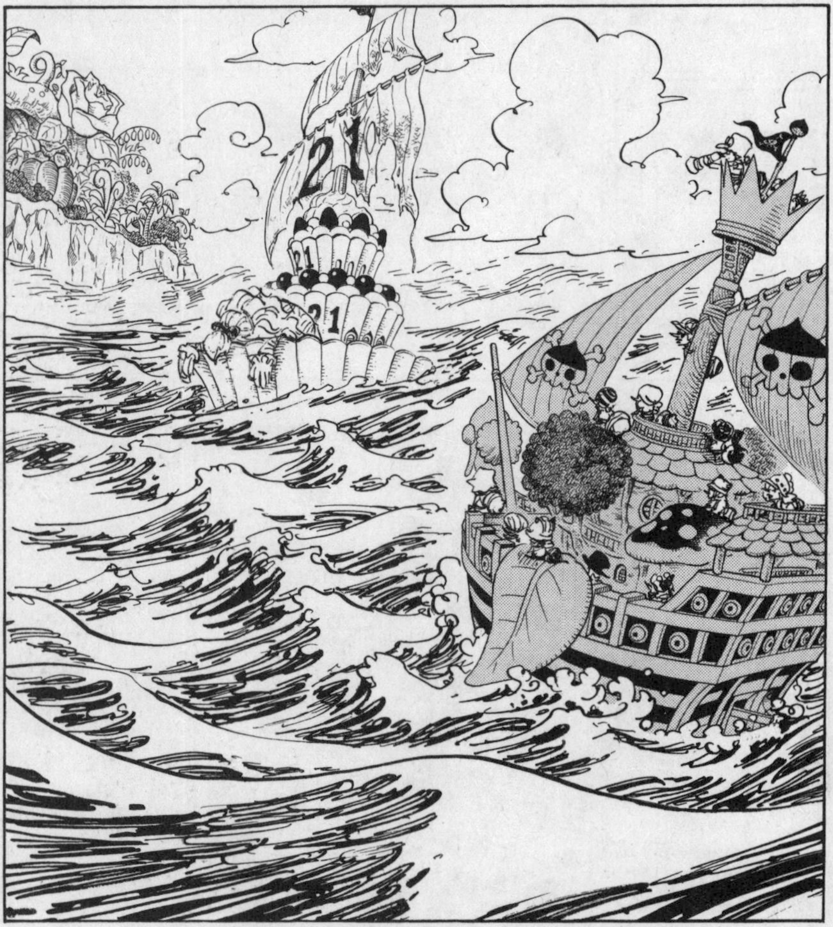

GANG BEGE'S OH MY FAMILY
VOL. 26: "THE TONTATTAS FIND A SHIP ADRIFT"

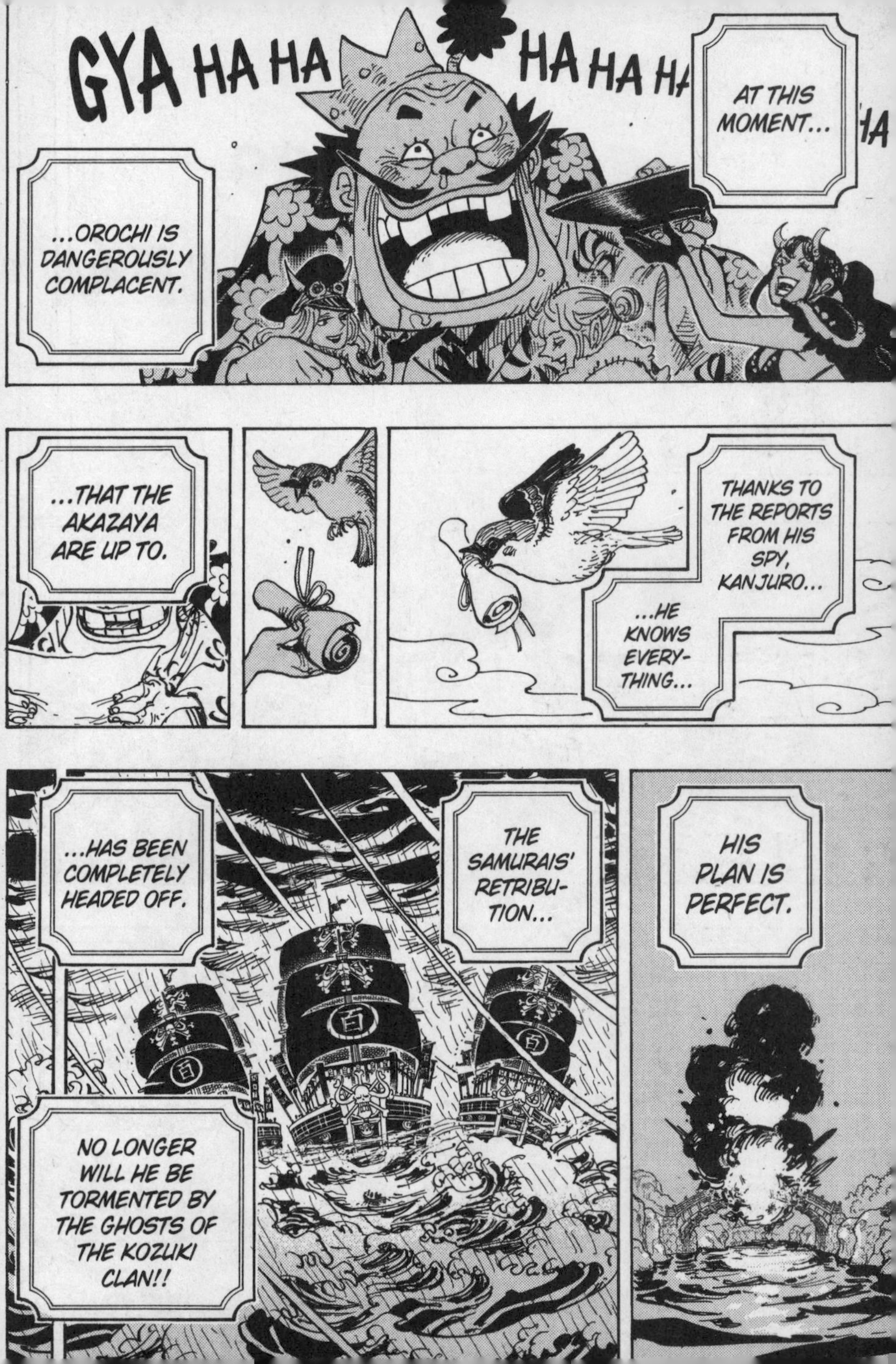
AT THIS MOMENT...
GYA HA HA HA HA HA HA
...OROCHI IS DANGEROUSLY COMPLACENT.
THANKS TO THE REPORTS FROM HIS SPY, KANJURO...
...HE KNOWS EVERYTHING...
...THAT THE AKAZAYA ARE UP TO.
HIS PLAN IS PERFECT.
THE SAMURAIS' RETRIBUTION...
...HAS BEEN COMPLETELY HEADED OFF.
NO LONGER WILL HE BE TORMENTED BY THE GHOSTS OF THE KOZUKI CLAN!!

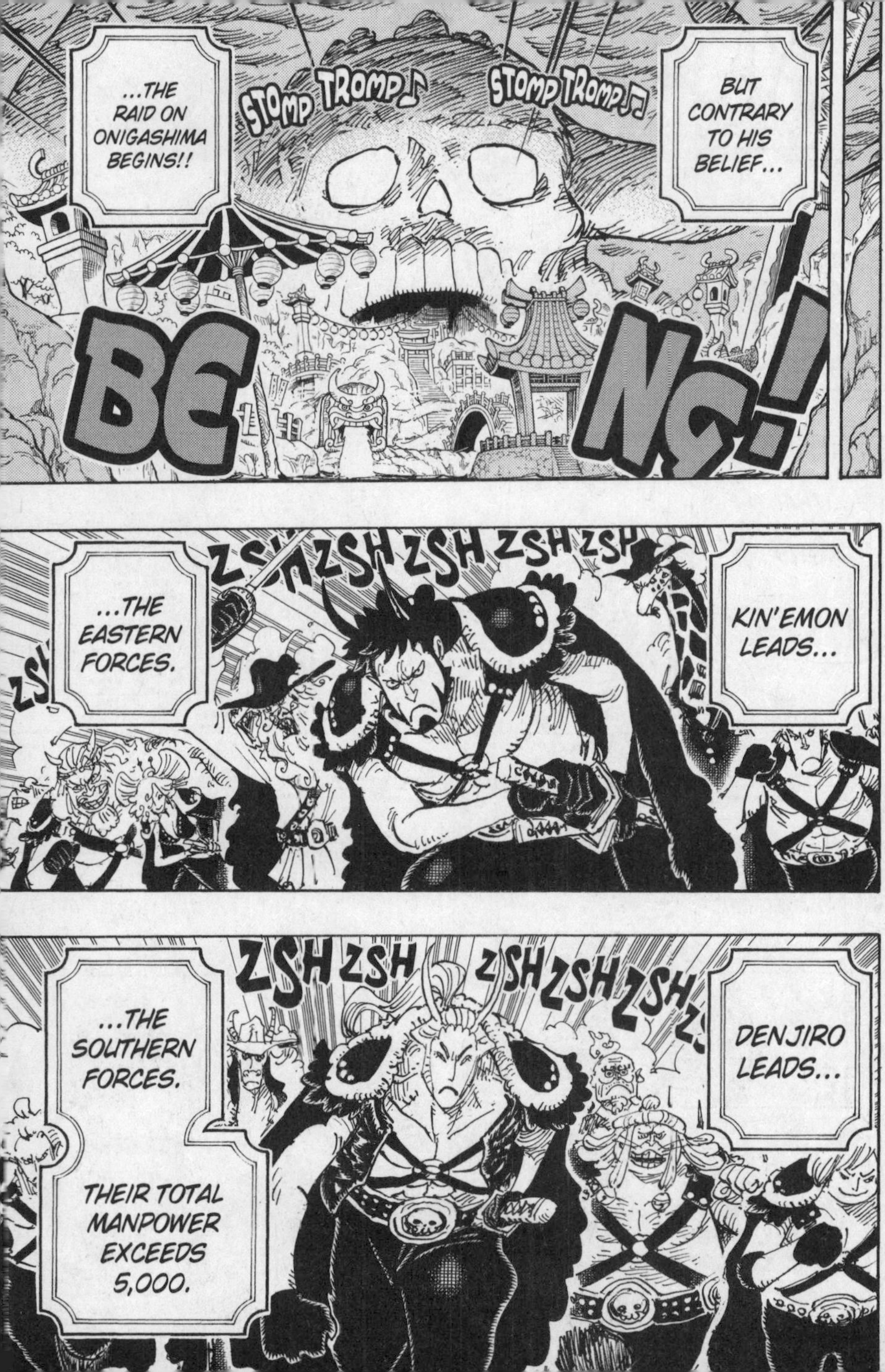
BUT CONTRARY TO HIS BELIEF...
STOMP TROMP♫
STOMP TROMP♪
...THE RAID ON ONIGASHIMA BEGINS!!
BENG!
KIN'EMON LEADS...
ZSH ZSH ZSH ZSH ZSP
...THE EASTERN FORCES.
DENJIRO LEADS...
ZSH ZSH ZSH ZSH
...THE SOUTHERN FORCES.
THEIR TOTAL MANPOWER EXCEEDS 5,000.

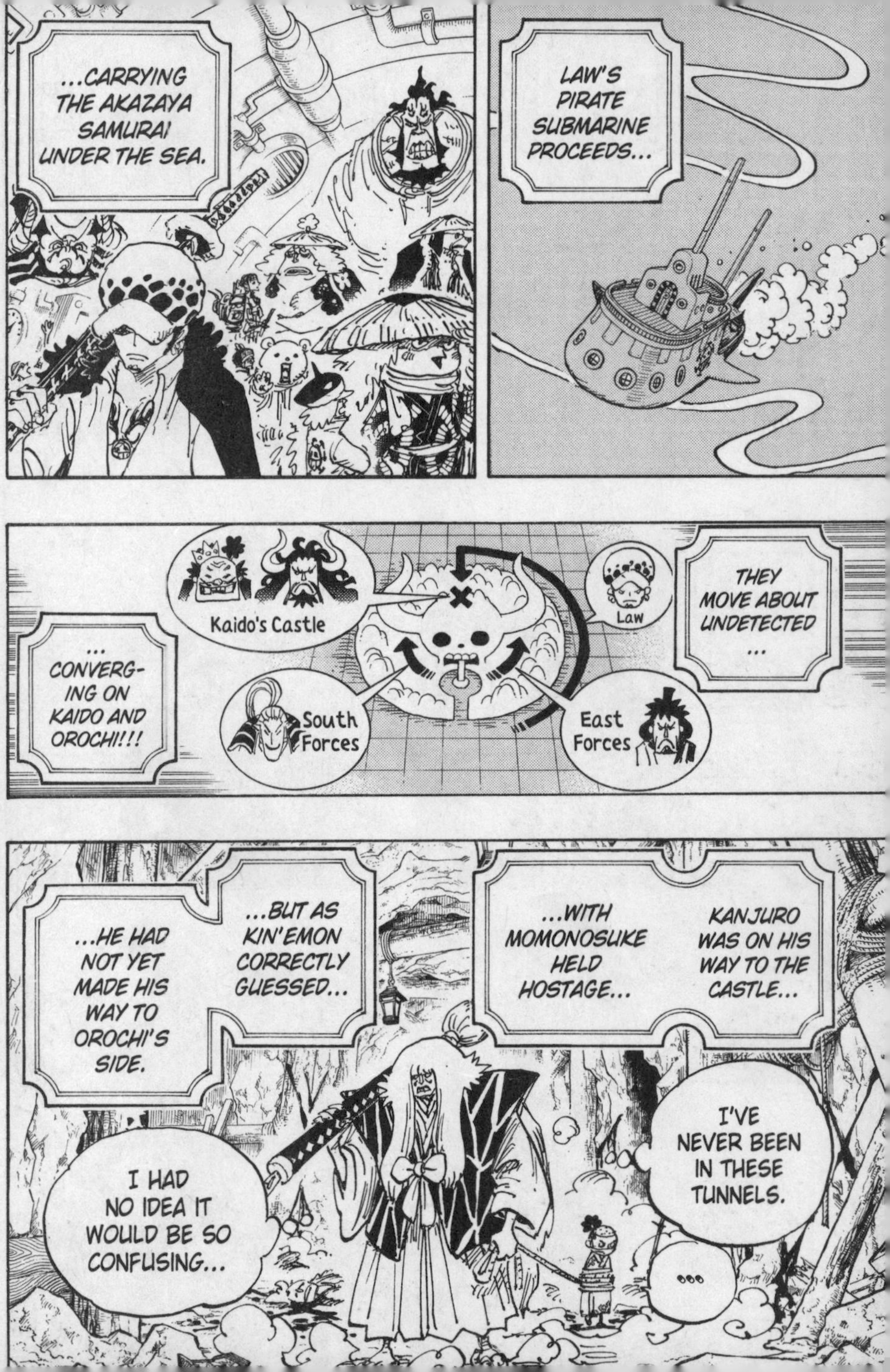
LAW'S PIRATE SUBMARINE PROCEEDS...
...CARRYING THE AKAZAYA SAMURAI UNDER THE SEA.
THEY MOVE ABOUT UNDETECTED ...
Law
Kaido's Castle
East Forces
South Forces
... CONVERG-ING ON KAIDO AND OROCHI!!!
KANJURO WAS ON HIS WAY TO THE CASTLE...
...WITH MOMONOSUKE HELD HOSTAGE...
...BUT AS KIN'EMON CORRECTLY GUESSED...
...HE HAD NOT YET MADE HIS WAY TO OROCHI'S SIDE.
I'VE NEVER BEEN IN THESE TUNNELS.
...
I HAD NO IDEA IT WOULD BE SO CONFUSING...

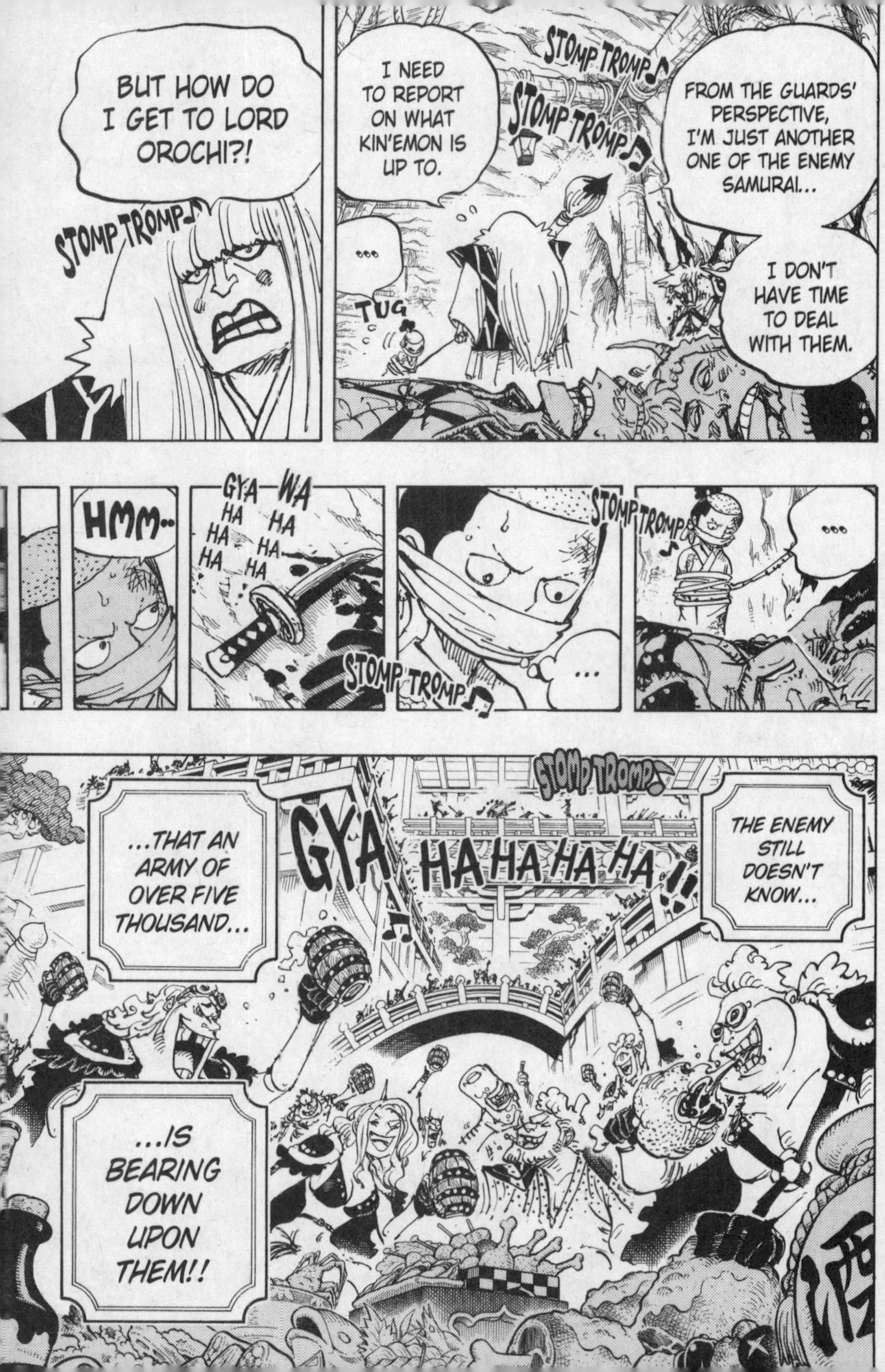
STOMP TROMP♪
STOMP TROMP♪
FROM THE GUARDS' PERSPECTIVE, I'M JUST ANOTHER ONE OF THE ENEMY SAMURAI...
I DON'T HAVE TIME TO DEAL WITH THEM.
I NEED TO REPORT ON WHAT KIN'EMON IS UP TO.
...
TUG
BUT HOW DO I GET TO LORD OROCHI?!
STOMP TROMP♪
STOMP TROMP♪
...
...
GYA HA HA HA
WA HA HA HA
STOMP TROMP♪
HMM..
STOMP TROMP♪
THE ENEMY STILL DOESN'T KNOW...
GYA HA HA HA HA HA!!
...THAT AN ARMY OF OVER FIVE THOUSAND...
...IS BEARING DOWN UPON THEM!!

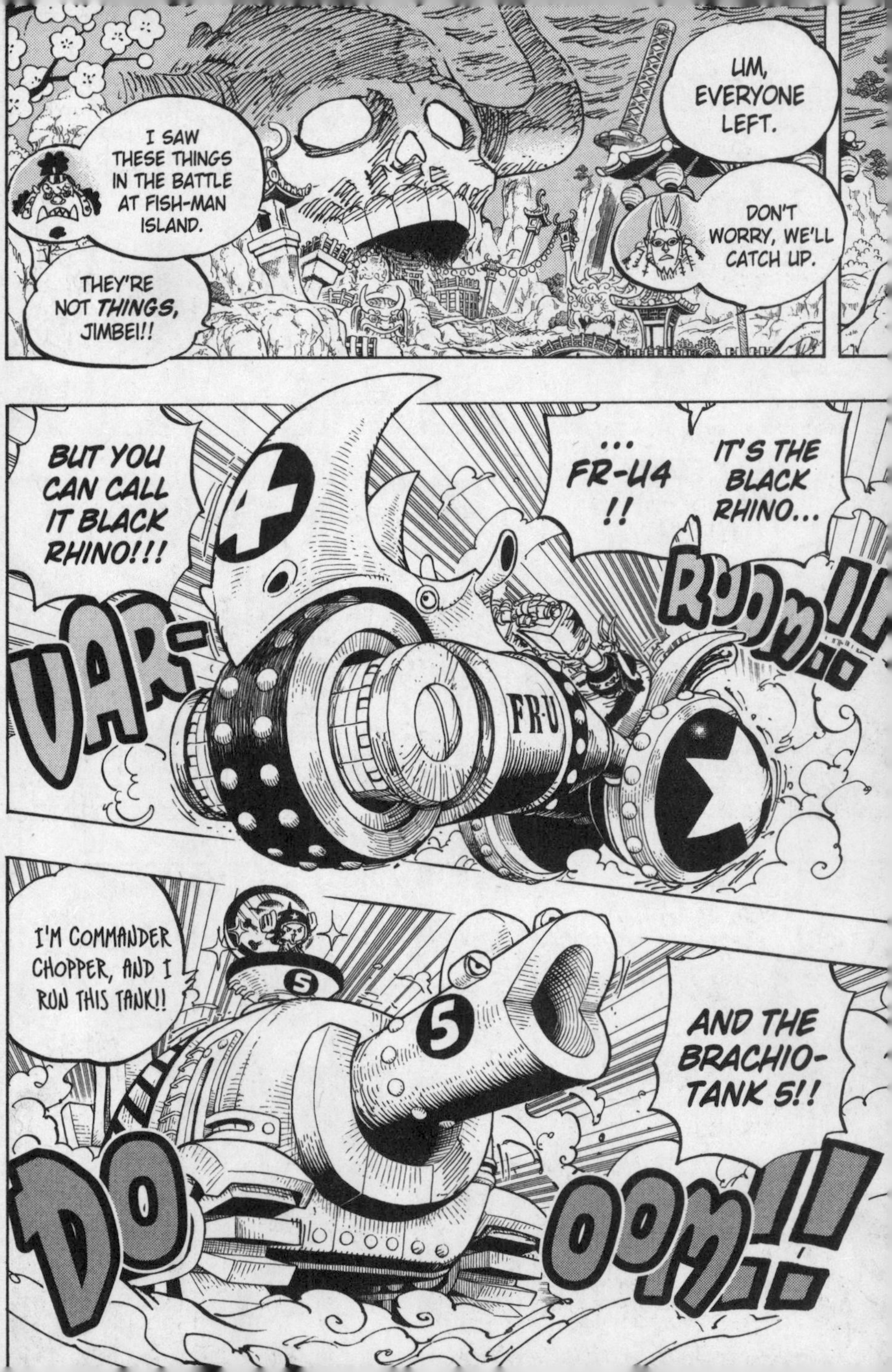
UM, EVERYONE LEFT.
DON'T WORRY, WE'LL CATCH UP.
I SAW THESE THINGS IN THE BATTLE AT FISH-MAN ISLAND.
THEY'RE NOT *THINGS*, JIMBEI!!
IT'S THE BLACK RHINO...
...FR-U4!!
BUT YOU CAN CALL IT BLACK RHINO!!!
RUOOM!!
FR-U
VAR-
AND THE BRACHIO-TANK 5!!
I'M COMMANDER CHOPPER, AND I RUN THIS TANK!!
DO-
OOM!!

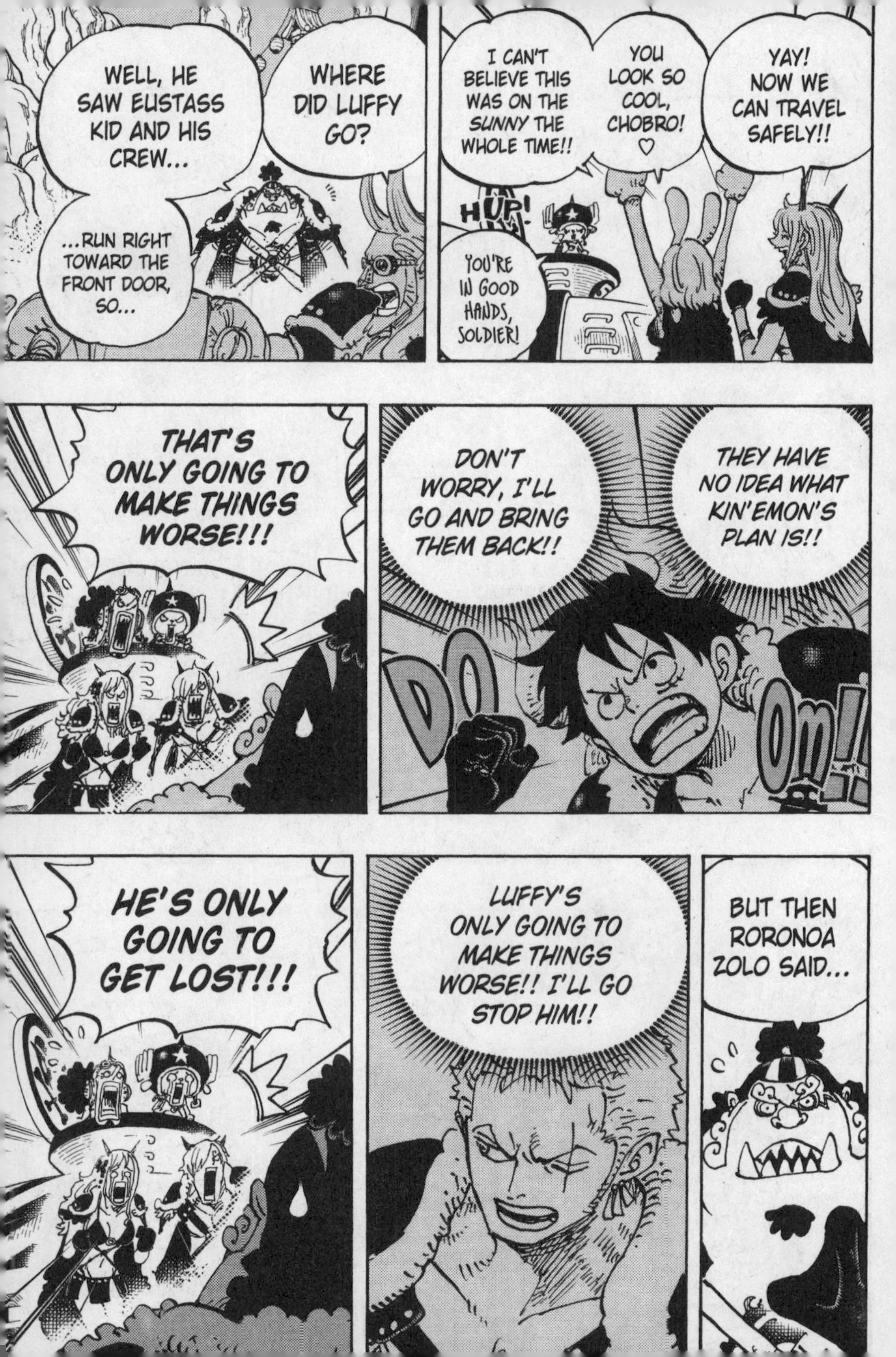
YAY! NOW WE CAN TRAVEL SAFELY!!
YOU LOOK SO COOL, CHOBRO! ♡
I CAN'T BELIEVE THIS WAS ON THE *SUNNY* THE WHOLE TIME!!
HUP!
YOU'RE IN GOOD HANDS, SOLDIER!
WHERE DID LUFFY GO?
WELL, HE SAW EUSTASS KID AND HIS CREW...
...RUN RIGHT TOWARD THE FRONT DOOR, SO...
THEY HAVE NO IDEA WHAT KIN'EMON'S PLAN IS!!
DON'T WORRY, I'LL GO AND BRING THEM BACK!!
DOOM!!
THAT'S ONLY GOING TO MAKE THINGS WORSE!!!
BUT THEN RORONOA ZOLO SAID...
LUFFY'S ONLY GOING TO MAKE THINGS WORSE!! I'LL GO STOP HIM!!
HE'S ONLY GOING TO GET LOST!!!

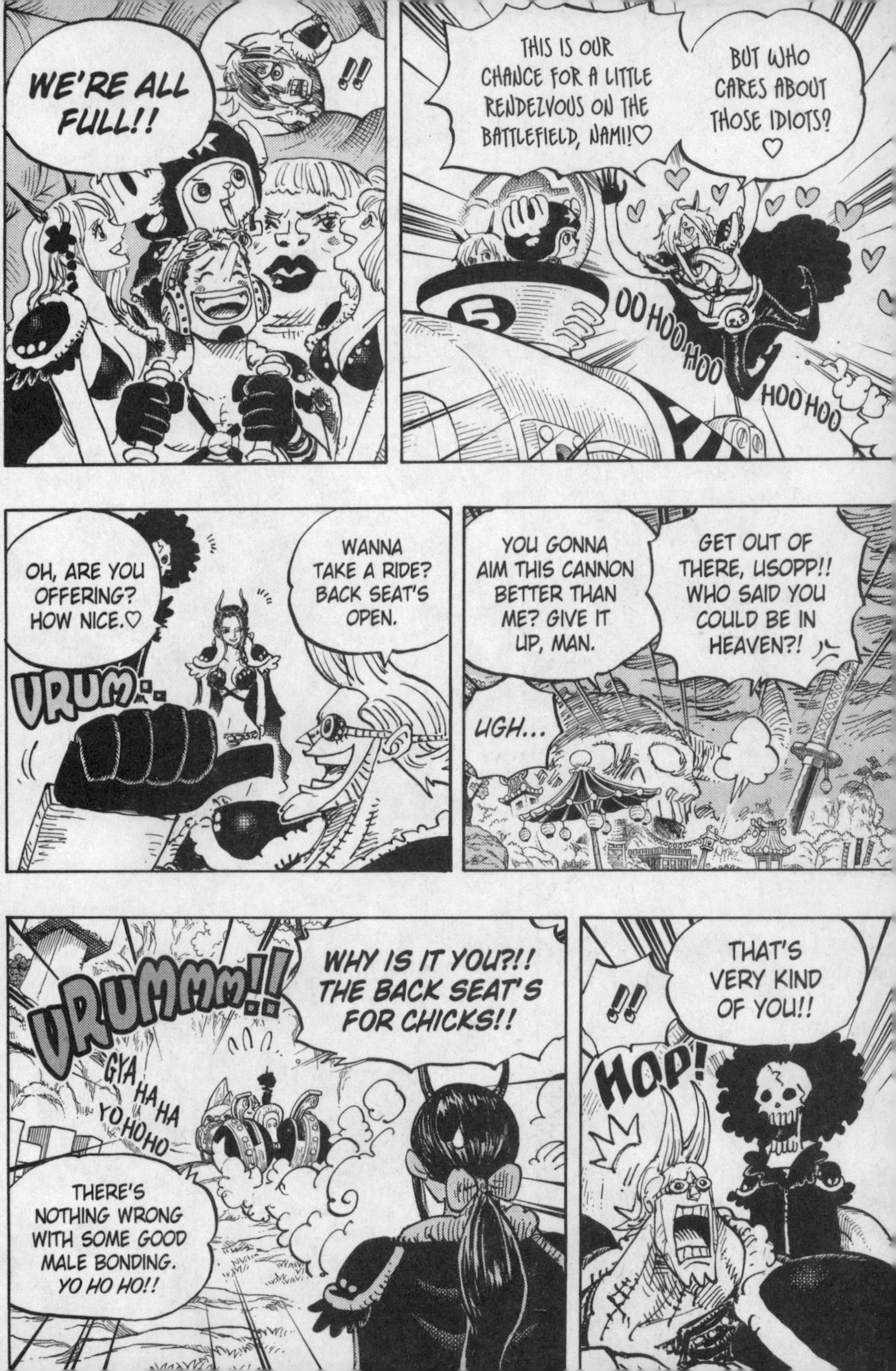
BUT WHO CARES ABOUT THOSE IDIOTS? ♡
THIS IS OUR CHANCE FOR A LITTLE RENDEZVOUS ON THE BATTLEFIELD, NAMI!♡
OOHOOHOOHOO
HOOHOO
!!
WE'RE ALL FULL!!
GET OUT OF THERE, USOPP!! WHO SAID YOU COULD BE IN HEAVEN?!
YOU GONNA AIM THIS CANNON BETTER THAN ME? GIVE IT UP, MAN.
UGH...
WANNA TAKE A RIDE? BACK SEAT'S OPEN.
OH, ARE YOU OFFERING? HOW NICE.♡
VRUM...
THAT'S VERY KIND OF YOU!!
!!
HOP!
WHY IS IT YOU?!! THE BACK SEAT'S FOR CHICKS!!
VRUMMM!!
GYA HA HA
YO HO HO
THERE'S NOTHING WRONG WITH SOME GOOD MALE BONDING. YO HO HO!!

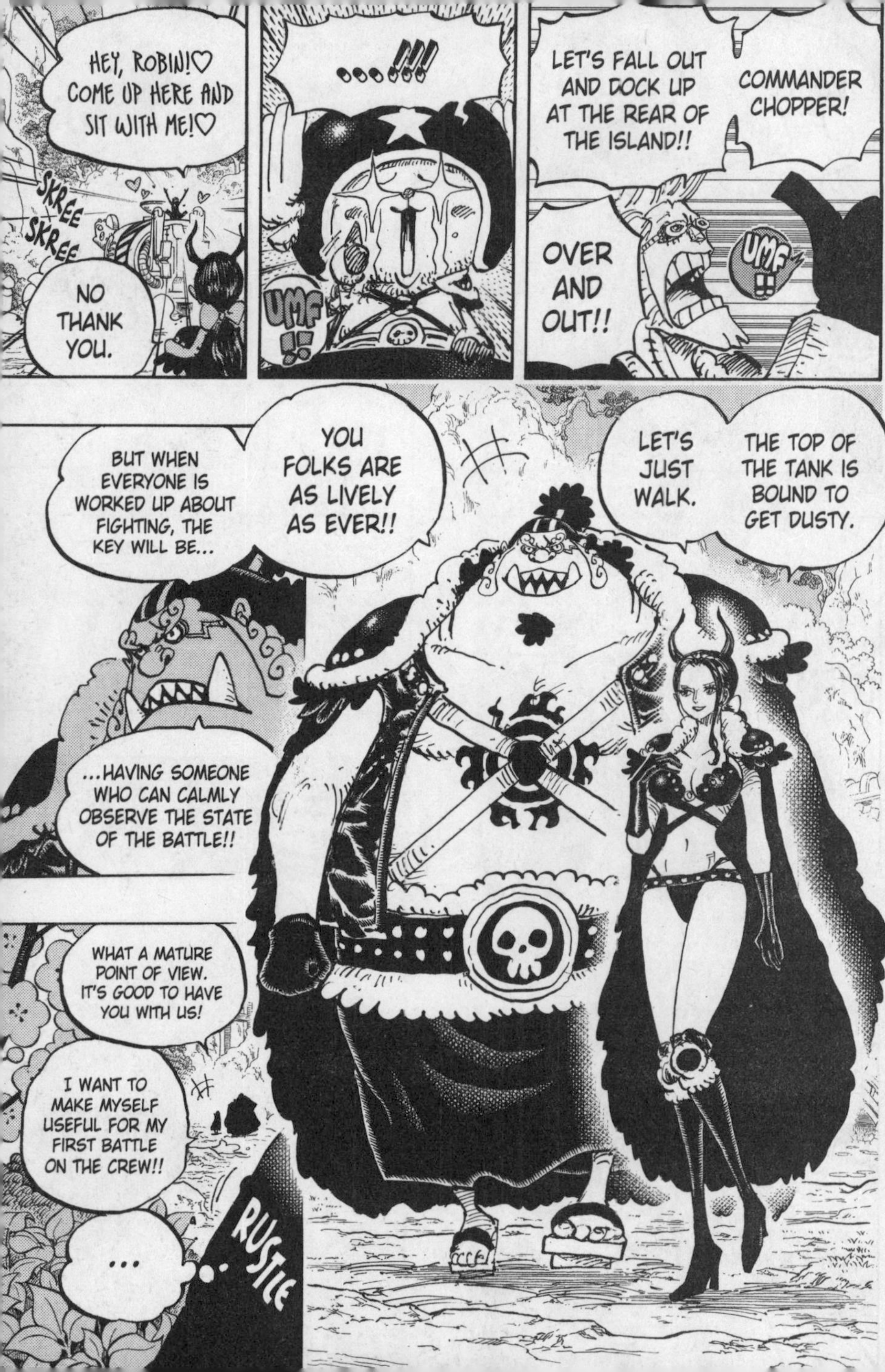
COMMANDER CHOPPER!
LET'S FALL OUT AND DOCK UP AT THE REAR OF THE ISLAND!!
OVER AND OUT!!
UMF
...!!!
UMF
HEY, ROBIN!♡ COME UP HERE AND SIT WITH ME!♡
SKREE SKREE
NO THANK YOU.
THE TOP OF THE TANK IS BOUND TO GET DUSTY.
LET'S JUST WALK.
YOU FOLKS ARE AS LIVELY AS EVER!!
BUT WHEN EVERYONE IS WORKED UP ABOUT FIGHTING, THE KEY WILL BE...
...HAVING SOMEONE WHO CAN CALMLY OBSERVE THE STATE OF THE BATTLE!!
WHAT A MATURE POINT OF VIEW. IT'S GOOD TO HAVE YOU WITH US!
I WANT TO MAKE MYSELF USEFUL FOR MY FIRST BATTLE ON THE CREW!!
...
RUSTLE

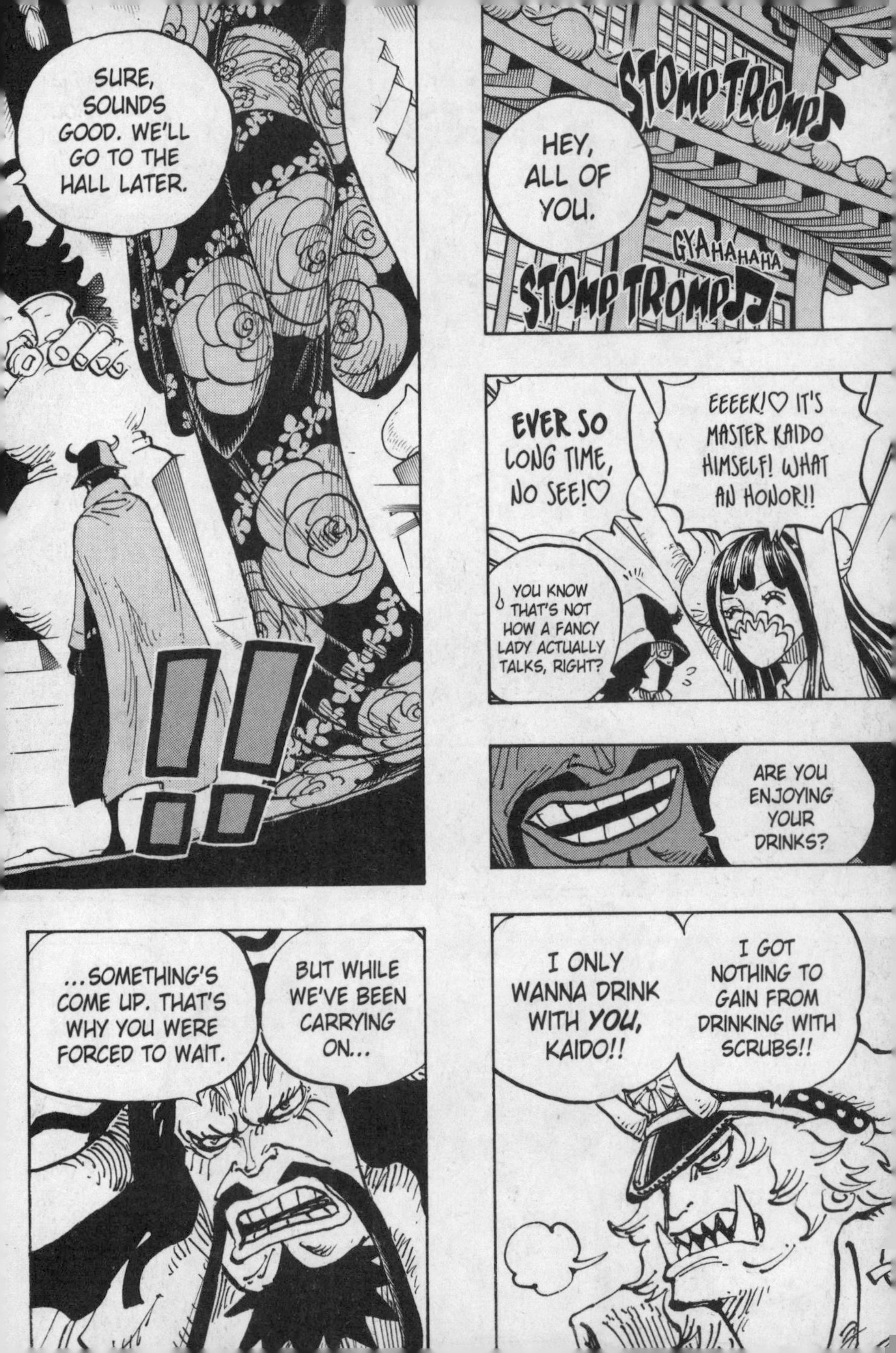
STOMP TROMP♪
HEY, ALL OF YOU.
GYAHAHAHA
STOMP TROMP♪♪
EEEEK!♡ IT'S MASTER KAIDO HIMSELF! WHAT AN HONOR!!
EVER SO LONG TIME, NO SEE!♡
YOU KNOW THAT'S NOT HOW A FANCY LADY ACTUALLY TALKS, RIGHT?
ARE YOU ENJOYING YOUR DRINKS?
SURE, SOUNDS GOOD. WE'LL GO TO THE HALL LATER.
!!
I GOT NOTHING TO GAIN FROM DRINKING WITH SCRUBS!!
I ONLY WANNA DRINK WITH *YOU*, KAIDO!!
BUT WHILE WE'VE BEEN CARRYING ON...
...SOMETHING'S COME UP. THAT'S WHY YOU WERE FORCED TO WAIT.

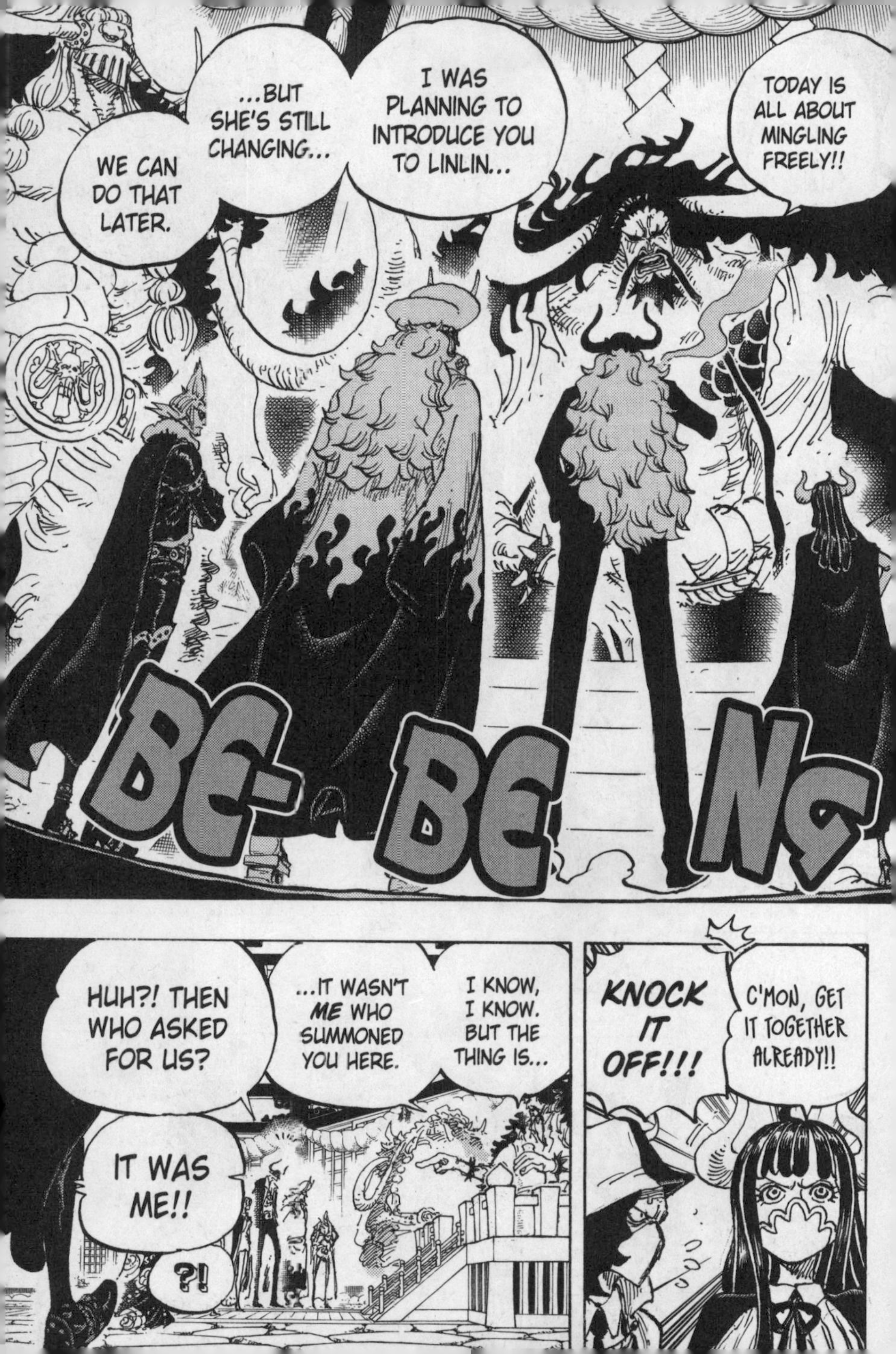
TODAY IS ALL ABOUT MINGLING FREELY!!
I WAS PLANNING TO INTRODUCE YOU TO LINLIN...
...BUT SHE'S STILL CHANGING...
WE CAN DO THAT LATER.
BE-BE-NG
C'MON, GET IT TOGETHER ALREADY!!
KNOCK IT OFF!!!
I KNOW, I KNOW. BUT THE THING IS...
...IT WASN'T *ME* WHO SUMMONED YOU HERE.
HUH?! THEN WHO ASKED FOR US?
IT WAS ME!!
?!

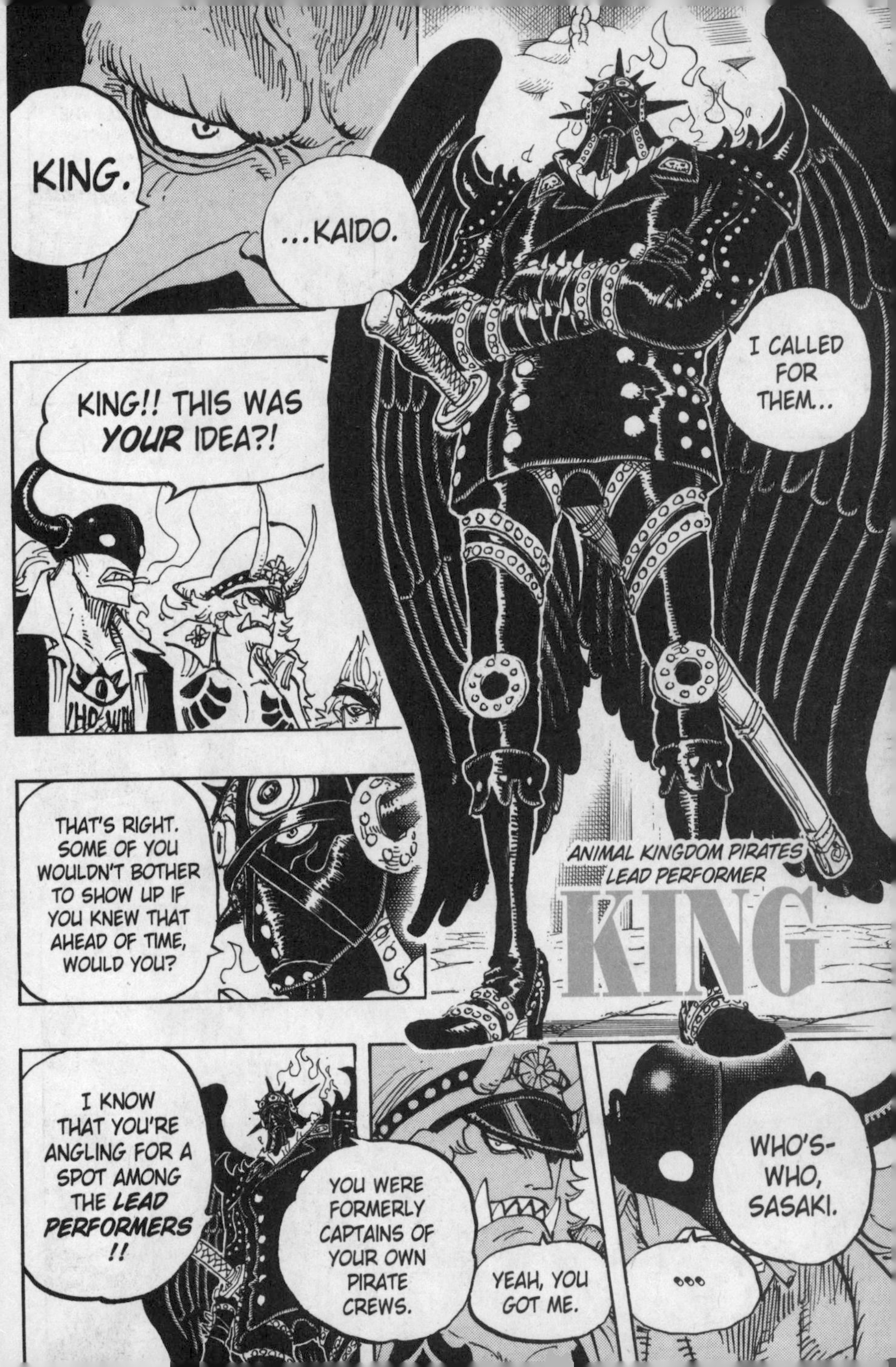
I CALLED FOR THEM...
ANIMAL KINGDOM PIRATES LEAD PERFORMER
KING
KING.
...KAIDO.
KING!! THIS WAS YOUR IDEA?!
THAT'S RIGHT. SOME OF YOU WOULDN'T BOTHER TO SHOW UP IF YOU KNEW THAT AHEAD OF TIME, WOULD YOU?
WHO'S-WHO, SASAKI.
...
YOU WERE FORMERLY CAPTAINS OF YOUR OWN PIRATE CREWS.
YEAH, YOU GOT ME.
I KNOW THAT YOU'RE ANGLING FOR A SPOT AMONG THE LEAD PERFORMERS!!

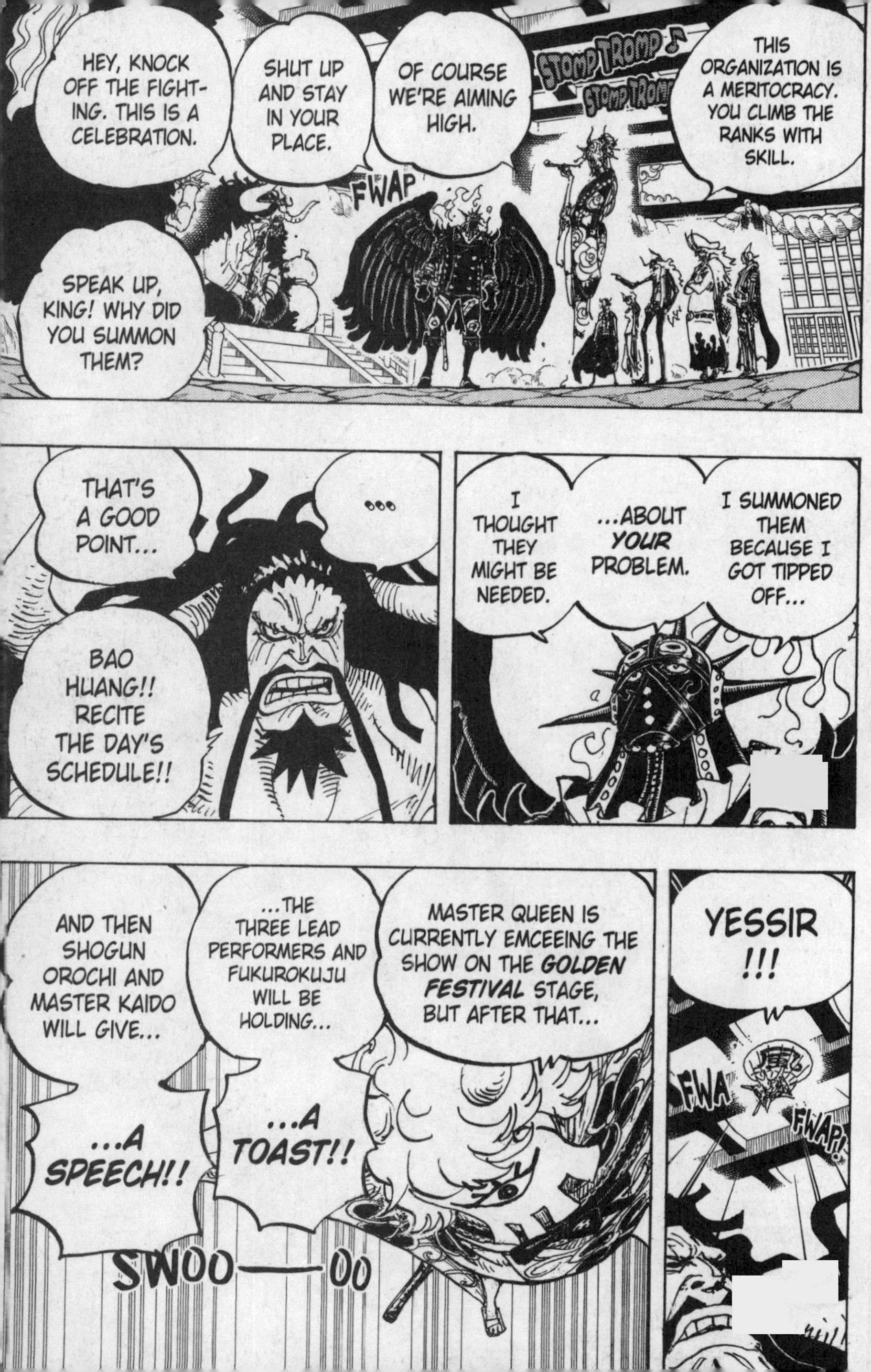
THIS ORGANIZATION IS A MERITOCRACY. YOU CLIMB THE RANKS WITH SKILL.
STOMP TROMP ♪
STOMP TROMP
OF COURSE WE'RE AIMING HIGH.
SHUT UP AND STAY IN YOUR PLACE.
HEY, KNOCK OFF THE FIGHT-ING. THIS IS A CELEBRATION.
FWAP
SPEAK UP, KING! WHY DID YOU SUMMON THEM?
I SUMMONED THEM BECAUSE I GOT TIPPED OFF...
...ABOUT *YOUR* PROBLEM.
I THOUGHT THEY MIGHT BE NEEDED.
...
THAT'S A GOOD POINT...
BAO HUANG!! RECITE THE DAY'S SCHEDULE!!
YESSIR!!!
FWA
FWAP!
MASTER QUEEN IS CURRENTLY EMCEEING THE SHOW ON THE *GOLDEN FESTIVAL* STAGE, BUT AFTER THAT...
...THE THREE LEAD PERFORMERS AND FUKUROKUJU WILL BE HOLDING...
AND THEN SHOGUN OROCHI AND MASTER KAIDO WILL GIVE...
...A TOAST!!
...A SPEECH!!
SWOO——OO

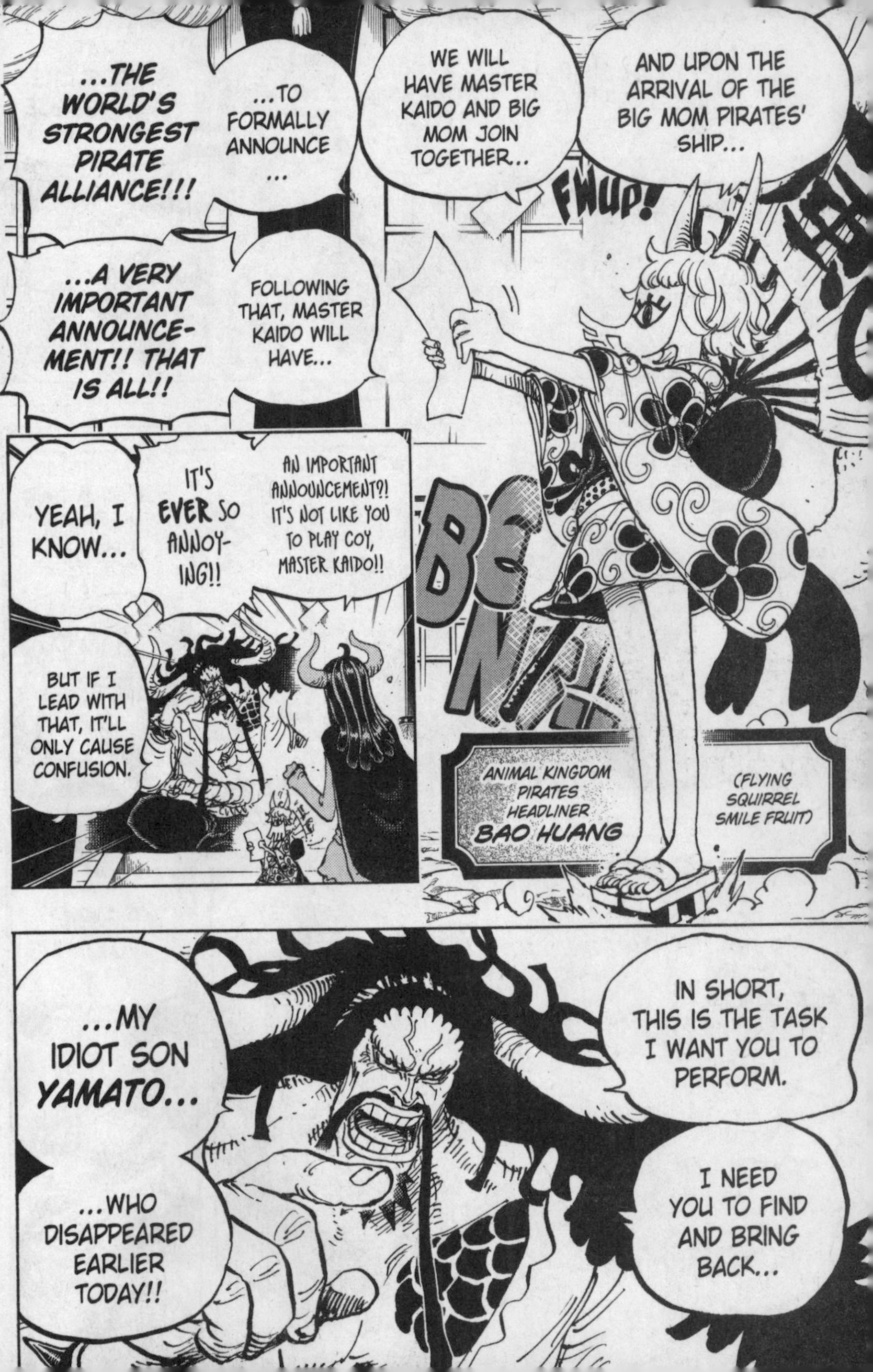
AND UPON THE ARRIVAL OF THE BIG MOM PIRATES' SHIP...
WE WILL HAVE MASTER KAIDO AND BIG MOM JOIN TOGETHER...
...TO FORMALLY ANNOUNCE ...
...THE WORLD'S STRONGEST PIRATE ALLIANCE!!!
FOLLOWING THAT, MASTER KAIDO WILL HAVE...
...A VERY IMPORTANT ANNOUNCE-MENT!! THAT IS ALL!!
FWUP!
BEN
ANIMAL KINGDOM PIRATES HEADLINER BAO HUANG
(FLYING SQUIRREL SMILE FRUIT)
AN IMPORTANT ANNOUNCEMENT?! IT'S NOT LIKE YOU TO PLAY COY, MASTER KAIDO!!
IT'S EVER SO ANNOY-ING!!
YEAH, I KNOW...
BUT IF I LEAD WITH THAT, IT'LL ONLY CAUSE CONFUSION.
IN SHORT, THIS IS THE TASK I WANT YOU TO PERFORM.
I NEED YOU TO FIND AND BRING BACK...
...MY IDIOT SON YAMATO...
...WHO DISAPPEARED EARLIER TODAY!!

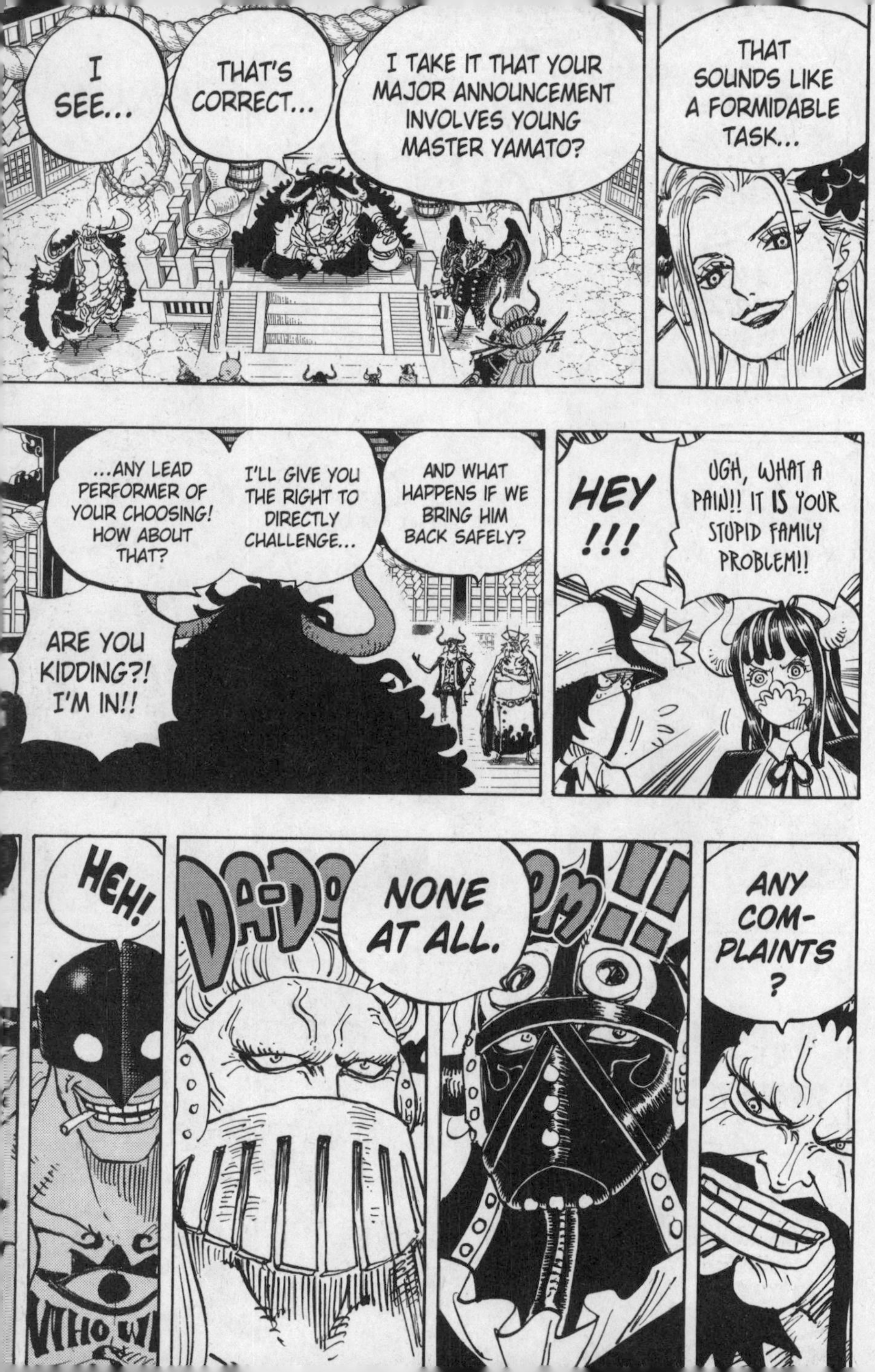
THAT SOUNDS LIKE A FORMIDABLE TASK...
I TAKE IT THAT YOUR MAJOR ANNOUNCEMENT INVOLVES YOUNG MASTER YAMATO?
THAT'S CORRECT...
I SEE...
UGH, WHAT A PAIN!! IT IS YOUR STUPID FAMILY PROBLEM!!
HEY !!!
AND WHAT HAPPENS IF WE BRING HIM BACK SAFELY?
I'LL GIVE YOU THE RIGHT TO DIRECTLY CHALLENGE...
...ANY LEAD PERFORMER OF YOUR CHOOSING! HOW ABOUT THAT?
ARE YOU KIDDING?! I'M IN!!
ANY COM-PLAINTS ?
DA-DO
OM!!
NONE AT ALL.
HEH!

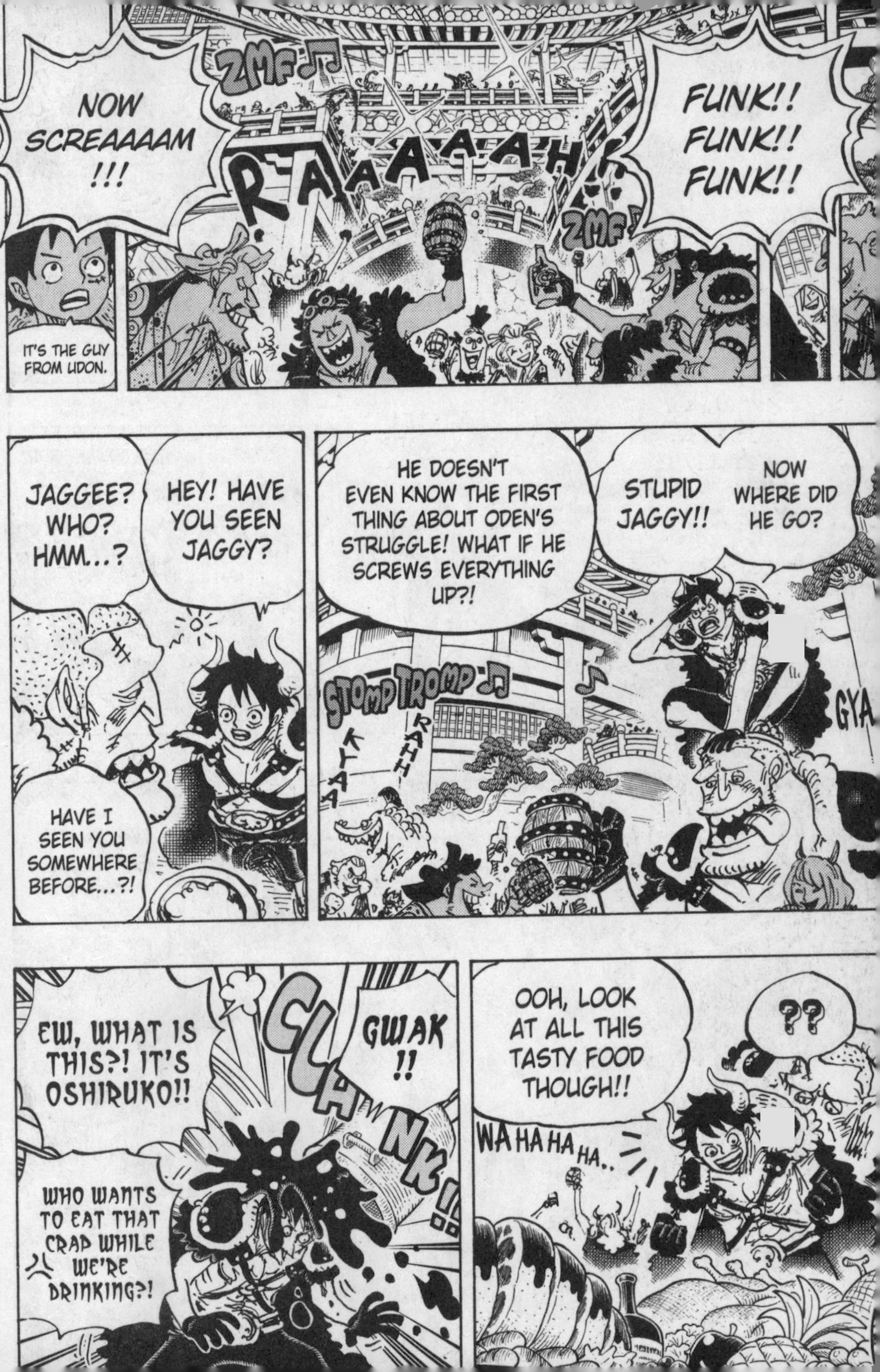
FUNK!! FUNK!! FUNK!!
ZMF
RAAAAAH
ZMF♫
NOW SCREAAAAM!!!
IT'S THE GUY FROM UDON.
NOW WHERE DID HE GO?
STUPID JAGGY!!
HE DOESN'T EVEN KNOW THE FIRST THING ABOUT ODEN'S STRUGGLE! WHAT IF HE SCREWS EVERYTHING UP?!
GYA
STOMP TROMP♫
RAHH!
KYAAA
HEY! HAVE YOU SEEN JAGGY?
JAGGEE? WHO? HMM...?
HAVE I SEEN YOU SOMEWHERE BEFORE...?!
??
OOH, LOOK AT ALL THIS TASTY FOOD THOUGH!!
WAHAHAHA...
GWAK!!
CLANK!!
EW, WHAT IS THIS?! IT'S OSHIRUKO!!
WHO WANTS TO EAT THAT CRAP WHILE WE'RE DRINKING?!

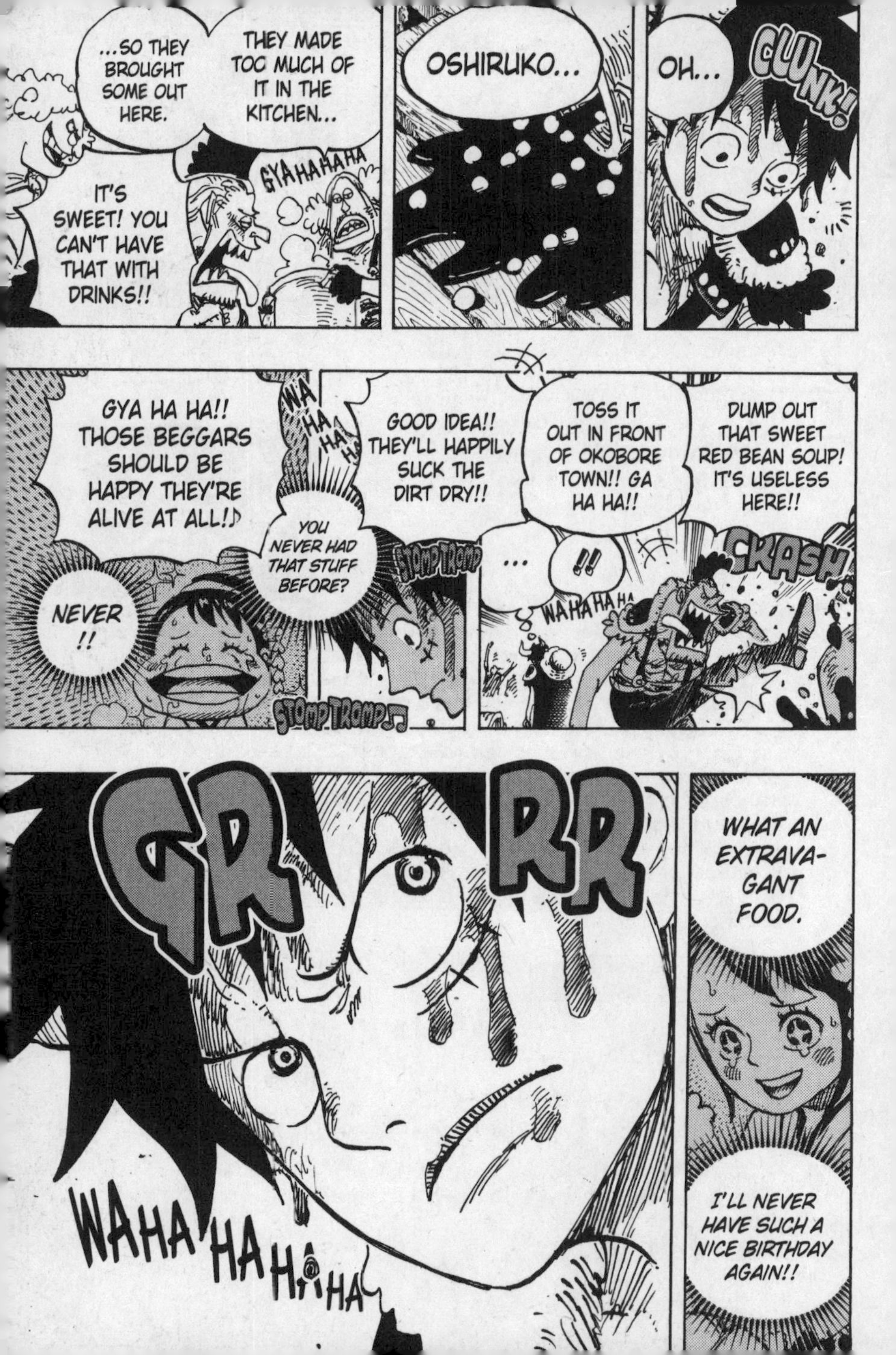
OH...
CLUNK!
OSHIRUKO...
THEY MADE TOO MUCH OF IT IN THE KITCHEN...
...SO THEY BROUGHT SOME OUT HERE.
GYA HAHAHA
IT'S SWEET! YOU CAN'T HAVE THAT WITH DRINKS!!
DUMP OUT THAT SWEET RED BEAN SOUP! IT'S USELESS HERE!!
TOSS IT OUT IN FRONT OF OKOBORE TOWN!! GA HA HA!!
CRASH
!!
...
WAHAHAHA
GOOD IDEA!! THEY'LL HAPPILY SUCK THE DIRT DRY!!
STOMP TROMP
STOMP TROMP♫
WA HA HA HA
GYA HA HA!! THOSE BEGGARS SHOULD BE HAPPY THEY'RE ALIVE AT ALL!♪
YOU NEVER HAD THAT STUFF BEFORE?
NEVER !!
WHAT AN EXTRAVA-GANT FOOD.
I'LL NEVER HAVE SUCH A NICE BIRTHDAY AGAIN!!
GRRR
WAHA HA HA HA

(Mito, Shiga)

質問コーナー

Q: Dear Odacchi!! Is it true that you'll quit drawing *One Piece* in five years? If true, it really hurts the fans to have that knowledge made public!! Lots of my fellow fans were crying at the sudden news! What's the big idea?! But most of all, I really want you to get your rest and relax!

--pari_bentham

A: Okay. It's not so much that I'm "quitting" as that the series will end when I've finished drawing the most exciting part of Luffy's adventures, which is the big story of what the One Piece is. But right now we're in a really exciting story in the land of Wano, but if Luffy manages to survive and sail away, I'll be drawing major international developments, the "biggest battle in One Piece history," which will be a thrilling and wild story the likes of which no one's read before. It'll be great!! So I put out a statement indicating that this very long story is actually moving toward an ending, so that you readers can mentally prepare yourselves. But for now, we're in Wano and it's really heating up, so sit back and enjoy it. I'll draw with all of my strength!!

Q: Hello, Oda Sensei!! I recently ate the Itch-Itch Fruit, Model Crotch. Now I'm itchy.

--Emu Fantasy

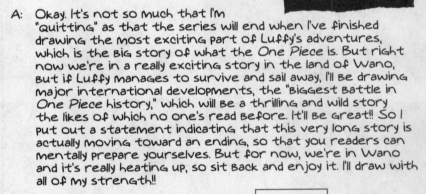

A: Got it. Next question.

Q: Here's that baked iron you ordered, sir.

--Katahajime

A: Ahh, finally! Nothing like a good baked iron in the winter! The best part is that you can eat them in one bite. Down the hatch!
Aieeee!!! Okay.

Chapter 980:
FIGHTING MUSIC

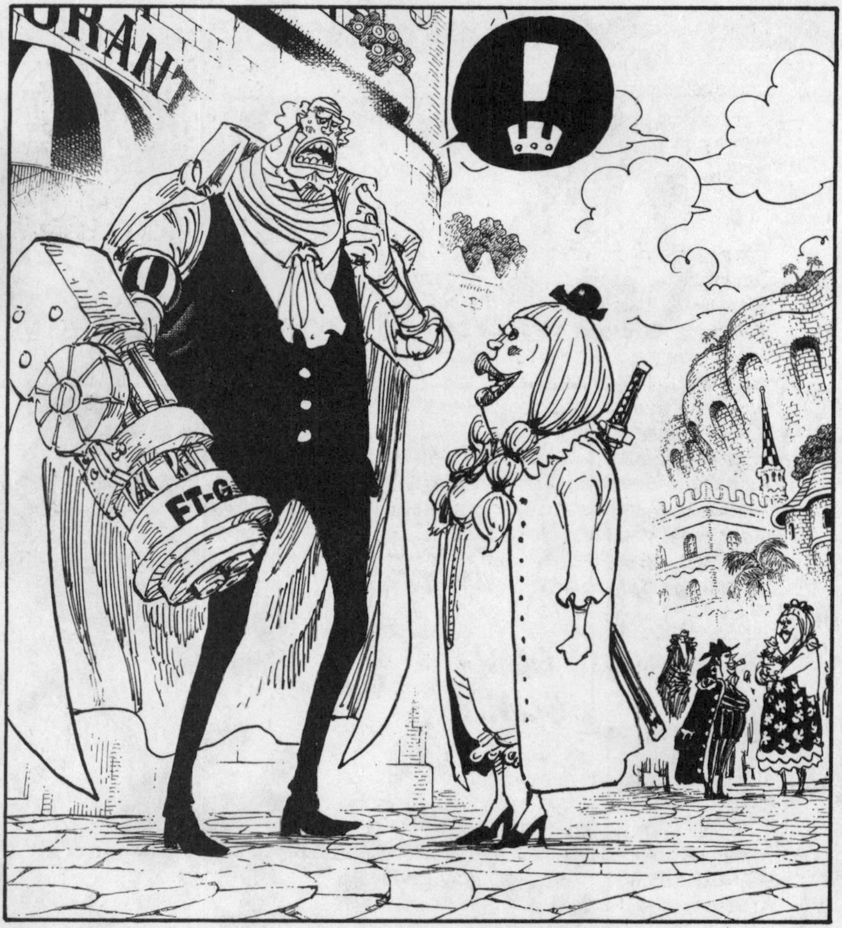

!
FT-G

GANG BEGE'S OH MY FAMILY
VOL. 27: "I LIKE YOU!!! MARRY ME!!!"

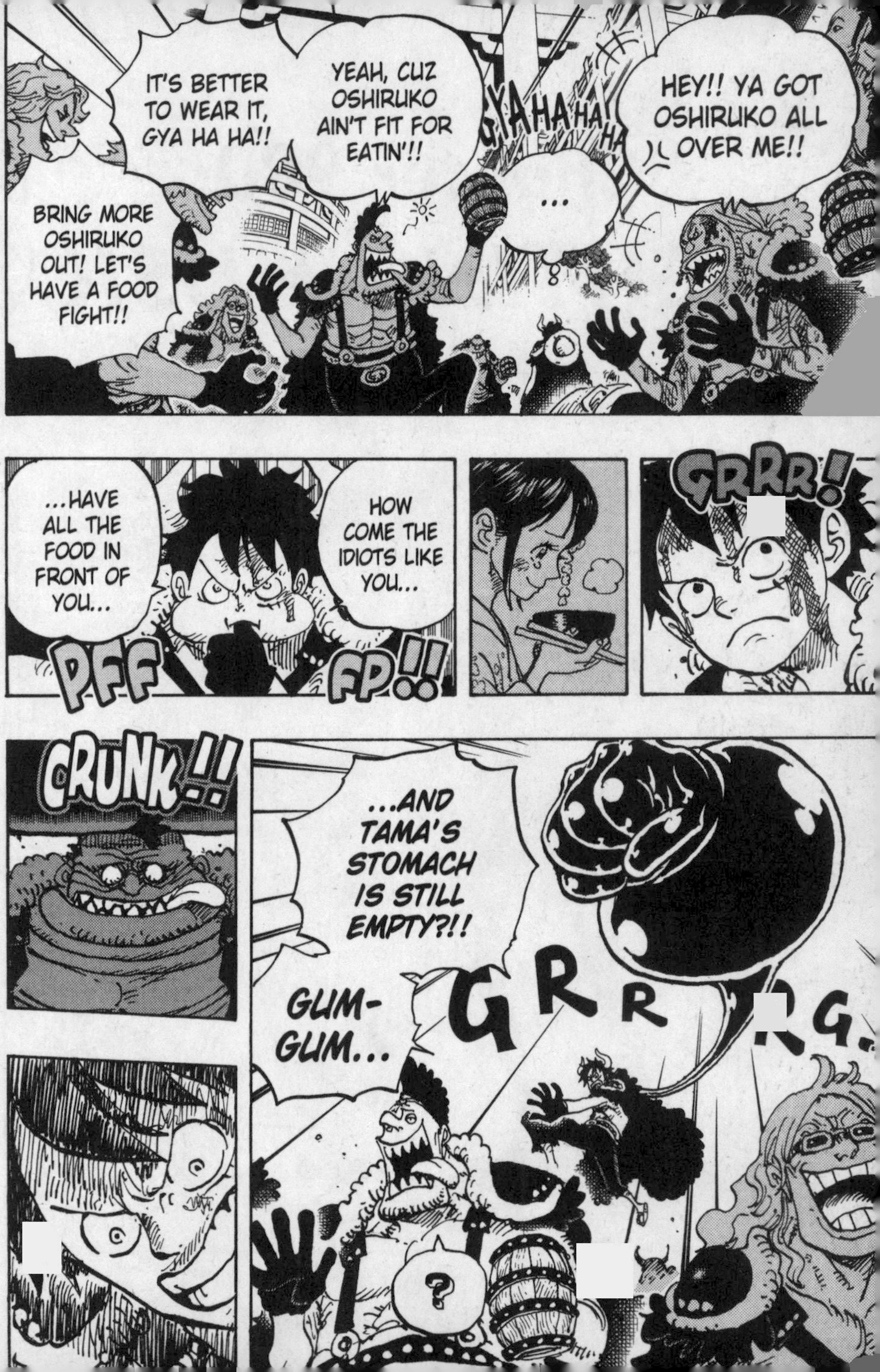
HEY!! YA GOT OSHIRUKO ALL OVER ME!!
GYAHAHAHA
...
YEAH, CUZ OSHIRUKO AIN'T FIT FOR EATIN'!!
IT'S BETTER TO WEAR IT, GYA HA HA!!
BRING MORE OSHIRUKO OUT! LET'S HAVE A FOOD FIGHT!!
GRRR!
HOW COME THE IDIOTS LIKE YOU...
...HAVE ALL THE FOOD IN FRONT OF YOU...
PFF FP!!
...AND TAMA'S STOMACH IS STILL EMPTY?!!
GRRRG..
GUM-GUM...
?
CRUNK!!

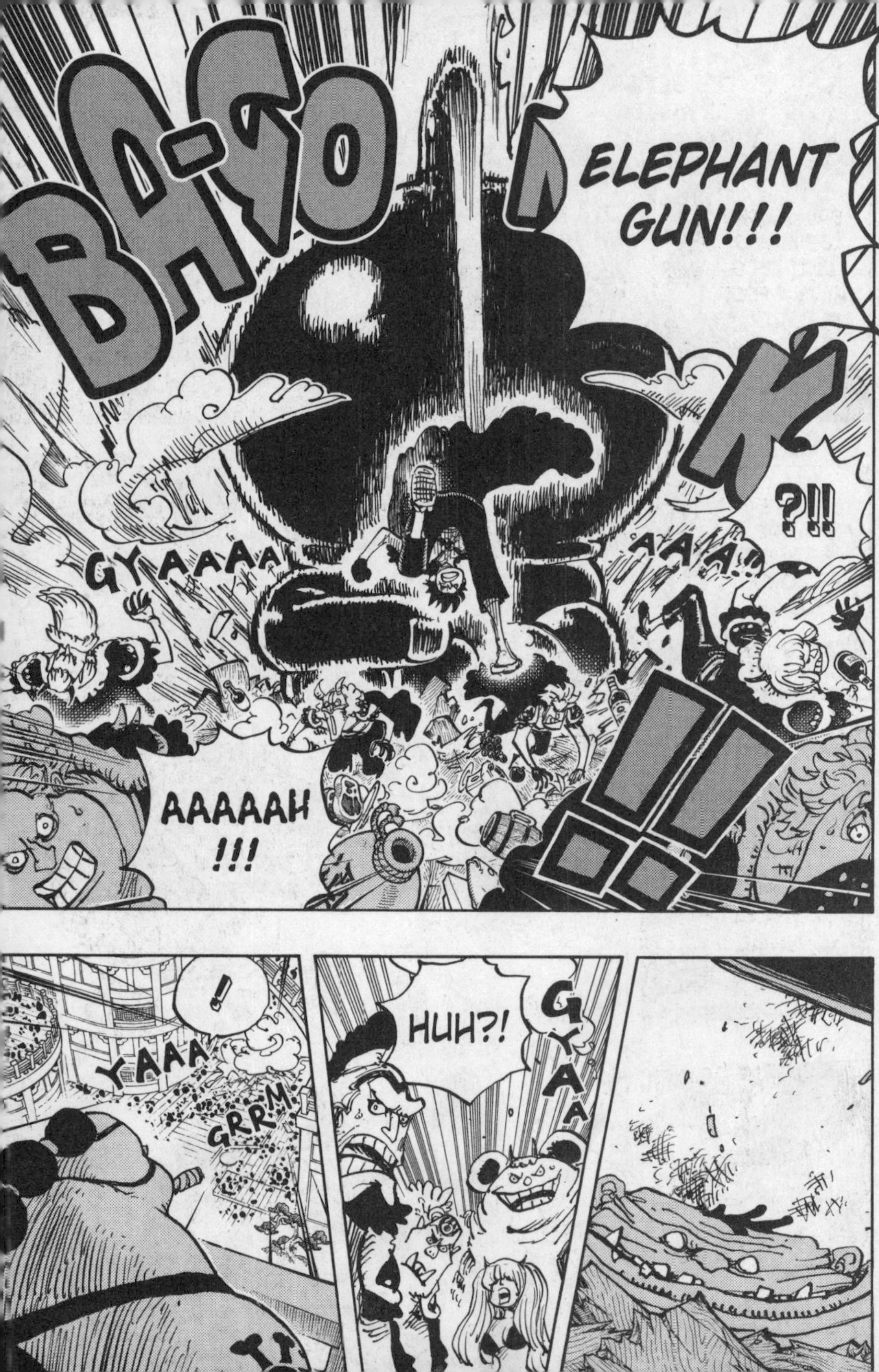
ELEPHANT GUN!!!
BA-GO
K
?!!
AAAA!!
GYAAAA
!!
AAAAAH !!!
GYAAA
HUH?!
!
YAAA
GRRM

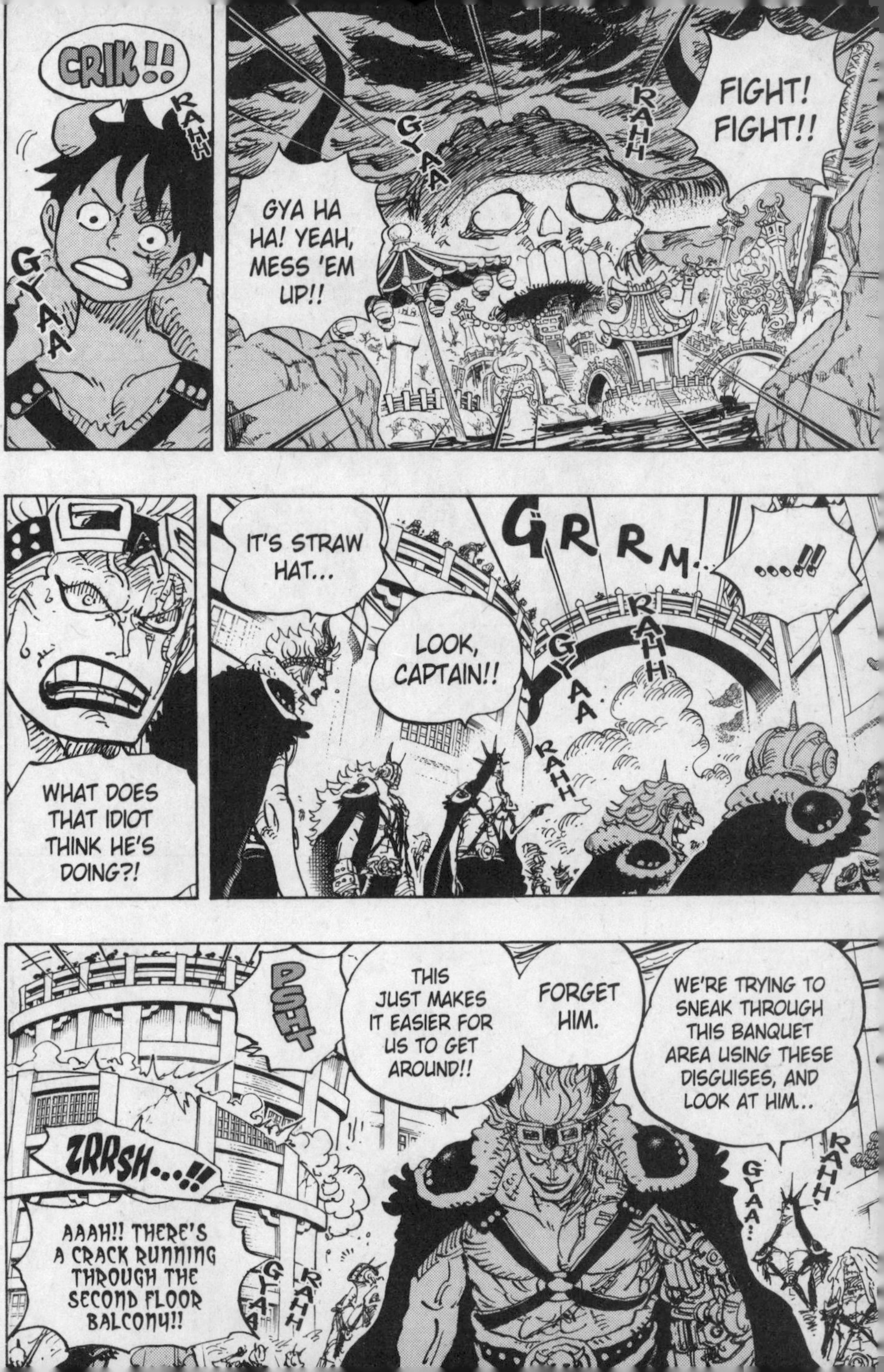
FIGHT! FIGHT!!
RAHH
GYAA
GYA HA HA! YEAH, MESS 'EM UP!!
CRIK!!
RAHH
GYAA
....!!
GRRRM...
IT'S STRAW HAT...
LOOK, CAPTAIN!!
RAHH
GYAA
RAHH
WHAT DOES THAT IDIOT THINK HE'S DOING?!
WE'RE TRYING TO SNEAK THROUGH THIS BANQUET AREA USING THESE DISGUISES, AND LOOK AT HIM...
FORGET HIM.
THIS JUST MAKES IT EASIER FOR US TO GET AROUND!!
RAHH
GYAA
PSHT
ZRRSH...!!
AAAH!! THERE'S A CRACK RUNNING THROUGH THE SECOND FLOOR BALCONY!!
RAHH
GYAA

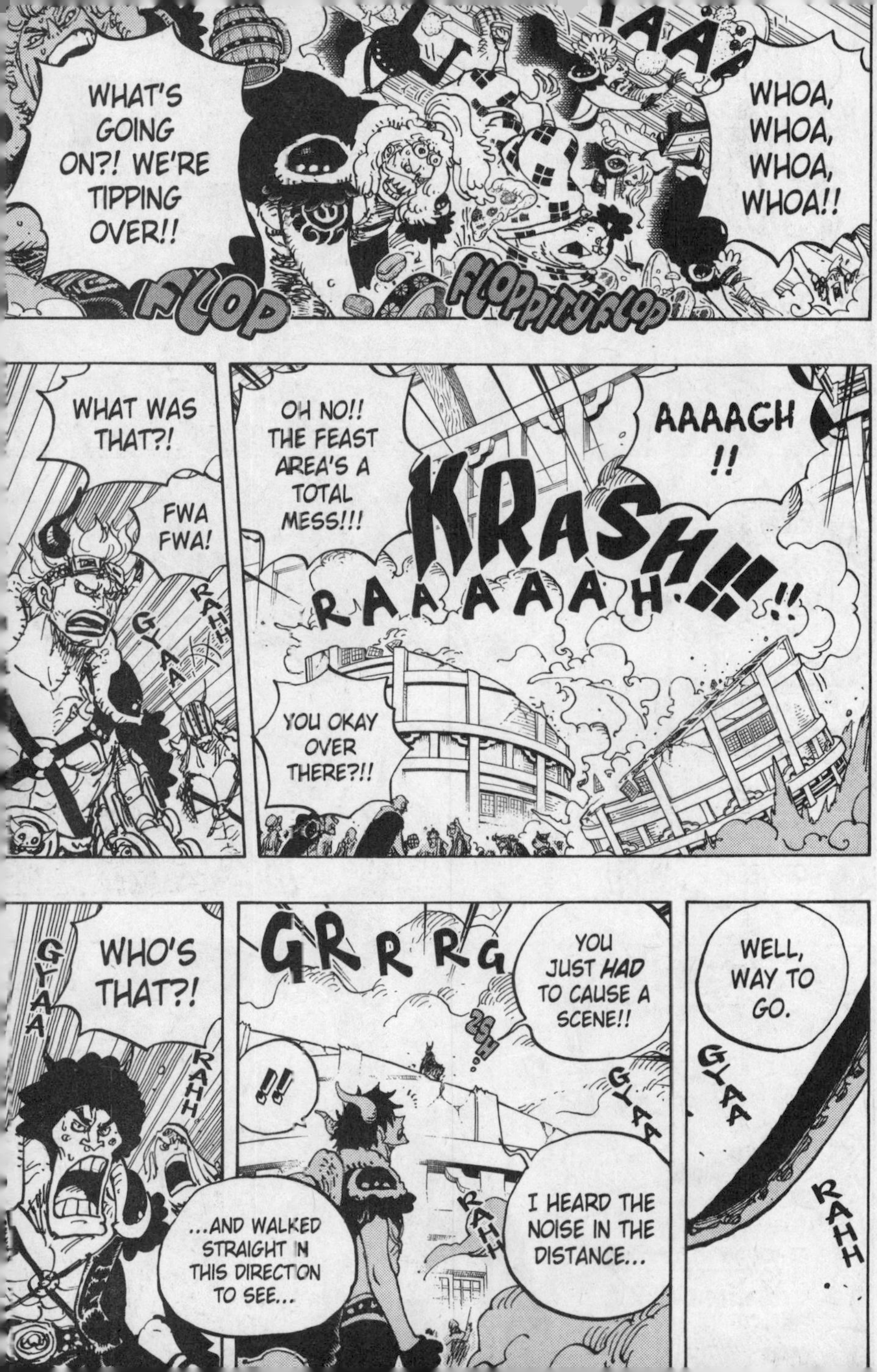
WHOA, WHOA, WHOA, WHOA!!
WHAT'S GOING ON?! WE'RE TIPPING OVER!!
FLOPPITY FLOP
FLOP
AAAAGH!!
KRASH!!
RAAAAAAH!!
OH NO!! THE FEAST AREA'S A TOTAL MESS!!!
YOU OKAY OVER THERE?!!
WHAT WAS THAT?!
FWA FWA!
GYAA
RAHH
WELL, WAY TO GO.
GYAA
RAHH
YOU JUST *HAD* TO CAUSE A SCENE!!
GRRRG
ZSH
!!
GYAA
I HEARD THE NOISE IN THE DISTANCE...
RAHH
...AND WALKED STRAIGHT IN THIS DIRECTION TO SEE...
WHO'S THAT?!
GYAA
RAHH

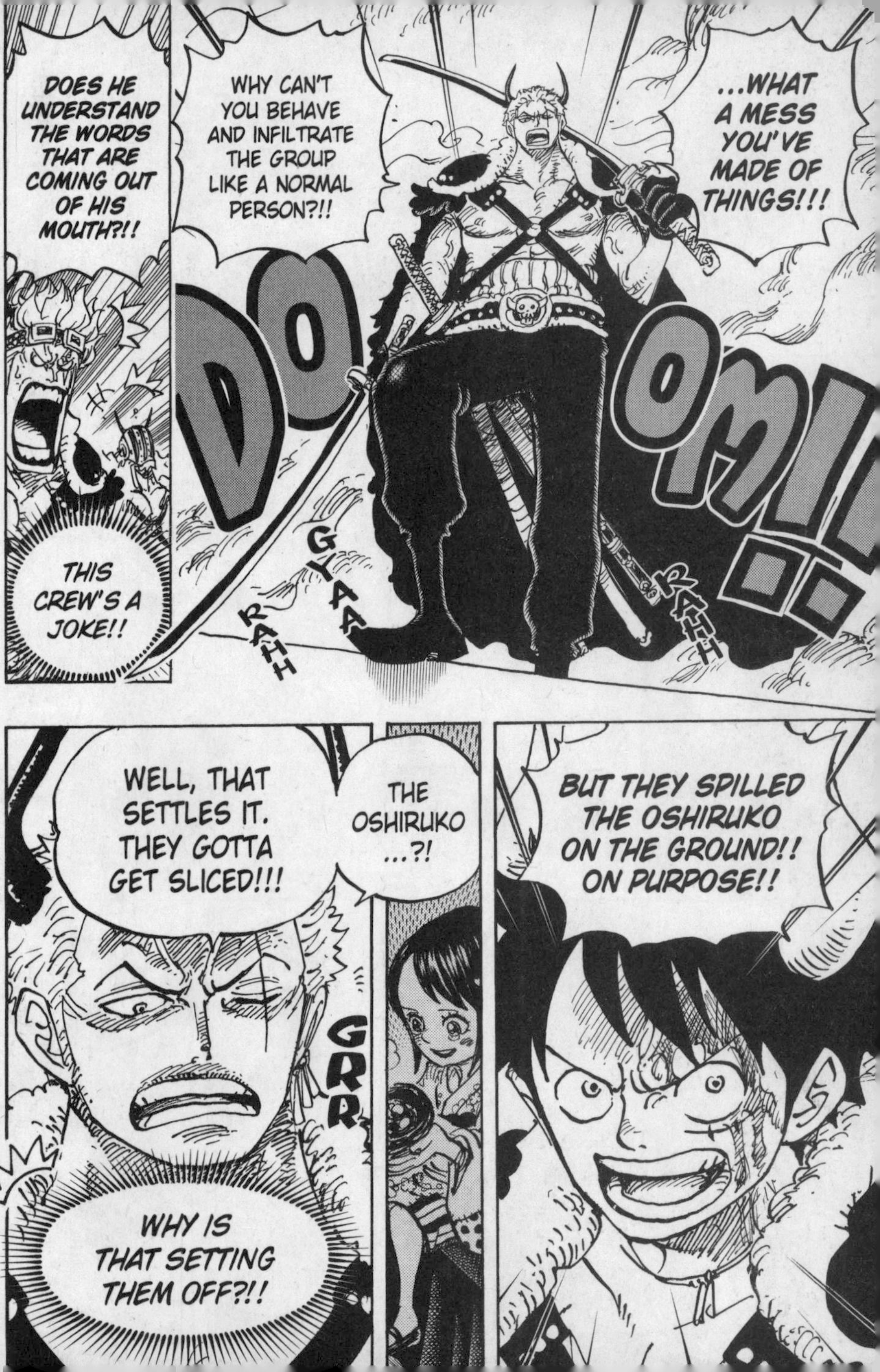
...WHAT A MESS YOU'VE MADE OF THINGS!!!
WHY CAN'T YOU BEHAVE AND INFILTRATE THE GROUP LIKE A NORMAL PERSON?!!
DOOM!!
GYAAA
RAHH
RAHH
DOES HE UNDERSTAND THE WORDS THAT ARE COMING OUT OF HIS MOUTH?!!
THIS CREW'S A JOKE!!
BUT THEY SPILLED THE OSHIRUKO ON THE GROUND!! ON PURPOSE!!
THE OSHIRUKO ...?!
WELL, THAT SETTLES IT. THEY GOTTA GET SLICED!!!
GRR
WHY IS THAT SETTING THEM OFF?!!

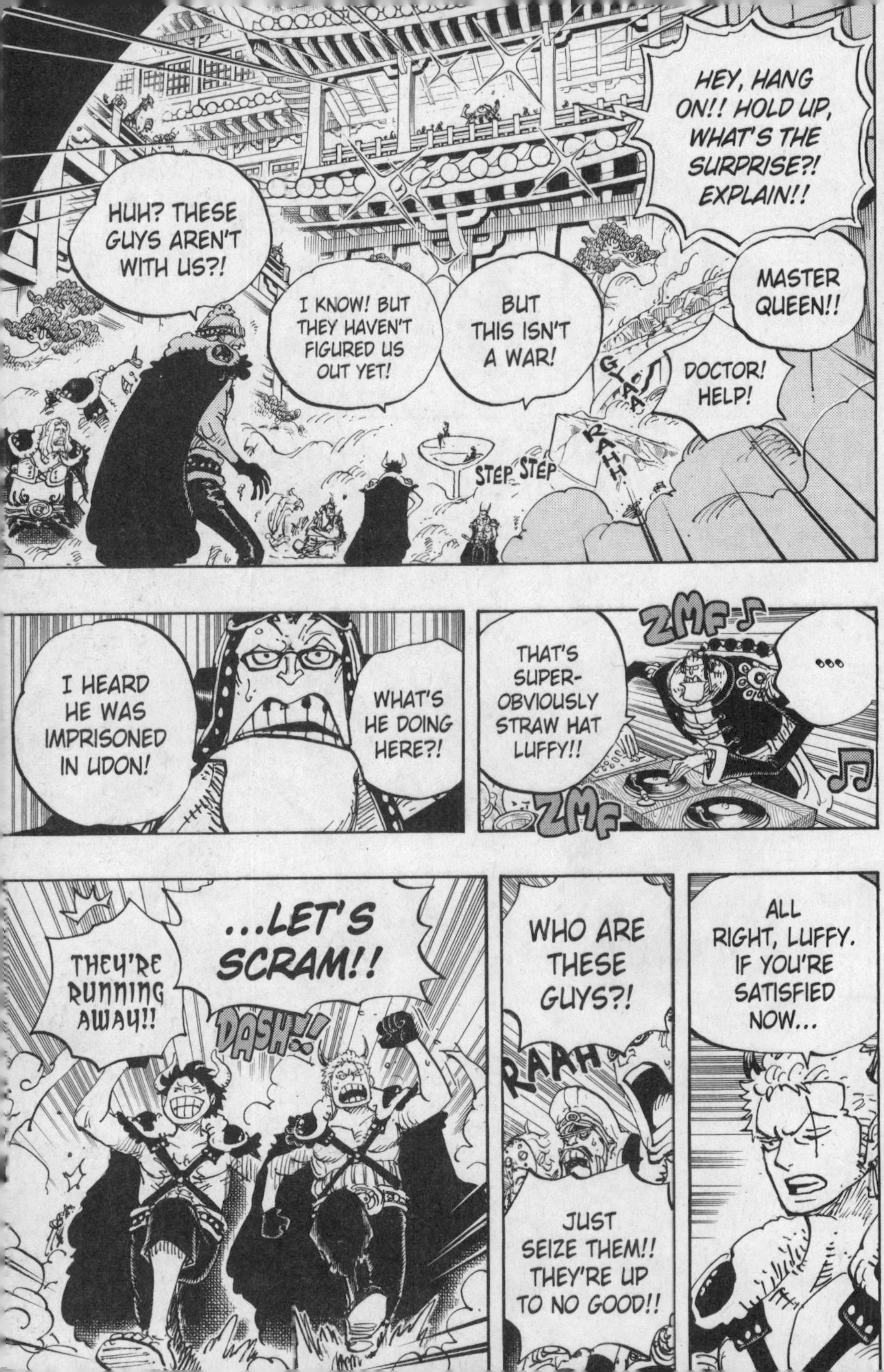
HEY, HANG ON!! HOLD UP, WHAT'S THE SURPRISE?! EXPLAIN!!
MASTER QUEEN!!
DOCTOR! HELP!
RAHH
STEP STEP
BUT THIS ISN'T A WAR!
I KNOW! BUT THEY HAVEN'T FIGURED US OUT YET!
HUH? THESE GUYS AREN'T WITH US?!
...
ZMF
THAT'S SUPER-OBVIOUSLY STRAW HAT LUFFY!!
ZMF
WHAT'S HE DOING HERE?!
I HEARD HE WAS IMPRISONED IN UDON!
ALL RIGHT, LUFFY. IF YOU'RE SATISFIED NOW...
WHO ARE THESE GUYS?!
RAAH
JUST SEIZE THEM!! THEY'RE UP TO NO GOOD!!
...LET'S SCRAM!!
THEY'RE RUNNING AWAY!!
DASH!!

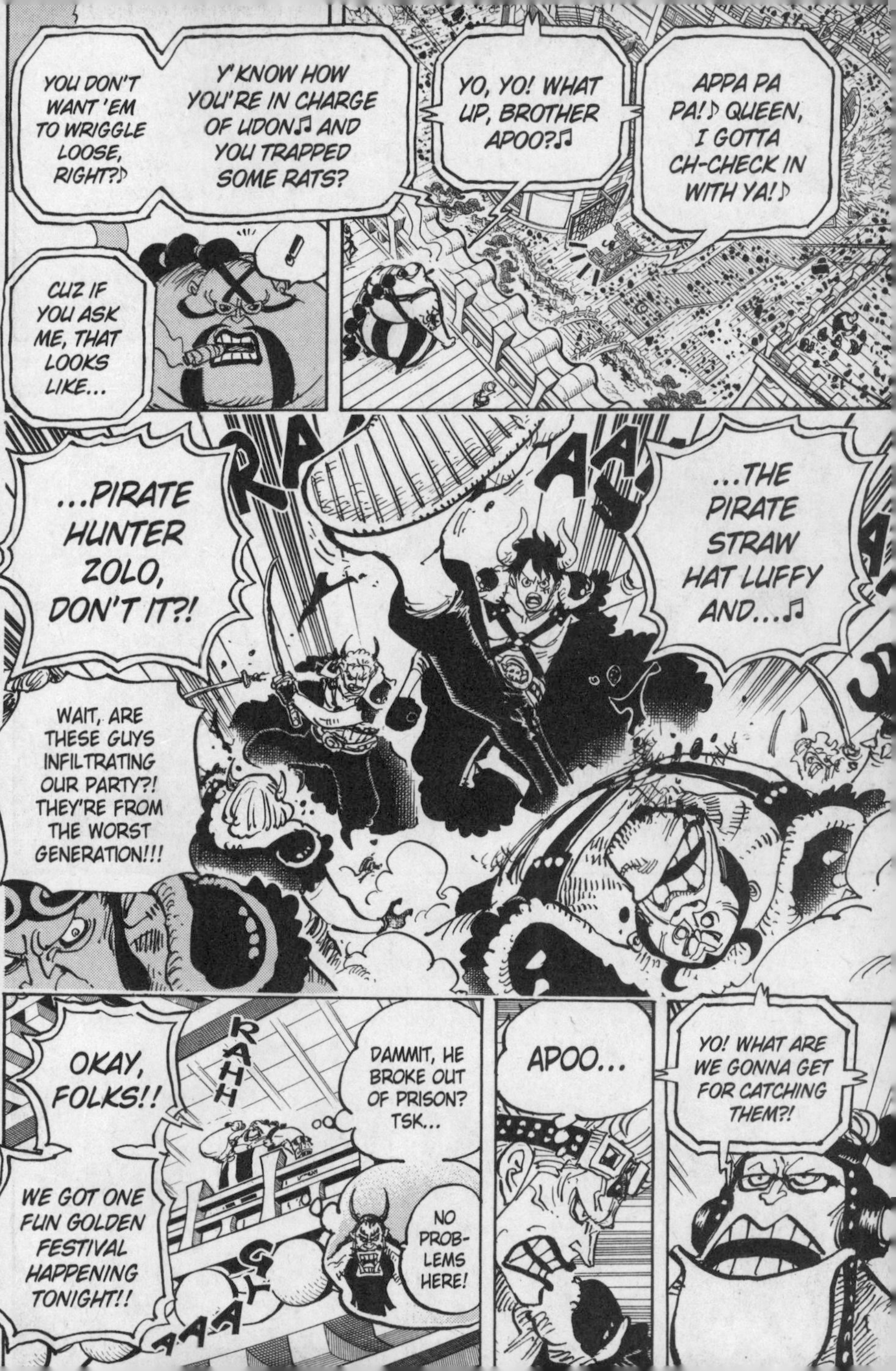
APPA PA PA!♪ QUEEN, I GOTTA CH-CHECK IN WITH YA!♪
YO, YO! WHAT UP, BROTHER APOO?♫
Y'KNOW HOW YOU'RE IN CHARGE OF UDON♫ AND YOU TRAPPED SOME RATS?
YOU DON'T WANT 'EM TO WRIGGLE LOOSE, RIGHT?♪
!
CUZ IF YOU ASK ME, THAT LOOKS LIKE...
...THE PIRATE STRAW HAT LUFFY AND...♫
...PIRATE HUNTER ZOLO, DON'T IT?!
WAIT, ARE THESE GUYS INFILTRATING OUR PARTY?! THEY'RE FROM THE WORST GENERATION!!!
YO! WHAT ARE WE GONNA GET FOR CATCHING THEM?!
APOO...
DAMMIT, HE BROKE OUT OF PRISON? TSK...
NO PROBLEMS HERE!
RAHH
OKAY, FOLKS!!
WE GOT ONE FUN GOLDEN FESTIVAL HAPPENING TONIGHT!!

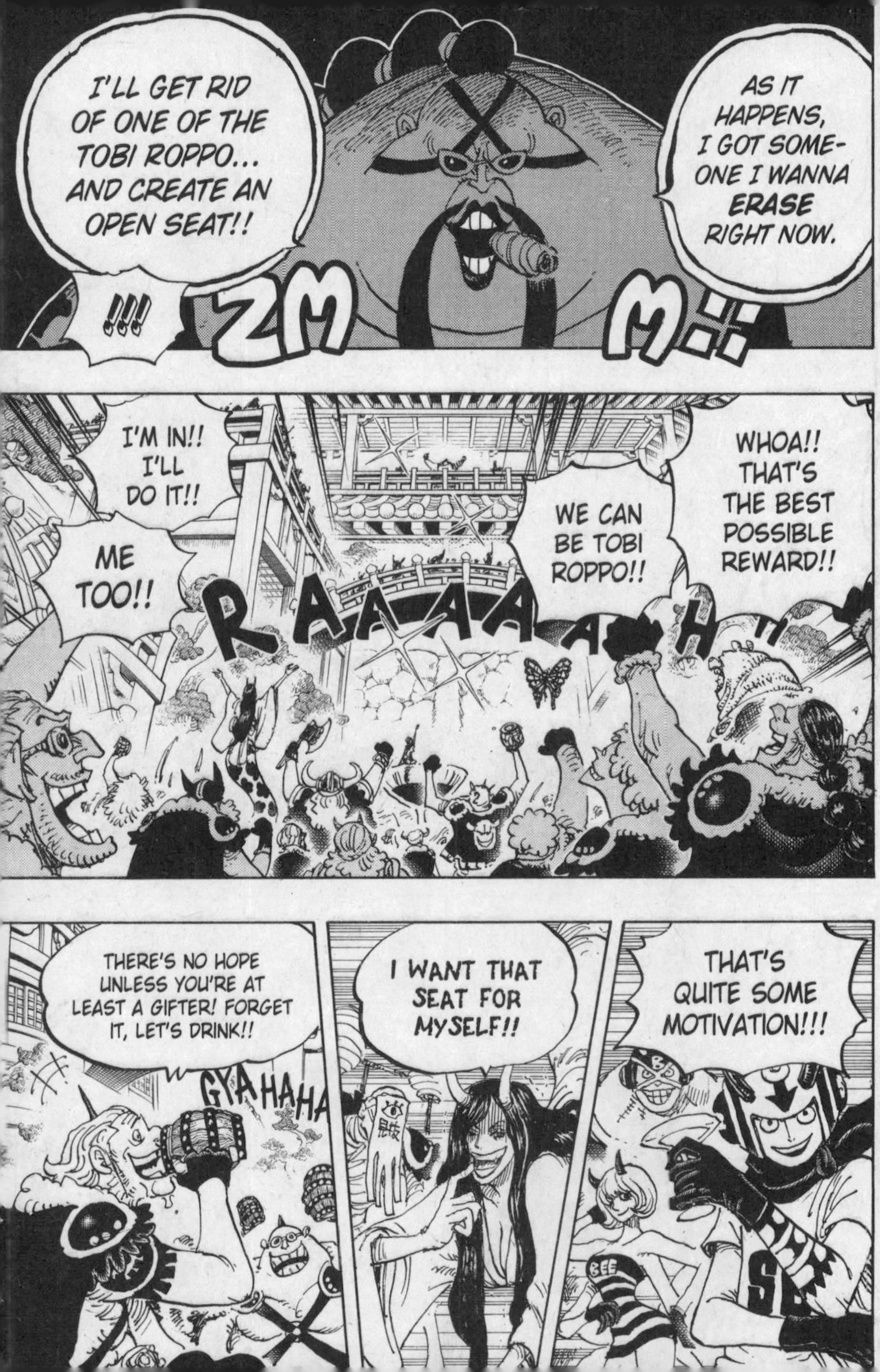
AS IT HAPPENS, I GOT SOME-ONE I WANNA ERASE RIGHT NOW.
I'LL GET RID OF ONE OF THE TOBI ROPPO... AND CREATE AN OPEN SEAT!!
!!!
ZMM..
WHOA!! THAT'S THE BEST POSSIBLE REWARD!!
WE CAN BE TOBI ROPPO!!
I'M IN!! I'LL DO IT!!
ME TOO!!
RAAAAAH
THAT'S QUITE SOME MOTIVATION!!!
I WANT THAT SEAT FOR MYSELF!!
THERE'S NO HOPE UNLESS YOU'RE AT LEAST A GIFTER! FORGET IT, LET'S DRINK!!
GYAHAHA

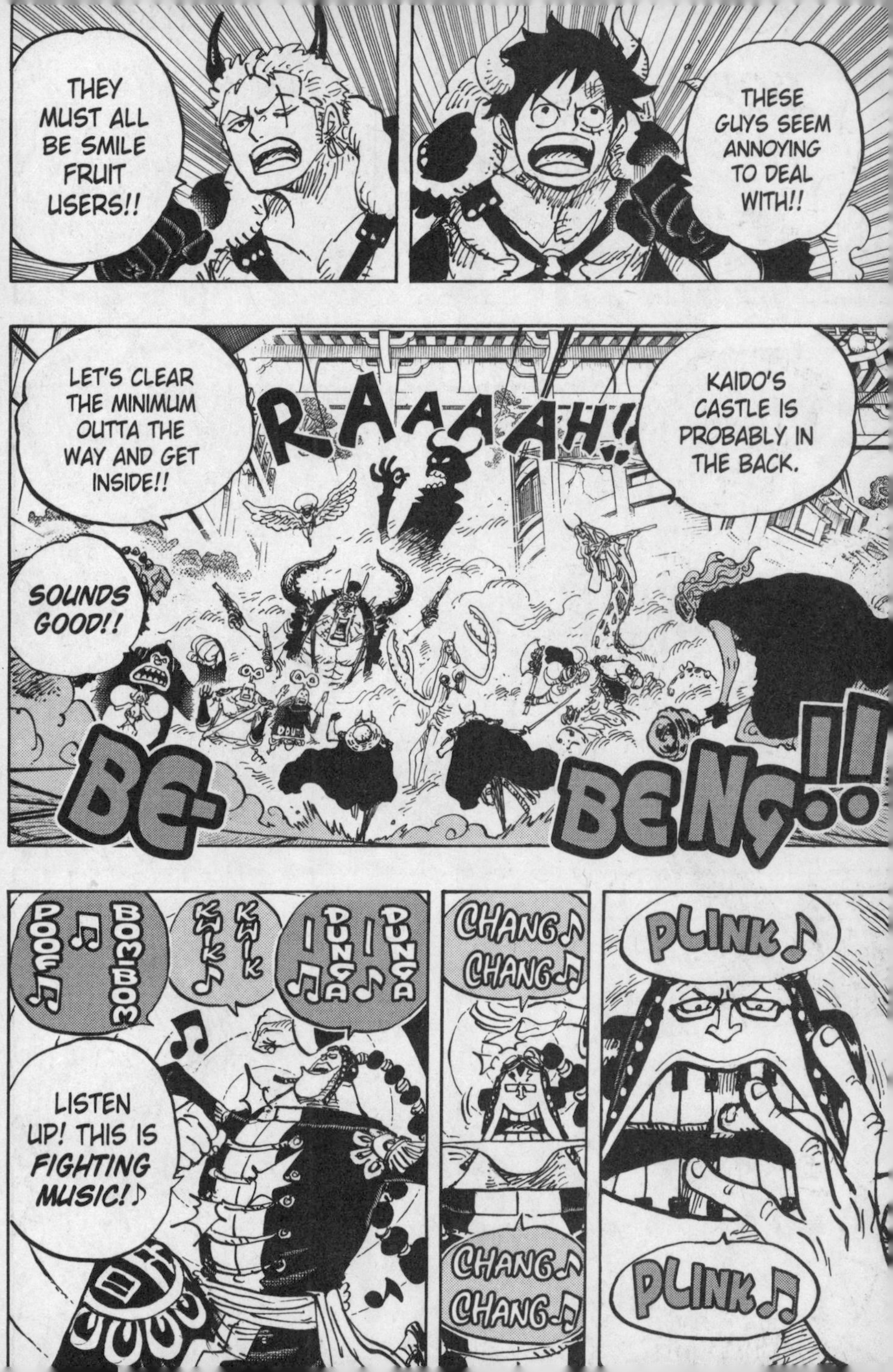
THESE GUYS SEEM ANNOYING TO DEAL WITH!!
THEY MUST ALL BE SMILE FRUIT USERS!!
KAIDO'S CASTLE IS PROBABLY IN THE BACK.
RAAAAH!!
LET'S CLEAR THE MINIMUM OUTTA THE WAY AND GET INSIDE!!
SOUNDS GOOD!!
BE-BENG!!
PLINK♪
PLINK♫
CHANG♪ CHANG♫
CHANG♪ CHANG♫
DUNGA-DUNGA♪ DUNGA-DUNGA♫
KWIK KWIK♪
BOM-BOM ♫
POOF♫
LISTEN UP! THIS IS FIGHTING MUSIC!♪

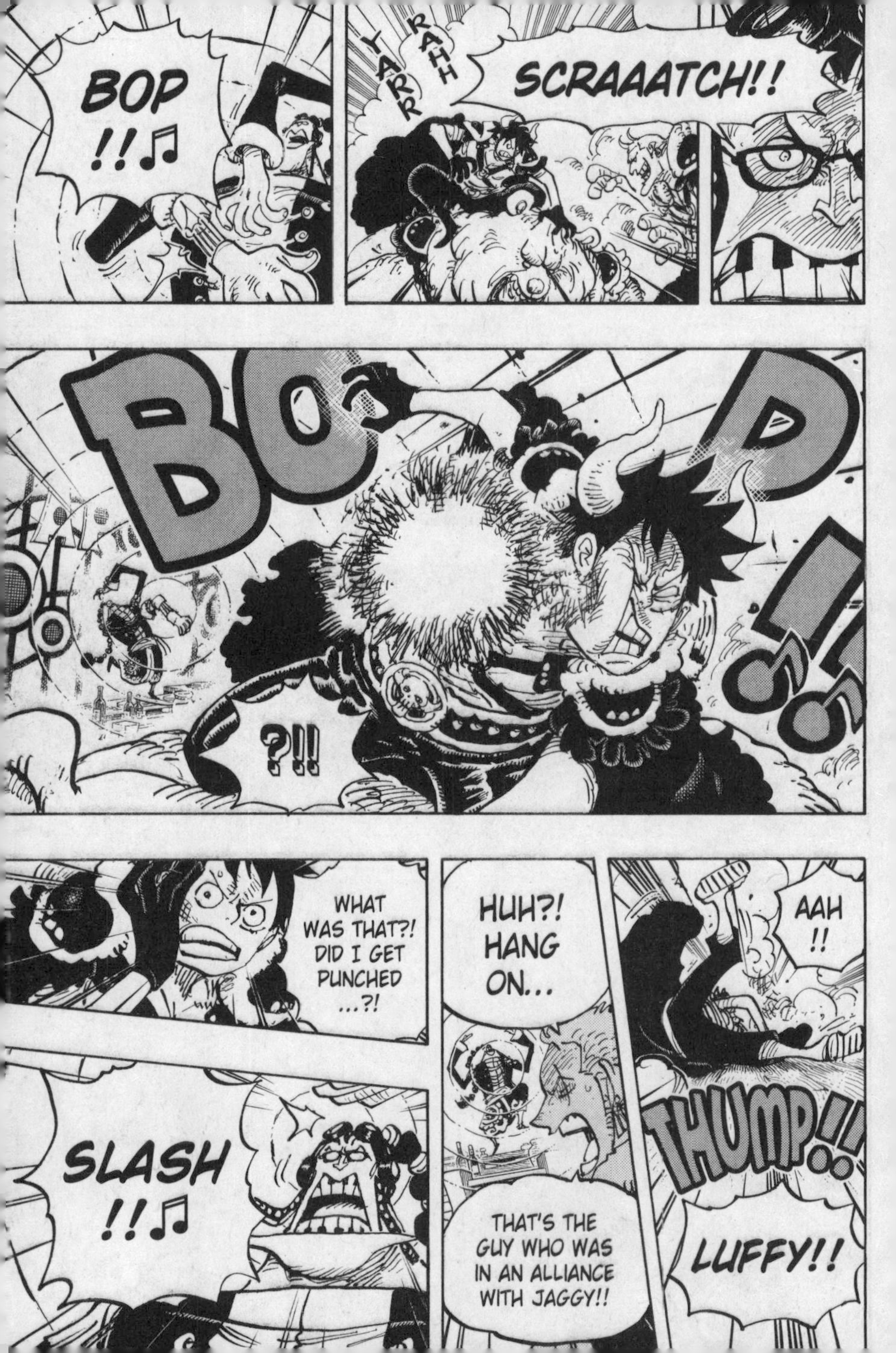

SCRAAATCH!!
RAHH
YARR
BOP!!♫
BOP!!♪♪
?!!
AAH!!
THUMP!!
LUFFY!!
HUH?! HANG ON...
THAT'S THE GUY WHO WAS IN AN ALLIANCE WITH JAGGY!!
WHAT WAS THAT?! DID I GET PUNCHED ...?!
SLASH!!♫

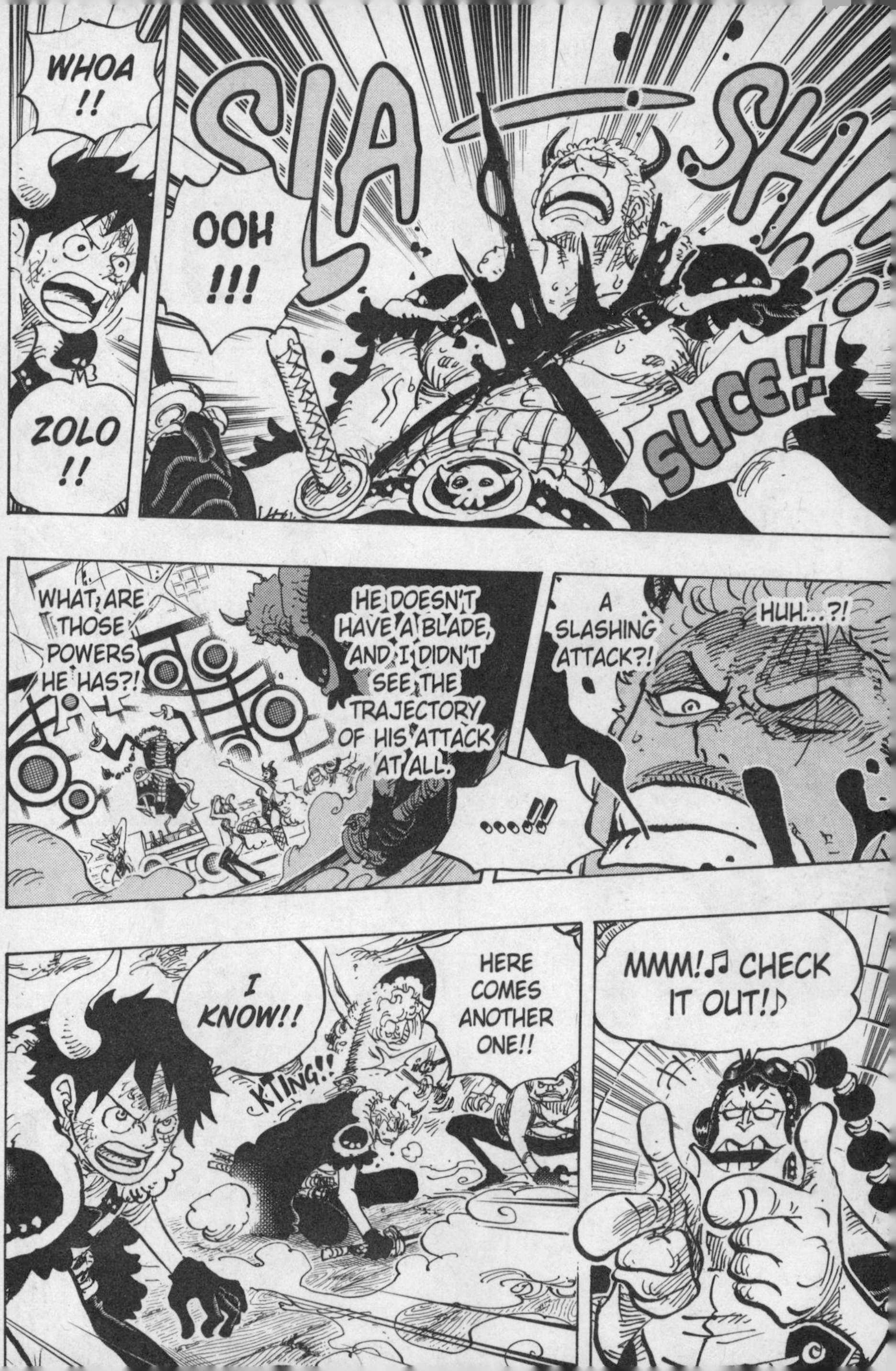

SLASH
SLICE!!
OOH !!!
WHOA !!
ZOLO !!
HUH...?!
A SLASHING ATTACK?!
....!!
HE DOESN'T HAVE A BLADE, AND I DIDN'T SEE THE TRAJECTORY OF HIS ATTACK AT ALL.
WHAT ARE THOSE POWERS HE HAS?!
MMM!♫ CHECK IT OUT!♪
HERE COMES ANOTHER ONE!!
KTING!!
I KNOW!!

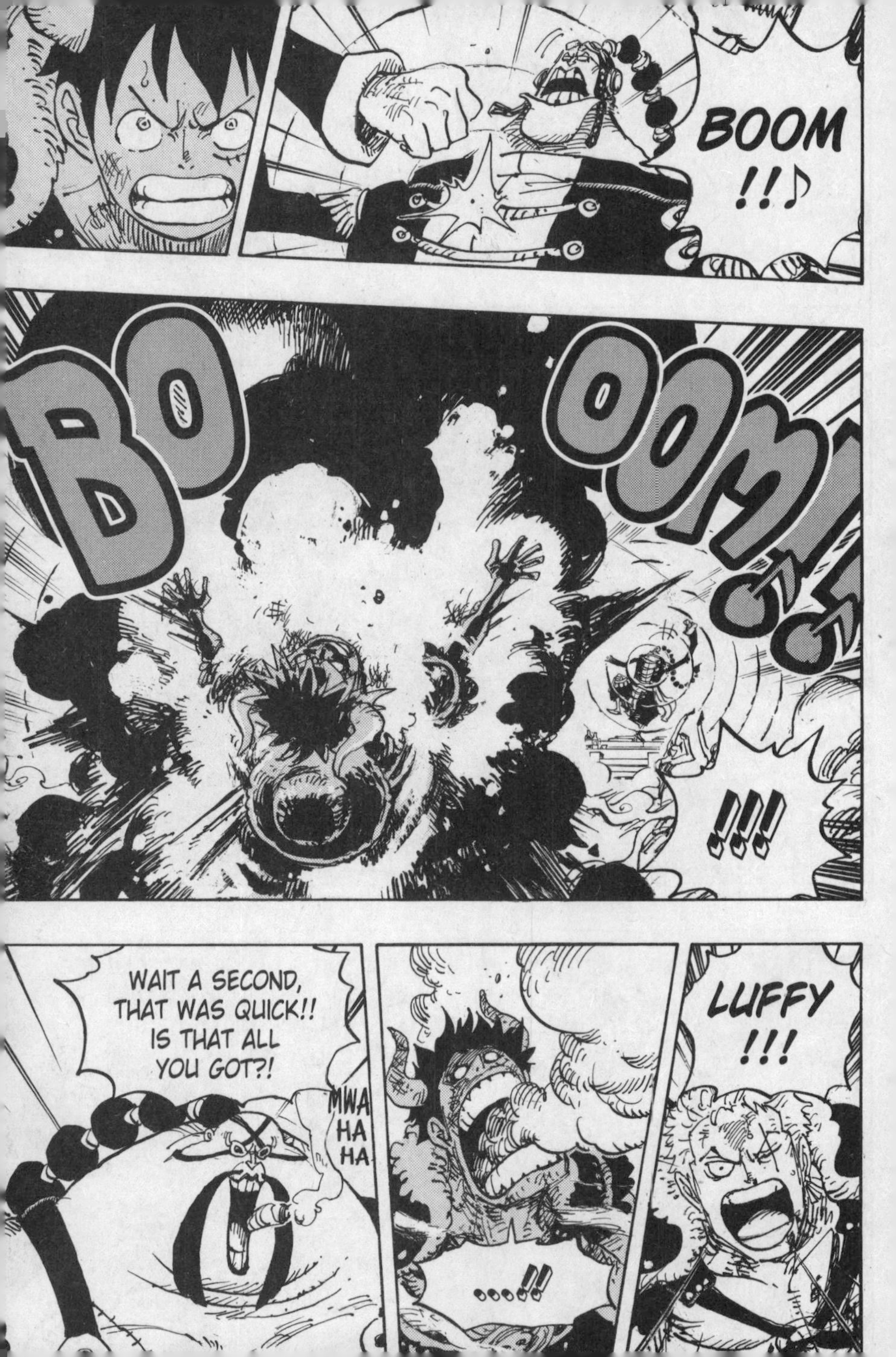
BOOM !!♪
BOOOM!!♪
!!!
LUFFY !!!
....!!
WAIT A SECOND, THAT WAS QUICK!! IS THAT ALL YOU GOT?!
MWA HA HA

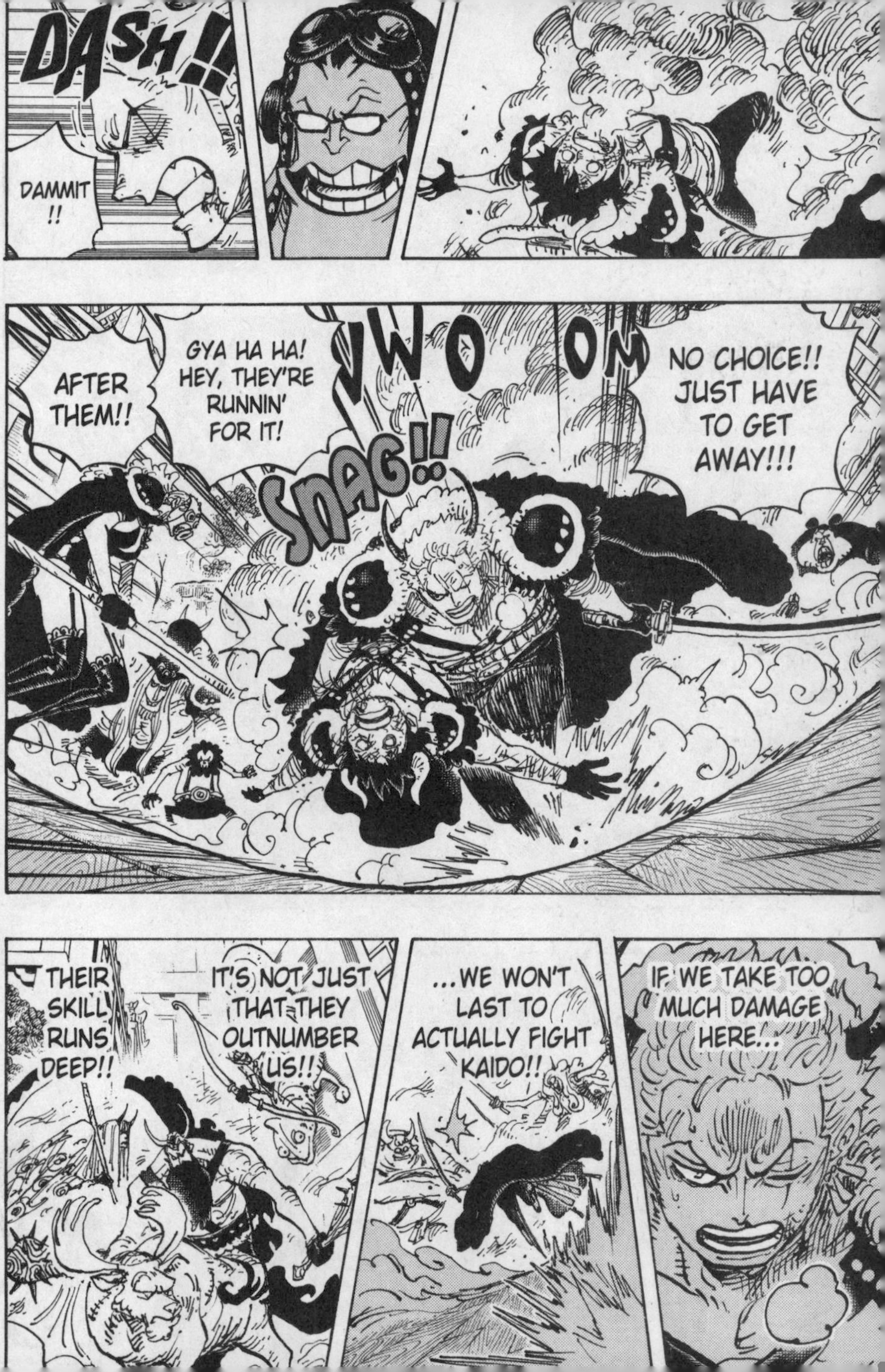
DASH!!
DAMMIT !!
NO CHOICE!! JUST HAVE TO GET AWAY!!!
VWOOM
GYA HA HA! HEY, THEY'RE RUNNIN' FOR IT!
AFTER THEM!!
SNAG!!
IF WE TAKE TOO MUCH DAMAGE HERE...
...WE WON'T LAST TO ACTUALLY FIGHT KAIDO!!
IT'S NOT JUST THAT THEY OUTNUMBER US!!
THEIR SKILL RUNS DEEP!!

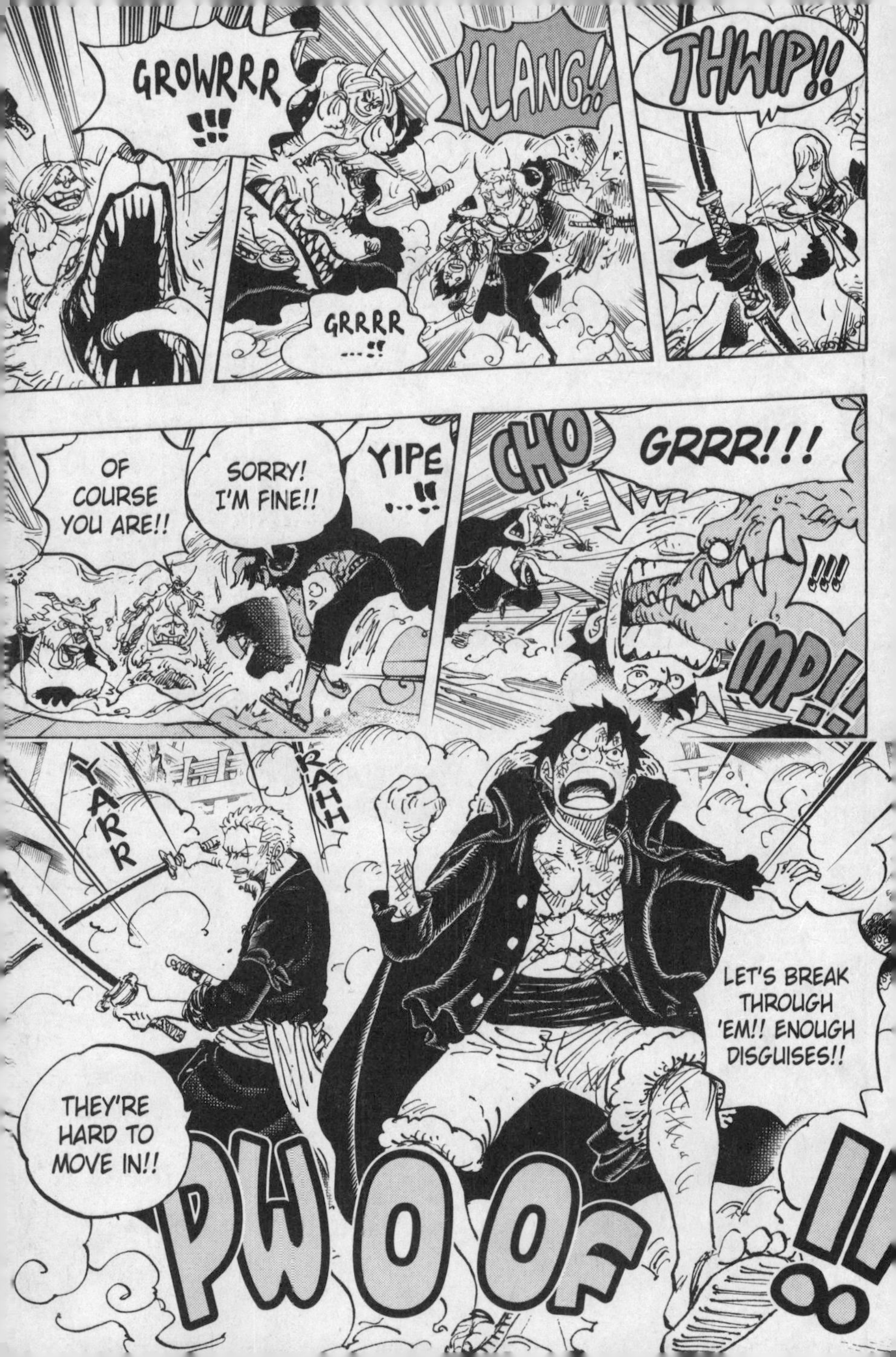
THWIP!!
KLANG!!
GRRRR...!!
GROWRRR!!!
CHO
GRRR!!!
!!!
MP!!
YIPE...!!
SORRY! I'M FINE!!
OF COURSE YOU ARE!!
RAHH
LET'S BREAK THROUGH 'EM!! ENOUGH DISGUISES!!
YARR
THEY'RE HARD TO MOVE IN!!
PWOOF!!

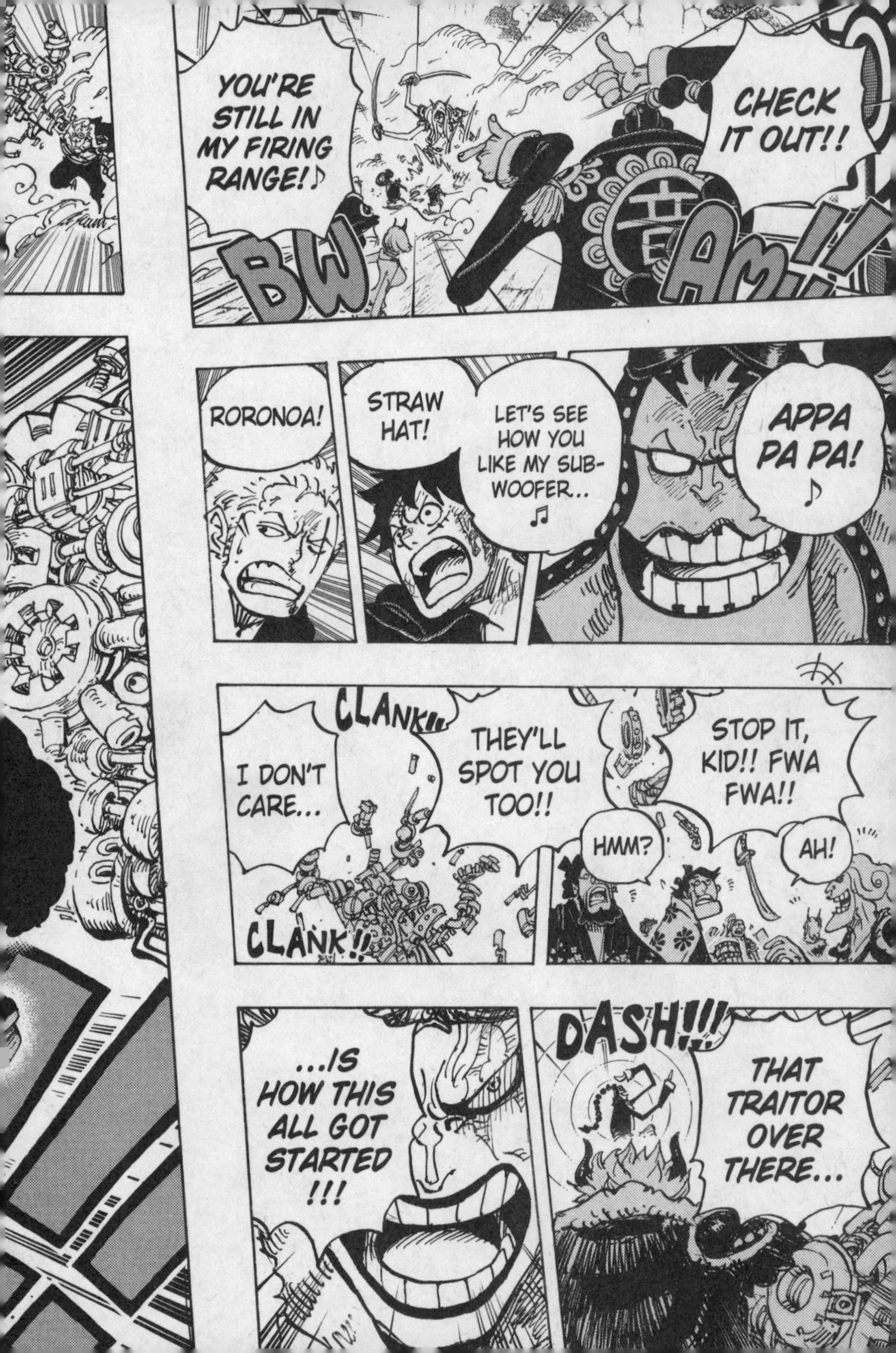
CHECK IT OUT!!
YOU'RE STILL IN MY FIRING RANGE!♪
BWAM!!
APPA PA PA! ♪
LET'S SEE HOW YOU LIKE MY SUB-WOOFER.. ♫
STRAW HAT!
RORONOA!
STOP IT, KID!! FWA FWA!!
AH!
HMM?
THEY'LL SPOT YOU TOO!!
CLANK!!
I DON'T CARE...
CLANK!!
DASH!!!
THAT TRAITOR OVER THERE...
...IS HOW THIS ALL GOT STARTED!!!

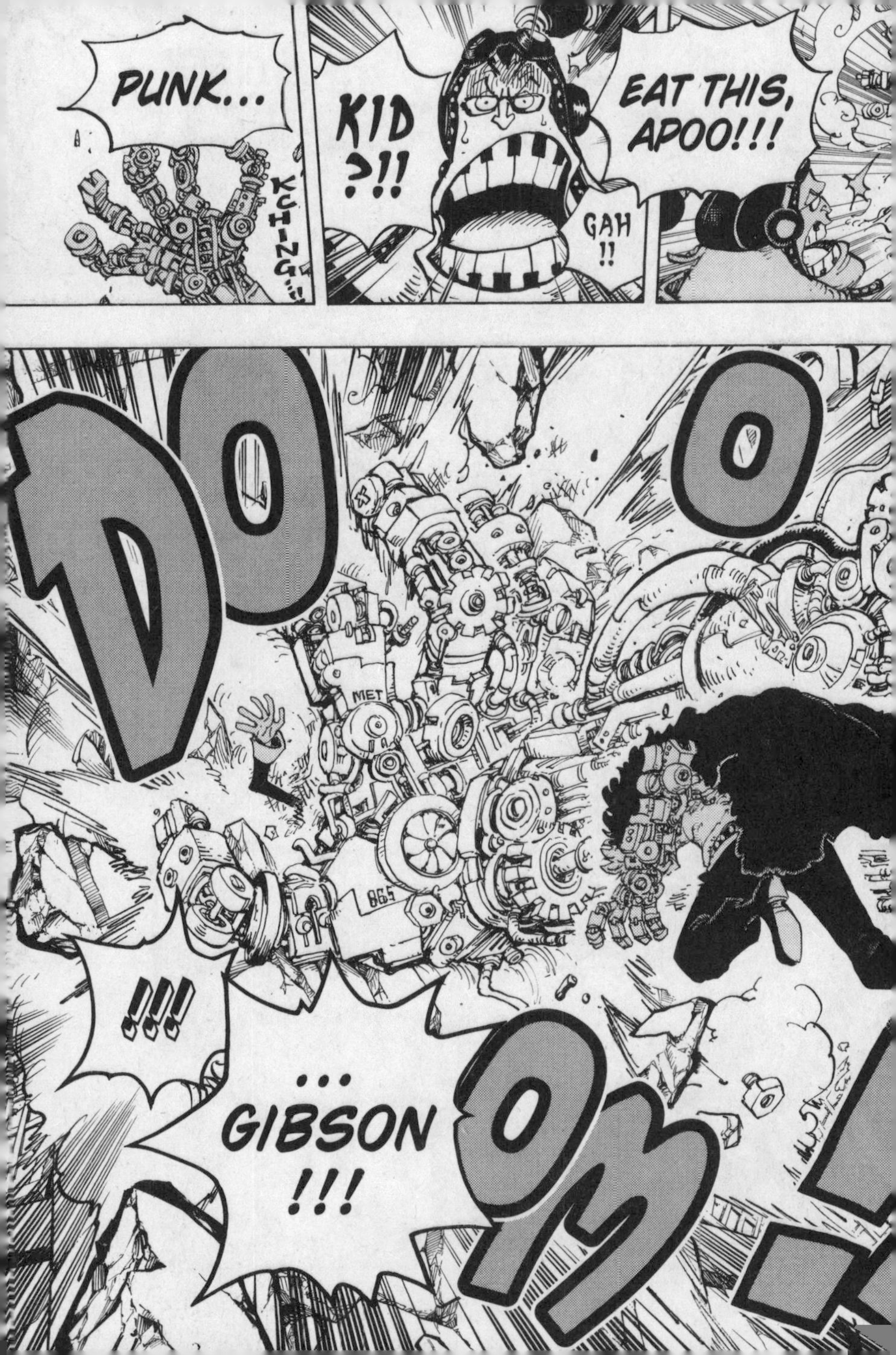
EAT THIS, APOO!!!
KID ?!!
GAH !!
PUNK...
KCHING...!!
!!!
... GIBSON !!!

JOINING THE FIGHT

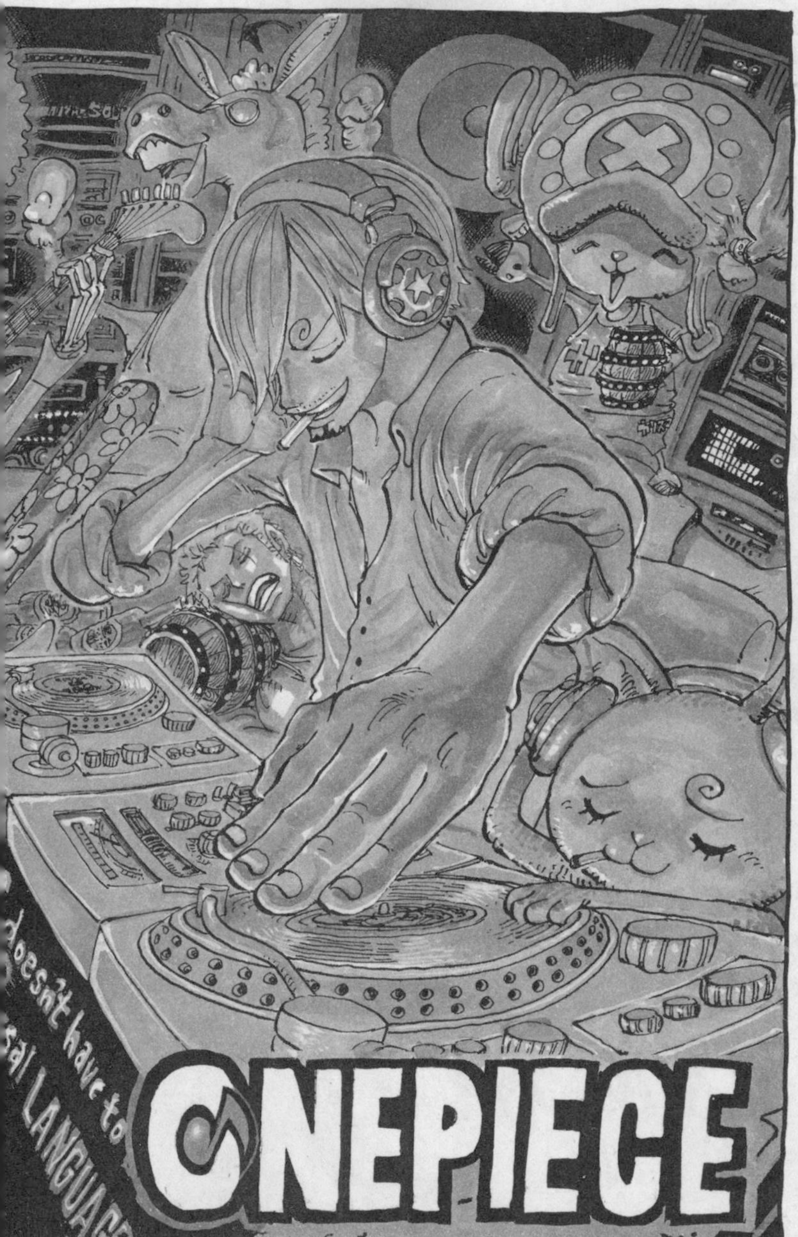
ONEPIECE
doesn't have to
sal LANGUAGE

Chapter 981:

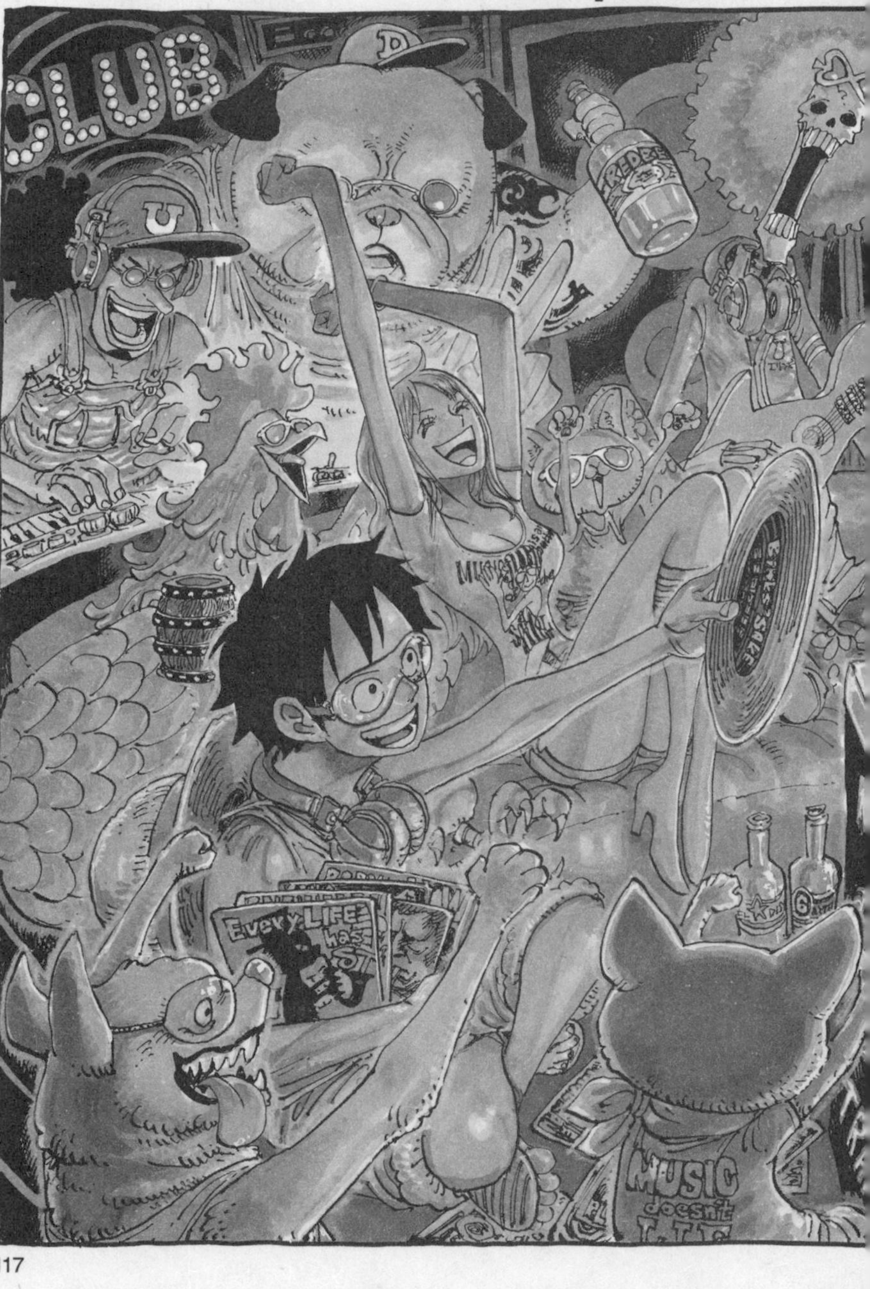
CLUB
MUSIC
doesn't

vol.97
ONE PIECE

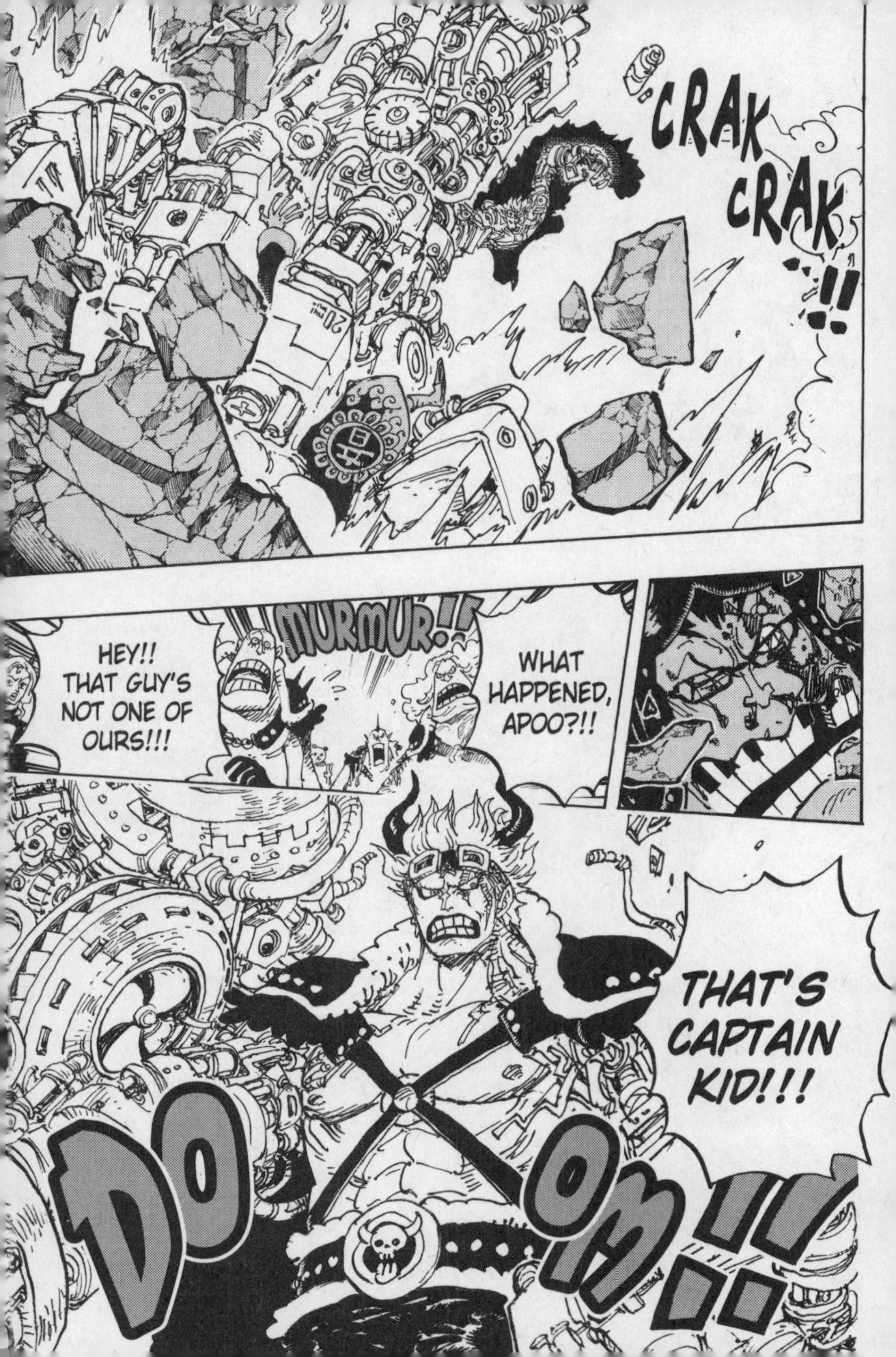
CRAK CRAK!!
WHAT HAPPENED, APOO?!!
MURMUR!!
HEY!! THAT GUY'S NOT ONE OF OURS!!!
THAT'S CAPTAIN KID!!!
DOOM!!

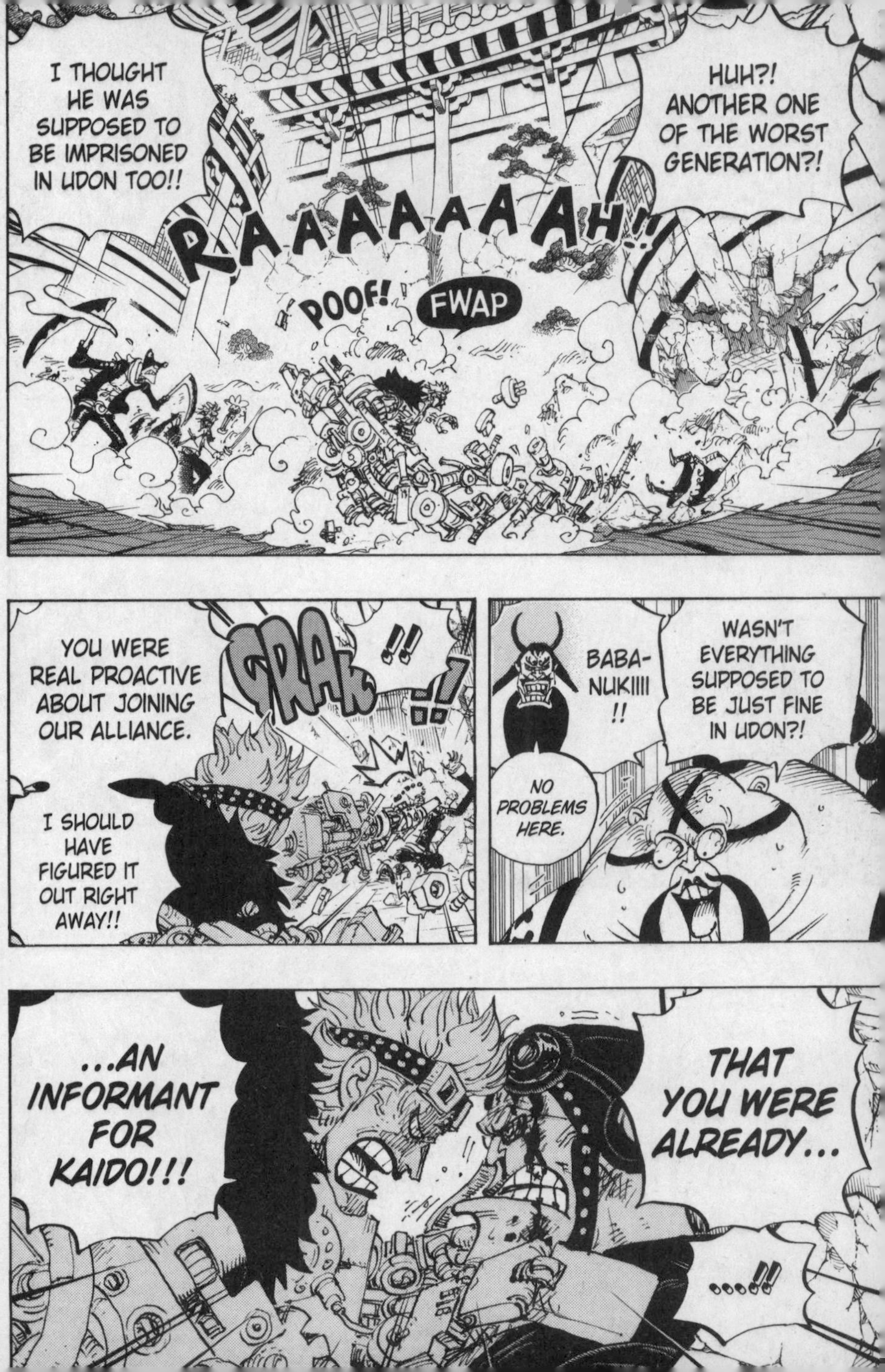
HUH?! ANOTHER ONE OF THE WORST GENERATION?!
I THOUGHT HE WAS SUPPOSED TO BE IMPRISONED IN UDON TOO!!
RAAAAAAAH!!
POOF!
FWAP
WASN'T EVERYTHING SUPPOSED TO BE JUST FINE IN UDON?!
BABA-NUKIIII !!
NO PROBLEMS HERE.
GRAK!!
YOU WERE REAL PROACTIVE ABOUT JOINING OUR ALLIANCE.
I SHOULD HAVE FIGURED IT OUT RIGHT AWAY!!
THAT YOU WERE ALREADY...
...AN INFORMANT FOR KAIDO!!!
...!!

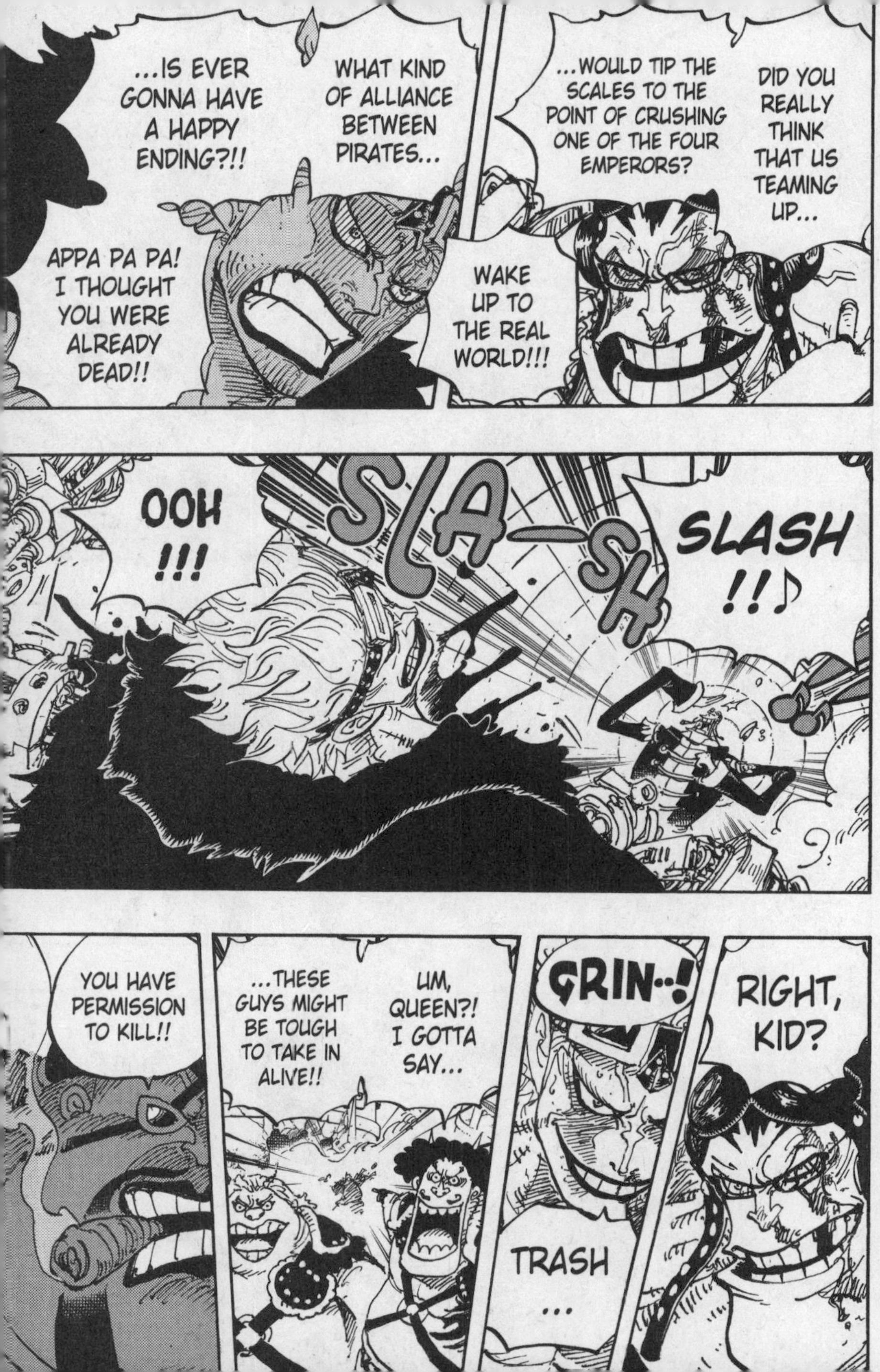

DID YOU REALLY THINK THAT US TEAMING UP...
...WOULD TIP THE SCALES TO THE POINT OF CRUSHING ONE OF THE FOUR EMPERORS?
WAKE UP TO THE REAL WORLD!!!
WHAT KIND OF ALLIANCE BETWEEN PIRATES...
...IS EVER GONNA HAVE A HAPPY ENDING?!!
APPA PA PA! I THOUGHT YOU WERE ALREADY DEAD!!
SLASH !!♪
SLA-SH
OOH !!!
RIGHT, KID?
GRIN..!
TRASH ...
UM, QUEEN?! I GOTTA SAY...
...THESE GUYS MIGHT BE TOUGH TO TAKE IN ALIVE!!
YOU HAVE PERMISSION TO KILL!!

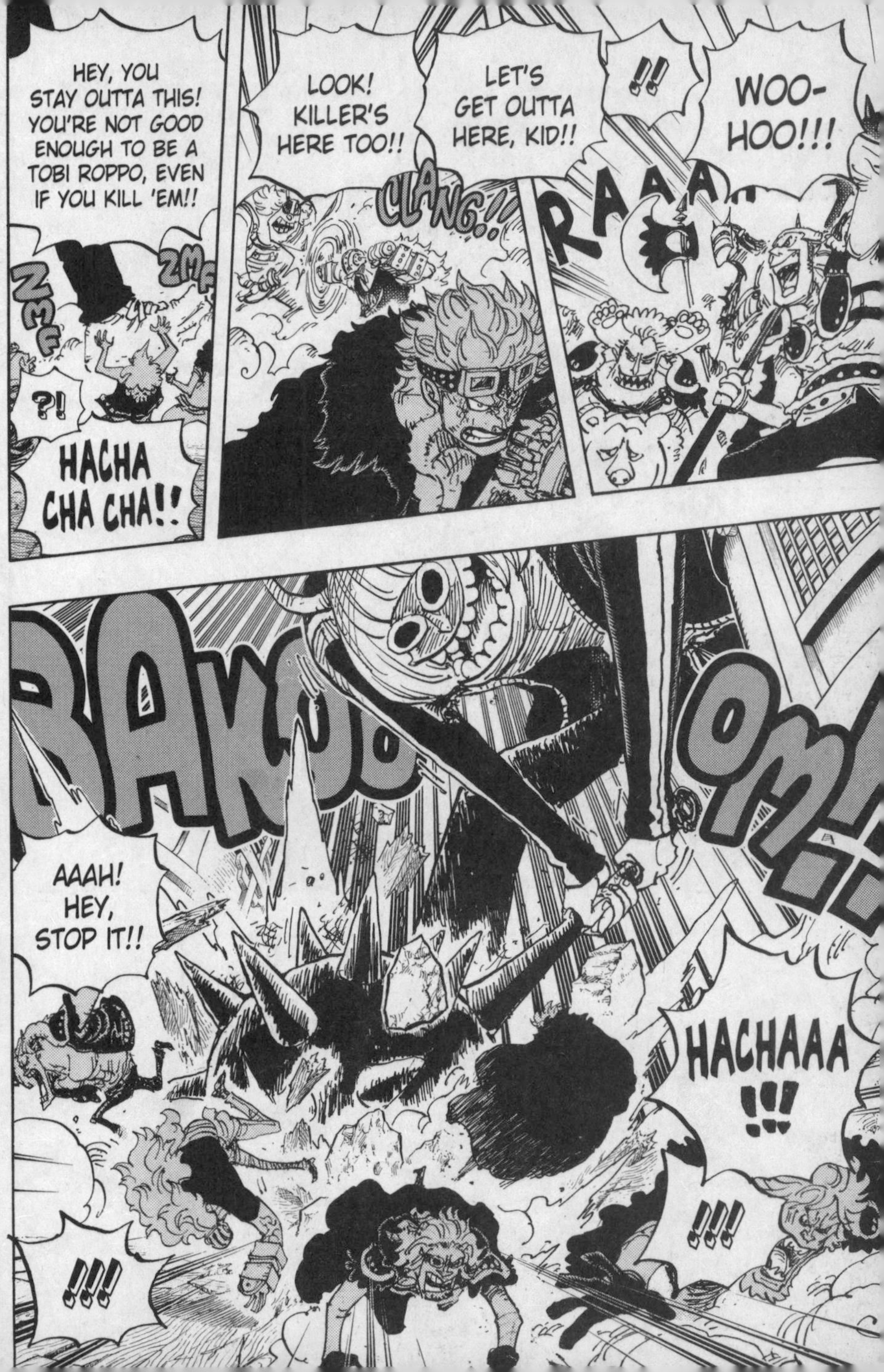
WOO-HOO!!!
!!
RAAA
LET'S GET OUTTA HERE, KID!!
LOOK! KILLER'S HERE TOO!!
CLANG!!
HEY, YOU STAY OUTTA THIS! YOU'RE NOT GOOD ENOUGH TO BE A TOBI ROPPO, EVEN IF YOU KILL 'EM!!
ZMF
ZMF
?!
HACHA CHA CHA!!
BAKOOOM!!
HACHAAA!!!
AAAH! HEY, STOP IT!!
!!!
!!!

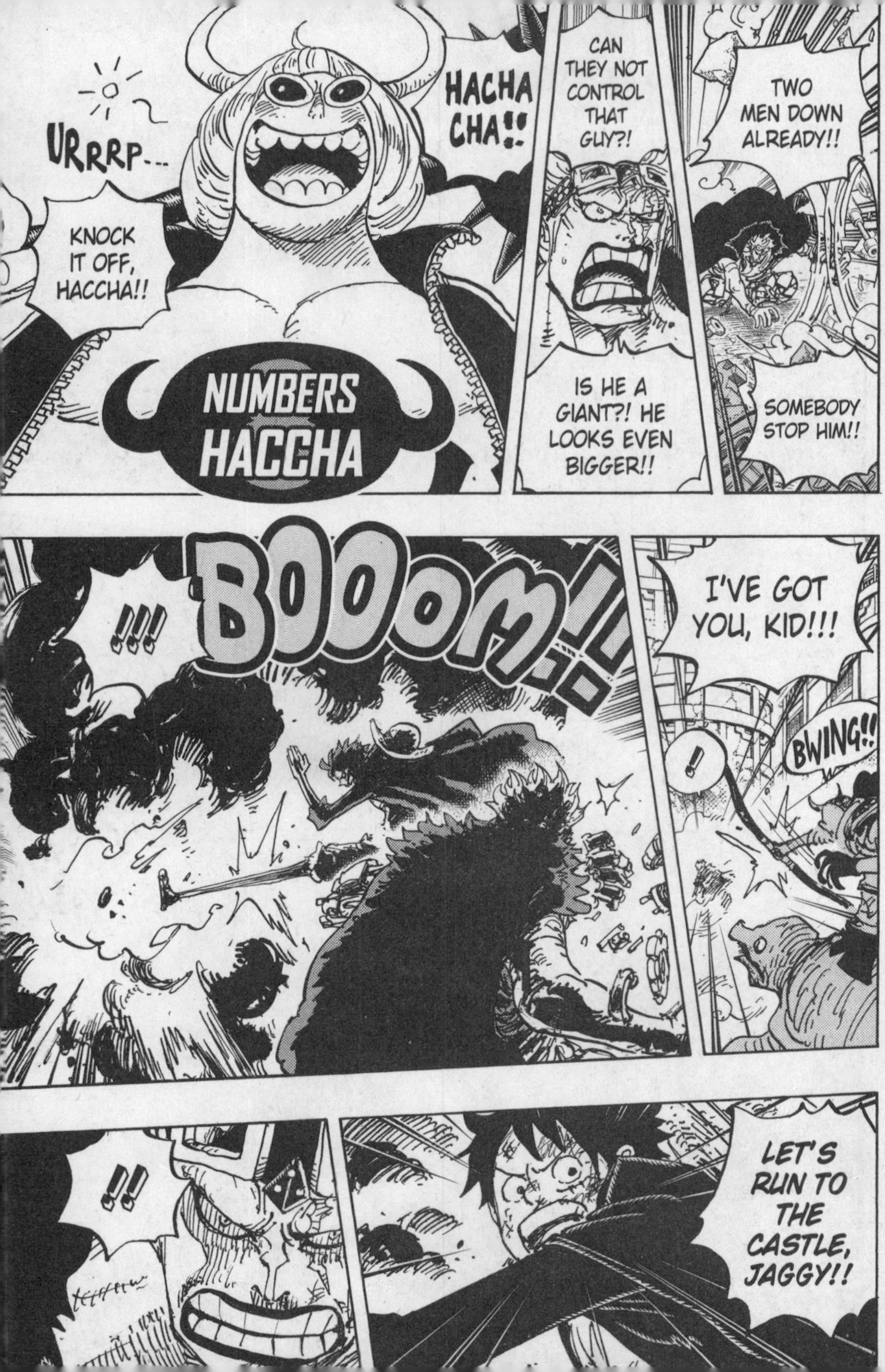
TWO MEN DOWN ALREADY!!
SOMEBODY STOP HIM!!
CAN THEY NOT CONTROL THAT GUY?!
IS HE A GIANT?! HE LOOKS EVEN BIGGER!!
HACHA CHA!!
URRRP...
KNOCK IT OFF, HACCHA!!
NUMBERS HACCHA
I'VE GOT YOU, KID!!!
BWING!!
!
BOOOM!!
!!!
LET'S RUN TO THE CASTLE, JAGGY!!
!!

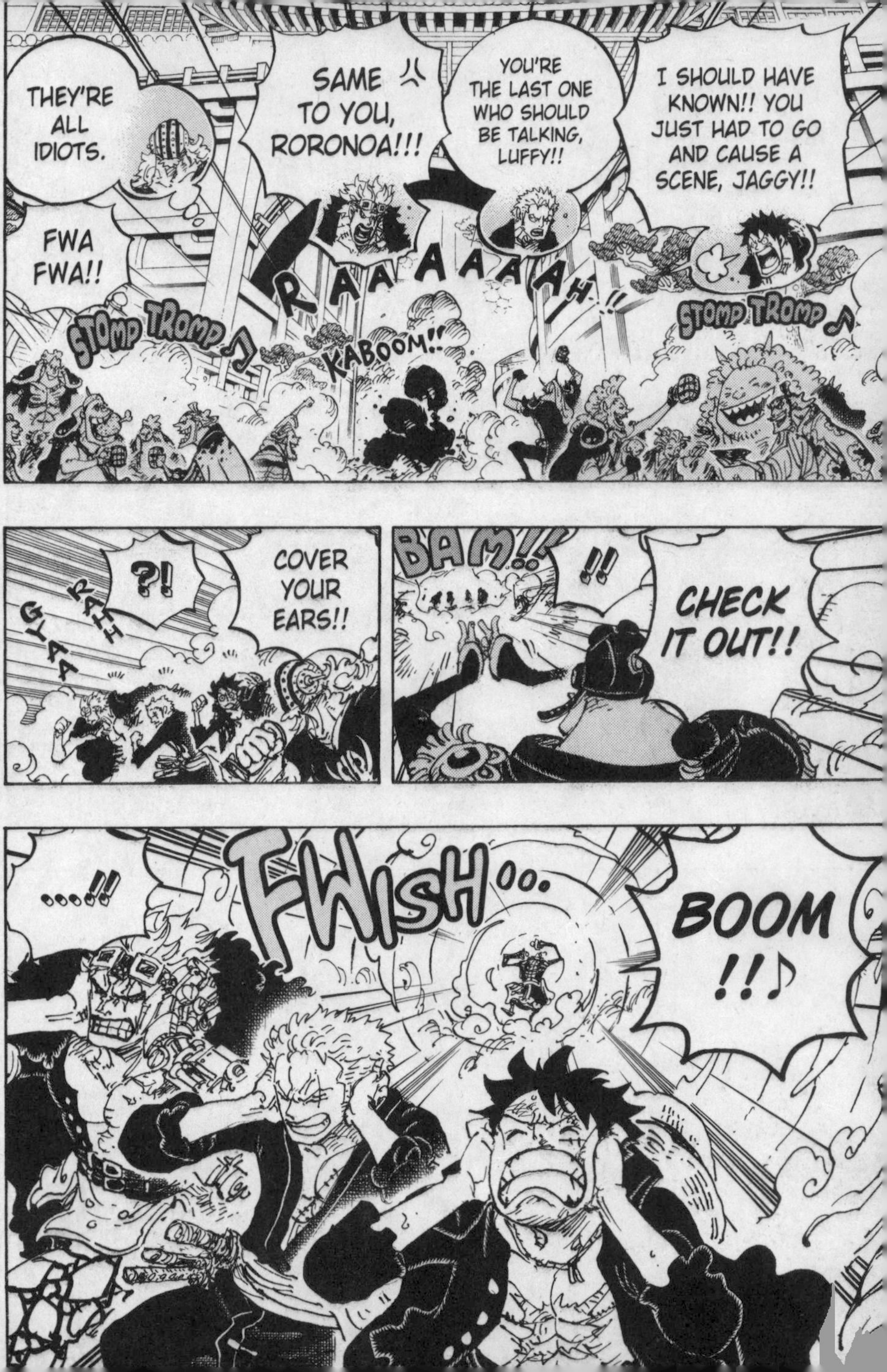
I SHOULD HAVE KNOWN!! YOU JUST HAD TO GO AND CAUSE A SCENE, JAGGY!!
STOMP TROMP♪
YOU'RE THE LAST ONE WHO SHOULD BE TALKING, LUFFY!!
RAAAAAAH!!
SAME TO YOU, RORONOA!!!
KABOOM!!
THEY'RE ALL IDIOTS.
FWA FWA!!
STOMP TROMP♫
CHECK IT OUT!!
!!
BAM!!
COVER YOUR EARS!!
?!
RAAH
GYAA
BOOM!!♪
FWISH
...!!

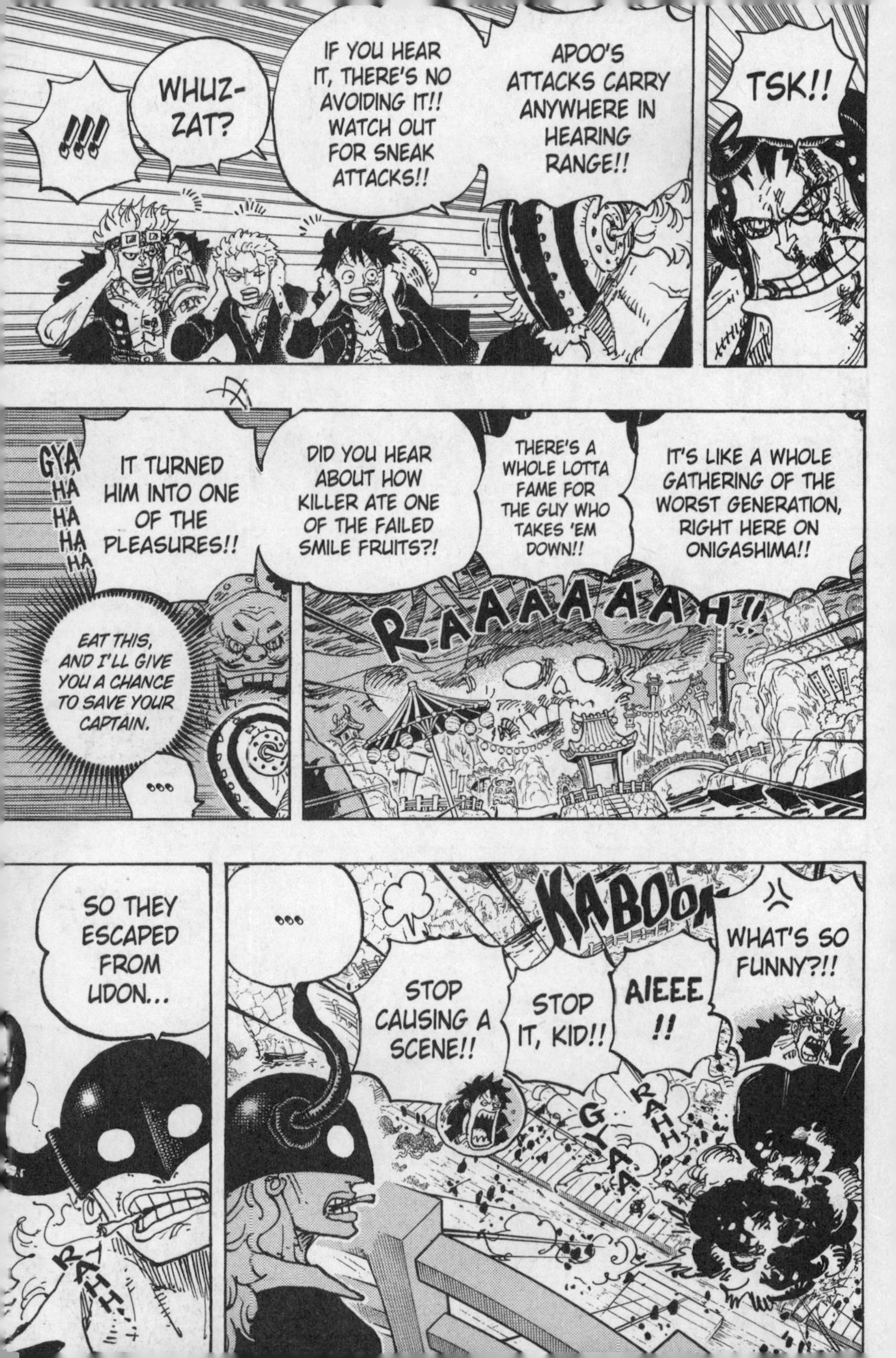
TSK!!
APOO'S ATTACKS CARRY ANYWHERE IN HEARING RANGE!!
IF YOU HEAR IT, THERE'S NO AVOIDING IT!! WATCH OUT FOR SNEAK ATTACKS!!
WHUZ-ZAT?
!!!
IT'S LIKE A WHOLE GATHERING OF THE WORST GENERATION, RIGHT HERE ON ONIGASHIMA!!
THERE'S A WHOLE LOTTA FAME FOR THE GUY WHO TAKES 'EM DOWN!!
DID YOU HEAR ABOUT HOW KILLER ATE ONE OF THE FAILED SMILE FRUITS?!
RAAAAAAAH!!
IT TURNED HIM INTO ONE OF THE PLEASURES!!
GYAHAHAHAHAHA
EAT THIS, AND I'LL GIVE YOU A CHANCE TO SAVE YOUR CAPTAIN.
...
WHAT'S SO FUNNY?!!
KABOOM
AIEEE!!
STOP IT, KID!!
STOP CAUSING A SCENE!!
...
GYAAA
RAHH
SO THEY ESCAPED FROM UDON...
RAHH!!

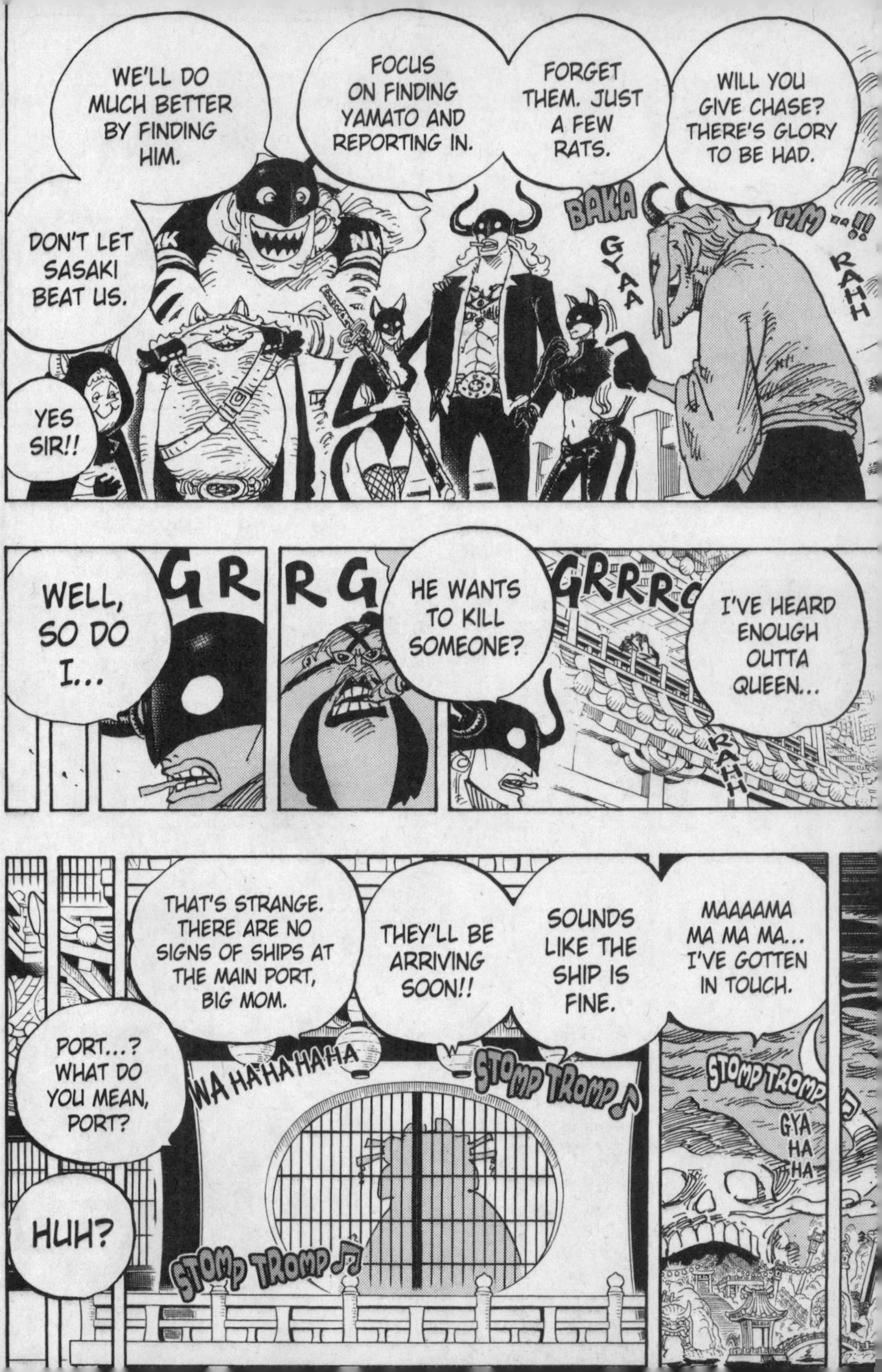

WILL YOU GIVE CHASE? THERE'S GLORY TO BE HAD.
HM..!!
RAHH
FORGET THEM. JUST A FEW RATS.
BAKA
GYAA
FOCUS ON FINDING YAMATO AND REPORTING IN.
WE'LL DO MUCH BETTER BY FINDING HIM.
DON'T LET SASAKI BEAT US.
YES SIR!!
I'VE HEARD ENOUGH OUTTA QUEEN...
GRRRO
RAHH
HE WANTS TO KILL SOMEONE?
RG
GR
WELL, SO DO I...
MAAAAMA MA MA MA... I'VE GOTTEN IN TOUCH.
STOMP TROMP
GYA HA HA HA
SOUNDS LIKE THE SHIP IS FINE.
STOMP TROMP
THEY'LL BE ARRIVING SOON!!
THAT'S STRANGE. THERE ARE NO SIGNS OF SHIPS AT THE MAIN PORT, BIG MOM.
WA HA HA HA HA HA
PORT...? WHAT DO YOU MEAN, PORT?
HUH?
STOMP TROMP

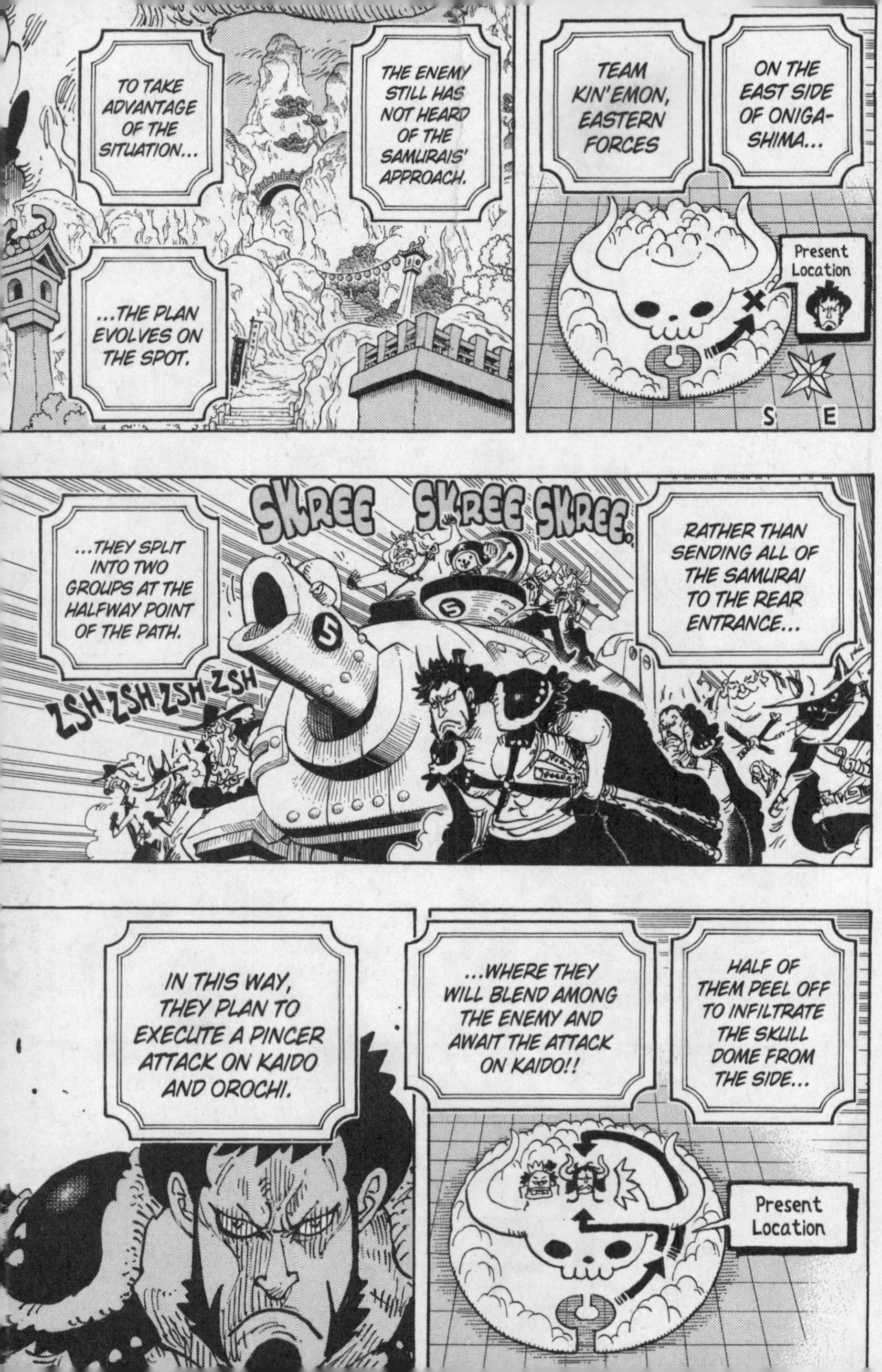
ON THE EAST SIDE OF ONIGA-SHIMA...
TEAM KIN'EMON, EASTERN FORCES
Present Location
S
E
THE ENEMY STILL HAS NOT HEARD OF THE SAMURAIS' APPROACH.
TO TAKE ADVANTAGE OF THE SITUATION...
...THE PLAN EVOLVES ON THE SPOT.
RATHER THAN SENDING ALL OF THE SAMURAI TO THE REAR ENTRANCE...
SKREE SKREE SKREE
...THEY SPLIT INTO TWO GROUPS AT THE HALFWAY POINT OF THE PATH.
ZSH ZSH ZSH ZSH
HALF OF THEM PEEL OFF TO INFILTRATE THE SKULL DOME FROM THE SIDE...
...WHERE THEY WILL BLEND AMONG THE ENEMY AND AWAIT THE ATTACK ON KAIDO!!
Present Location
IN THIS WAY, THEY PLAN TO EXECUTE A PINCER ATTACK ON KAIDO AND OROCHI.

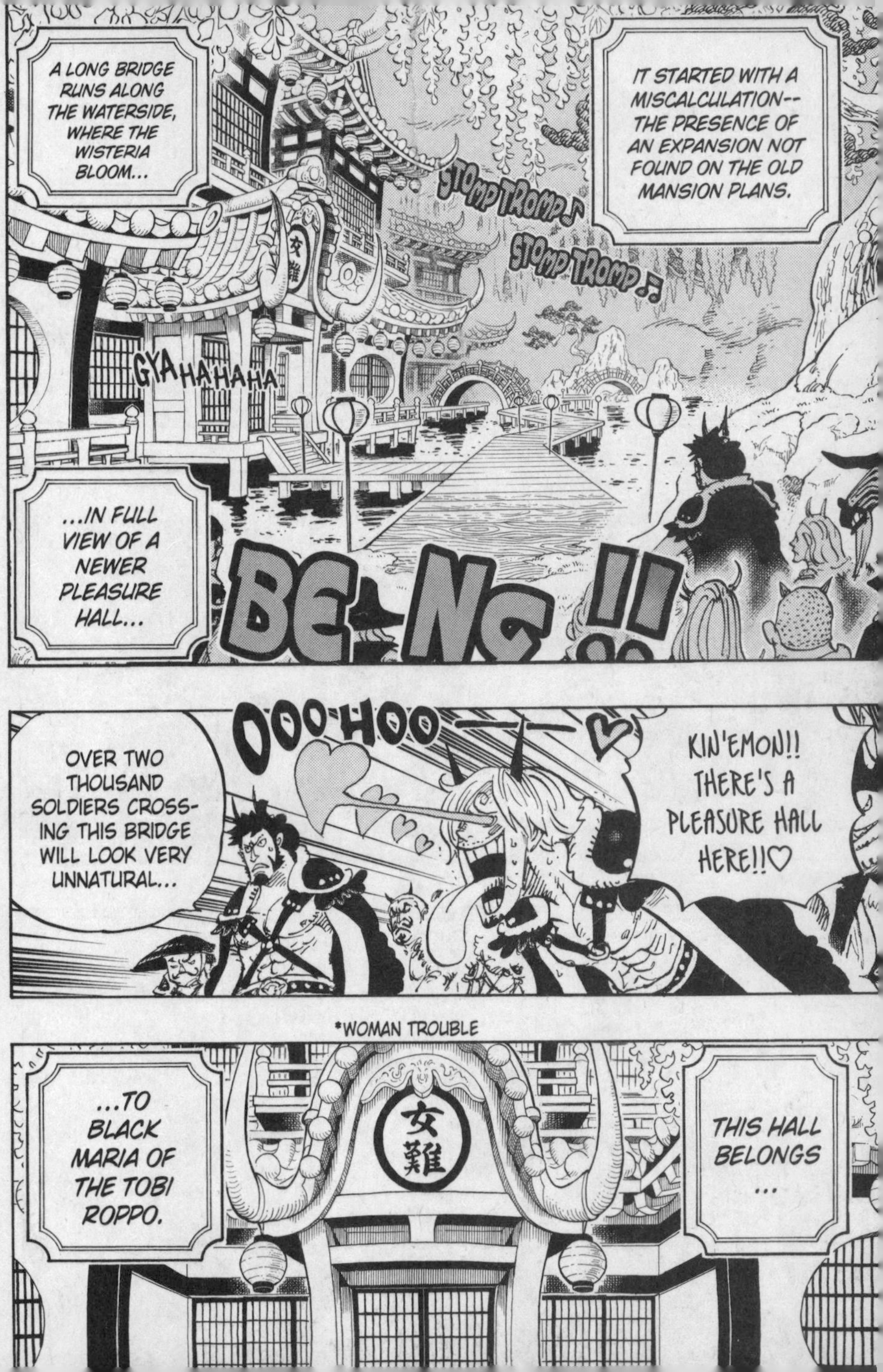
IT STARTED WITH A MISCALCULATION-- THE PRESENCE OF AN EXPANSION NOT FOUND ON THE OLD MANSION PLANS.
STOMP TROMP♪
STOMP TROMP♫
A LONG BRIDGE RUNS ALONG THE WATERSIDE, WHERE THE WISTERIA BLOOM...
GYAHAHAHA
...IN FULL VIEW OF A NEWER PLEASURE HALL...
BE-NG!!
KIN'EMON!! THERE'S A PLEASURE HALL HERE!!♡
OOO-HOO—♡
OVER TWO THOUSAND SOLDIERS CROSSING THIS BRIDGE WILL LOOK VERY UNNATURAL...
*WOMAN TROUBLE
THIS HALL BELONGS ...
女難
...TO BLACK MARIA OF THE TOBI ROPPO.

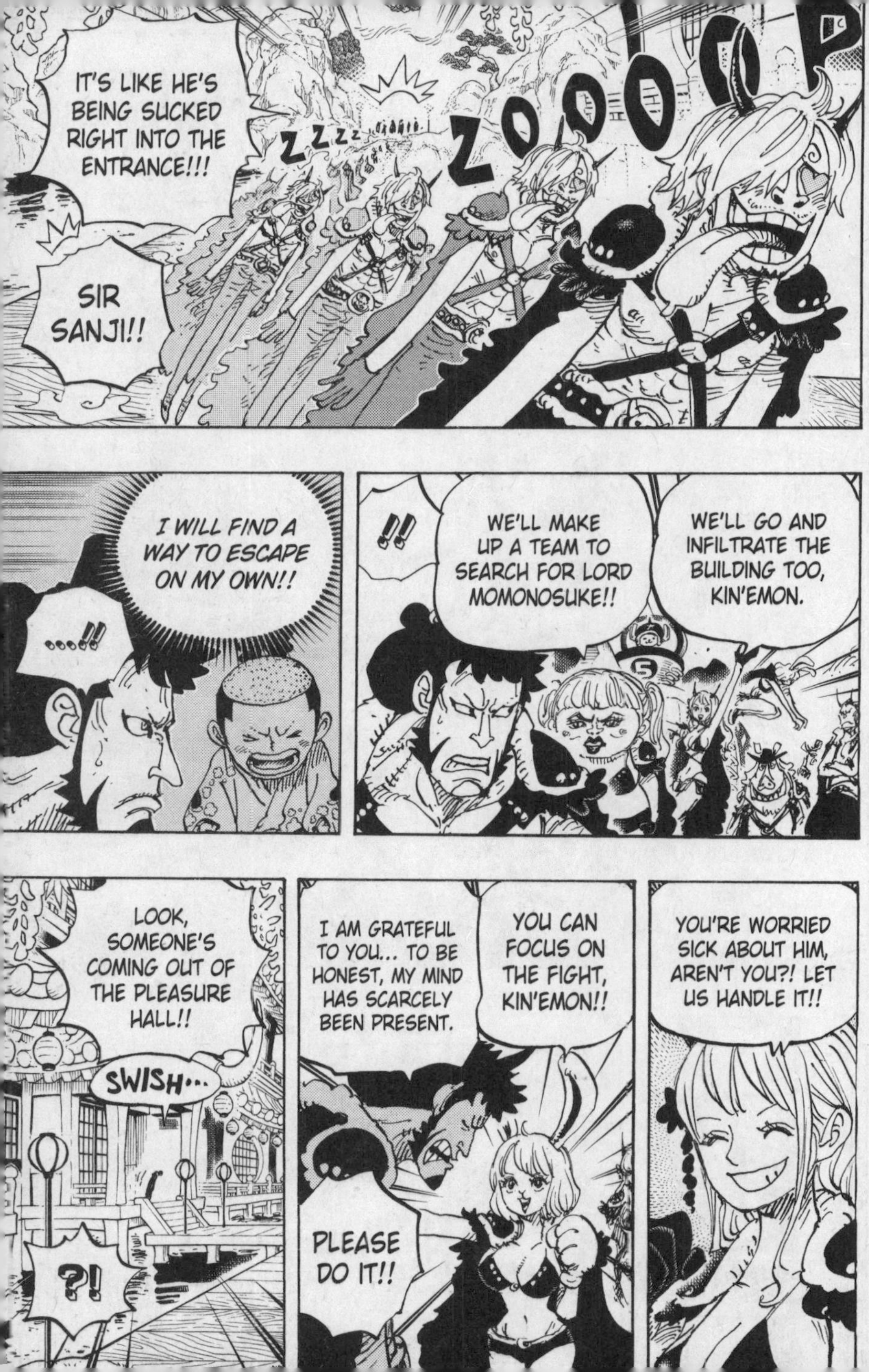
ZOOOOOP
ZZZz
IT'S LIKE HE'S BEING SUCKED RIGHT INTO THE ENTRANCE!!!
SIR SANJI!!
WE'LL GO AND INFILTRATE THE BUILDING TOO, KIN'EMON.
WE'LL MAKE UP A TEAM TO SEARCH FOR LORD MOMONOSUKE!!
!!
I WILL FIND A WAY TO ESCAPE ON MY OWN!!
...!!
YOU'RE WORRIED SICK ABOUT HIM, AREN'T YOU?! LET US HANDLE IT!!
YOU CAN FOCUS ON THE FIGHT, KIN'EMON!!
I AM GRATEFUL TO YOU... TO BE HONEST, MY MIND HAS SCARCELY BEEN PRESENT.
PLEASE DO IT!!
LOOK, SOMEONE'S COMING OUT OF THE PLEASURE HALL!!
SWISH...
?!

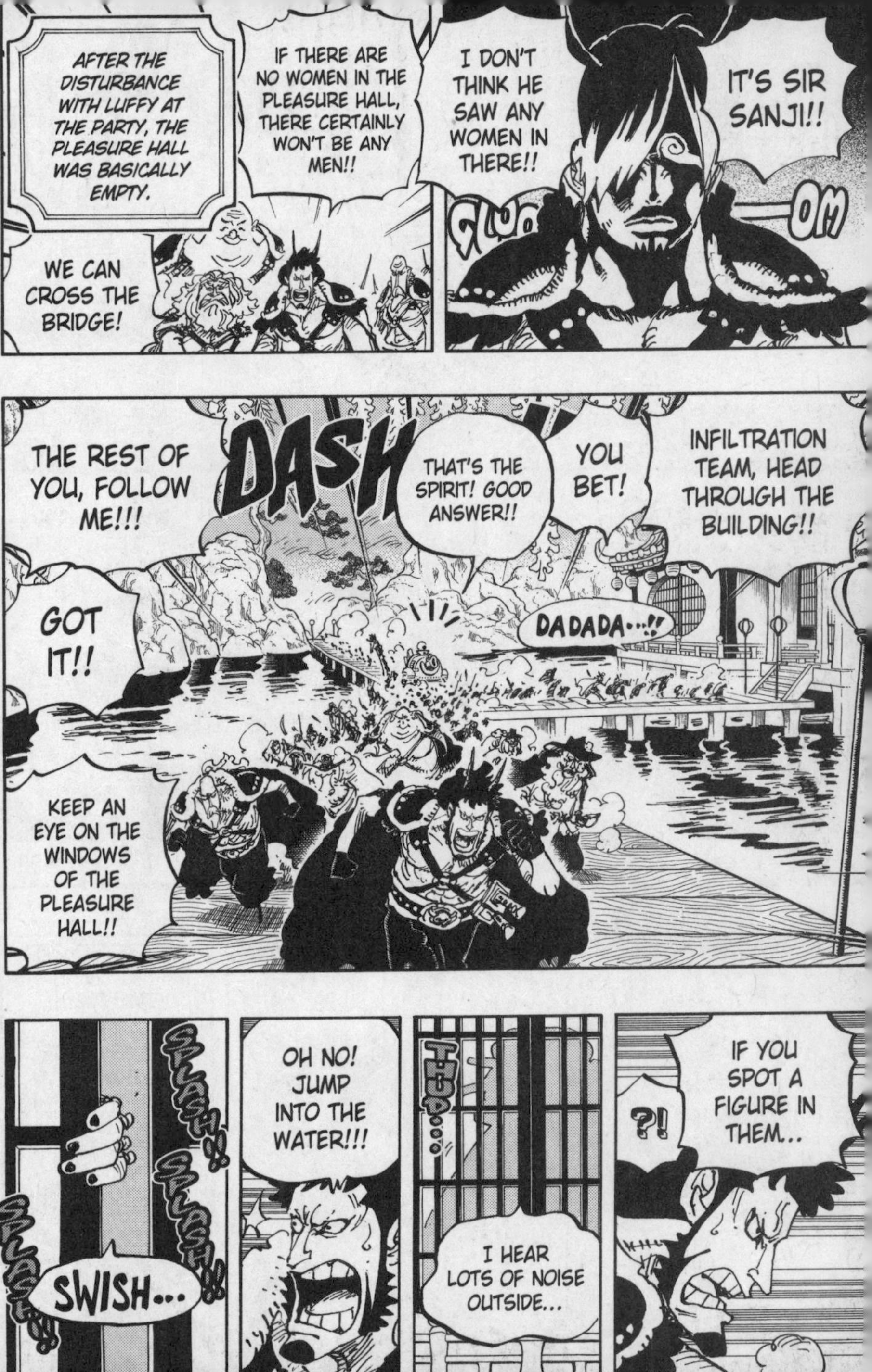
IT'S SIR SANJI!!
I DON'T THINK HE SAW ANY WOMEN IN THERE!!
IF THERE ARE NO WOMEN IN THE PLEASURE HALL, THERE CERTAINLY WON'T BE ANY MEN!!
AFTER THE DISTURBANCE WITH LUFFY AT THE PARTY, THE PLEASURE HALL WAS BASICALLY EMPTY.
WE CAN CROSS THE BRIDGE!
INFILTRATION TEAM, HEAD THROUGH THE BUILDING!!
YOU BET!
THAT'S THE SPIRIT! GOOD ANSWER!!
DASH
THE REST OF YOU, FOLLOW ME!!!
DADADA...!!
GOT IT!!
KEEP AN EYE ON THE WINDOWS OF THE PLEASURE HALL!!
IF YOU SPOT A FIGURE IN THEM...
?!
THUD...
I HEAR LOTS OF NOISE OUTSIDE...
OH NO! JUMP INTO THE WATER!!!
SPLASH!!
SPLASH!!
SPLASH!!
SWISH...

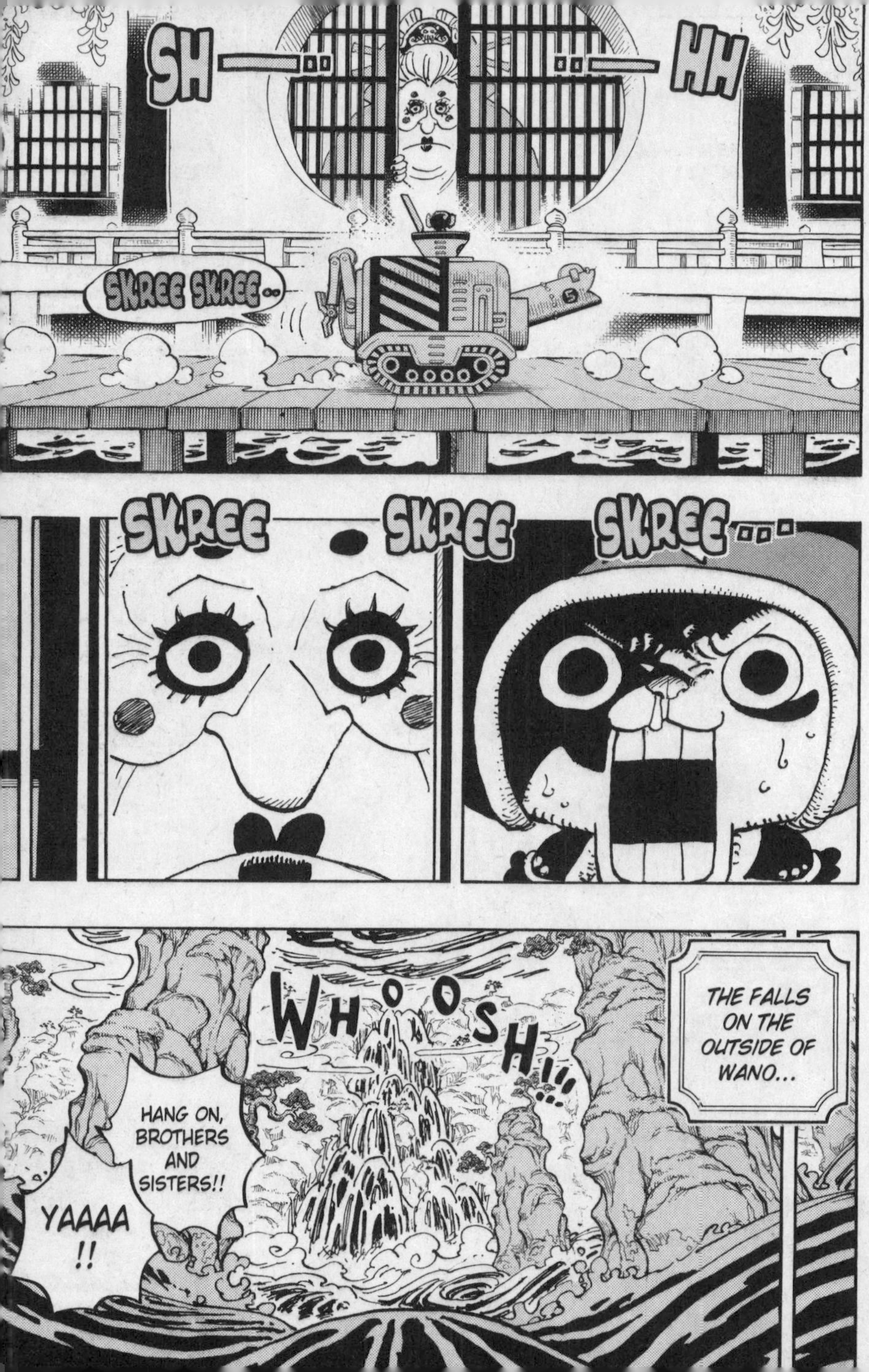
SH—.. ..—HH
SKREE SKREE..
SKREE SKREE SKREE...
THE FALLS ON THE OUTSIDE OF WANO...
WHOOSH!!!
HANG ON, BROTHERS AND SISTERS!!
YAAAA!!

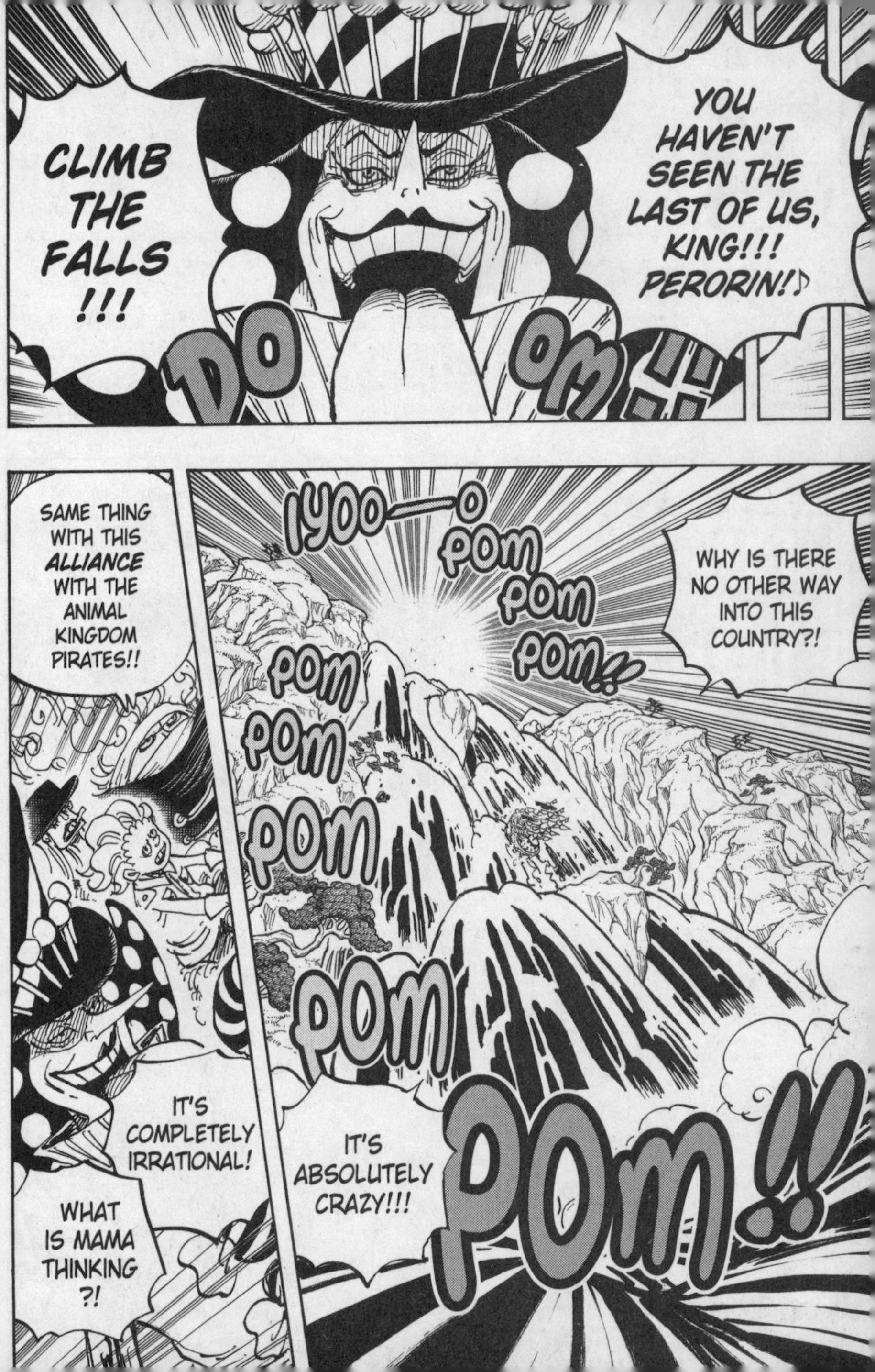
YOU HAVEN'T SEEN THE LAST OF US, KING!!! PERORIN!♪
CLIMB THE FALLS!!!
DOOM!!
WHY IS THERE NO OTHER WAY INTO THIS COUNTRY?!
IYOO—O POM POM POM!!
POM POM POM POM POM!!
IT'S ABSOLUTELY CRAZY!!!
SAME THING WITH THIS *ALLIANCE* WITH THE ANIMAL KINGDOM PIRATES!!
IT'S COMPLETELY IRRATIONAL!
WHAT IS MAMA THINKING?!

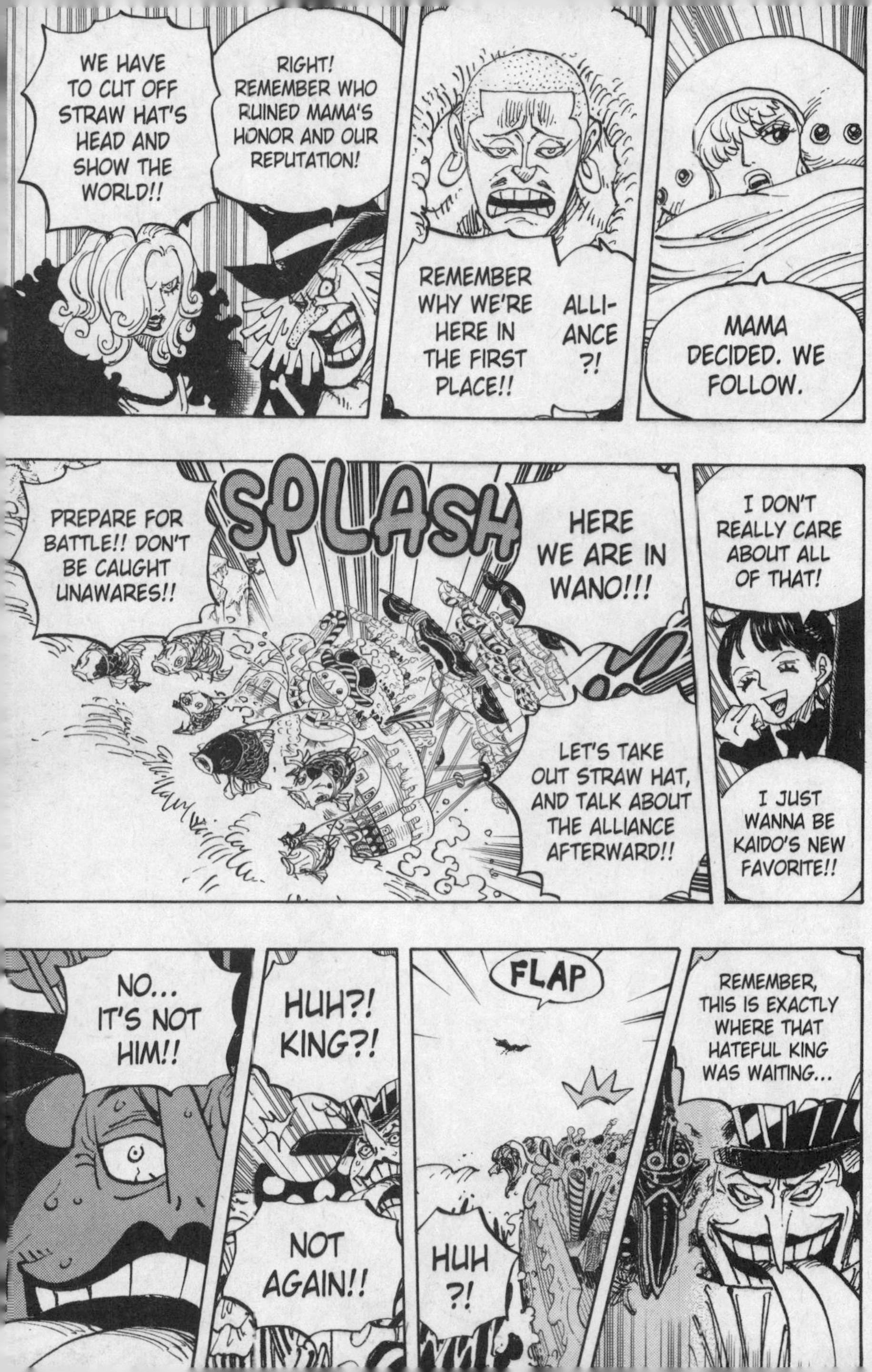
MAMA DECIDED. WE FOLLOW.
ALLI-ANCE ?!
REMEMBER WHY WE'RE HERE IN THE FIRST PLACE!!
RIGHT! REMEMBER WHO RUINED MAMA'S HONOR AND OUR REPUTATION!
WE HAVE TO CUT OFF STRAW HAT'S HEAD AND SHOW THE WORLD!!
I DON'T REALLY CARE ABOUT ALL OF THAT!
I JUST WANNA BE KAIDO'S NEW FAVORITE!!
HERE WE ARE IN WANO!!!
SPLASH
PREPARE FOR BATTLE!! DON'T BE CAUGHT UNAWARES!!
LET'S TAKE OUT STRAW HAT, AND TALK ABOUT THE ALLIANCE AFTERWARD!!
REMEMBER, THIS IS EXACTLY WHERE THAT HATEFUL KING WAS WAITING...
FLAP
HUH ?!
HUH?! KING?!
NOT AGAIN!!
NO... IT'S NOT HIM!!

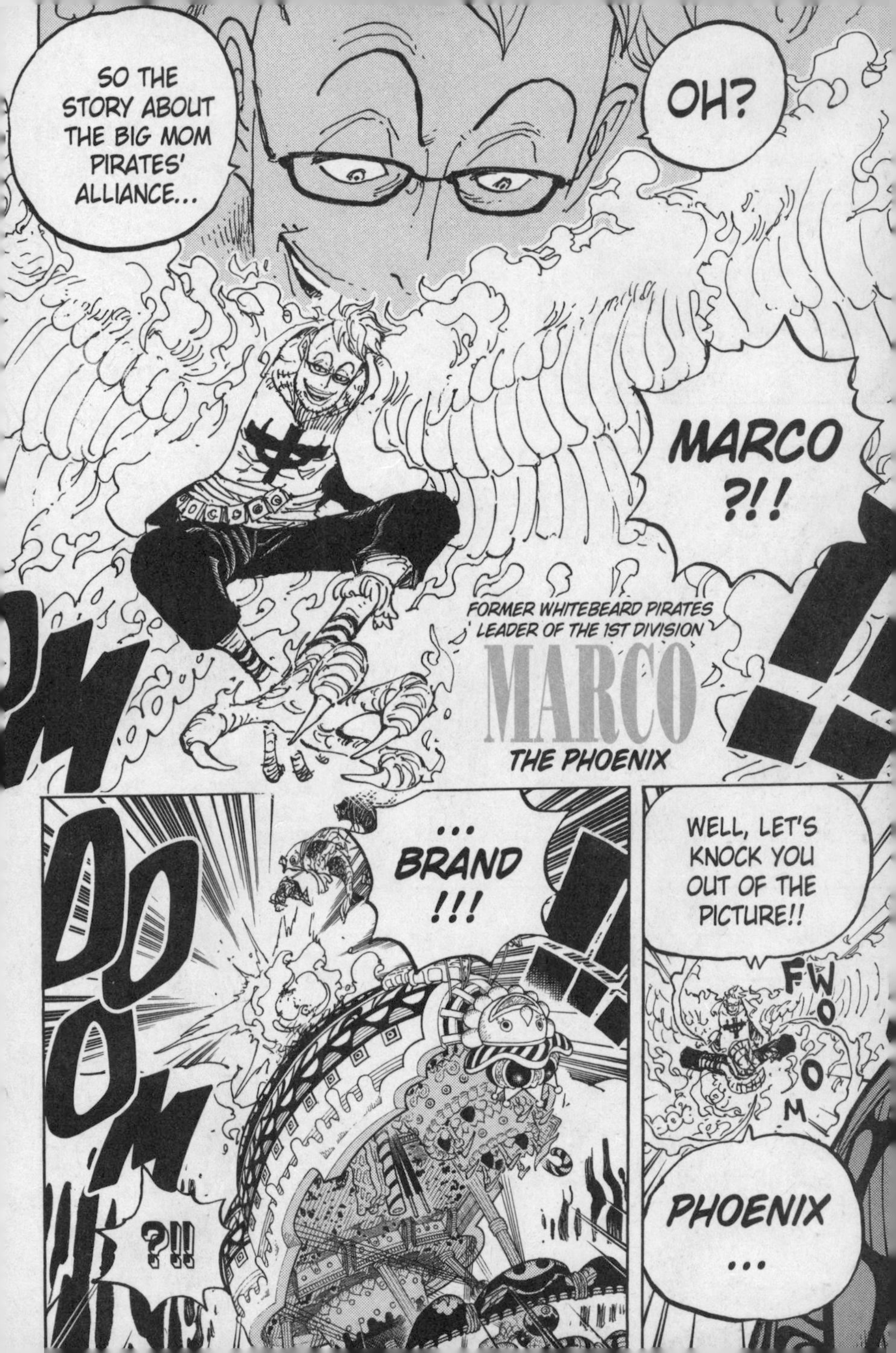
OH?
SO THE STORY ABOUT THE BIG MOM PIRATES' ALLIANCE...
MARCO ?!!
FORMER WHITEBEARD PIRATES LEADER OF THE 1ST DIVISION
MARCO
THE PHOENIX
WELL, LET'S KNOCK YOU OUT OF THE PICTURE!!
FWOOM
PHOENIX ...
... BRAND !!!
DOOM
?!!

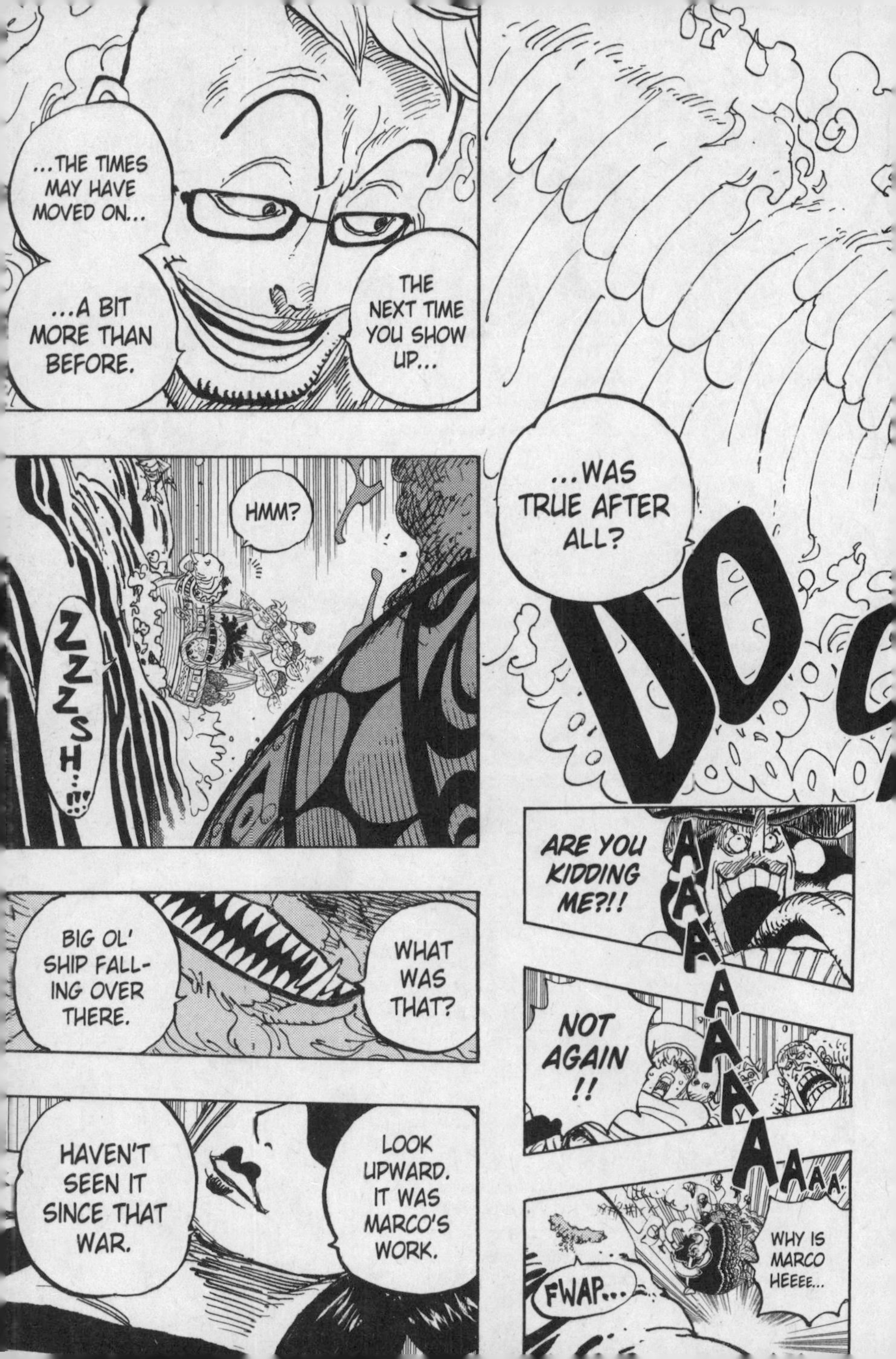
...WAS TRUE AFTER ALL?
DOO
ARE YOU KIDDING ME?!!
AAAAAAAAAA
NOT AGAIN !!
WHY IS MARCO HEEEE...
FWAP...
THE NEXT TIME YOU SHOW UP...
...THE TIMES MAY HAVE MOVED ON...
...A BIT MORE THAN BEFORE.
HMM?
ZZZSH...!!!
WHAT WAS THAT?
BIG OL' SHIP FALL-ING OVER THERE.
LOOK UPWARD. IT WAS MARCO'S WORK.
HAVEN'T SEEN IT SINCE THAT WAR.

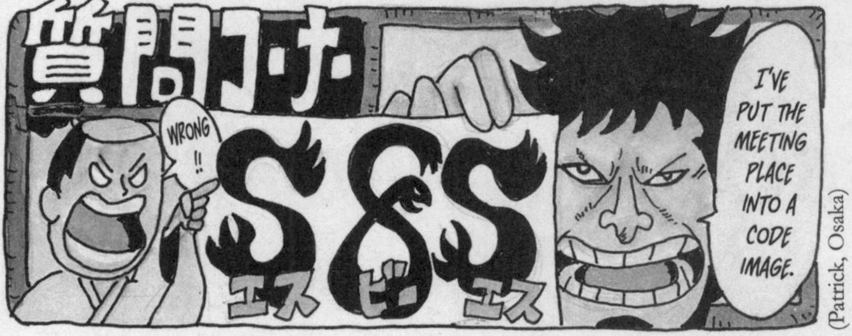
質問コーナー
WRONG !!
SBS
エスビーエス
I'VE PUT THE MEETING PLACE INTO A CODE IMAGE.

(Patrick, Osaka)

Q: Oda Sensei!! In May of 2020, they discovered that Spinosaurus actually swam in the ocean!! Since you're so busy, I just thought I'd drop you a line to let you know. ♡
Hey, wait!!!! You already fixed his tail in chapter 983!!!! Geez, man! When do you find the time to watch the news?!!

--Yuchabin

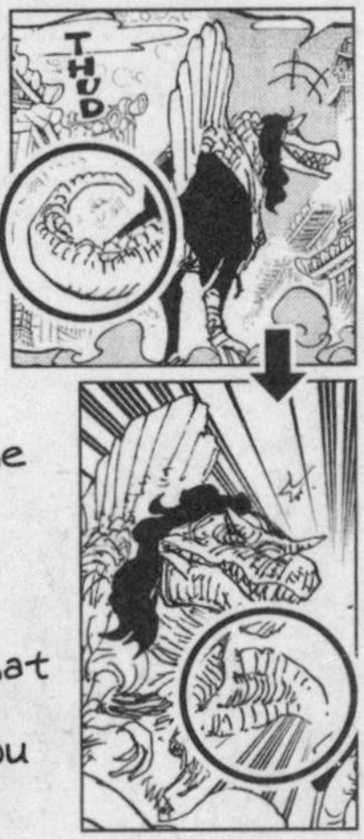
THUD

A: Oh, you noticed? That's right, between Page One's first and second appearance, they discovered a fossil of the Spinosaurus that filled in what had only been a guess before. Now it has a different skeletal structure!! I freaked out at first, but then I thought that if I changed it real smooth and sneaky-like, nobody would notice. I should have figured you would, LOL. Paleontology evolves by the day.

Q: As a matter of fact, the next person to join the Straw Hat Crew will be me.

--Momo Daifuku

A: Really?!! Wow, such confidence!! But you're only twelve...

Q: As content restrictions get tighter around the world these days, it makes me so happy that we've got a segment here that is completely free of any of that. Speaking of which, can I smell Onami's used bath towel? I'm worried that her kunoichi outfit might be cut a little too short.

--Sanadacchi

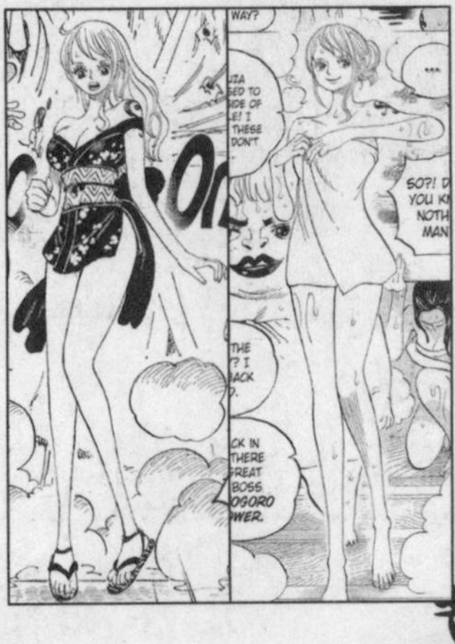

A: Sanada!!! Hey! Security! Why did you let this guy in here?! I told you to send him away, didn't I?! We have proper restrictions here!! And perverted statements are against the rules!! I want a squeaky-clean image for this segment!! Get lost, Sanada!!

Chapter 982:

SCOUNDREL MEETS SCOUNDREL

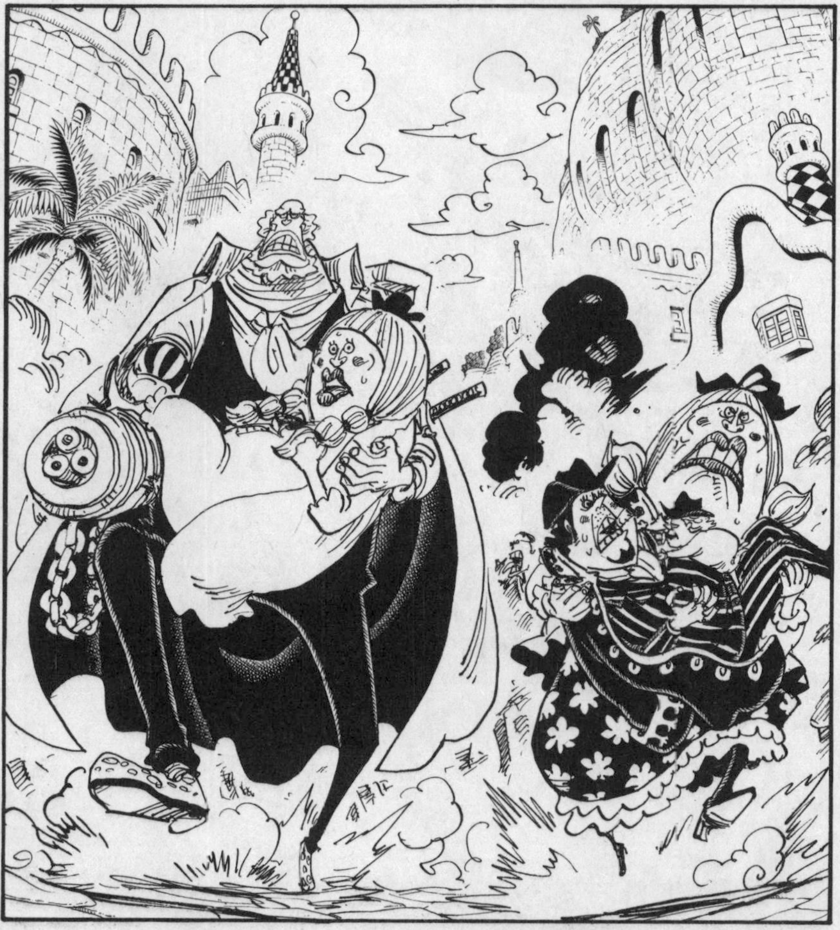

GANG BEGE'S OH MY FAMILY
VOL. 28: "RUN AWAY FROM THE NAVY!!"

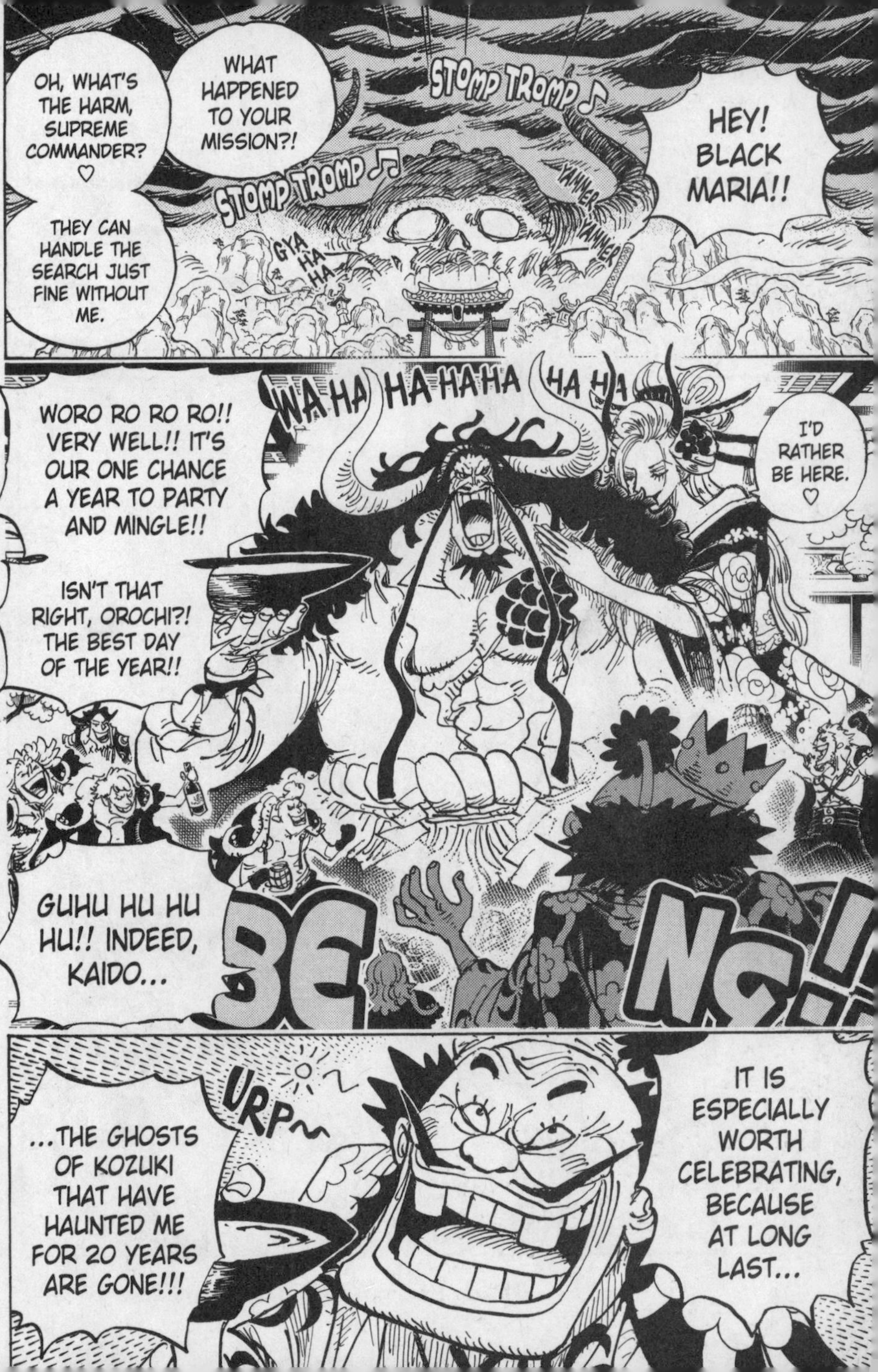
HEY! BLACK MARIA!!
STOMP TROMP ♫
WHAT HAPPENED TO YOUR MISSION?!
YAMMER YAMMER
STOMP TROMP ♫
OH, WHAT'S THE HARM, SUPREME COMMANDER? ♡
THEY CAN HANDLE THE SEARCH JUST FINE WITHOUT ME.
GYA HA HA
I'D RATHER BE HERE. ♡
WA HA HA HAHA HA HA
WORO RO RO RO!! VERY WELL!! IT'S OUR ONE CHANCE A YEAR TO PARTY AND MINGLE!!
ISN'T THAT RIGHT, OROCHI?! THE BEST DAY OF THE YEAR!!
NG!!
BE
GUHU HU HU HU!! INDEED, KAIDO...
IT IS ESPECIALLY WORTH CELEBRATING, BECAUSE AT LONG LAST...
URP~
...THE GHOSTS OF KOZUKI THAT HAVE HAUNTED ME FOR 20 YEARS ARE GONE!!!

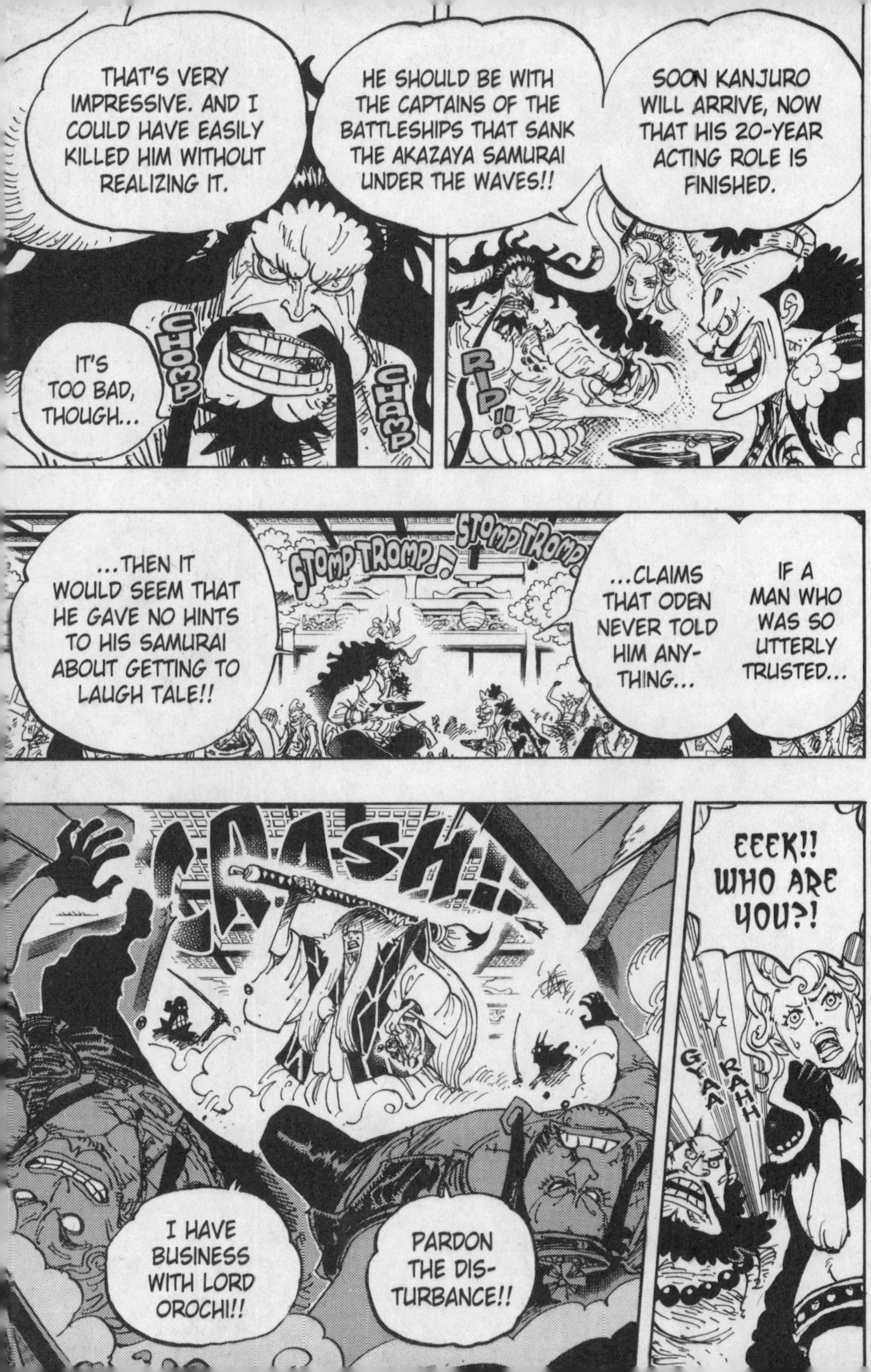

SOON KANJURO WILL ARRIVE, NOW THAT HIS 20-YEAR ACTING ROLE IS FINISHED.
HE SHOULD BE WITH THE CAPTAINS OF THE BATTLESHIPS THAT SANK THE AKAZAYA SAMURAI UNDER THE WAVES!!
RIP!!
THAT'S VERY IMPRESSIVE. AND I COULD HAVE EASILY KILLED HIM WITHOUT REALIZING IT.
CHOMP
CHAMP
IT'S TOO BAD, THOUGH...
IF A MAN WHO WAS SO UTTERLY TRUSTED...
...CLAIMS THAT ODEN NEVER TOLD HIM ANY-THING...
STOMP TROMP
STOMP TROMP
...THEN IT WOULD SEEM THAT HE GAVE NO HINTS TO HIS SAMURAI ABOUT GETTING TO LAUGH TALE!!
EEEK!! WHO ARE YOU?!
GYAA
RAHH
CRASH!!
PARDON THE DIS-TURBANCE!!
I HAVE BUSINESS WITH LORD OROCHI!!

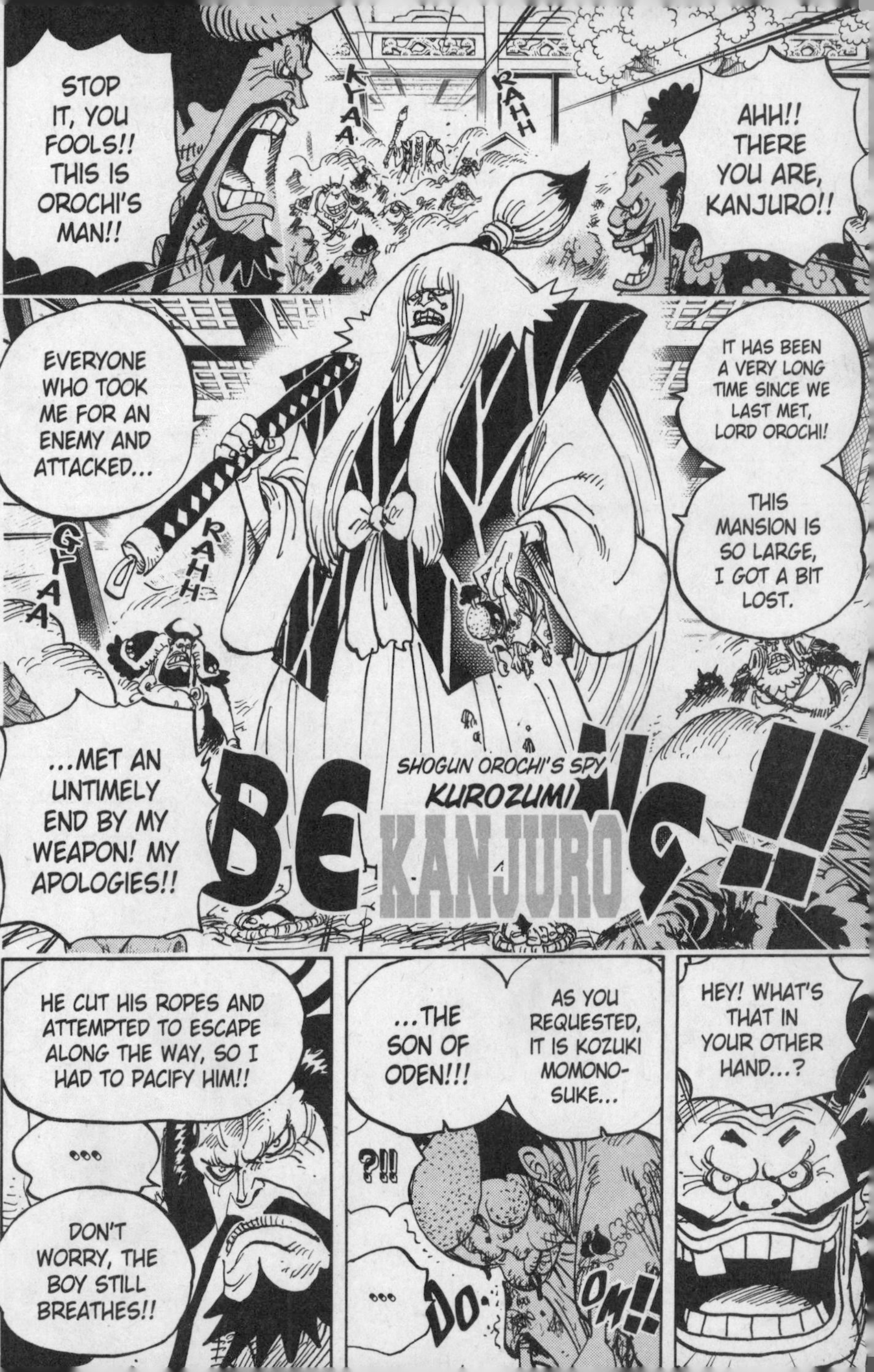
AHH!! THERE YOU ARE, KANJURO!!
RAHH
KYAA
STOP IT, YOU FOOLS!! THIS IS OROCHI'S MAN!!
IT HAS BEEN A VERY LONG TIME SINCE WE LAST MET, LORD OROCHI!
THIS MANSION IS SO LARGE, I GOT A BIT LOST.
EVERYONE WHO TOOK ME FOR AN ENEMY AND ATTACKED...
RAHH
KYAA
...MET AN UNTIMELY END BY MY WEAPON! MY APOLOGIES!!
SHOGUN OROCHI'S SPY
KUROZUMI KANJURO
BE
!!
HEY! WHAT'S THAT IN YOUR OTHER HAND...?
AS YOU REQUESTED, IT IS KOZUKI MOMONO-SUKE...
...THE SON OF ODEN!!!
?!!
...
DO
OM!!
HE CUT HIS ROPES AND ATTEMPTED TO ESCAPE ALONG THE WAY, SO I HAD TO PACIFY HIM!!
...
DON'T WORRY, THE BOY STILL BREATHES!!

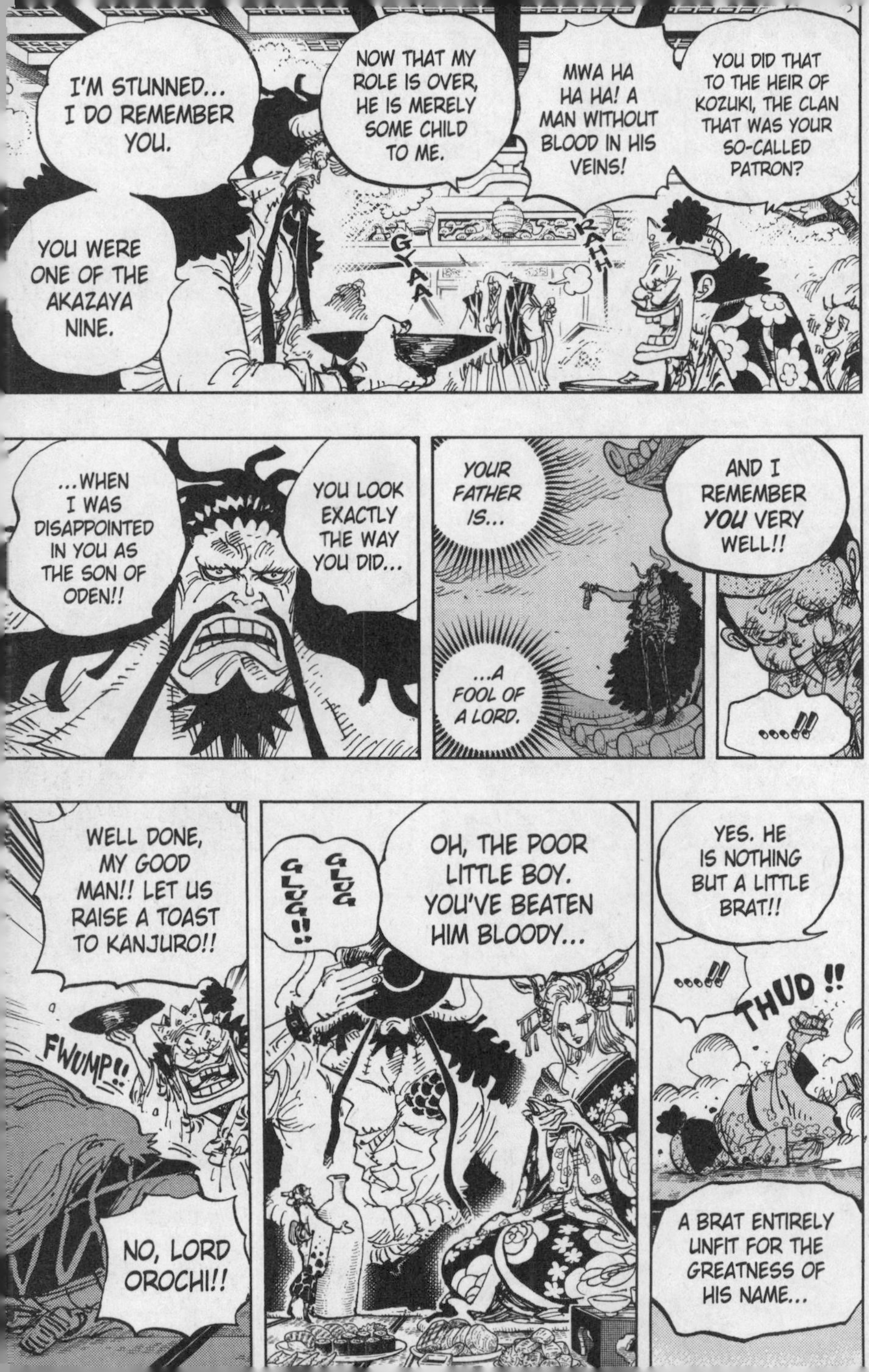
YOU DID THAT TO THE HEIR OF KOZUKI, THE CLAN THAT WAS YOUR SO-CALLED PATRON?
MWA HA HA HA! A MAN WITHOUT BLOOD IN HIS VEINS!
RAHH
GYAA
NOW THAT MY ROLE IS OVER, HE IS MERELY SOME CHILD TO ME.
I'M STUNNED... I DO REMEMBER YOU.
YOU WERE ONE OF THE AKAZAYA NINE.
AND I REMEMBER YOU VERY WELL!!
...!!
YOUR FATHER IS...
...A FOOL OF A LORD.
YOU LOOK EXACTLY THE WAY YOU DID...
...WHEN I WAS DISAPPOINTED IN YOU AS THE SON OF ODEN!!
YES. HE IS NOTHING BUT A LITTLE BRAT!!
...!!
THUD!!
A BRAT ENTIRELY UNFIT FOR THE GREATNESS OF HIS NAME...
OH, THE POOR LITTLE BOY. YOU'VE BEATEN HIM BLOODY...
GLUG GLUG!!
WELL DONE, MY GOOD MAN!! LET US RAISE A TOAST TO KANJURO!!
FWUMP!!
NO, LORD OROCHI!!

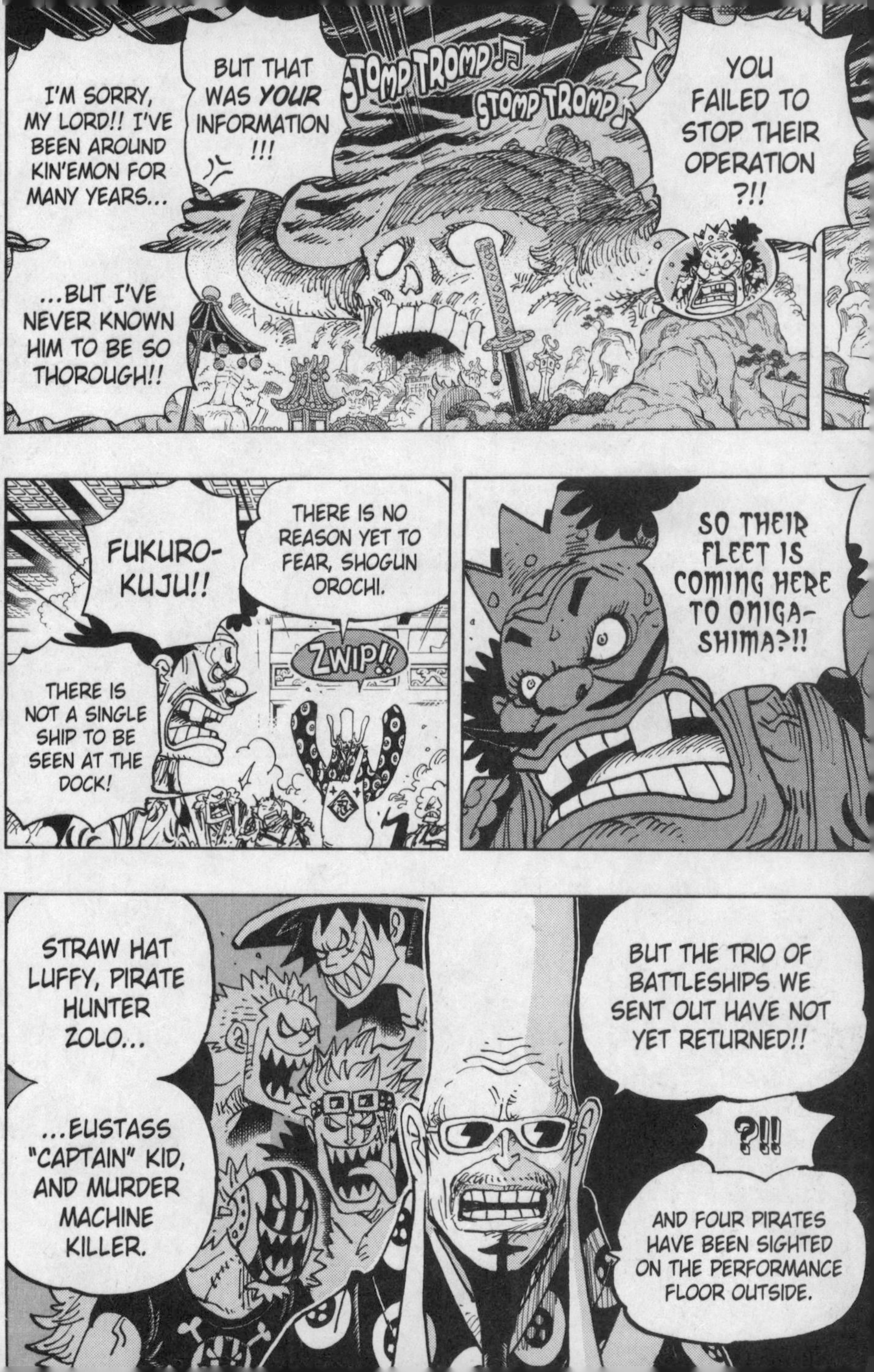
YOU FAILED TO STOP THEIR OPERATION ?!!
STOMP TROMP♫
STOMP TROMP♪
BUT THAT WAS *YOUR* INFORMATION !!!
I'M SORRY, MY LORD!! I'VE BEEN AROUND KIN'EMON FOR MANY YEARS...
...BUT I'VE NEVER KNOWN HIM TO BE SO THOROUGH!!
SO THEIR FLEET IS COMING HERE TO ONIGA-SHIMA?!!
THERE IS NO REASON YET TO FEAR, SHOGUN OROCHI.
FUKURO-KUJU!!
ZWIP!!
THERE IS NOT A SINGLE SHIP TO BE SEEN AT THE DOCK!
BUT THE TRIO OF BATTLESHIPS WE SENT OUT HAVE NOT YET RETURNED!!
?!!
AND FOUR PIRATES HAVE BEEN SIGHTED ON THE PERFORMANCE FLOOR OUTSIDE.
STRAW HAT LUFFY, PIRATE HUNTER ZOLO...
...EUSTASS "CAPTAIN" KID, AND MURDER MACHINE KILLER.

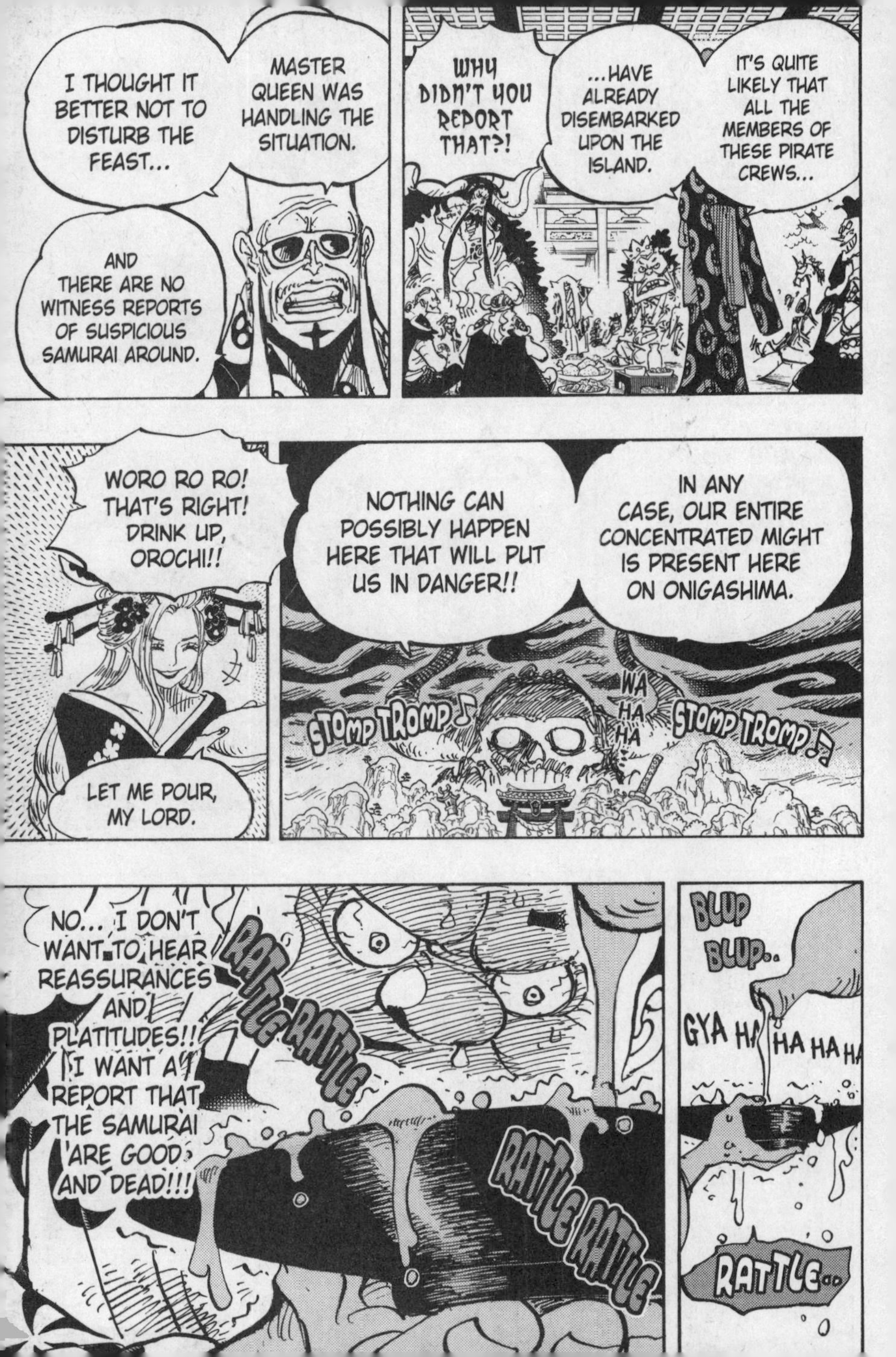
IT'S QUITE LIKELY THAT ALL THE MEMBERS OF THESE PIRATE CREWS...
...HAVE ALREADY DISEMBARKED UPON THE ISLAND.
WHY DIDN'T YOU REPORT THAT?!
MASTER QUEEN WAS HANDLING THE SITUATION.
I THOUGHT IT BETTER NOT TO DISTURB THE FEAST...
AND THERE ARE NO WITNESS REPORTS OF SUSPICIOUS SAMURAI AROUND.
IN ANY CASE, OUR ENTIRE CONCENTRATED MIGHT IS PRESENT HERE ON ONIGASHIMA.
NOTHING CAN POSSIBLY HAPPEN HERE THAT WILL PUT US IN DANGER!!
STOMP TROMP
WA HA HA
STOMP TROMP
WORO RO RO! THAT'S RIGHT! DRINK UP, OROCHI!!
LET ME POUR, MY LORD.
BLUP
BLUP..
GYA HA HA HA HA
RATTLE..
RATTLE RATTLE
RATTLE RATTLE
NO... I DON'T WANT TO HEAR REASSURANCES AND PLATITUDES!!! I WANT A REPORT THAT THE SAMURAI ARE GOOD AND DEAD!!!

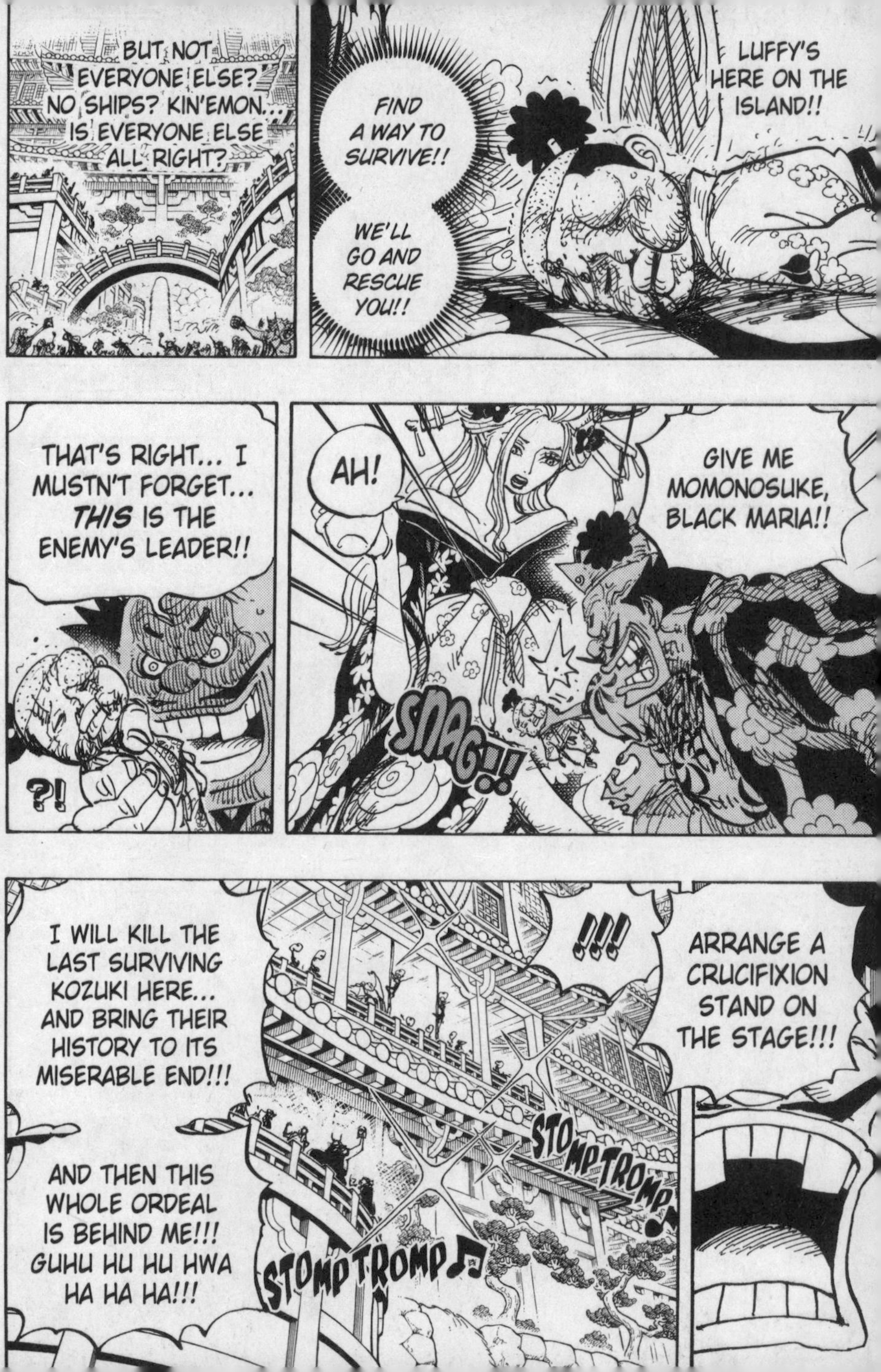

LUFFY'S HERE ON THE ISLAND!!
FIND A WAY TO SURVIVE!!
WE'LL GO AND RESCUE YOU!!
BUT NOT EVERYONE ELSE? NO SHIPS? KIN'EMON... IS EVERYONE ELSE ALL RIGHT?
GIVE ME MOMONOSUKE, BLACK MARIA!!
AH!
SNAG!!
THAT'S RIGHT... I MUSTN'T FORGET... *THIS* IS THE ENEMY'S LEADER!!
?!
ARRANGE A CRUCIFIXION STAND ON THE STAGE!!!
!!!
I WILL KILL THE LAST SURVIVING KOZUKI HERE... AND BRING THEIR HISTORY TO ITS MISERABLE END!!!
STOMP TROMP
AND THEN THIS WHOLE ORDEAL IS BEHIND ME!!! GUHU HU HU HWA HA HA HA!!!
STOMP TROMP♫

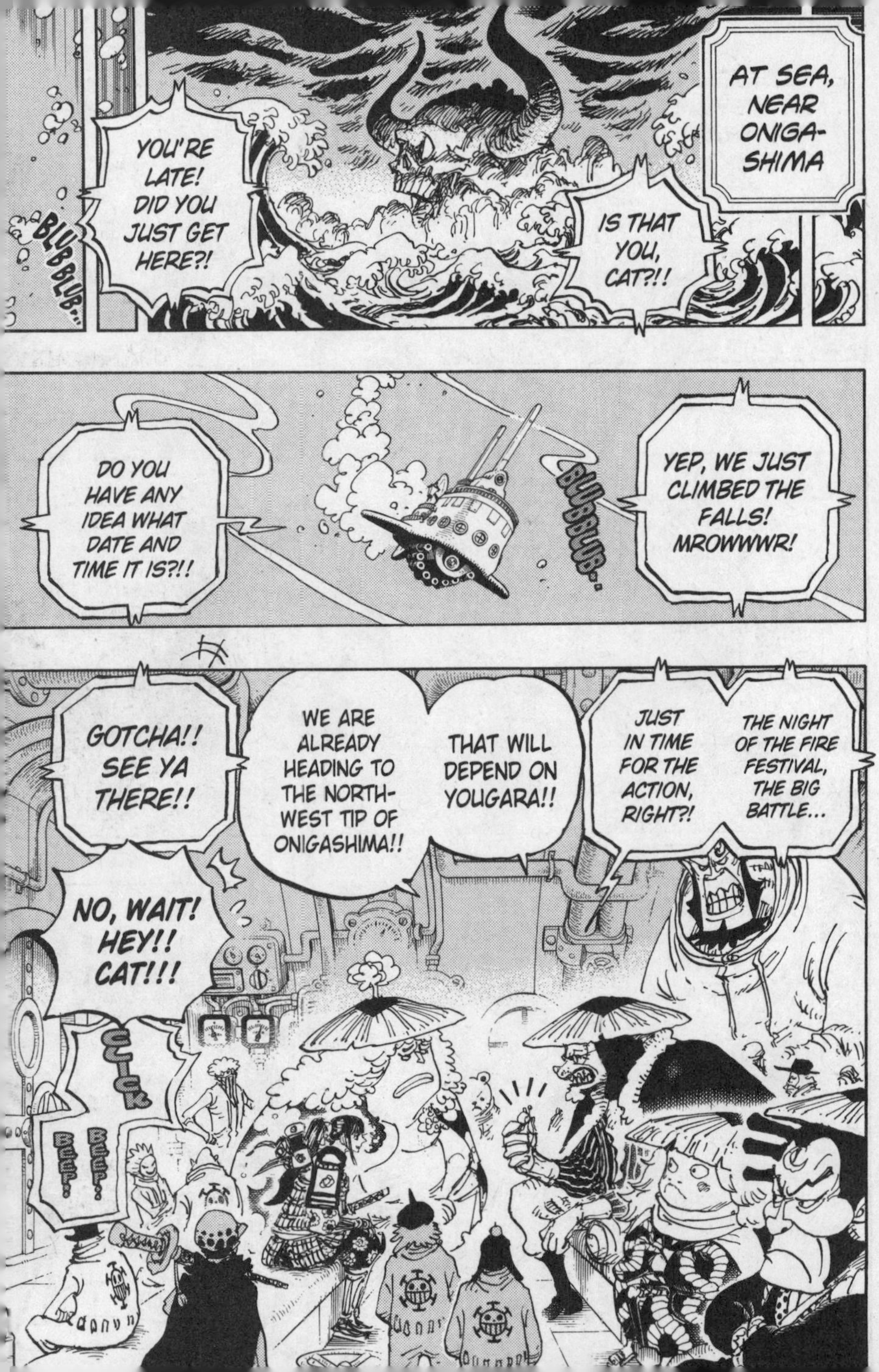
AT SEA, NEAR ONIGA-SHIMA
IS THAT YOU, CAT?!!
YOU'RE LATE! DID YOU JUST GET HERE?!
BLUB BLUB...
YEP, WE JUST CLIMBED THE FALLS! MROWWWR!
BLUBBLUB...
DO YOU HAVE ANY IDEA WHAT DATE AND TIME IT IS?!!
THE NIGHT OF THE FIRE FESTIVAL, THE BIG BATTLE...
JUST IN TIME FOR THE ACTION, RIGHT?!
THAT WILL DEPEND ON YOUGARA!!
WE ARE ALREADY HEADING TO THE NORTH-WEST TIP OF ONIGASHIMA!!
GOTCHA!! SEE YA THERE!!
NO, WAIT! HEY!! CAT!!!
CLICK
BEEP... BEEP...

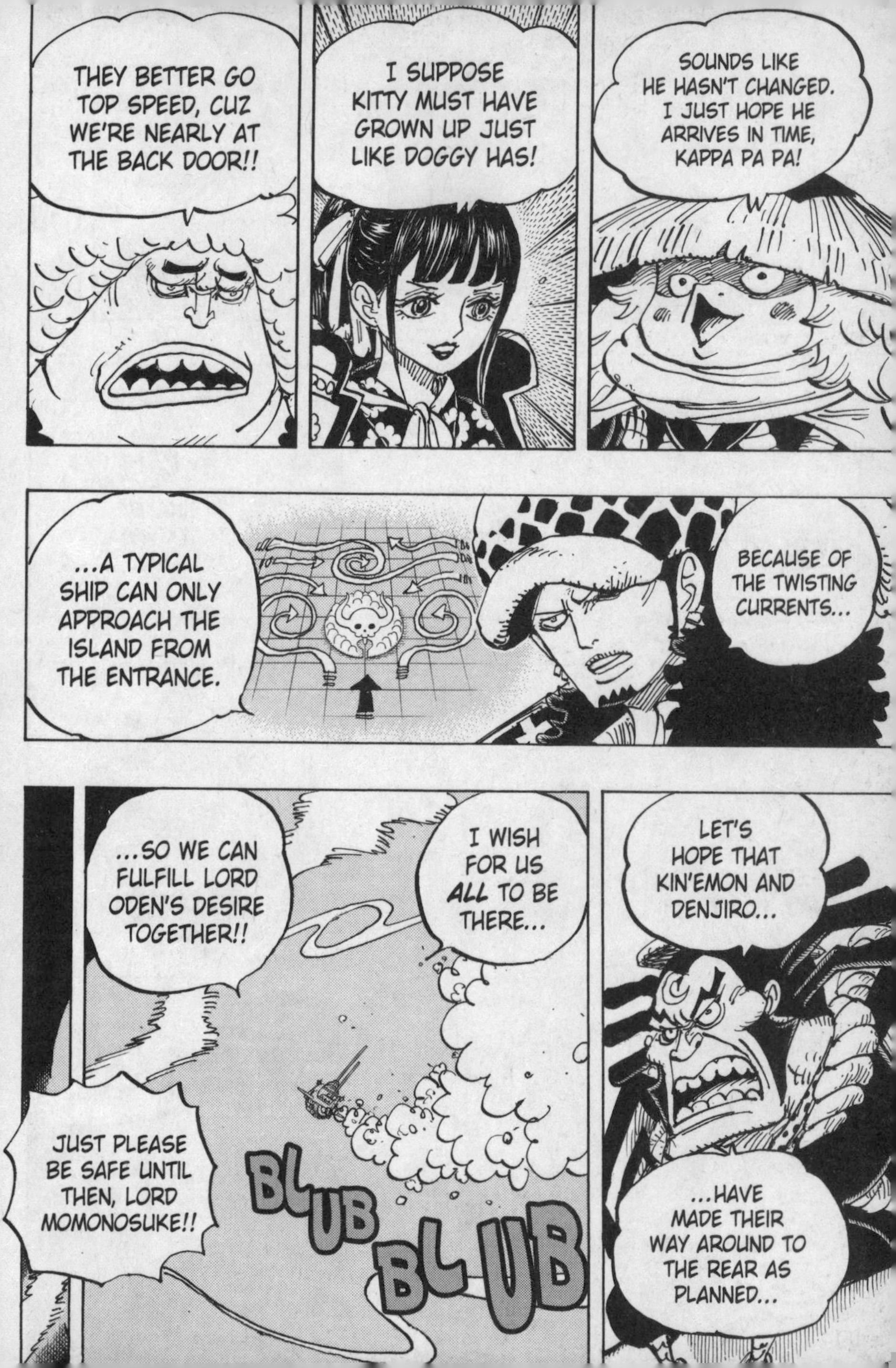
SOUNDS LIKE HE HASN'T CHANGED. I JUST HOPE HE ARRIVES IN TIME, KAPPA PA PA!
I SUPPOSE KITTY MUST HAVE GROWN UP JUST LIKE DOGGY HAS!
THEY BETTER GO TOP SPEED, CUZ WE'RE NEARLY AT THE BACK DOOR!!
BECAUSE OF THE TWISTING CURRENTS...
...A TYPICAL SHIP CAN ONLY APPROACH THE ISLAND FROM THE ENTRANCE.
LET'S HOPE THAT KIN'EMON AND DENJIRO...
...HAVE MADE THEIR WAY AROUND TO THE REAR AS PLANNED...
I WISH FOR US *ALL* TO BE THERE...
...SO WE CAN FULFILL LORD ODEN'S DESIRE TOGETHER!!
BLUB
BLUB
JUST PLEASE BE SAFE UNTIL THEN, LORD MOMONOSUKE!!

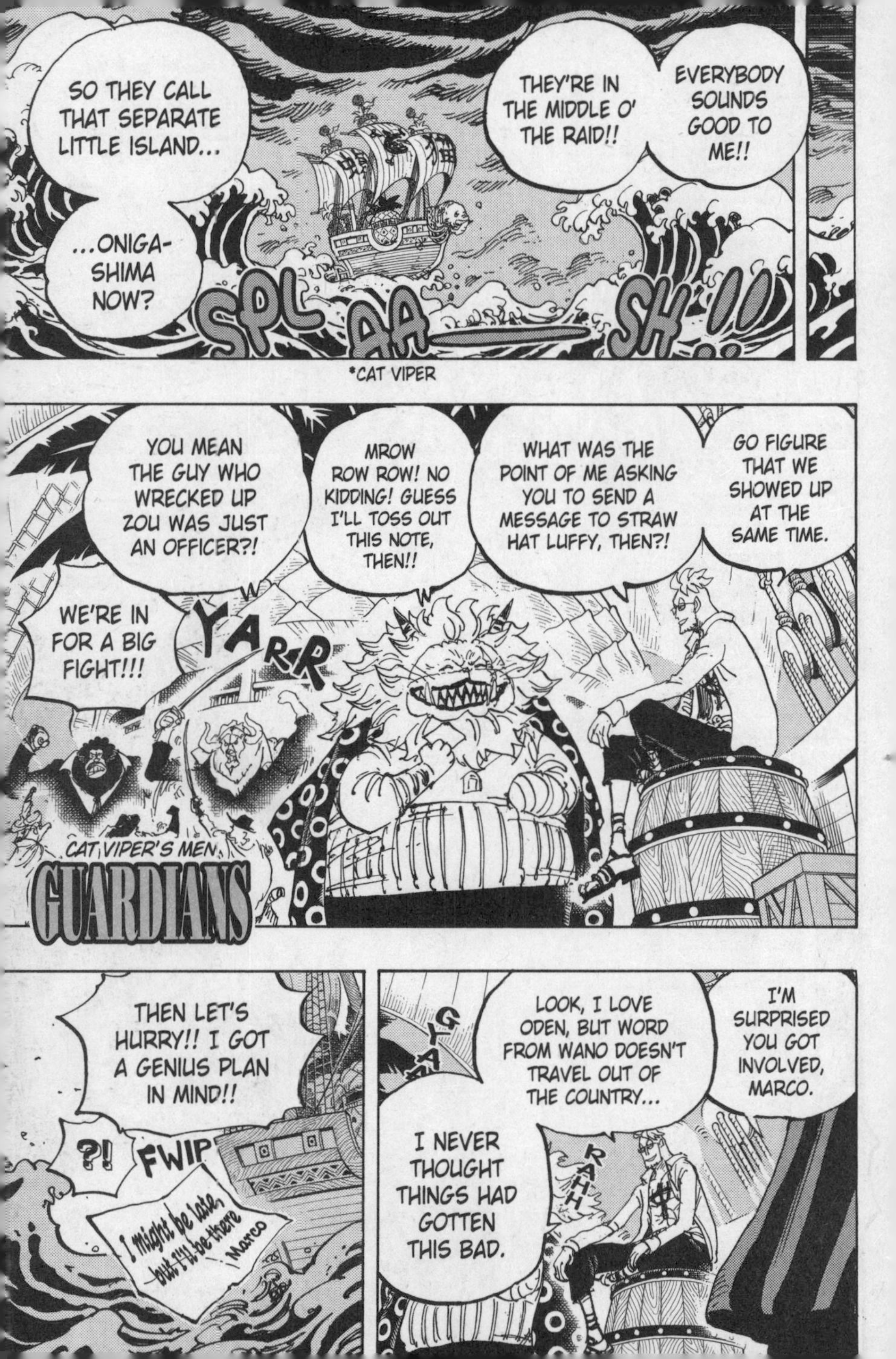
EVERYBODY SOUNDS GOOD TO ME!!
THEY'RE IN THE MIDDLE O' THE RAID!!
SO THEY CALL THAT SEPARATE LITTLE ISLAND...
...ONIGA-SHIMA NOW?
SPLAASH!!
*CAT VIPER
GO FIGURE THAT WE SHOWED UP AT THE SAME TIME.
WHAT WAS THE POINT OF ME ASKING YOU TO SEND A MESSAGE TO STRAW HAT LUFFY, THEN?!
MROW ROW ROW! NO KIDDING! GUESS I'LL TOSS OUT THIS NOTE, THEN!!
YOU MEAN THE GUY WHO WRECKED UP ZOU WAS JUST AN OFFICER?!
YARRR
WE'RE IN FOR A BIG FIGHT!!!
CAT VIPER'S MEN
GUARDIANS
I'M SURPRISED YOU GOT INVOLVED, MARCO.
LOOK, I LOVE ODEN, BUT WORD FROM WANO DOESN'T TRAVEL OUT OF THE COUNTRY...
GYAA
RAHH
I NEVER THOUGHT THINGS HAD GOTTEN THIS BAD.
THEN LET'S HURRY!! I GOT A GENIUS PLAN IN MIND!!
?!
FWIP
I might be late, but I'll be there
Marco

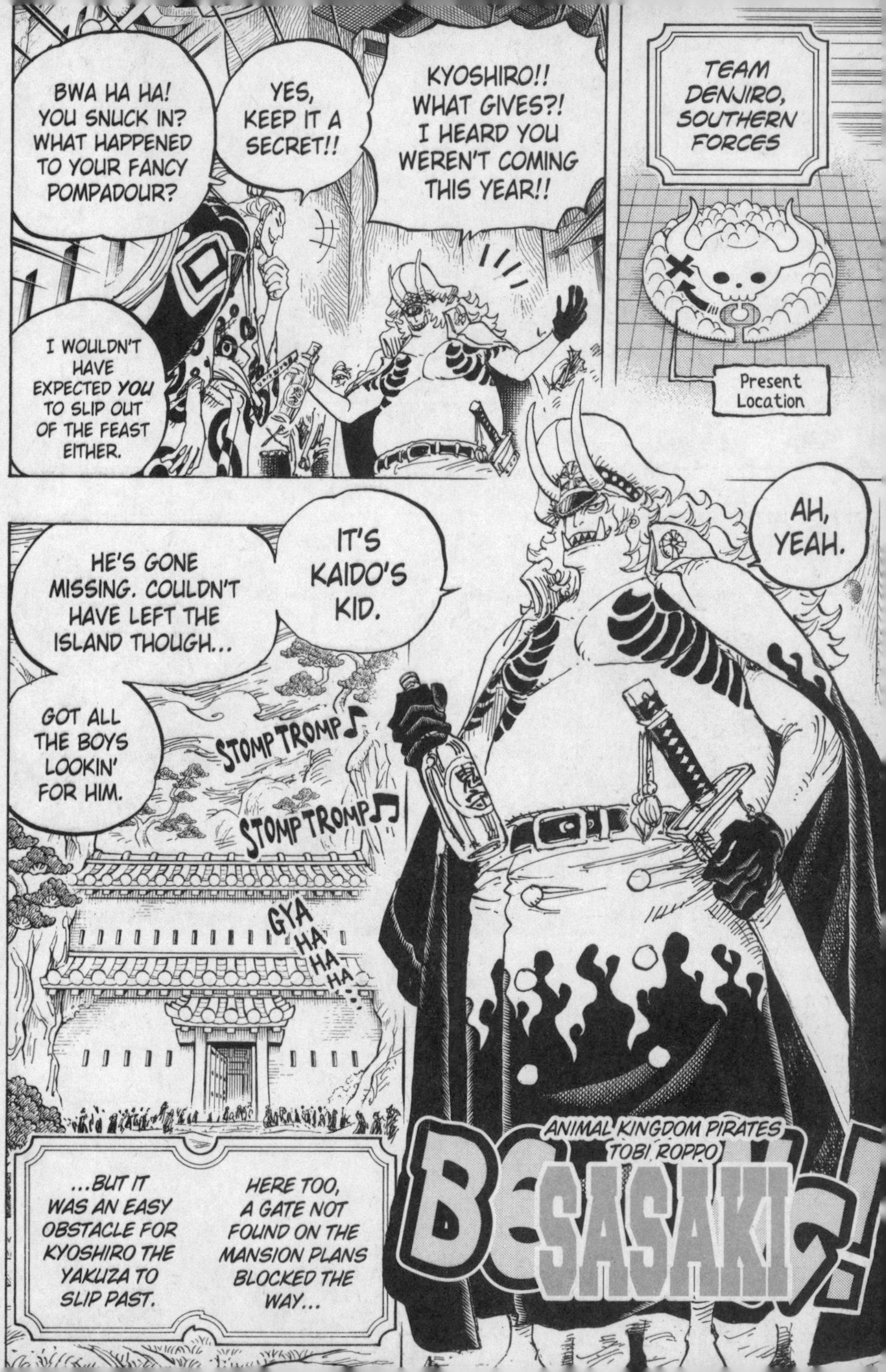
TEAM DENJIRO, SOUTHERN FORCES
Present Location
KYOSHIRO!! WHAT GIVES?! I HEARD YOU WEREN'T COMING THIS YEAR!!
YES, KEEP IT A SECRET!!
BWA HA HA! YOU SNUCK IN? WHAT HAPPENED TO YOUR FANCY POMPADOUR?
I WOULDN'T HAVE EXPECTED *YOU* TO SLIP OUT OF THE FEAST EITHER.
AH, YEAH.
IT'S KAIDO'S KID.
HE'S GONE MISSING. COULDN'T HAVE LEFT THE ISLAND THOUGH...
GOT ALL THE BOYS LOOKIN' FOR HIM.
STOMP TROMP
STOMP TROMP
GYA HA HA HA
ANIMAL KINGDOM PIRATES TOBI ROPPO
SASAKI
HERE TOO, A GATE NOT FOUND ON THE MANSION PLANS BLOCKED THE WAY...
...BUT IT WAS AN EASY OBSTACLE FOR KYOSHIRO THE YAKUZA TO SLIP PAST.

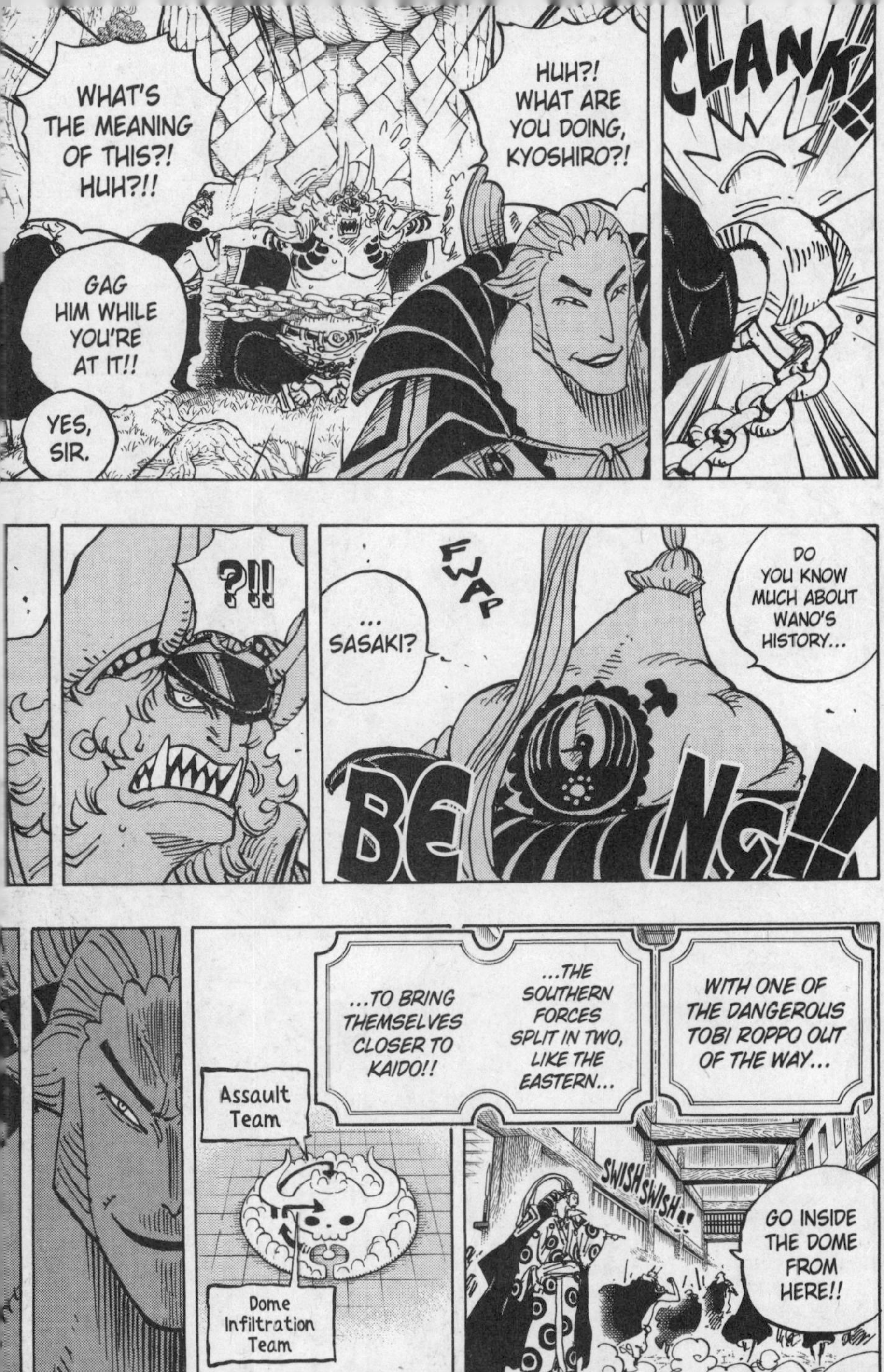
CLANK!!
HUH?! WHAT ARE YOU DOING, KYOSHIRO?!
WHAT'S THE MEANING OF THIS?! HUH?!!
GAG HIM WHILE YOU'RE AT IT!!
YES, SIR.
DO YOU KNOW MUCH ABOUT WANO'S HISTORY...
FWAP
... SASAKI?
BE
NG!!
?!!
WITH ONE OF THE DANGEROUS TOBI ROPPO OUT OF THE WAY...
...THE SOUTHERN FORCES SPLIT IN TWO, LIKE THE EASTERN...
...TO BRING THEMSELVES CLOSER TO KAIDO!!
SWISH SWISH!!
GO INSIDE THE DOME FROM HERE!!
Assault Team
Dome Infiltration Team

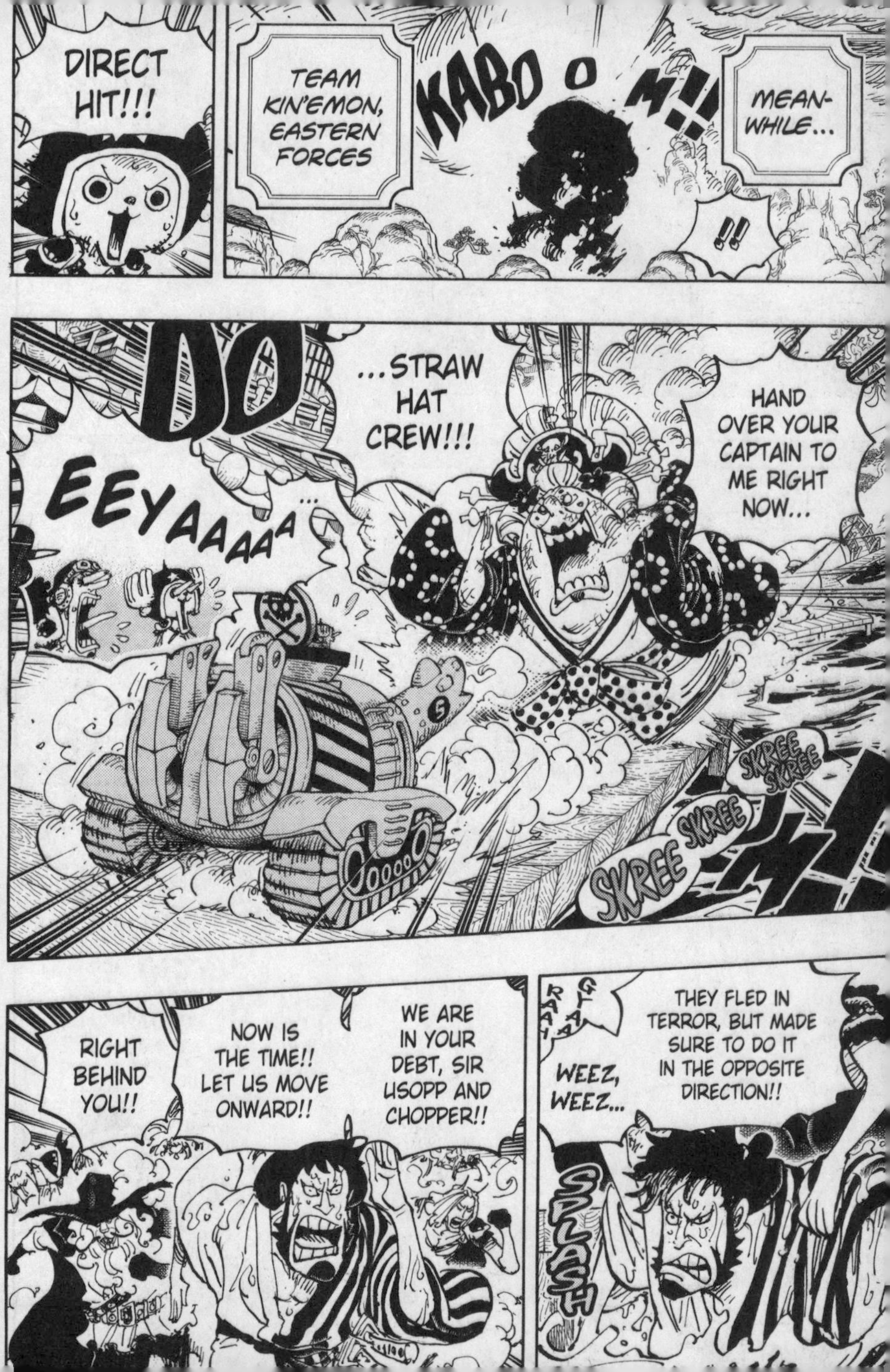
MEAN-WHILE...
!!
KABOOM!!
TEAM KIN'EMON, EASTERN FORCES
DIRECT HIT!!!
HAND OVER YOUR CAPTAIN TO ME RIGHT NOW...
...STRAW HAT CREW!!!
EEYAAAAA...
SKREE SKREE
SKREE SKREE
SKREE
THEY FLED IN TERROR, BUT MADE SURE TO DO IT IN THE OPPOSITE DIRECTION!!
WEEZ, WEEZ...
SPLASH
WE ARE IN YOUR DEBT, SIR USOPP AND CHOPPER!!
NOW IS THE TIME!! LET US MOVE ONWARD!!
RIGHT BEHIND YOU!!

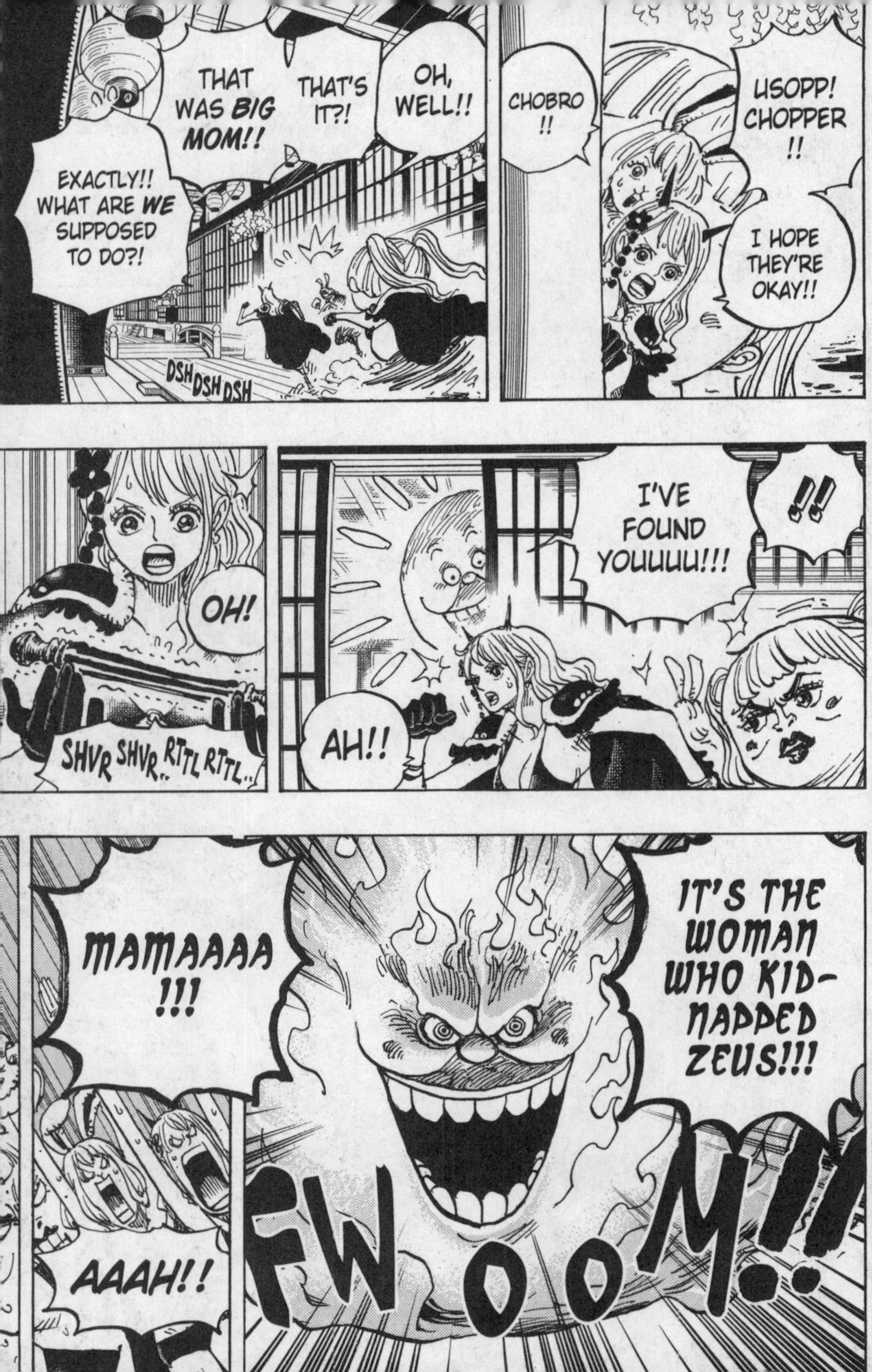
USOPP! CHOPPER !!
CHOBRO !!
I HOPE THEY'RE OKAY!!
OH, WELL!!
THAT'S IT?!
THAT WAS BIG MOM!!
EXACTLY!! WHAT ARE WE SUPPOSED TO DO?!
DSH DSH DSH
!!
I'VE FOUND YOUUUU!!!
AH!!
OH!
SHVR SHVR.. RTTL RTTL..
IT'S THE WOMAN WHO KID-NAPPED ZEUS!!!
FWOOM!!
MAMAAAA !!!
AAAH!!

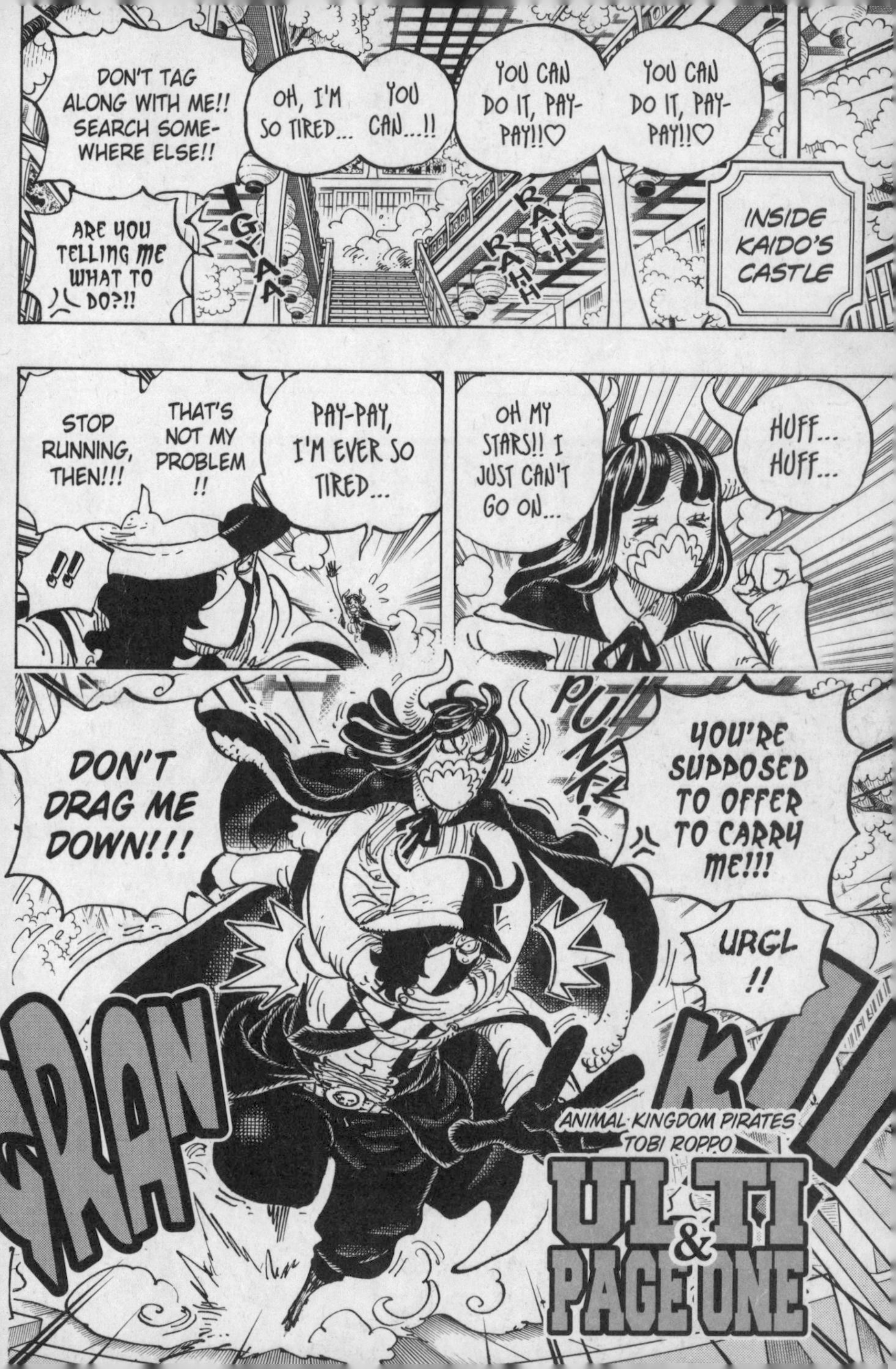
INSIDE KAIDO'S CASTLE
YOU CAN DO IT, PAY-PAY!!♡
YOU CAN DO IT, PAY-PAY!!♡
RAHH RAHH
OH, I'M SO TIRED...
YOU CAN...!!
GYAA
DON'T TAG ALONG WITH ME!! SEARCH SOME-WHERE ELSE!!
ARE YOU TELLING ME WHAT TO DO?!!
HUFF... HUFF...
OH MY STARS!! I JUST CAN'T GO ON...
PAY-PAY, I'M EVER SO TIRED...
THAT'S NOT MY PROBLEM !!
STOP RUNNING, THEN!!!
!!
YOU'RE SUPPOSED TO OFFER TO CARRY ME!!!
PUNK!
DON'T DRAG ME DOWN!!!
URGL !!
ANIMAL KINGDOM PIRATES TOBI ROPPO
ULTI & PAGE ONE

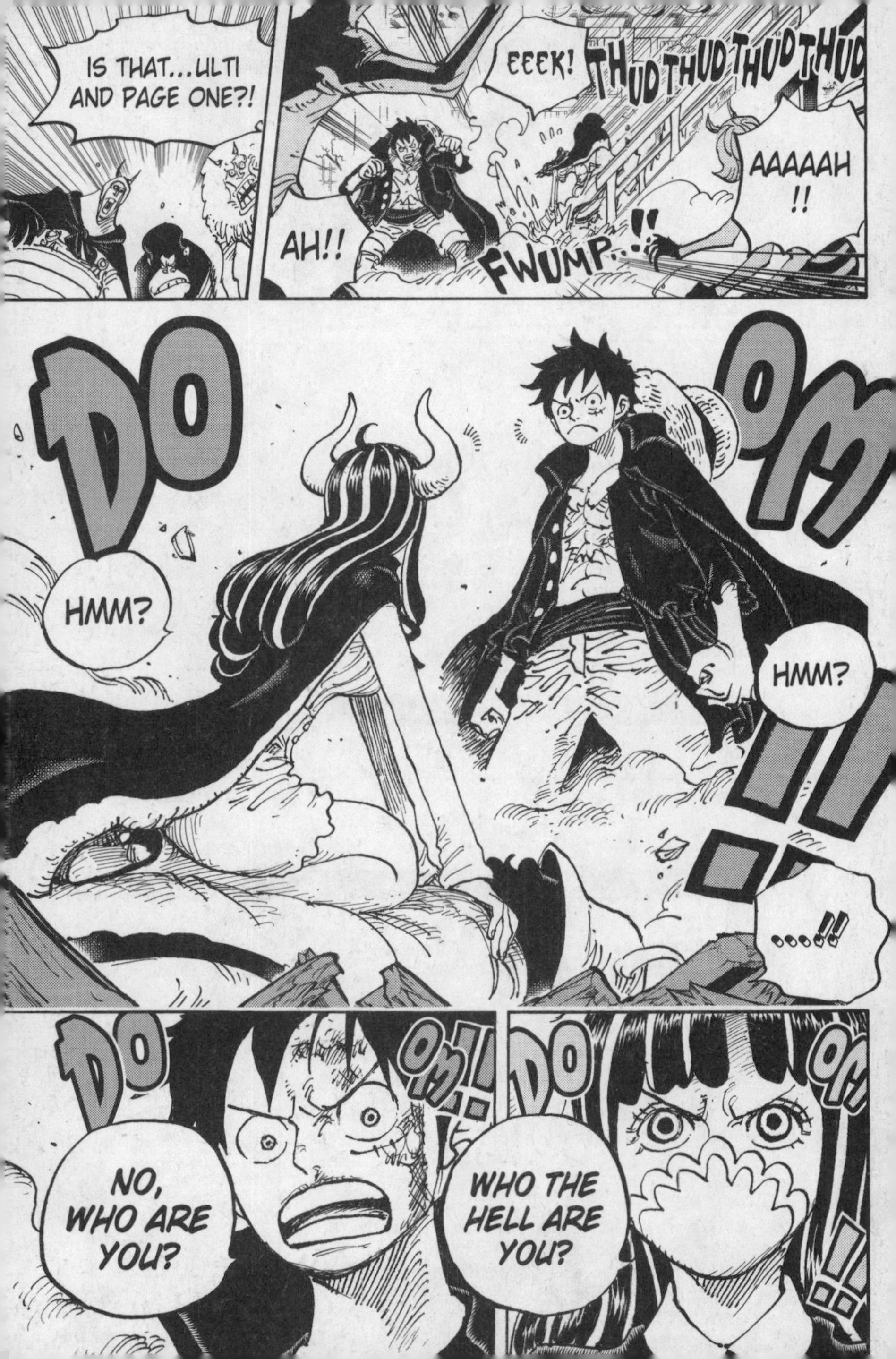
THUD THUD THUD THUD
AAAAAH !!
EEEK!
FWUMP..!!
AH!!
IS THAT...ULTI AND PAGE ONE?!
DOOM!!
HMM?
....!!
HMM?
DOOM!!
WHO THE HELL ARE YOU?
DOOM!!
NO, WHO ARE YOU?

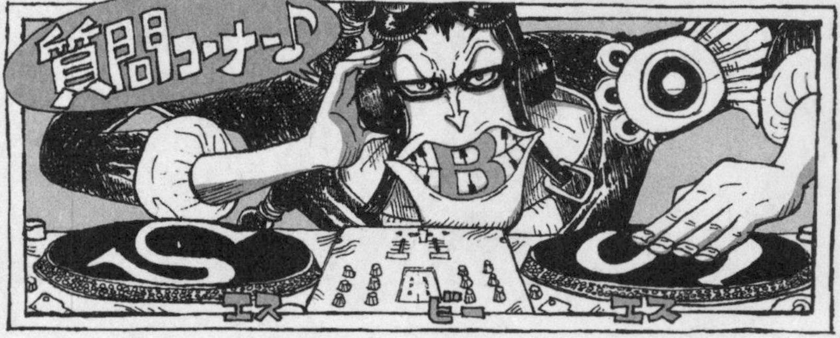
質問コーナー♪
エス
ビー
エス

(DJ Boss, Tochigi)

Q: Nice to meet you, Odacchi!! The full lineup of the Tobi Roppo as introduced in chapter 978 is so cool, I just had to write you a letter! Like I'm sure everyone else is asking, I want to know their height, age and favorite food!!

--Haruki Genia

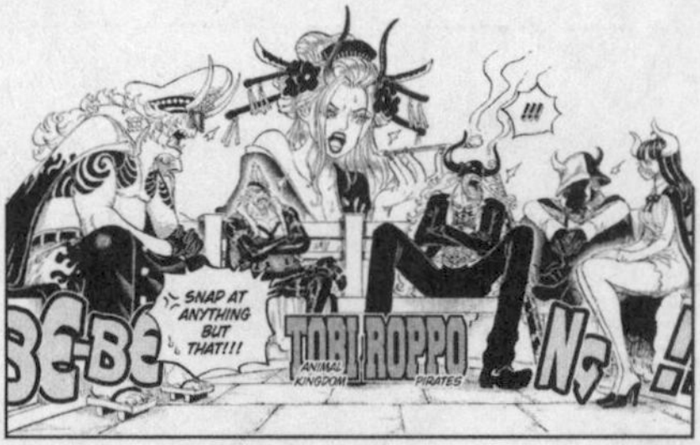
!!!
SNAP AT ANYTHING BUT THAT!!!
BE-BE
TOBI ROPPO
ANIMAL KINGDOM
PIRATES
NG
!!

A: Ah, all right. People really seem to love the Tobi Roppo. Why are they so popular? Save some compliments for Master Queen too!!

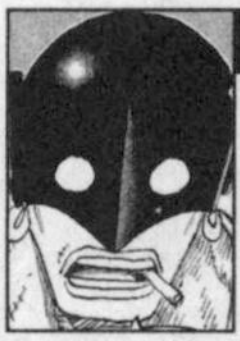

Who's-Who
11'0"
38 years old
Crab paella

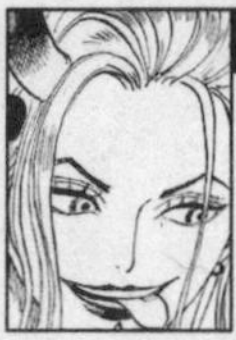

Black Maria
26'11"
29 years old
Glazed rice dumplings

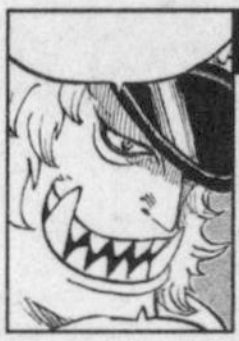

Sasaki
10'5"
34 years old
Asparagus

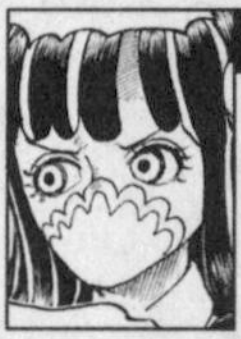

Ulti
5'8"
22 years old
Tornado potato

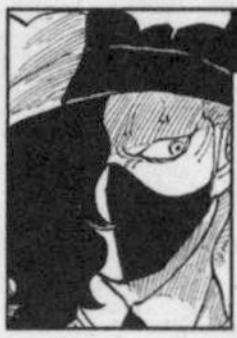

Page One
5'7"
20 years old
Nachos

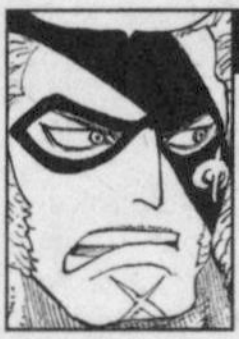

X. (Diez) Drake
7'8"
33 years old
Chicken and rice

Q: In volume 96, you introduced the main members of the Roger Pirates, but the character you called "Nozudon" was previously introduced in the data book Blue Deep under the name of "Seagull," which is what I've known him as... What am I supposed to do now?

--Ohta, Captain of the Toppi Fleet

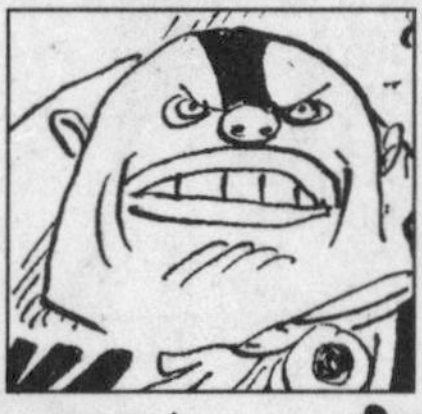

A: Huh?! ...Oh!!
Ahhh... Him? Ha hah, yes, yes, I see. You mean Seagull Ganz Nozudon? That's a good question. Well... Y-you can call him whatever name you want... Or you could not bother to memorize his name at all... It's up to you...

Chapter 983: THUNDER

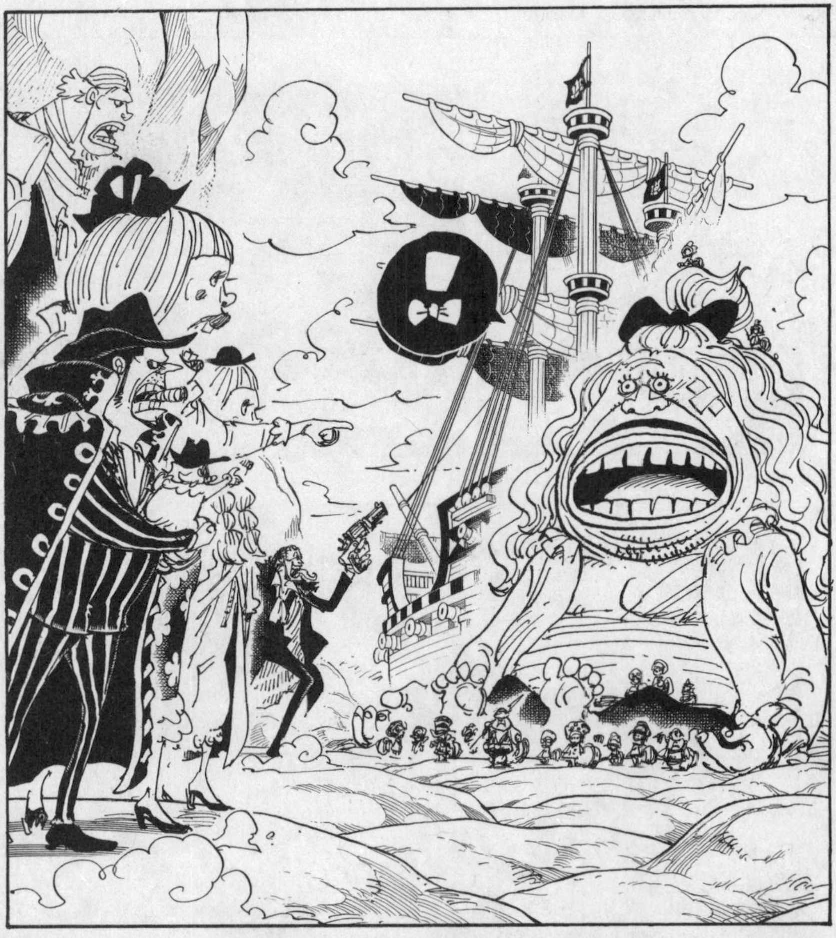

GANG BEGE'S OH MY FAMILY
VOL. 29: "IT'S THAT ONE GUY FROM THE PORT"

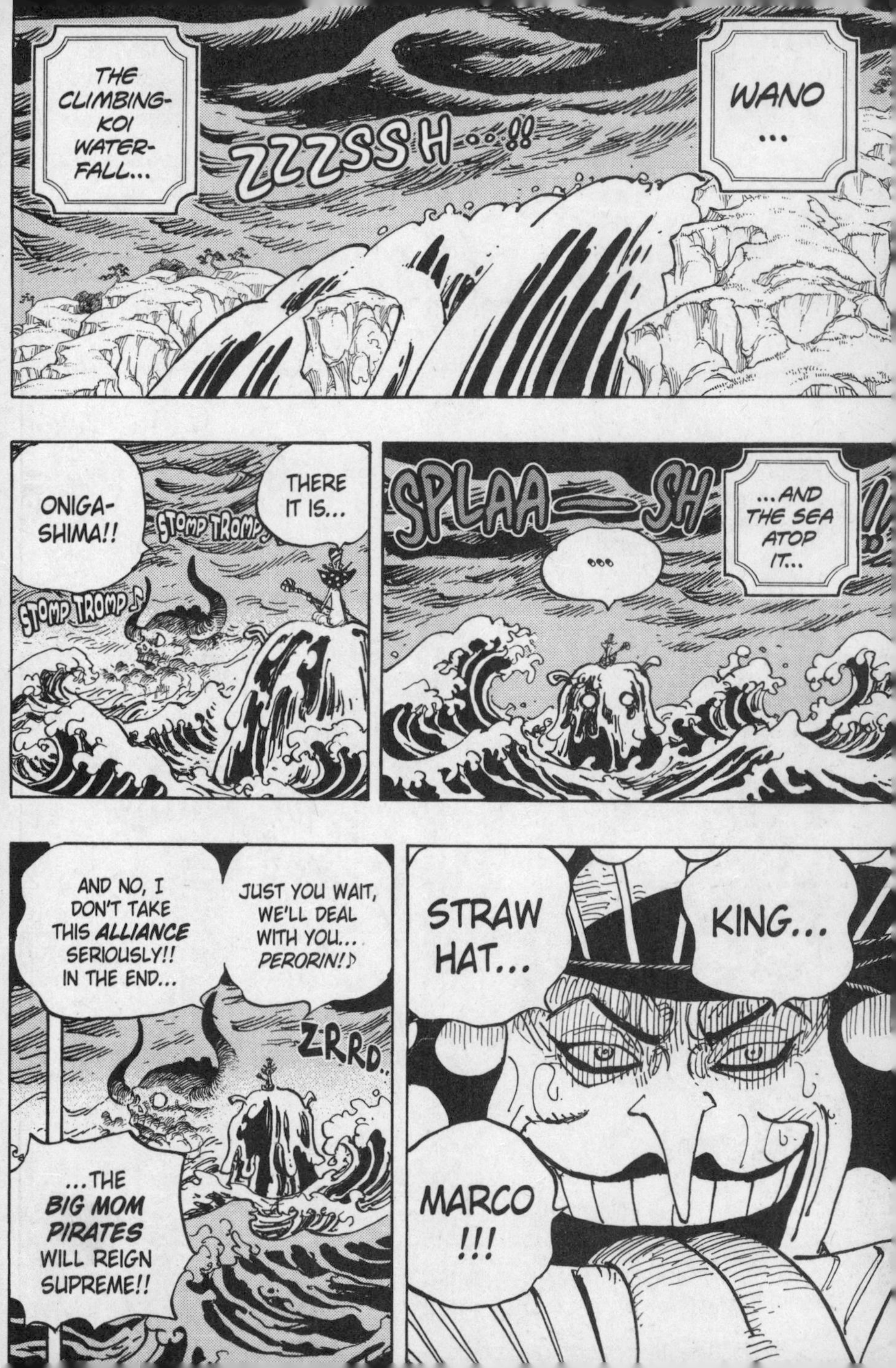
WANO ...
ZZZSSH...!!
THE CLIMBING-KOI WATERFALL...
...AND THE SEA ATOP IT...
SPLAA—SH
...
THERE IT IS...
ONIGA-SHIMA!!
STOMP TROMP
STOMP TROMP♪
KING...
STRAW HAT...
MARCO!!!
JUST YOU WAIT, WE'LL DEAL WITH YOU... PERORIN!♪
AND NO, I DON'T TAKE THIS ALLIANCE SERIOUSLY!! IN THE END...
ZRRD..
...THE BIG MOM PIRATES WILL REIGN SUPREME!!

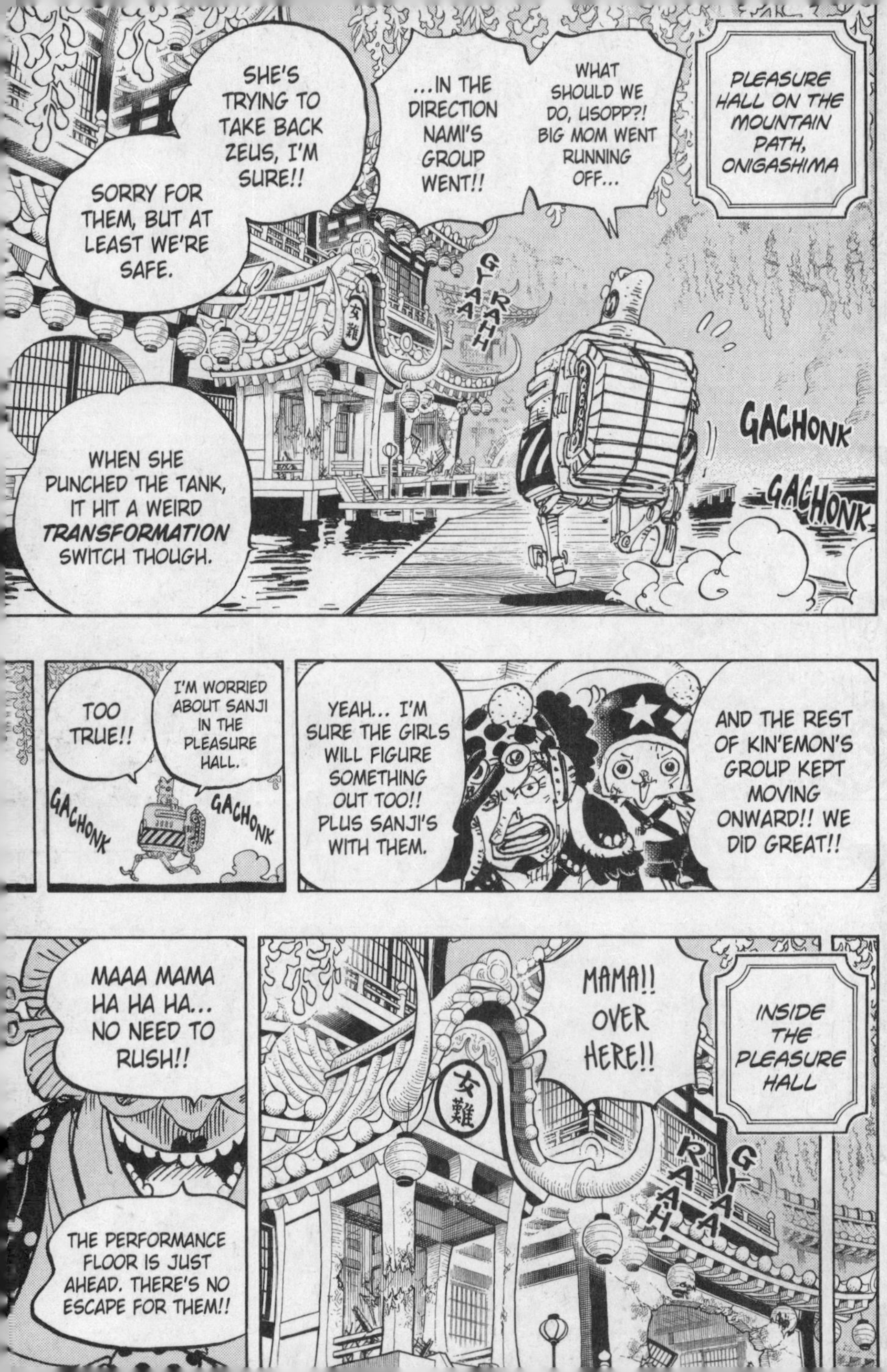
PLEASURE HALL ON THE MOUNTAIN PATH, ONIGASHIMA
WHAT SHOULD WE DO, USOPP?! BIG MOM WENT RUNNING OFF...
...IN THE DIRECTION NAMI'S GROUP WENT!!
SHE'S TRYING TO TAKE BACK ZEUS, I'M SURE!!
SORRY FOR THEM, BUT AT LEAST WE'RE SAFE.
女難
GYAA RAHH
GACHONK
GACHONK
WHEN SHE PUNCHED THE TANK, IT HIT A WEIRD *TRANSFORMATION* SWITCH THOUGH.
AND THE REST OF KIN'EMON'S GROUP KEPT MOVING ONWARD!! WE DID GREAT!!
YEAH... I'M SURE THE GIRLS WILL FIGURE SOMETHING OUT TOO!! PLUS SANJI'S WITH THEM.
I'M WORRIED ABOUT SANJI IN THE PLEASURE HALL.
TOO TRUE!!
GACHONK
GACHONK
INSIDE THE PLEASURE HALL
MAMA!! OVER HERE!!
GYAA RAAH
女難
MAAA MAMA HA HA HA... NO NEED TO RUSH!!
THE PERFORMANCE FLOOR IS JUST AHEAD. THERE'S NO ESCAPE FOR THEM!!

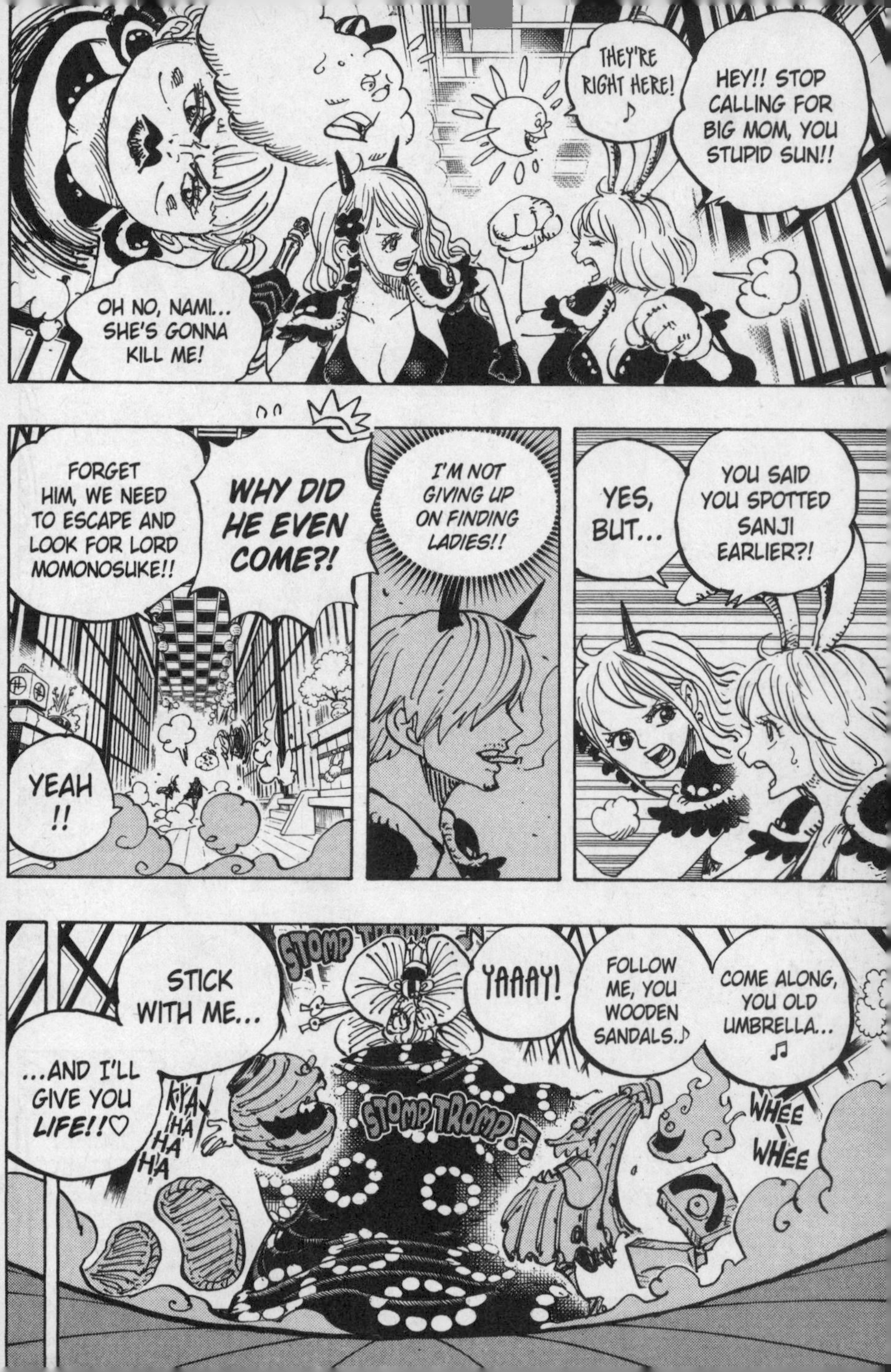
HEY!! STOP CALLING FOR BIG MOM, YOU STUPID SUN!!
THEY'RE RIGHT HERE! ♪
OH NO, NAMI... SHE'S GONNA KILL ME!
YOU SAID YOU SPOTTED SANJI EARLIER?!
YES, BUT...
I'M NOT GIVING UP ON FINDING LADIES!!
WHY DID HE EVEN COME?!
FORGET HIM, WE NEED TO ESCAPE AND LOOK FOR LORD MOMONOSUKE!!
YEAH!!
COME ALONG, YOU OLD UMBRELLA... ♫
FOLLOW ME, YOU WOODEN SANDALS.♪
YAAAY!
STOMP
WHEE WHEE
STOMP TROMP♫
STICK WITH ME...
...AND I'LL GIVE YOU LIFE!!♡
KYA HA HA HA

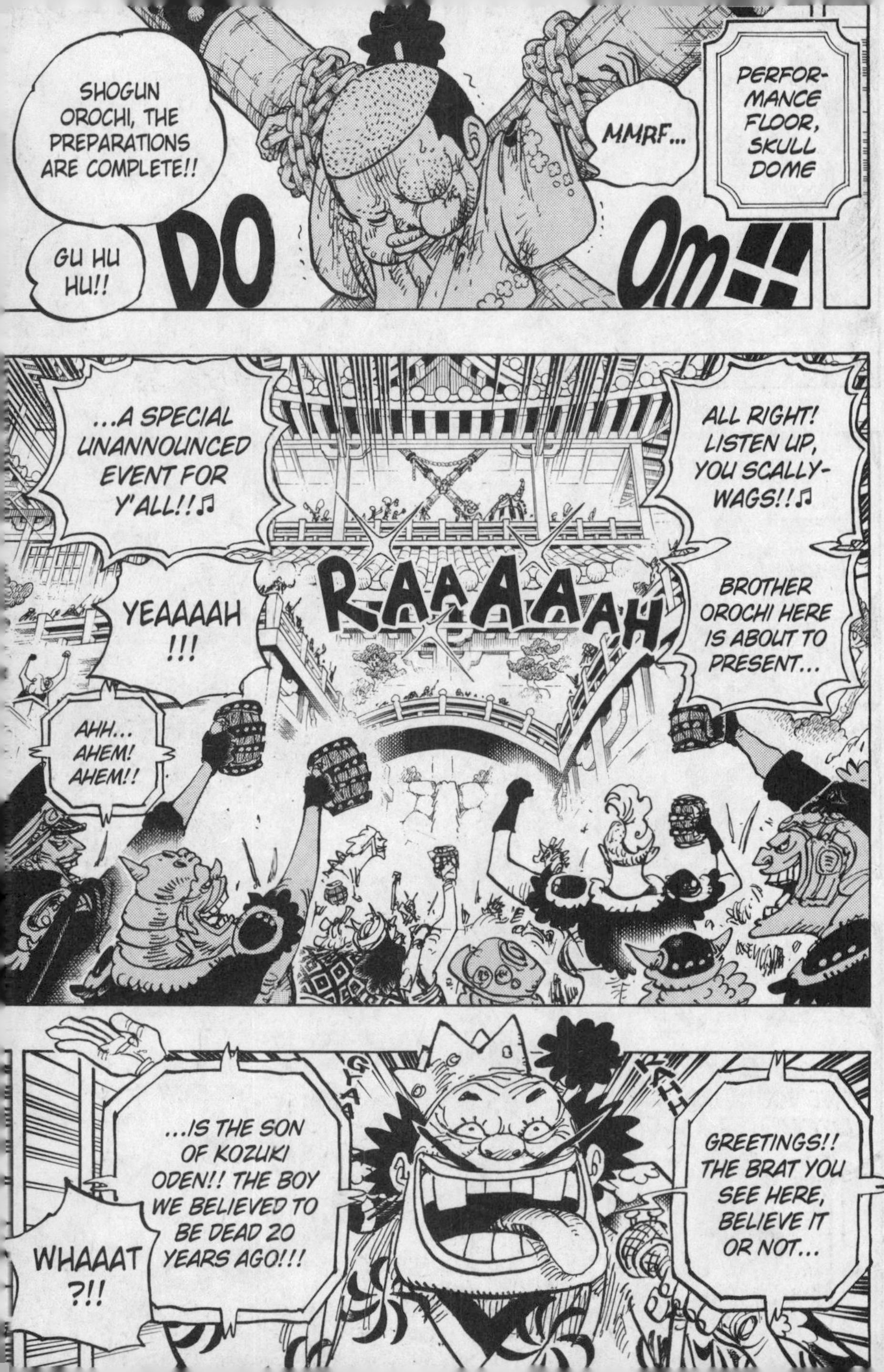
PERFOR-
MANCE
FLOOR,
SKULL
DOME
MMRF...
SHOGUN OROCHI, THE PREPARATIONS ARE COMPLETE!!
GU HU HU!!
DOOM!!
ALL RIGHT! LISTEN UP, YOU SCALLY-WAGS!!♫
BROTHER OROCHI HERE IS ABOUT TO PRESENT...
...A SPECIAL UNANNOUNCED EVENT FOR Y'ALL!!♫
RAAAAAH
YEAAAAH!!!
AHH... AHEM! AHEM!!
GREETINGS!! THE BRAT YOU SEE HERE, BELIEVE IT OR NOT...
...IS THE SON OF KOZUKI ODEN!! THE BOY WE BELIEVED TO BE DEAD 20 YEARS AGO!!!
WHAAAT?!!

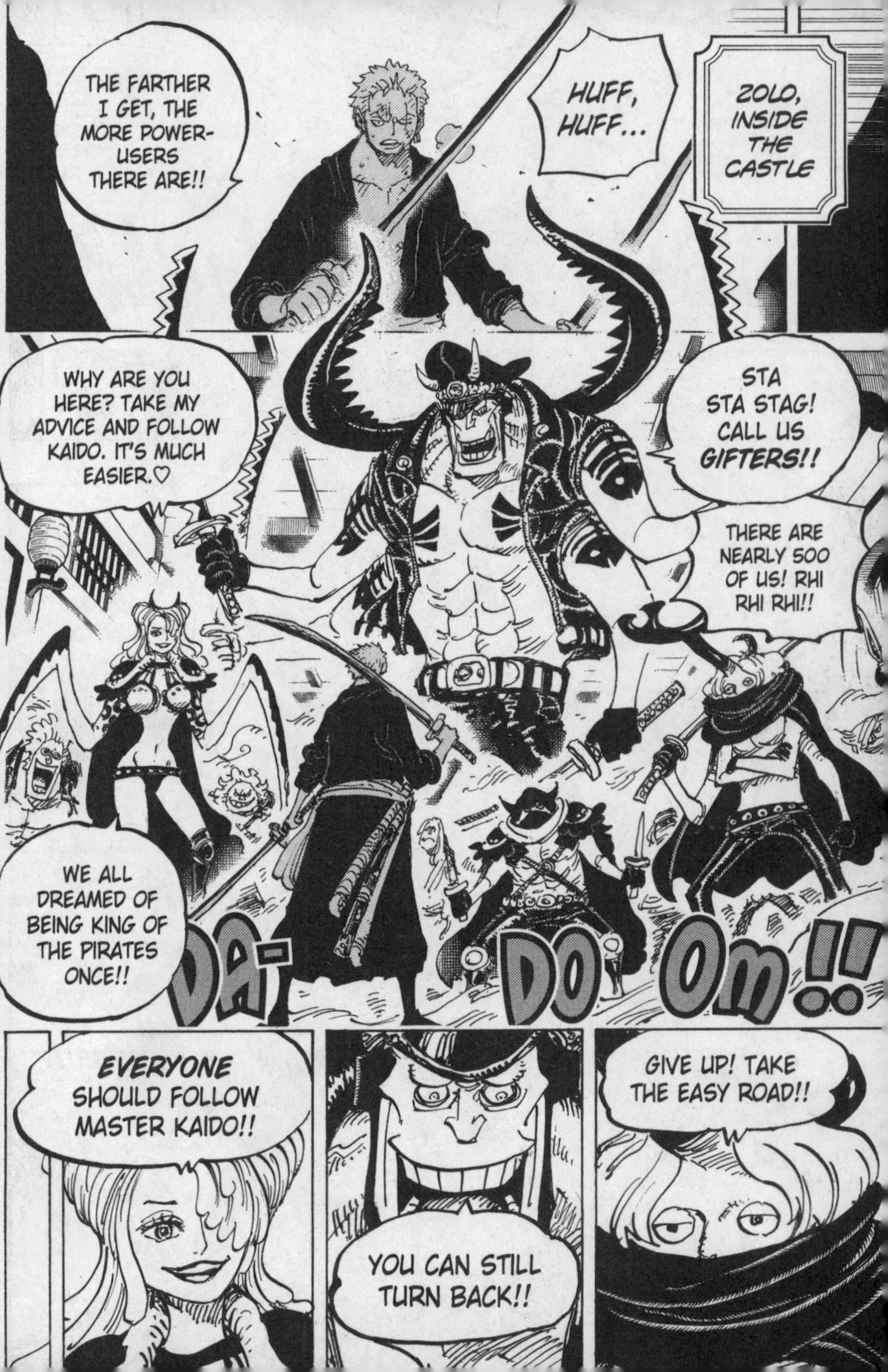

ZOLO, INSIDE THE CASTLE
HUFF, HUFF...
THE FARTHER I GET, THE MORE POWER-USERS THERE ARE!!
STA STA STAG! CALL US *GIFTERS!!*
WHY ARE YOU HERE? TAKE MY ADVICE AND FOLLOW KAIDO. IT'S MUCH EASIER.♡
THERE ARE NEARLY 500 OF US! RHI RHI RHI!!
WE ALL DREAMED OF BEING KING OF THE PIRATES ONCE!!
DA-DO-OM!!
GIVE UP! TAKE THE EASY ROAD!!
YOU CAN STILL TURN BACK!!
EVERYONE SHOULD FOLLOW MASTER KAIDO!!

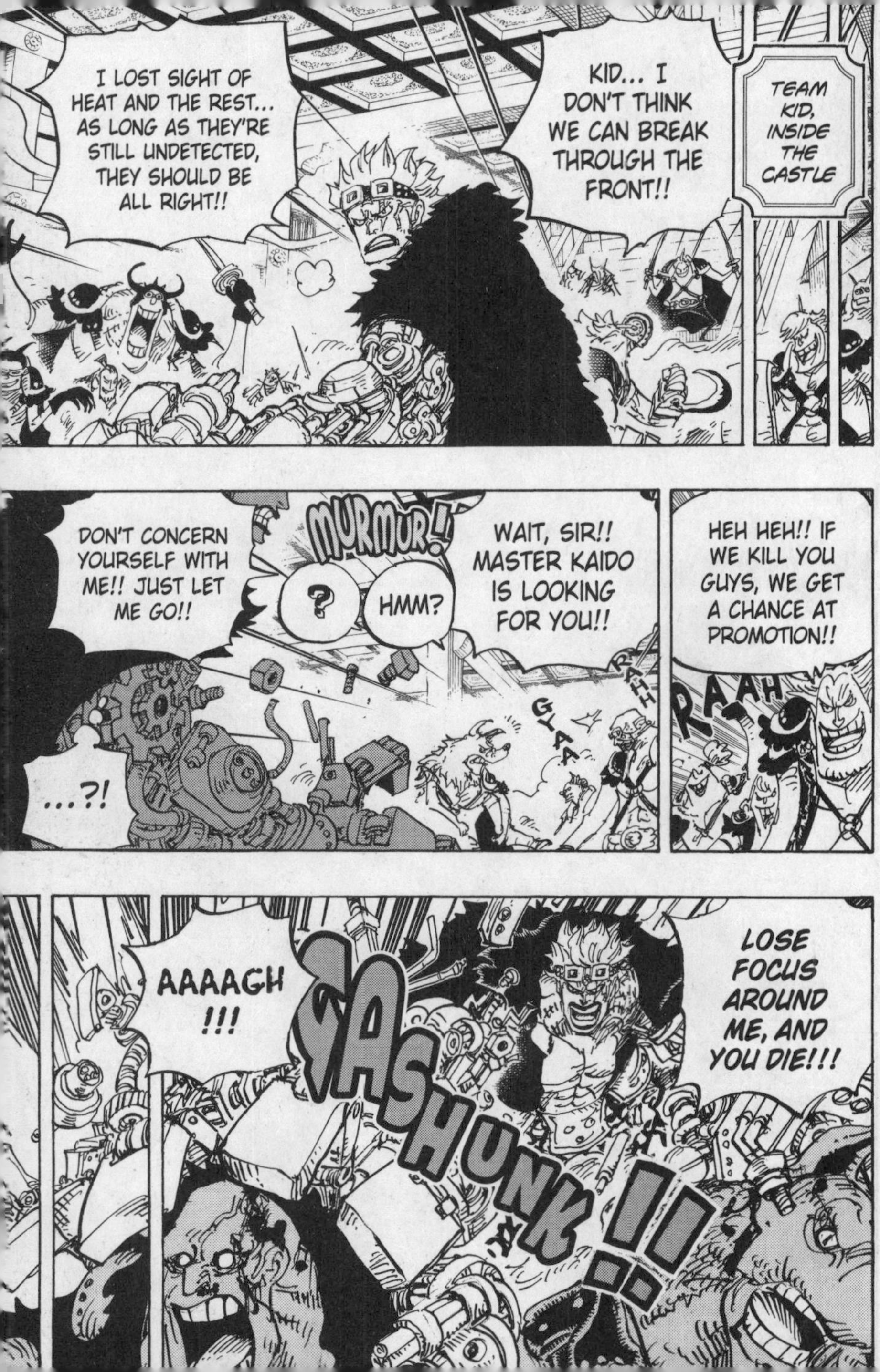
TEAM KID, INSIDE THE CASTLE
KID... I DON'T THINK WE CAN BREAK THROUGH THE FRONT!!
I LOST SIGHT OF HEAT AND THE REST... AS LONG AS THEY'RE STILL UNDETECTED, THEY SHOULD BE ALL RIGHT!!
HEH HEH!! IF WE KILL YOU GUYS, WE GET A CHANCE AT PROMOTION!!
RAAH
WAIT, SIR!! MASTER KAIDO IS LOOKING FOR YOU!!
RAHH
GYAA
HMM?
?
MURMUR!
DON'T CONCERN YOURSELF WITH ME!! JUST LET ME GO!!
...?!
LOSE FOCUS AROUND ME, AND YOU DIE!!!
KASHUNK!!
AAAAGH!!!

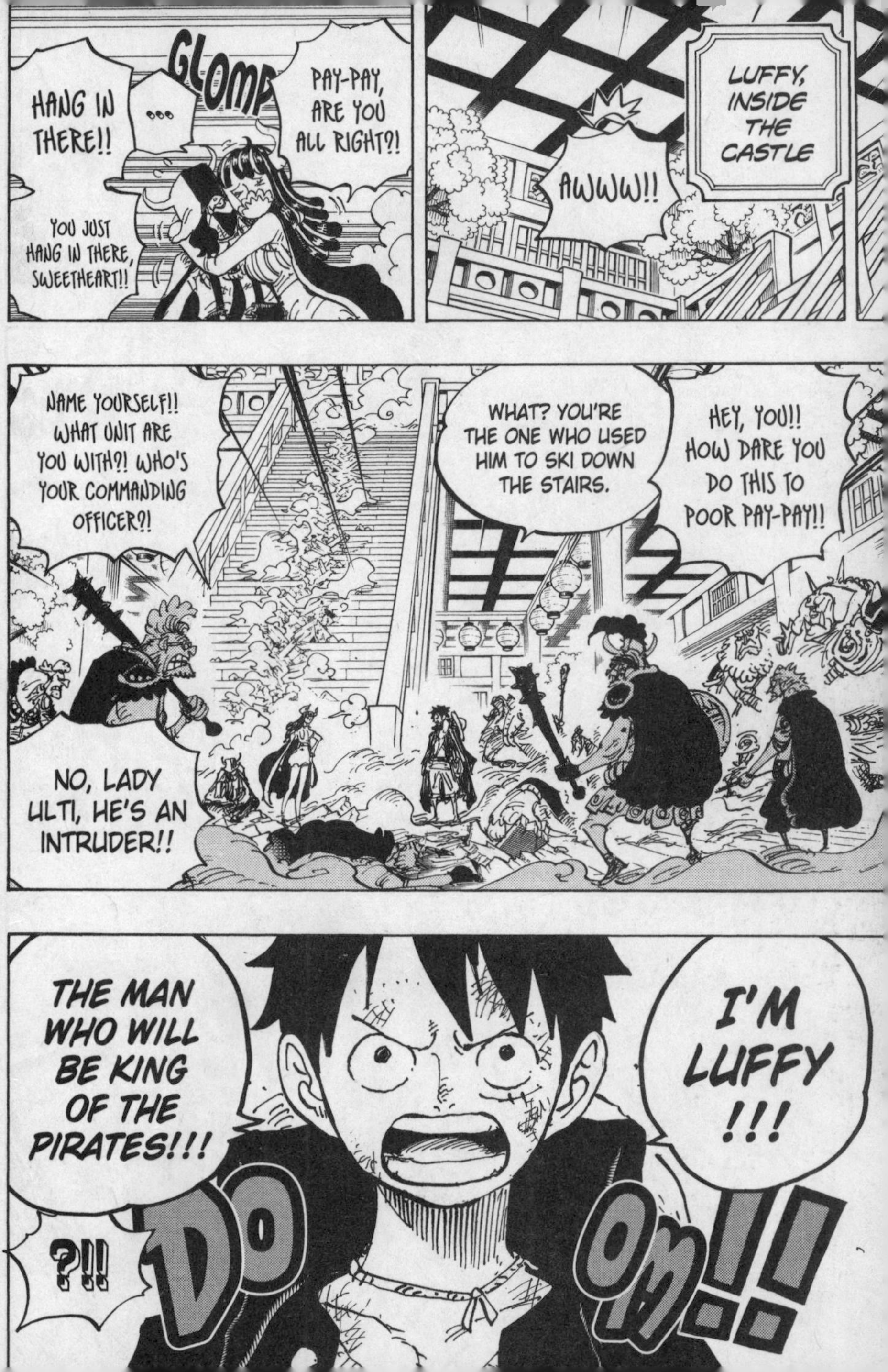
LUFFY, INSIDE THE CASTLE
AWWW!!
PAY-PAY, ARE YOU ALL RIGHT?!
GLOMP
...
HANG IN THERE!!
YOU JUST HANG IN THERE, SWEETHEART!!
HEY, YOU!! HOW DARE YOU DO THIS TO POOR PAY-PAY!!
WHAT? YOU'RE THE ONE WHO USED HIM TO SKI DOWN THE STAIRS.
NAME YOURSELF!! WHAT UNIT ARE YOU WITH?! WHO'S YOUR COMMANDING OFFICER?!
NO, LADY ULTI, HE'S AN INTRUDER!!
I'M LUFFY!!!
THE MAN WHO WILL BE KING OF THE PIRATES!!!
DOOM!!
?!!

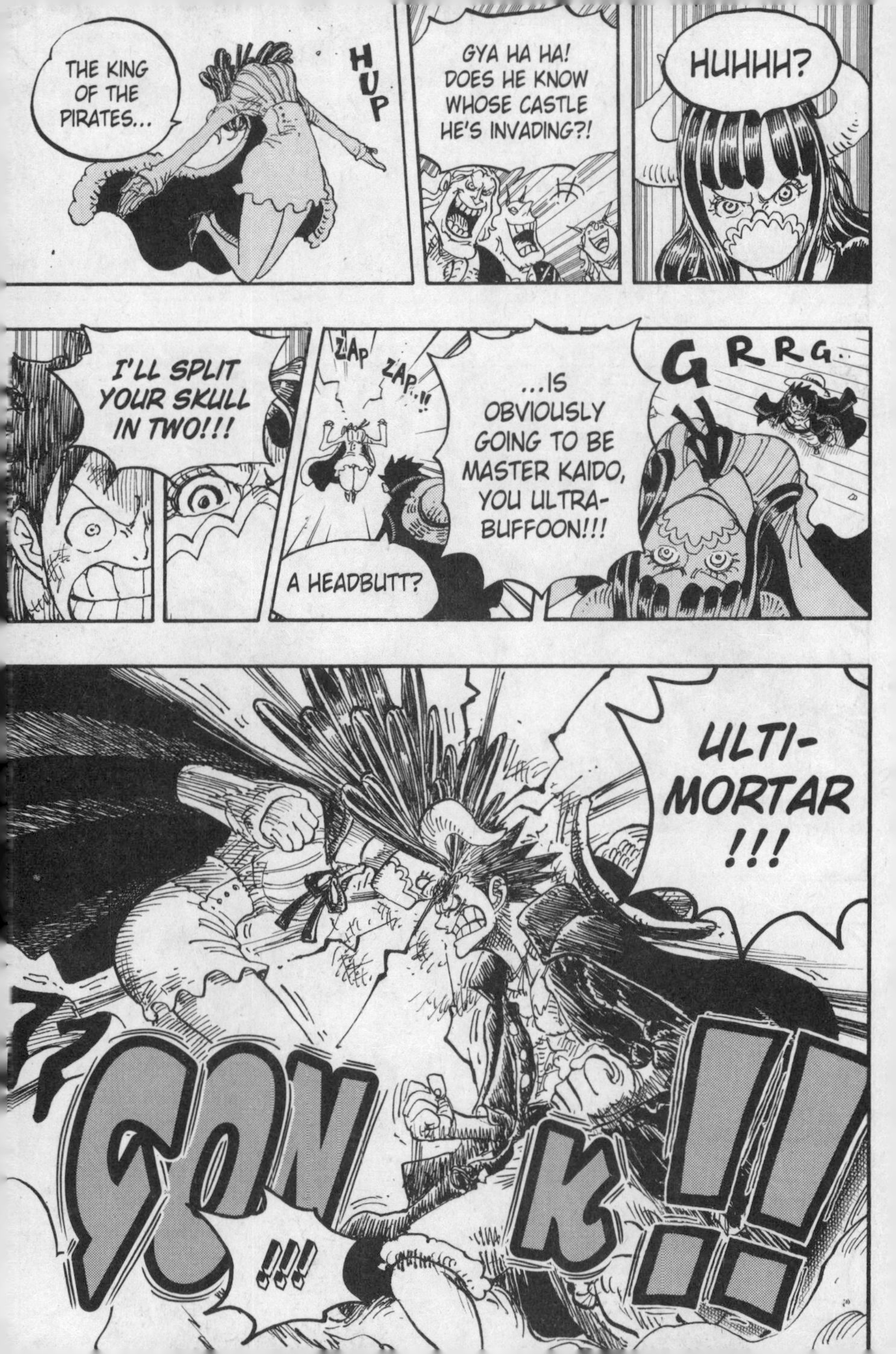
HUHHH?
GYA HA HA! DOES HE KNOW WHOSE CASTLE HE'S INVADING?!
HUP
THE KING OF THE PIRATES...
GRRRG..
...IS OBVIOUSLY GOING TO BE MASTER KAIDO, YOU ULTRA-BUFFOON!!!
ZAP ZAP..!!
A HEADBUTT?
I'LL SPLIT YOUR SKULL IN TWO!!!
ULTI-MORTAR!!!
GONK!!!!!!

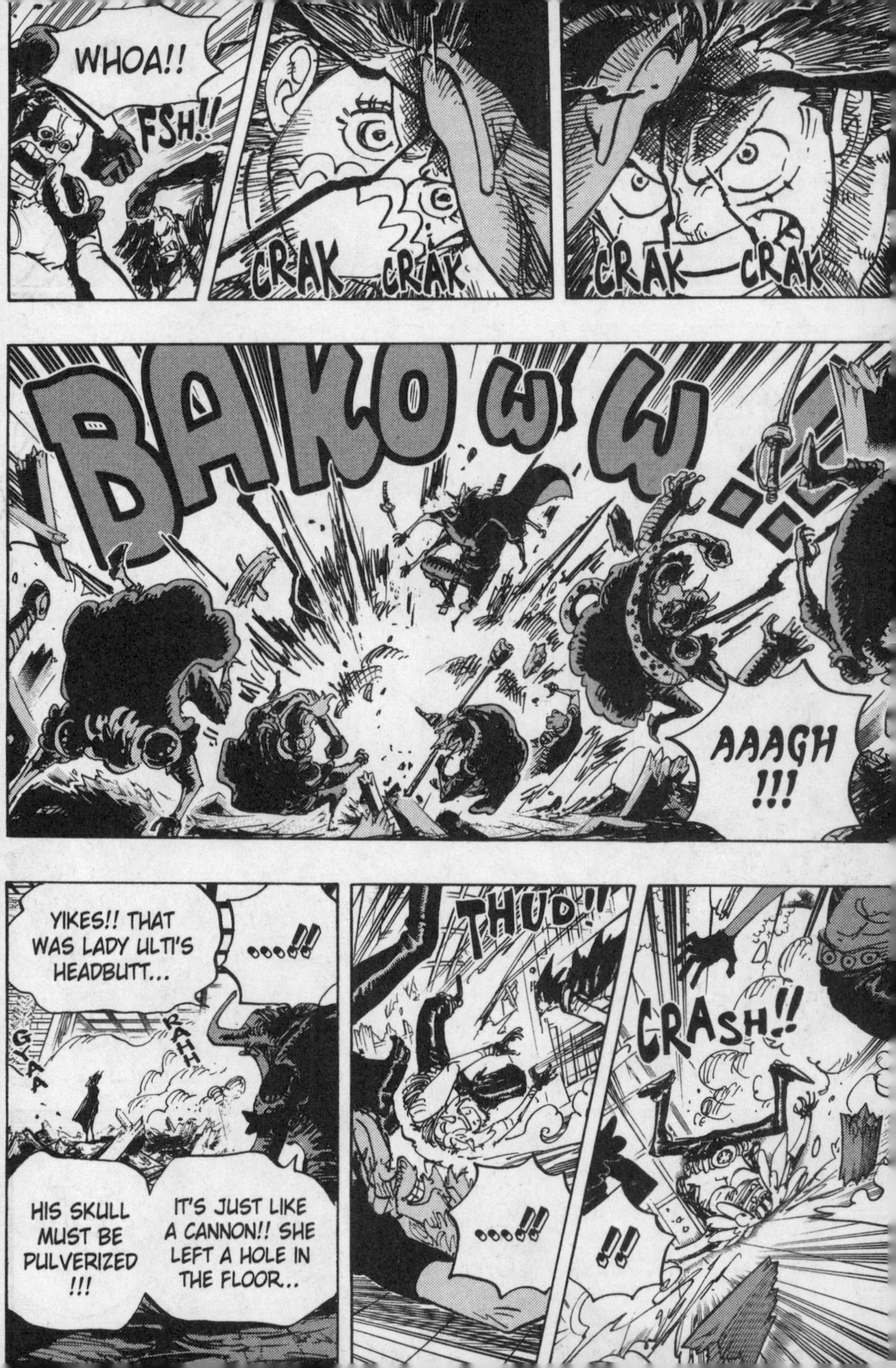
CRAK CRAK
CRAK CRAK
WHOA!!
FSH!!
BAKOWW!!
AAAGH!!!
CRASH!!
!!
THUD!!
....!!
YIKES!! THAT WAS LADY ULTI'S HEADBUTT...
....!!
RAHH
GYAA
IT'S JUST LIKE A CANNON!! SHE LEFT A HOLE IN THE FLOOR...
HIS SKULL MUST BE PULVERIZED!!!

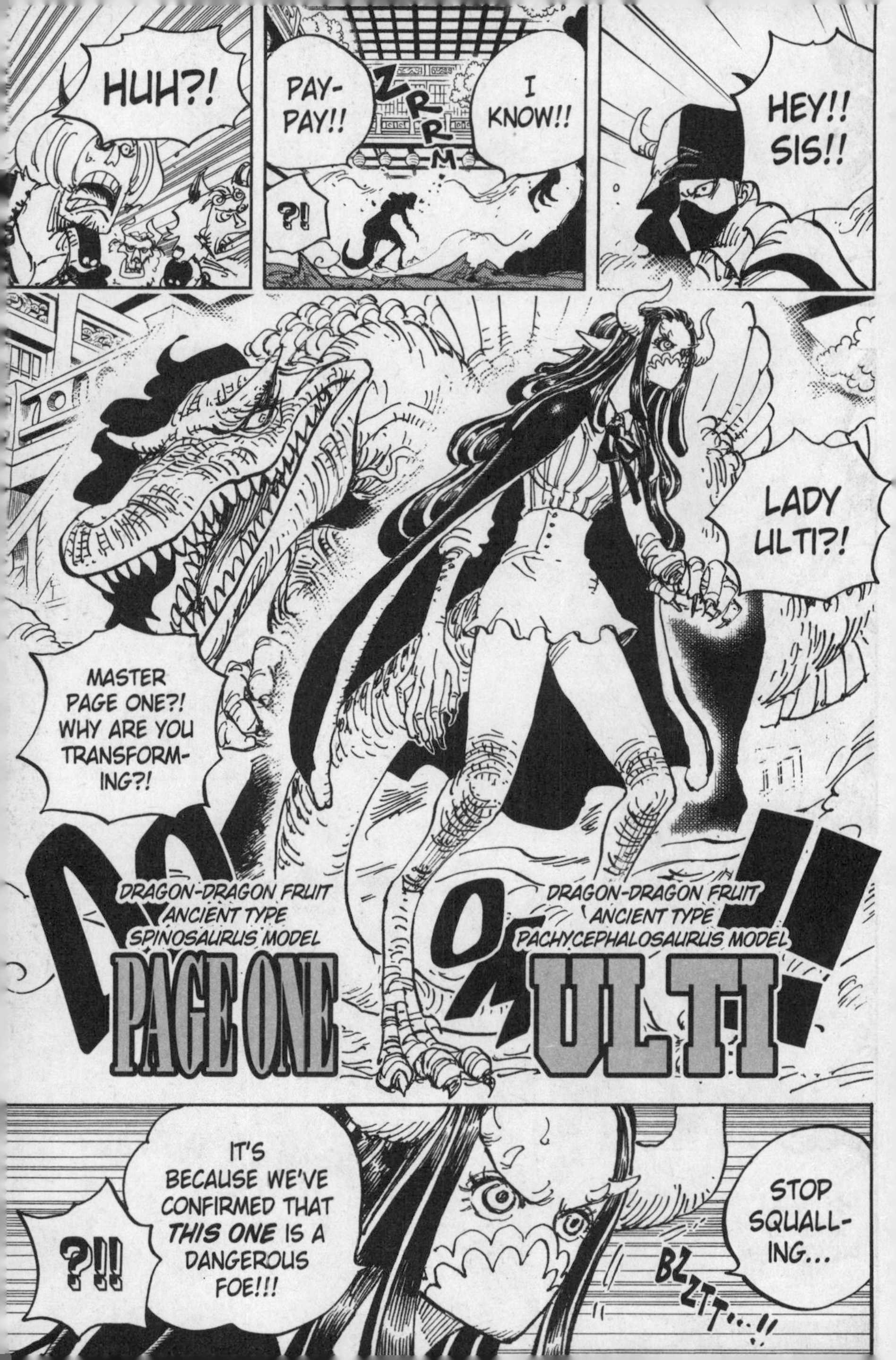

HEY!! SIS!!
I KNOW!!
PAY-PAY!!
ZRRM
?!
HUH?!
LADY ULTI?!
MASTER PAGE ONE?! WHY ARE YOU TRANSFORM-ING?!
DRAGON-DRAGON FRUIT ANCIENT TYPE PACHYCEPHALOSAURUS MODEL
ULTI
DRAGON-DRAGON FRUIT ANCIENT TYPE SPINOSAURUS MODEL
PAGE ONE
STOP SQUALL-ING...
BZZTT...!!
IT'S BECAUSE WE'VE CONFIRMED THAT *THIS ONE* IS A DANGEROUS FOE!!!
?!!

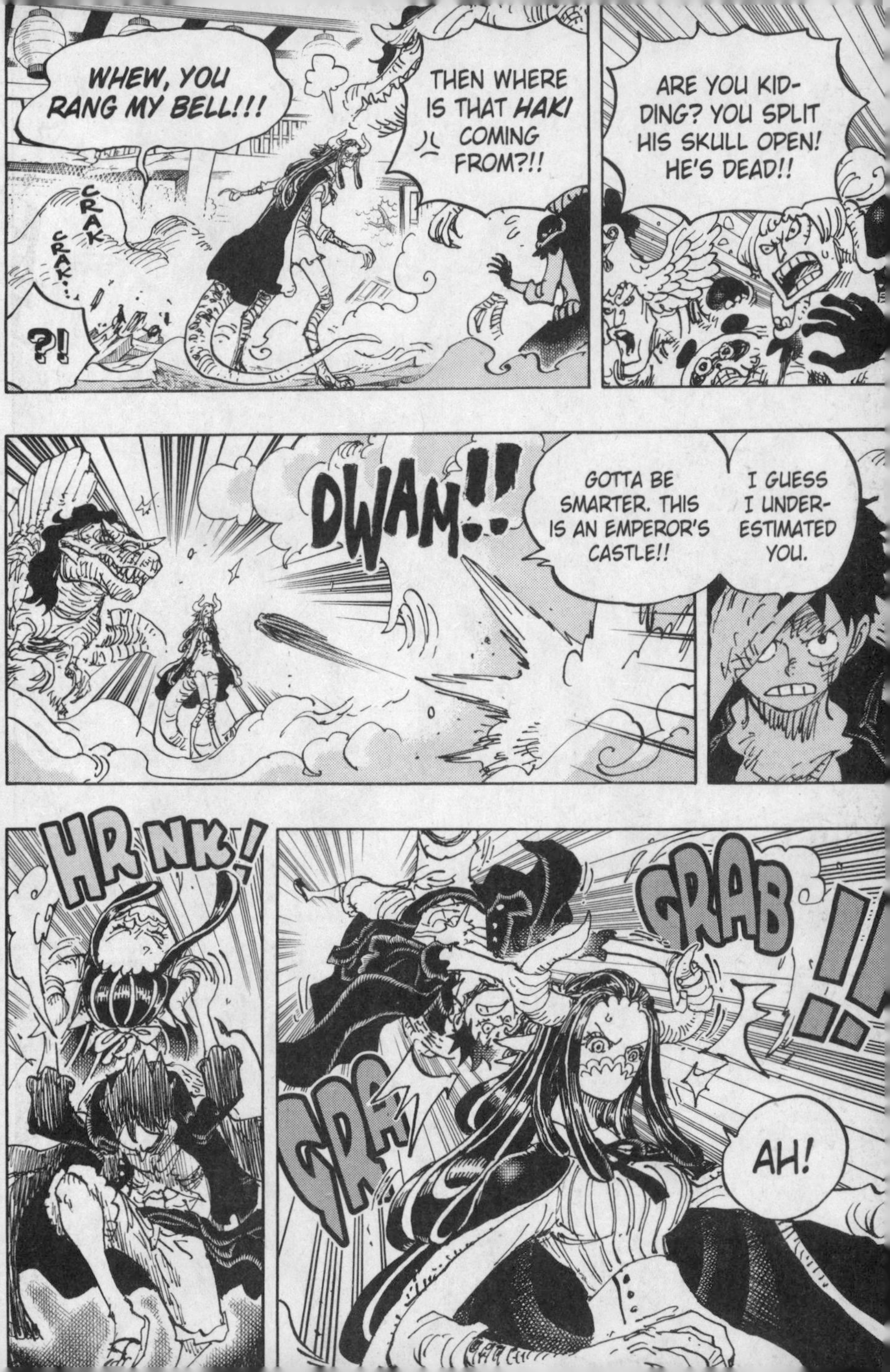
ARE YOU KID-
DING? YOU SPLIT
HIS SKULL OPEN!
HE'S DEAD!!
THEN WHERE IS THAT *HAKI* COMING FROM?!!
WHEW, YOU RANG MY BELL!!!
CRAK
CRAK...
?!
I GUESS I UNDER-ESTIMATED YOU.
GOTTA BE SMARTER. THIS IS AN EMPEROR'S CASTLE!!
DWAM!!
GRAB!!
AH!
GRA
HRNK!

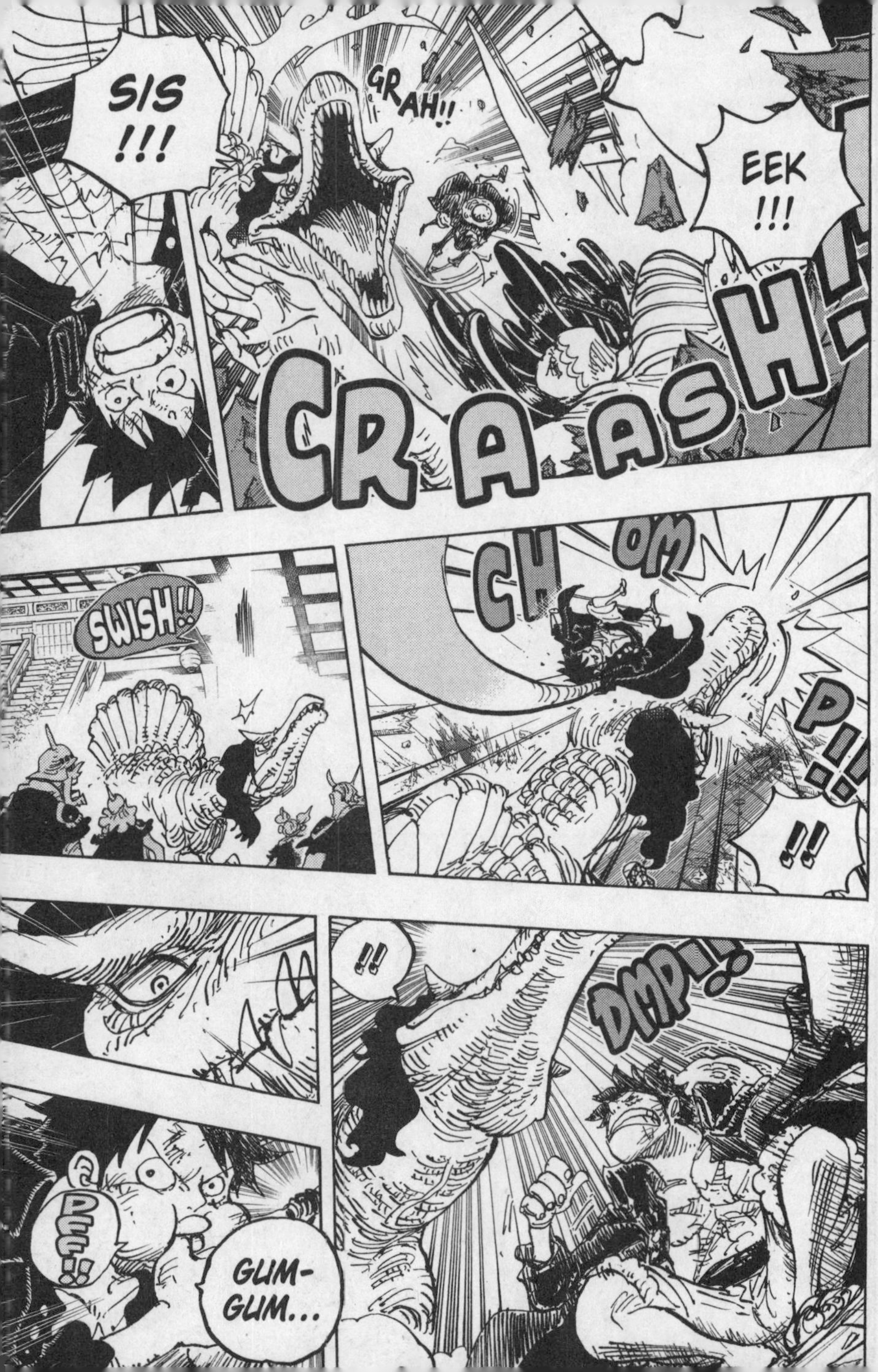
EEK !!!
GRAH!!
CRAASH!!
SIS !!!
CHOMP!!
!!
SWISH!!
DMP!!
!!
PFF!!
GUM-GUM...

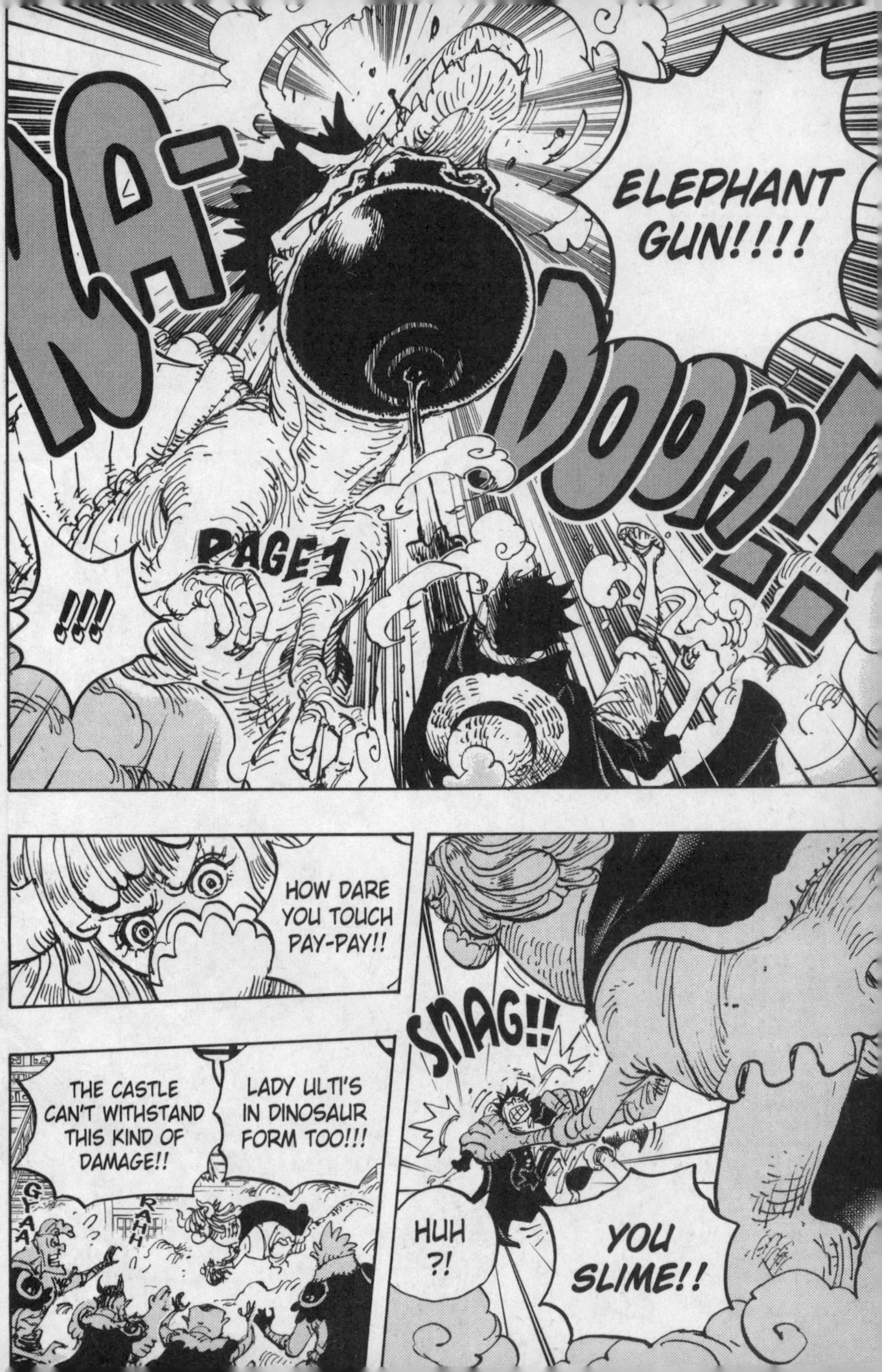
ELEPHANT GUN!!!!
DOOM!!
HA-
PAGE 1
!!!
SNAG!!
YOU SLIME!!
HUH ?!
HOW DARE YOU TOUCH PAY-PAY!!
LADY ULTI'S IN DINOSAUR FORM TOO!!!
THE CASTLE CAN'T WITHSTAND THIS KIND OF DAMAGE!!
RAHH
GYAA

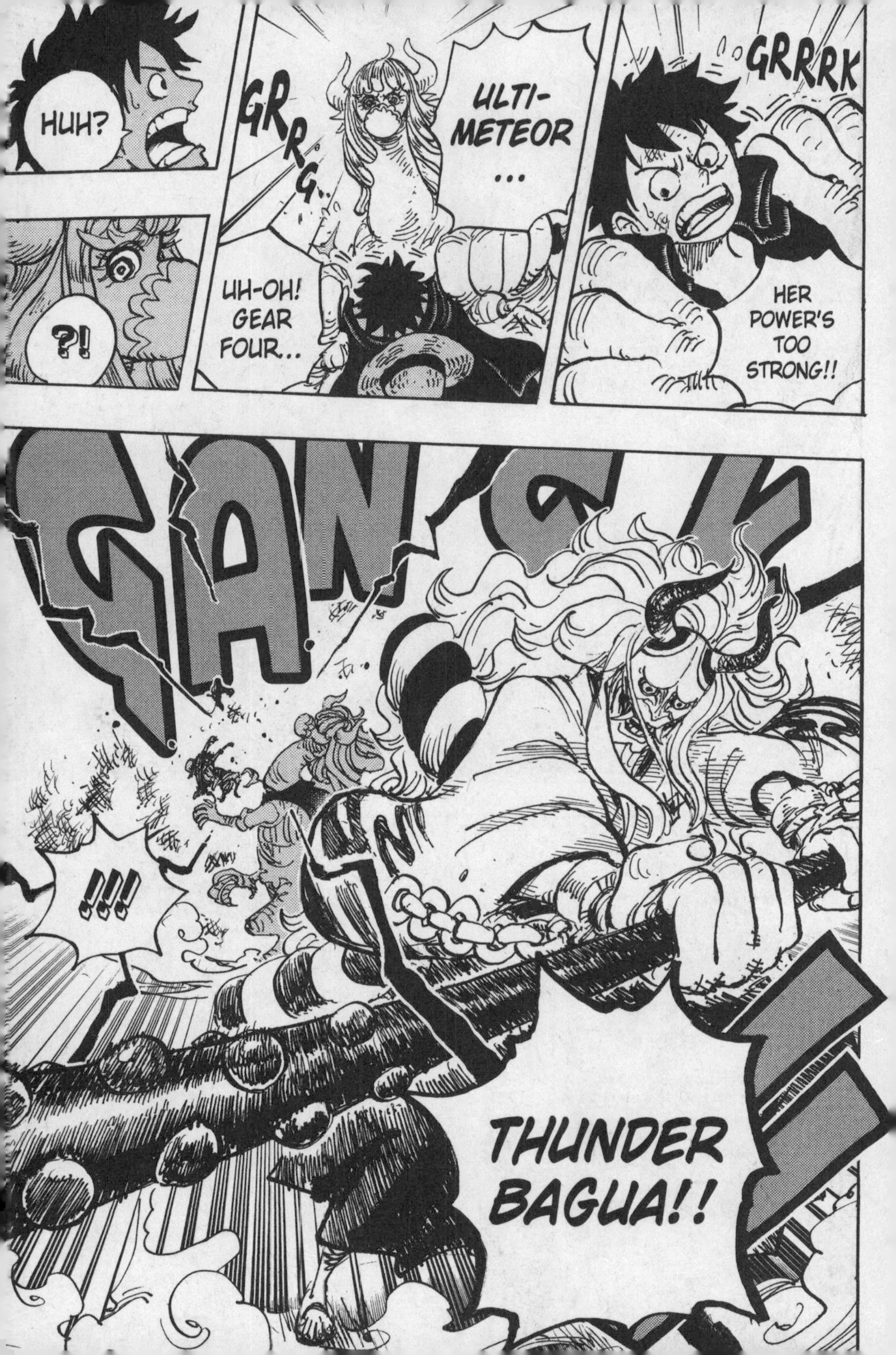
GRRRK
HER POWER'S TOO STRONG!!
ULTI-METEOR ...
GRRG..
UH-OH! GEAR FOUR...
HUH?
?!
!!!
THUNDER BAGUA!!

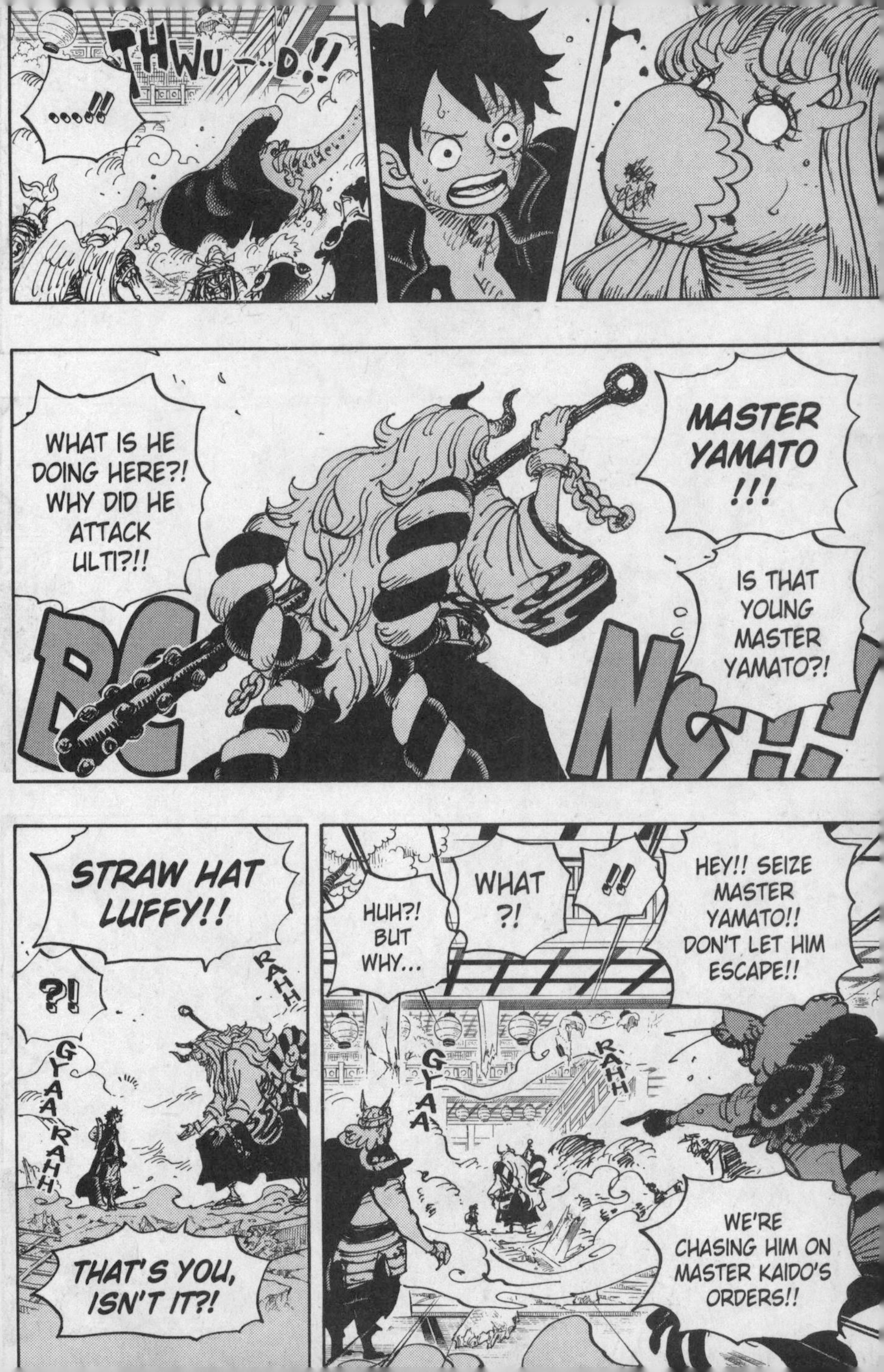

THWU--D!!
....!!
MASTER YAMATO!!!
IS THAT YOUNG MASTER YAMATO?!
WHAT IS HE DOING HERE?! WHY DID HE ATTACK ULTI?!!
HEY!! SEIZE MASTER YAMATO!! DON'T LET HIM ESCAPE!!
!!
WHAT?!
HUH?! BUT WHY...
RAHH
GYAA
WE'RE CHASING HIM ON MASTER KAIDO'S ORDERS!!
STRAW HAT LUFFY!!
RAHH
?!
GYAARAHH
THAT'S YOU, ISN'T IT?!

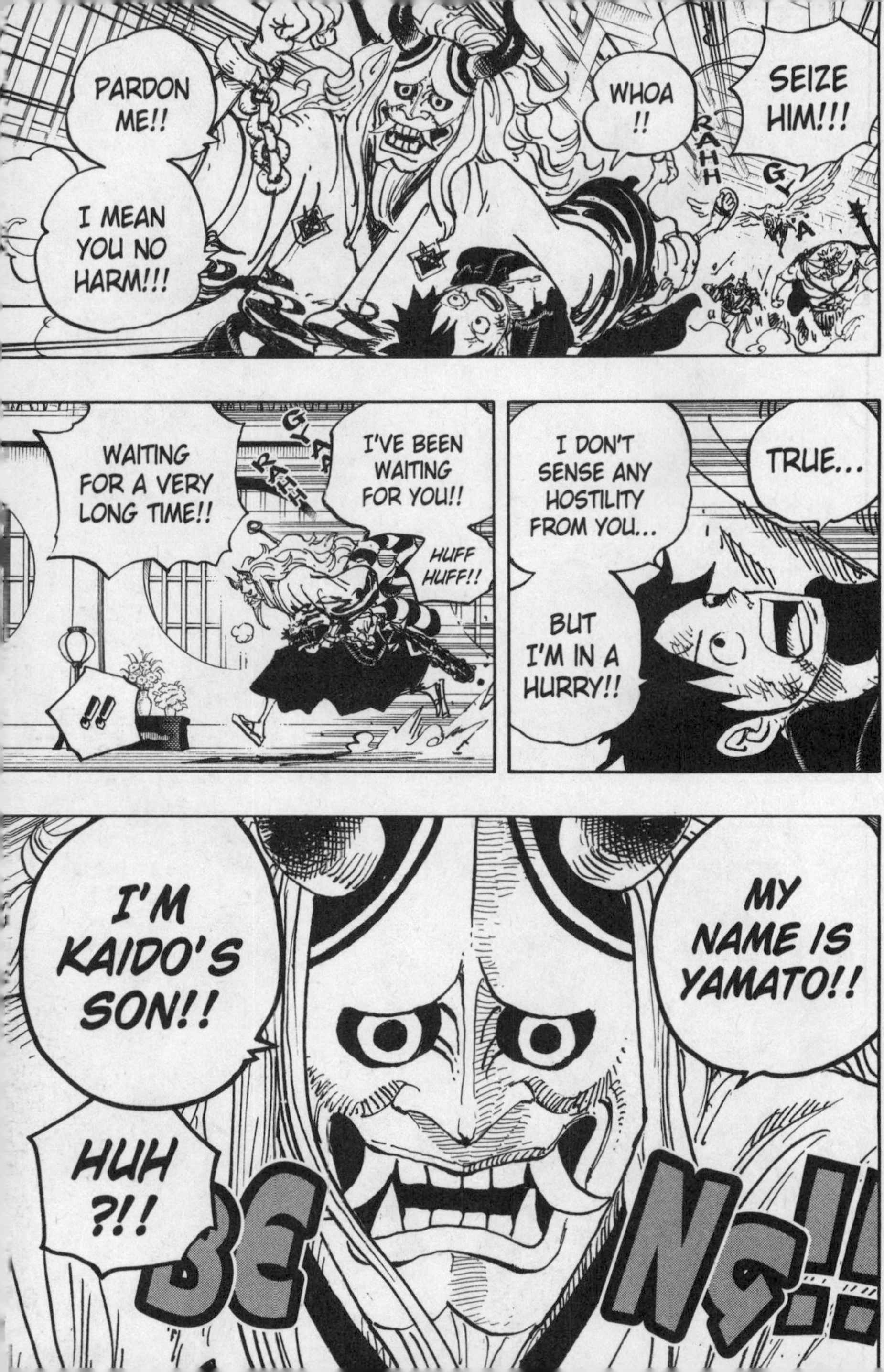
SEIZE HIM!!!
GYA
RAHH
WHOA !!
PARDON ME!!
I MEAN YOU NO HARM!!!
TRUE...
I DON'T SENSE ANY HOSTILITY FROM YOU...
BUT I'M IN A HURRY!!
I'VE BEEN WAITING FOR YOU!!
HUFF HUFF!!
GYAA
RAHH
WAITING FOR A VERY LONG TIME!!
!!
MY NAME IS YAMATO!!
I'M KAIDO'S SON!!
HUH ?!!

SBS Question Corner

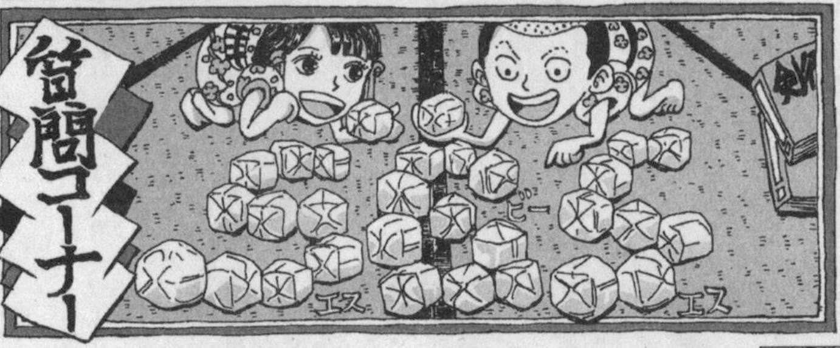

質問コーナー

(Buchonosuke, Tochigi)

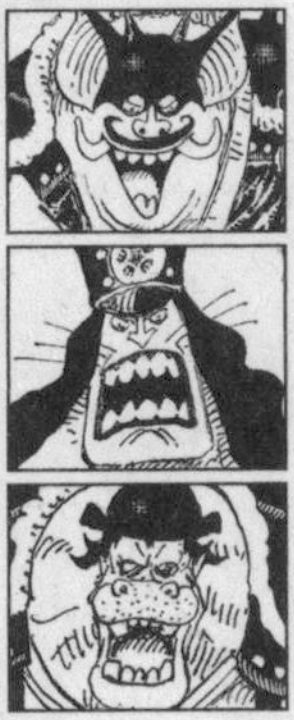

Q: Are all of the Gifters able to transform between animal form and human form freely? Or does it depend on the fruit?

--Kenkichi

A: It depends on the fruit. Smile fruits are grown artificially, so they're unstable in every way. They will get animal strength, but the fact that you see them fighting with the lion on their stomach or eaten constantly by their hippo should serve as evidence that they can't completely control the animal part. Many of them are very strong, but in short, Smile fruits are a big gamble.

Q: Huh? Does nobody want to see what Sanji would look like at age 40 and age 60? Then I guess I'll ask! Can you draw what Chopper will look like in the future?! Please!!

--420 Land

A: You wanna see? Here you go.

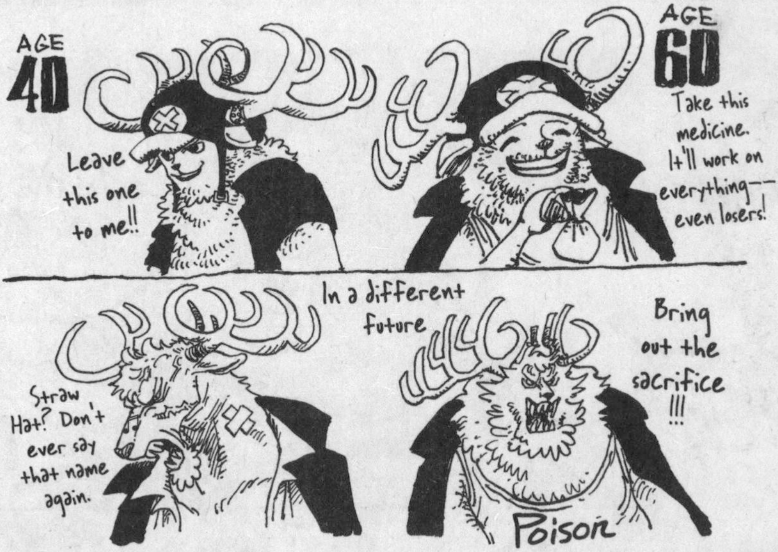

AGE 40
Leave this one to me!!
AGE 60
Take this medicine. It'll work on everything-- even losers!
In a different future
Straw Hat? Don't ever say that name again.
Bring out the sacrifice !!!
Poison

And that's all for the SBS! See you next volume!!

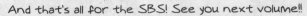

Chapter 984:
MY BIBLE

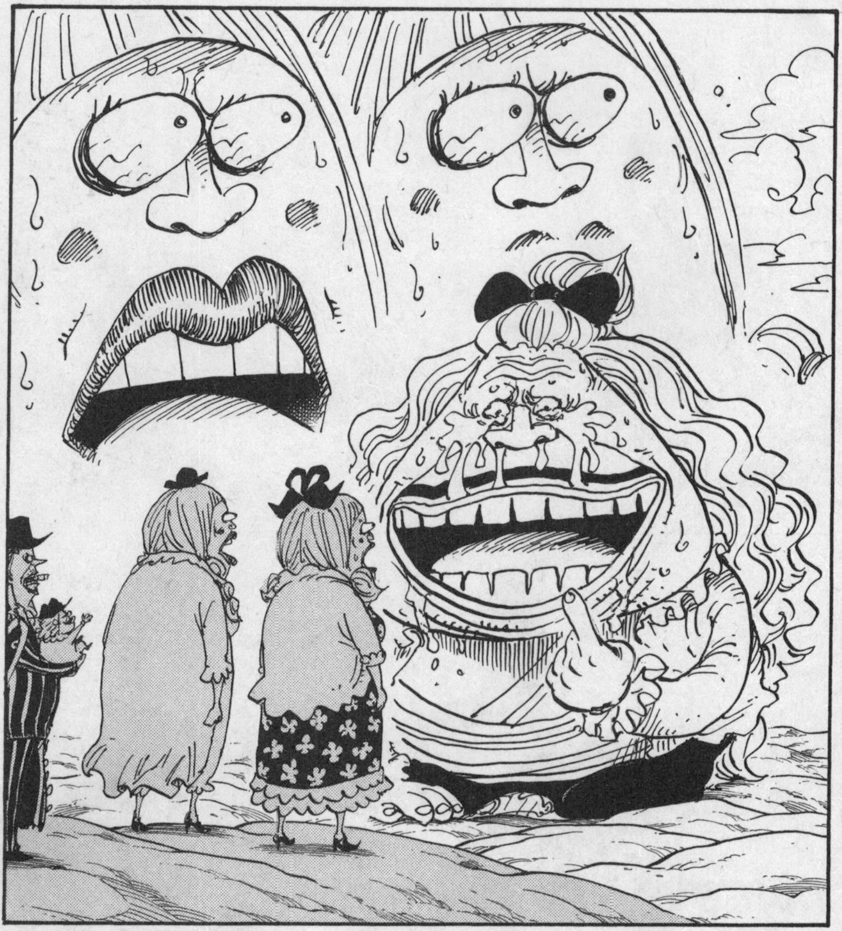

GANG BEGE'S OH MY FAMILY
VOL. 30: "IT'S ME!! I'M YOUR FATHER!!!"

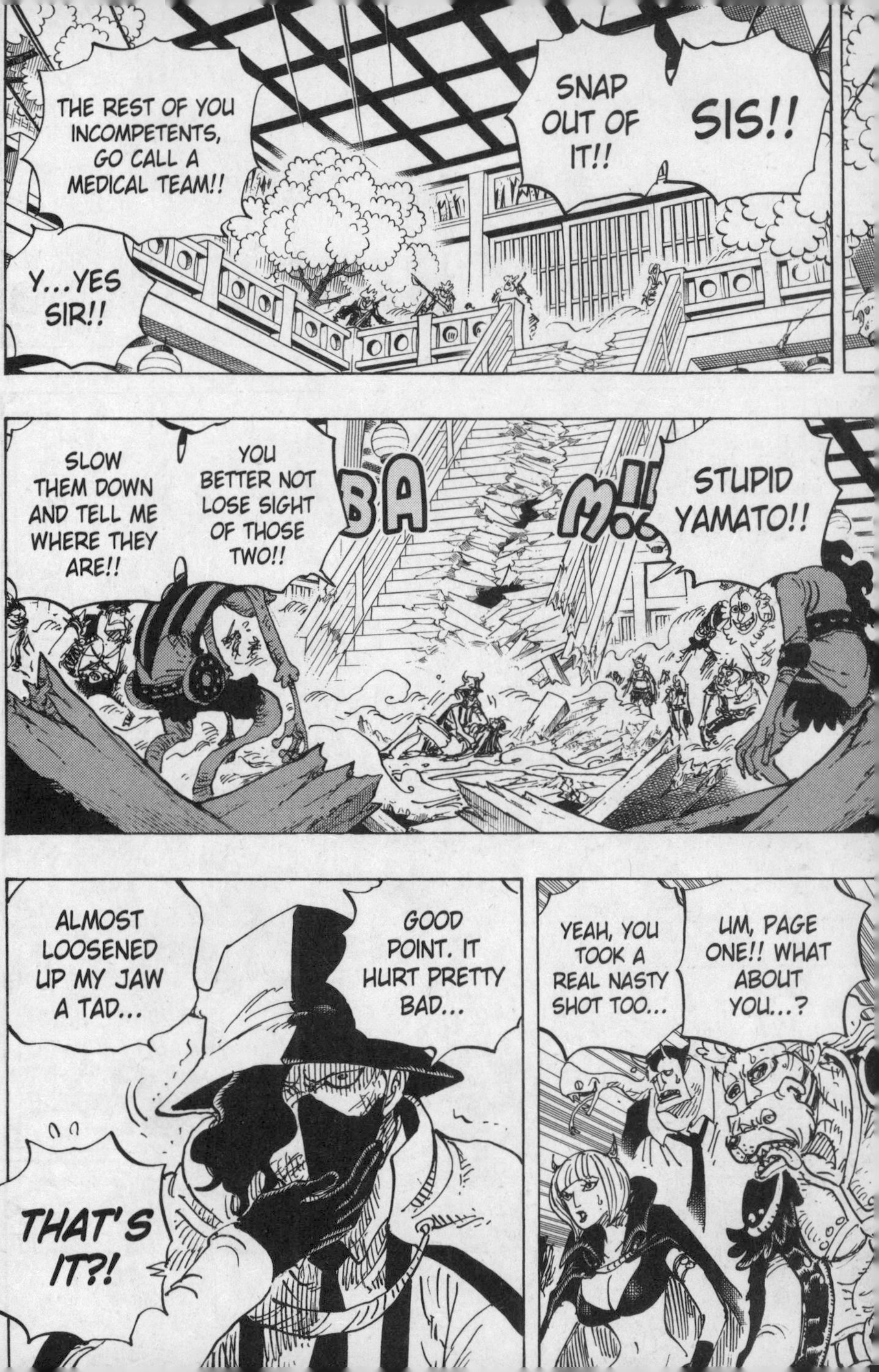
SNAP OUT OF IT!!
SIS!!
THE REST OF YOU INCOMPETENTS, GO CALL A MEDICAL TEAM!!
Y...YES SIR!!
STUPID YAMATO!!
BAM!!
YOU BETTER NOT LOSE SIGHT OF THOSE TWO!!
SLOW THEM DOWN AND TELL ME WHERE THEY ARE!!
UM, PAGE ONE!! WHAT ABOUT YOU...?
YEAH, YOU TOOK A REAL NASTY SHOT TOO...
GOOD POINT. IT HURT PRETTY BAD...
ALMOST LOOSENED UP MY JAW A TAD...
THAT'S IT?!

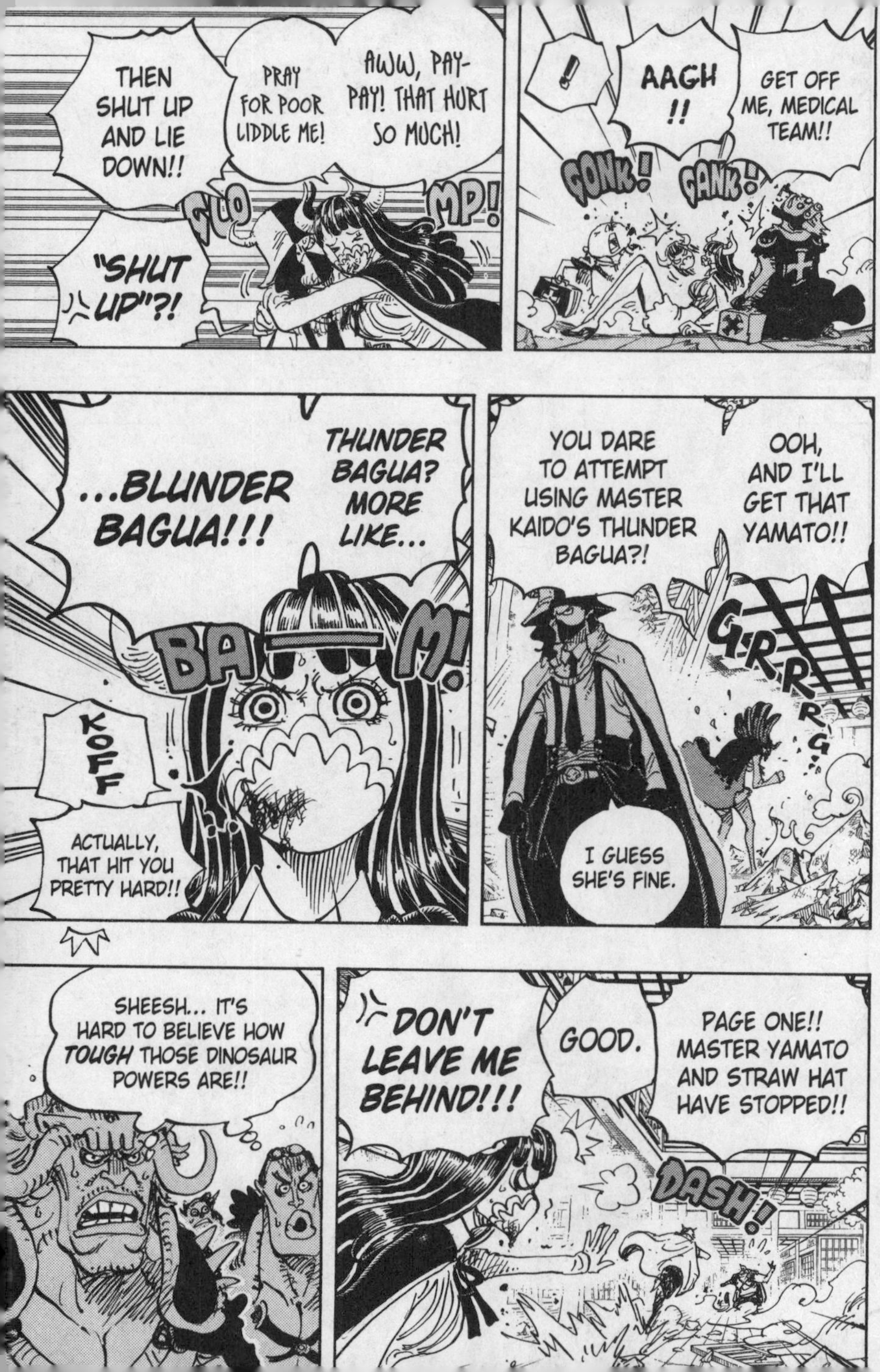
!
AAGH !!
GET OFF ME, MEDICAL TEAM!!
GANK!
GONK!
AWW, PAY-PAY! THAT HURT SO MUCH!
PRAY FOR POOR LIDDLE ME!
THEN SHUT UP AND LIE DOWN!!
GLOMP!
"SHUT UP"?!
OOH, AND I'LL GET THAT YAMATO!!
YOU DARE TO ATTEMPT USING MASTER KAIDO'S THUNDER BAGUA?!
GRRRRG
I GUESS SHE'S FINE.
THUNDER BAGUA? MORE LIKE...
...BLUNDER BAGUA!!!
BAM!
KOFF
ACTUALLY, THAT HIT YOU PRETTY HARD!!
PAGE ONE!! MASTER YAMATO AND STRAW HAT HAVE STOPPED!!
GOOD.
DON'T LEAVE ME BEHIND!!!
DASH!
SHEESH... IT'S HARD TO BELIEVE HOW TOUGH THOSE DINOSAUR POWERS ARE!!

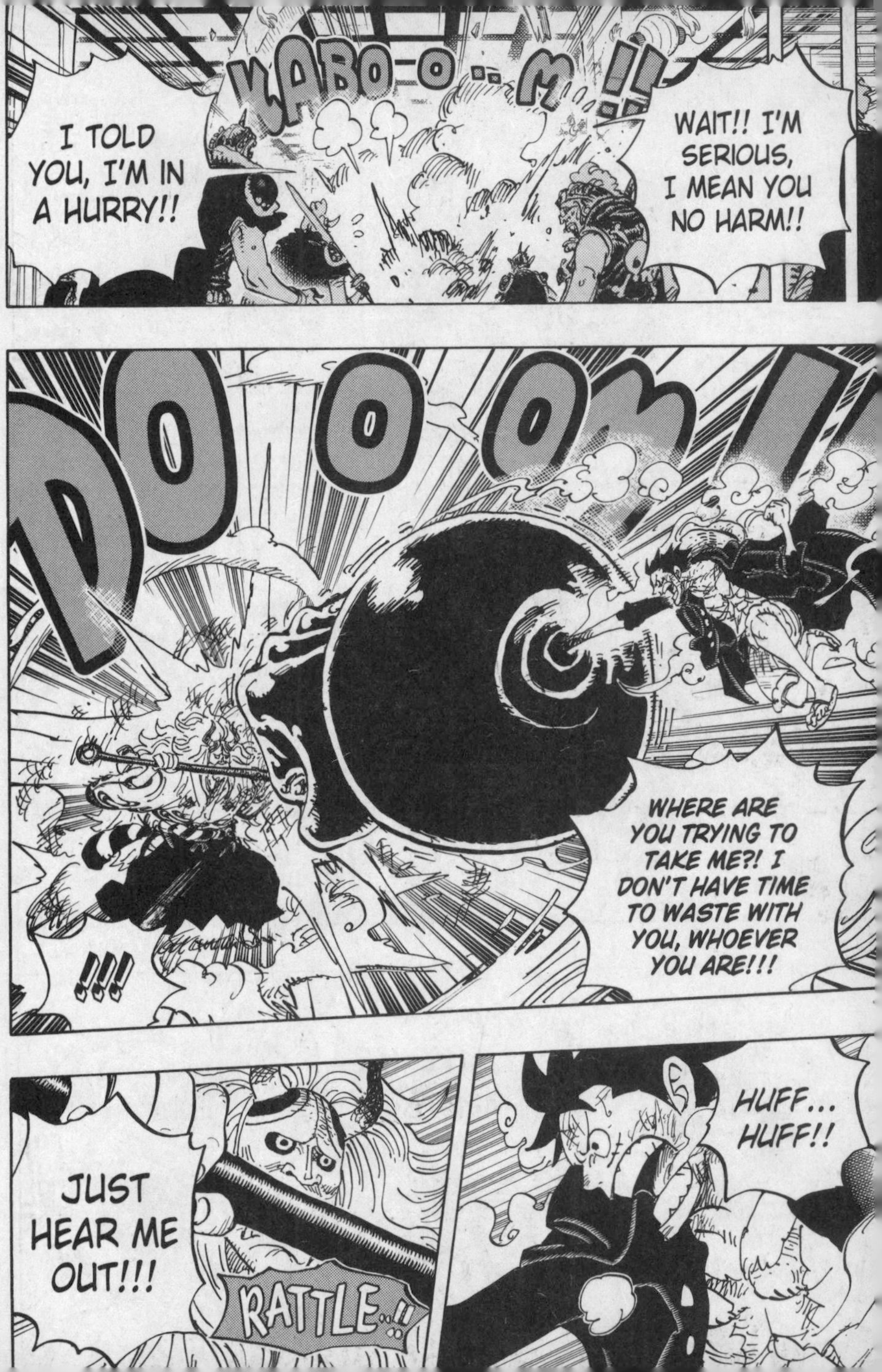
KABO-O..M!!
WAIT!! I'M SERIOUS, I MEAN YOU NO HARM!!
I TOLD YOU, I'M IN A HURRY!!
DOOOM!!
WHERE ARE YOU TRYING TO TAKE ME?! I DON'T HAVE TIME TO WASTE WITH YOU, WHOEVER YOU ARE!!!
!!!
HUFF... HUFF!!
JUST HEAR ME OUT!!!
RATTLE..!!

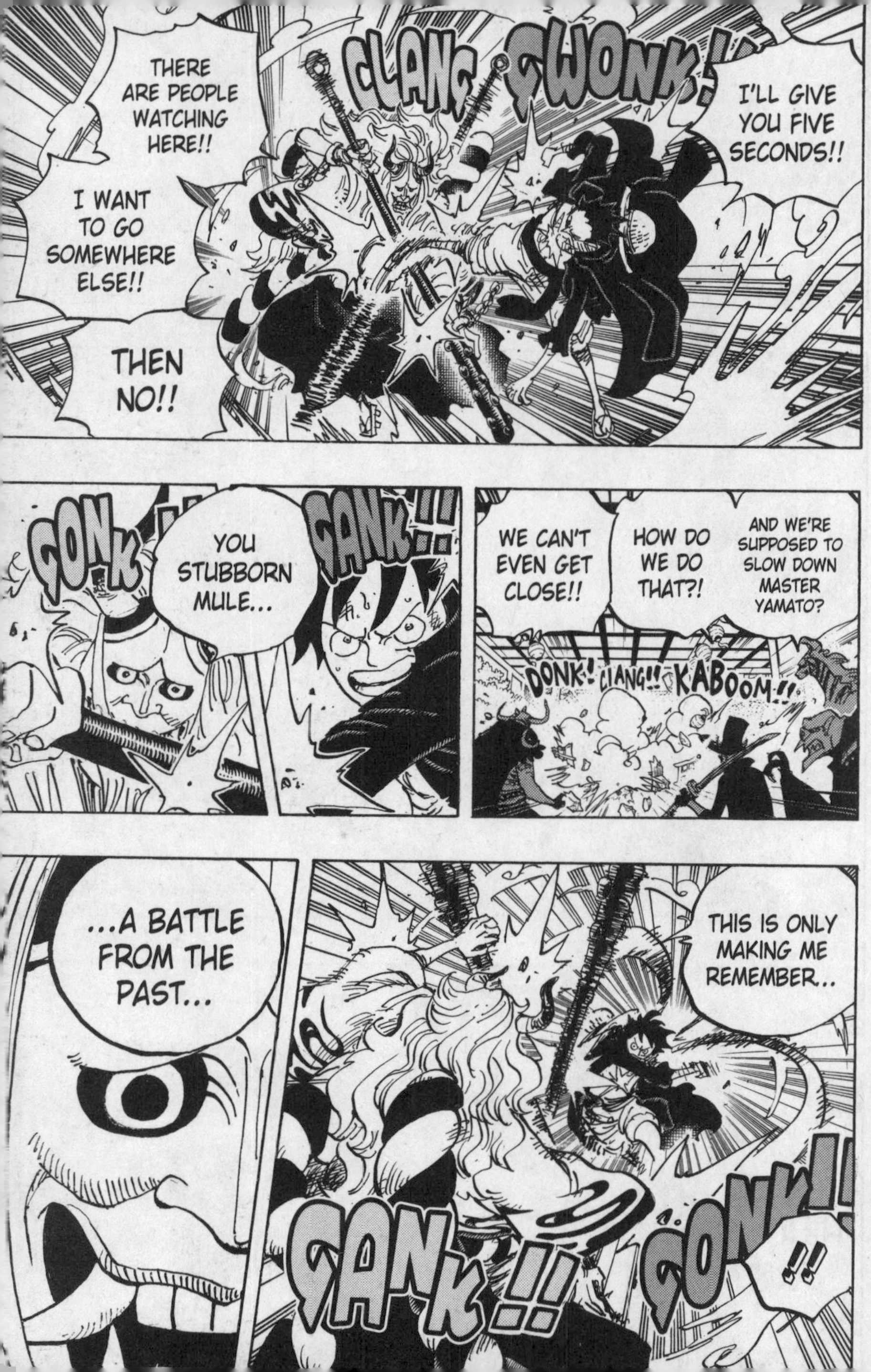
GWONK!!
CLANG
I'LL GIVE YOU FIVE SECONDS!!
THERE ARE PEOPLE WATCHING HERE!!
I WANT TO GO SOMEWHERE ELSE!!
THEN NO!!
AND WE'RE SUPPOSED TO SLOW DOWN MASTER YAMATO?
HOW DO WE DO THAT?!
WE CAN'T EVEN GET CLOSE!!
KABOOM!!
CLANG!!
DONK!
GANK!!
YOU STUBBORN MULE...
GONK
THIS IS ONLY MAKING ME REMEMBER...
GONK!!
GANK!!
...A BATTLE FROM THE PAST...

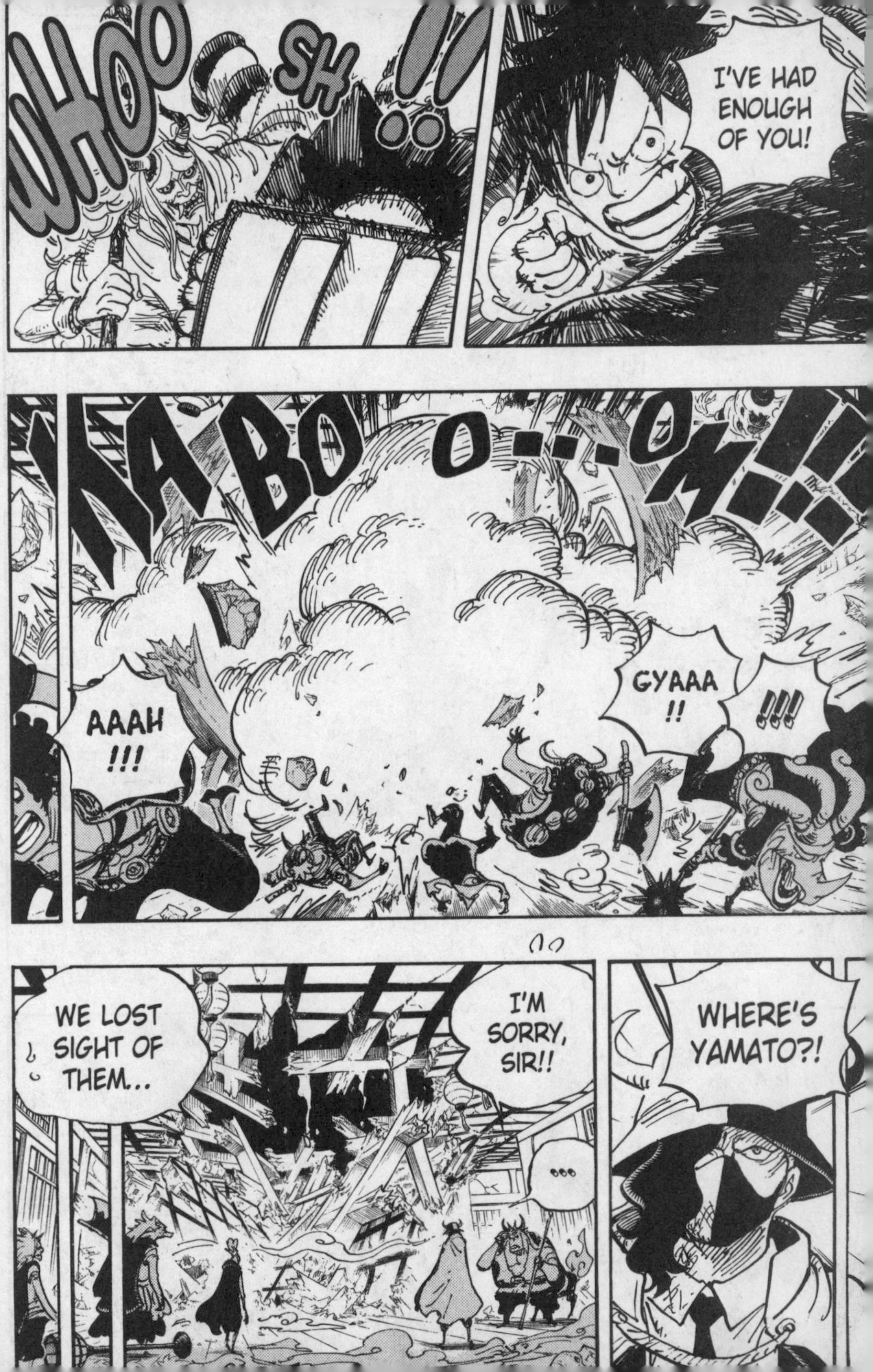
I'VE HAD ENOUGH OF YOU!
WHOOOSH!!
KABOO...OM!!!
!!!
GYAAA !!
AAAH !!!
WHERE'S YAMATO?!
I'M SORRY, SIR!!
...
WE LOST SIGHT OF THEM...

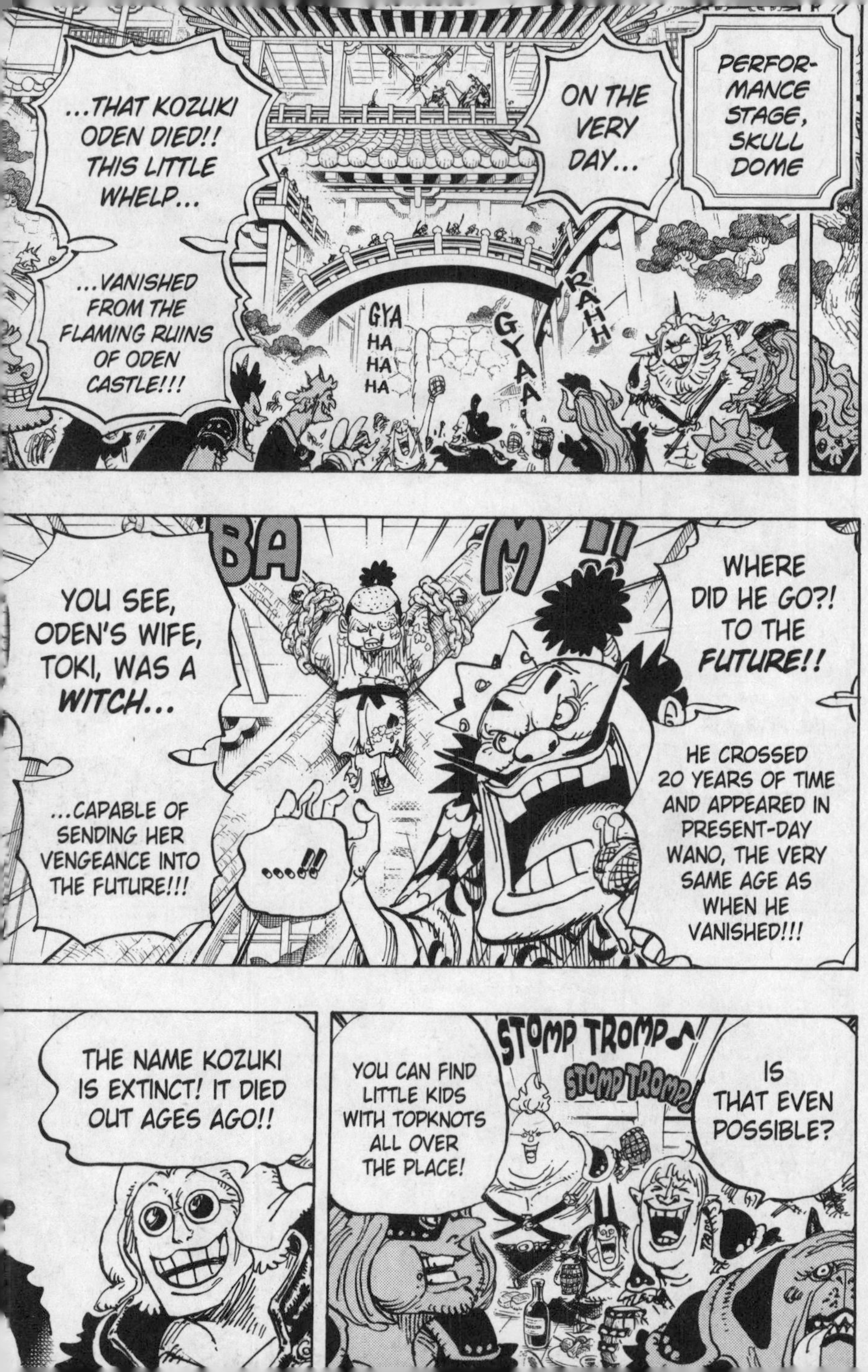
PERFORMANCE STAGE, SKULL DOME
ON THE VERY DAY...
...THAT KOZUKI ODEN DIED!! THIS LITTLE WHELP...
...VANISHED FROM THE FLAMING RUINS OF ODEN CASTLE!!!
RAHH
GYAA
GYA HA HA HA
BAM!!
WHERE DID HE GO?! TO THE FUTURE!!
HE CROSSED 20 YEARS OF TIME AND APPEARED IN PRESENT-DAY WANO, THE VERY SAME AGE AS WHEN HE VANISHED!!!
YOU SEE, ODEN'S WIFE, TOKI, WAS A WITCH...
...CAPABLE OF SENDING HER VENGEANCE INTO THE FUTURE!!!
....!!
IS THAT EVEN POSSIBLE?
STOMP TROMP♪
STOMP TROMP
YOU CAN FIND LITTLE KIDS WITH TOPKNOTS ALL OVER THE PLACE!
THE NAME KOZUKI IS EXTINCT! IT DIED OUT AGES AGO!!

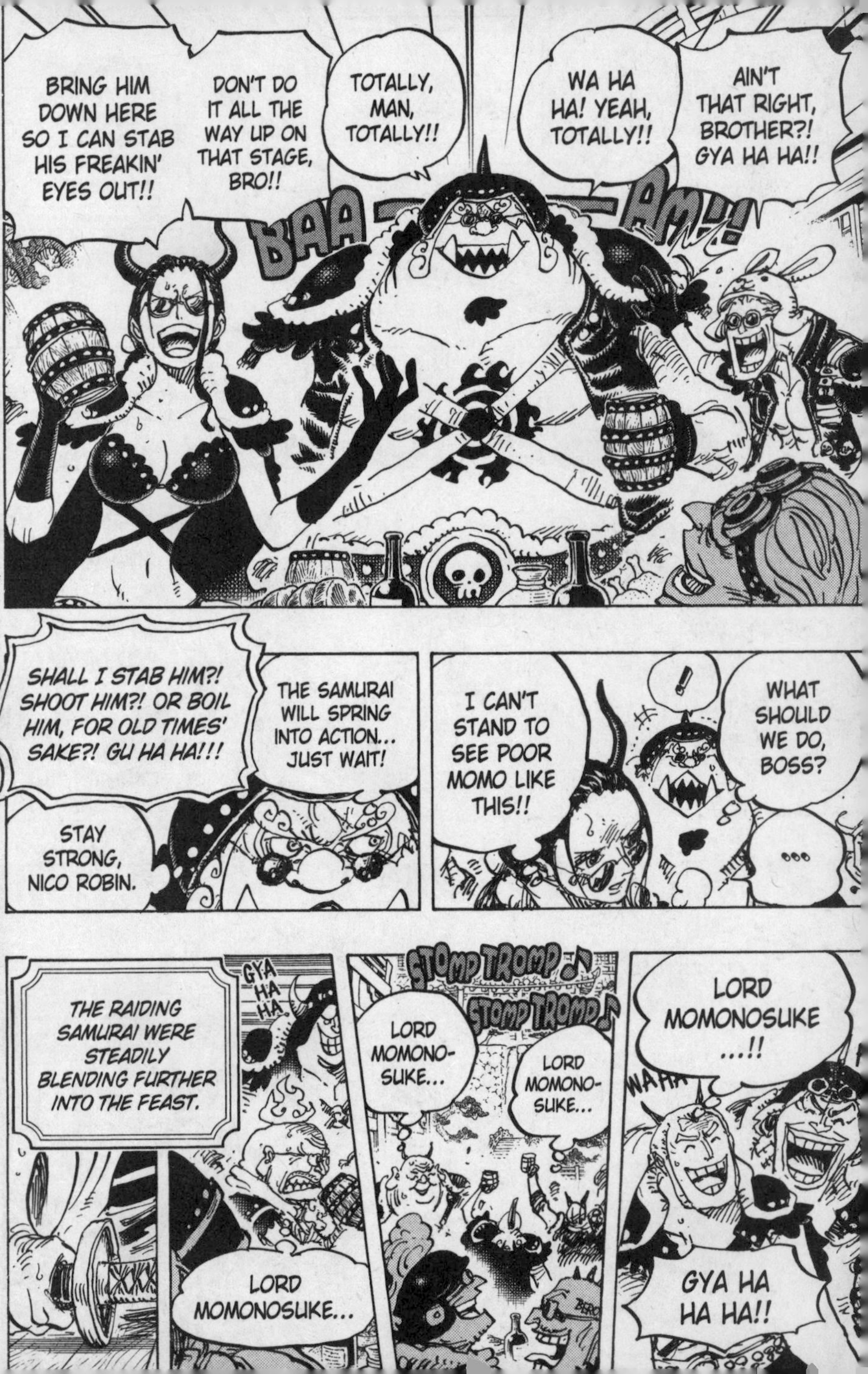
AIN'T THAT RIGHT, BROTHER?! GYA HA HA!!
WA HA HA! YEAH, TOTALLY!!
BAA— —AM!!
TOTALLY, MAN, TOTALLY!!
DON'T DO IT ALL THE WAY UP ON THAT STAGE, BRO!!
BRING HIM DOWN HERE SO I CAN STAB HIS FREAKIN' EYES OUT!!
WHAT SHOULD WE DO, BOSS?
!
I CAN'T STAND TO SEE POOR MOMO LIKE THIS!!
...
SHALL I STAB HIM?! SHOOT HIM?! OR BOIL HIM, FOR OLD TIMES' SAKE?! GU HA HA!!!
THE SAMURAI WILL SPRING INTO ACTION... JUST WAIT!
STAY STRONG, NICO ROBIN.
LORD MOMONOSUKE ...!!
WAHA
GYA HA HA HA!!
STOMP TROMP♪
STOMP TROMP♪
LORD MOMONO-SUKE...
LORD MOMONO-SUKE...
GYA HA HA
THE RAIDING SAMURAI WERE STEADILY BLENDING FURTHER INTO THE FEAST.
LORD MOMONOSUKE...

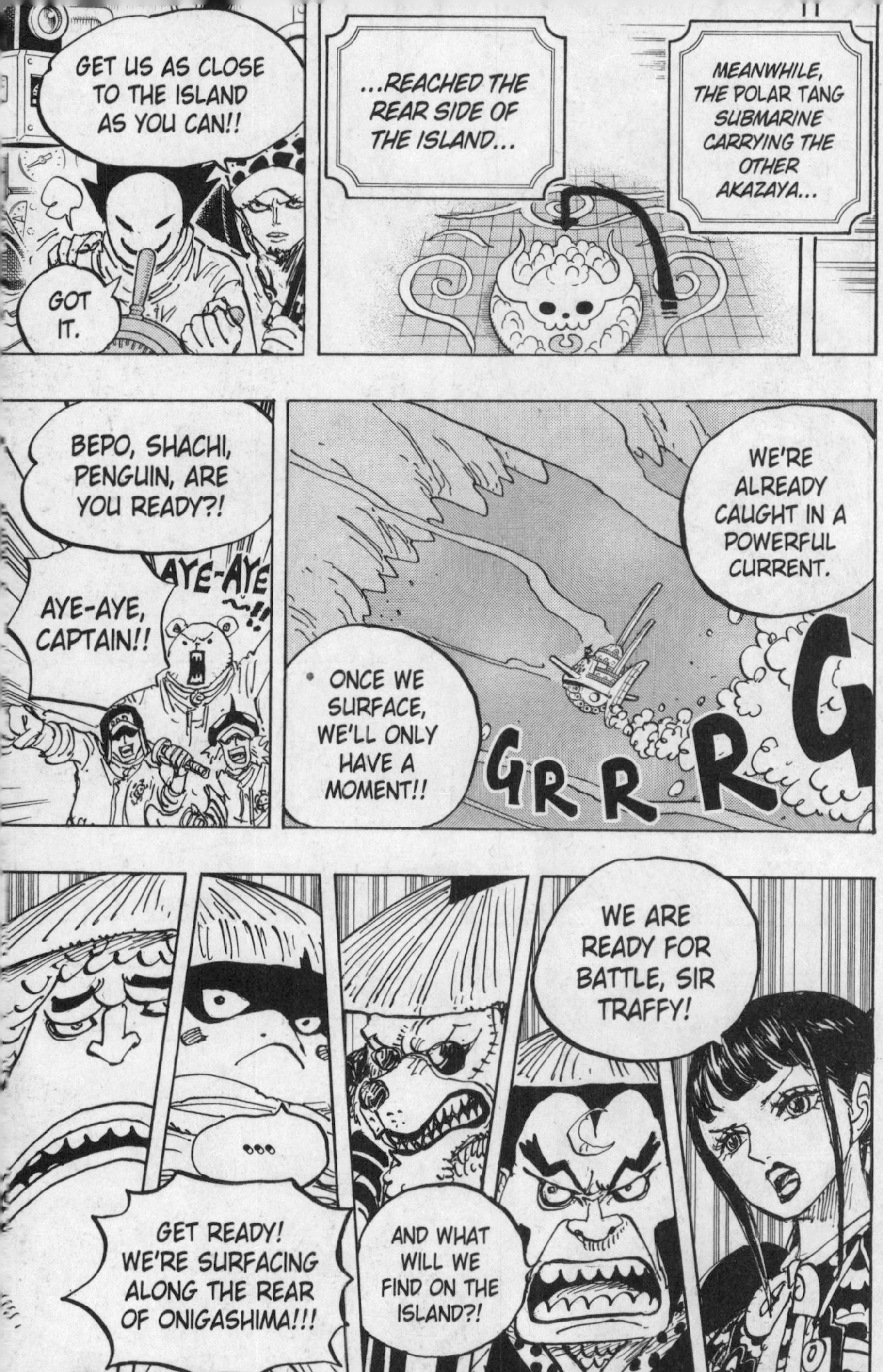
MEANWHILE, THE POLAR TANG SUBMARINE CARRYING THE OTHER AKAZAYA...
...REACHED THE REAR SIDE OF THE ISLAND...
GET US AS CLOSE TO THE ISLAND AS YOU CAN!!
GOT IT.
WE'RE ALREADY CAUGHT IN A POWERFUL CURRENT.
ONCE WE SURFACE, WE'LL ONLY HAVE A MOMENT!!
GRRRG
BEPO, SHACHI, PENGUIN, ARE YOU READY?!
AYE-AYE~!!
AYE-AYE, CAPTAIN!!
WE ARE READY FOR BATTLE, SIR TRAFFY!
AND WHAT WILL WE FIND ON THE ISLAND?!
...
GET READY! WE'RE SURFACING ALONG THE REAR OF ONIGASHIMA!!!

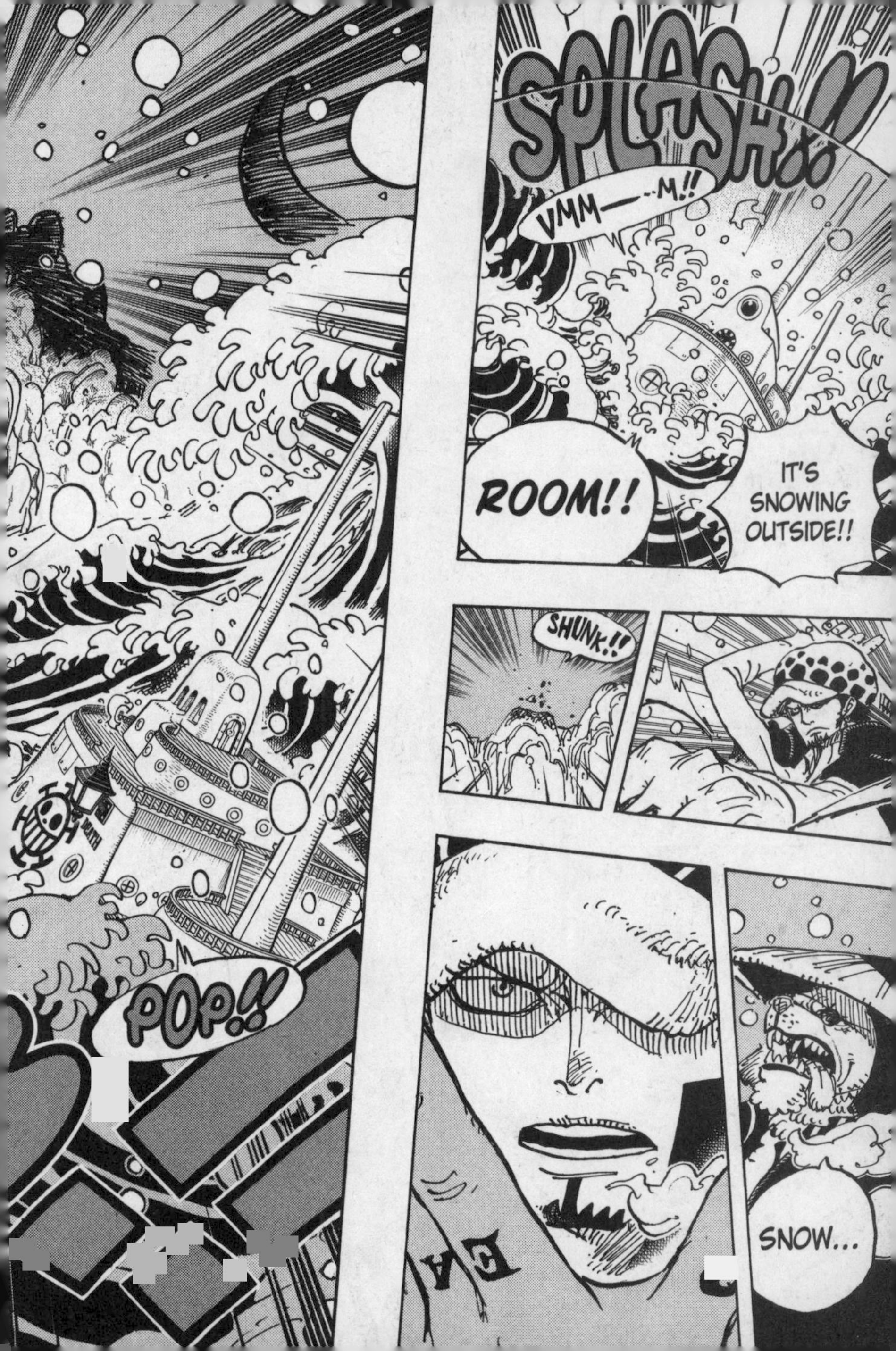
SPLASH!!
VMM———M!!
IT'S SNOWING OUTSIDE!!
ROOM!!
SHUNK!!
SNOW...
POP!!

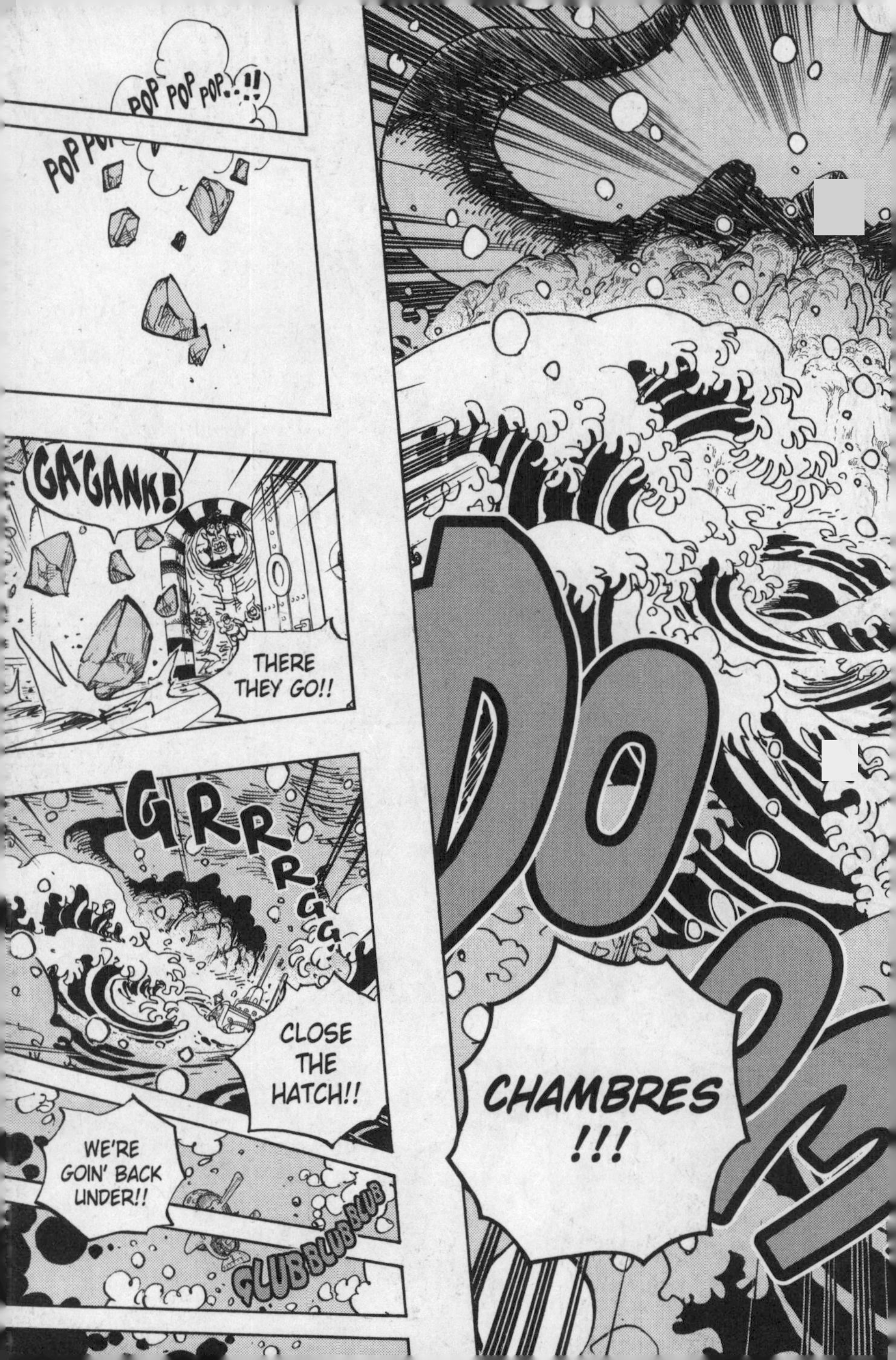
CHAMBRES !!!
POP POP POP..!!
POP POP
GA-GANK!
THERE THEY GO!!
GRRRRGG
CLOSE THE HATCH!!
WE'RE GOIN' BACK UNDER!!
GLUB BLUB BLUB

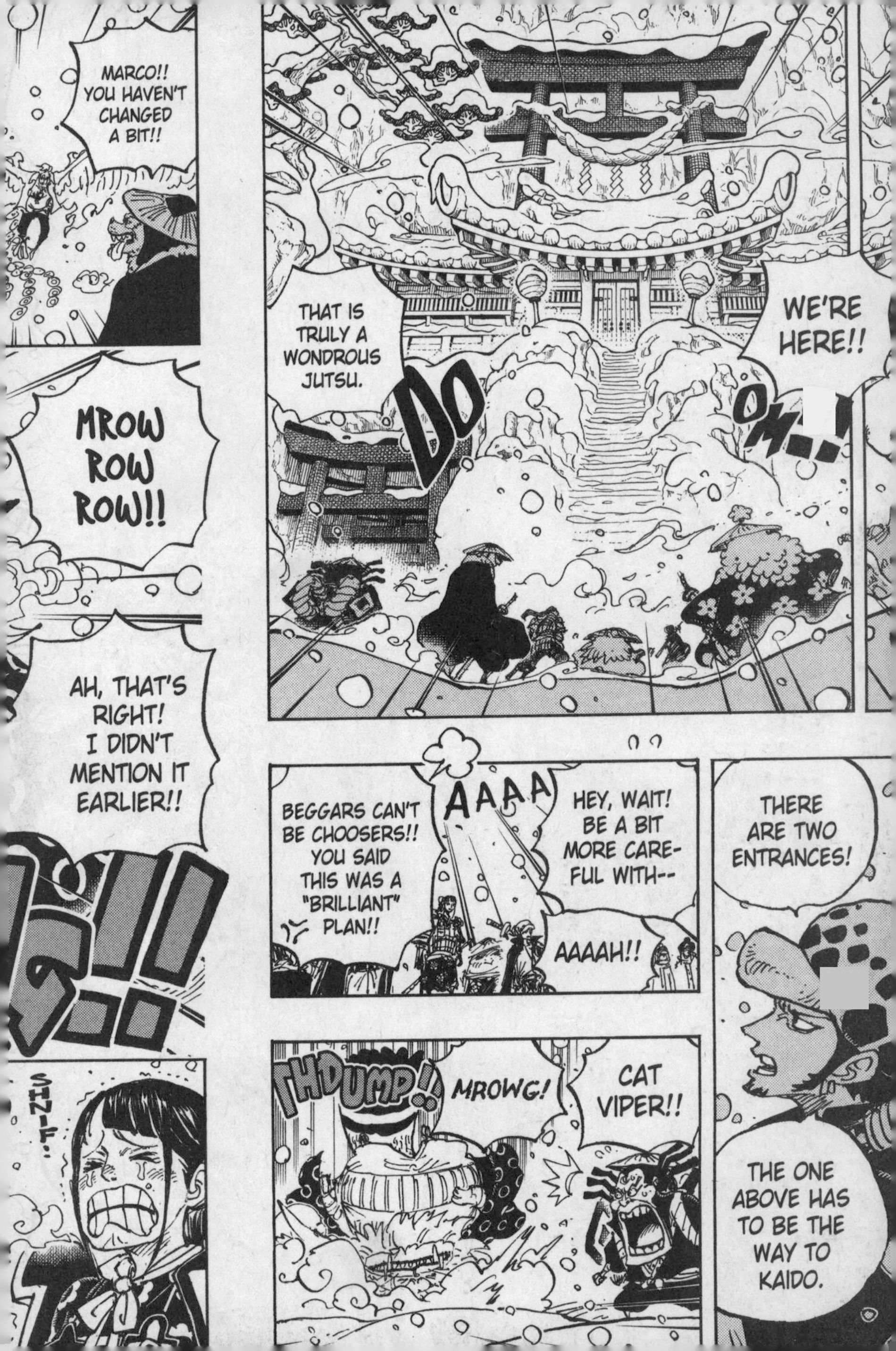
WE'RE HERE!!
OM..!!
DO
THAT IS TRULY A WONDROUS JUTSU.
THERE ARE TWO ENTRANCES!
THE ONE ABOVE HAS TO BE THE WAY TO KAIDO.
HEY, WAIT! BE A BIT MORE CARE-FUL WITH--
AAAA
BEGGARS CAN'T BE CHOOSERS!! YOU SAID THIS WAS A "BRILLIANT" PLAN!!
AAAAH!!
CAT VIPER!!
MROWG!
THDUMP!!
MARCO!! YOU HAVEN'T CHANGED A BIT!!
MROW ROW ROW!!
AH, THAT'S RIGHT! I DIDN'T MENTION IT EARLIER!!
SHNIF..

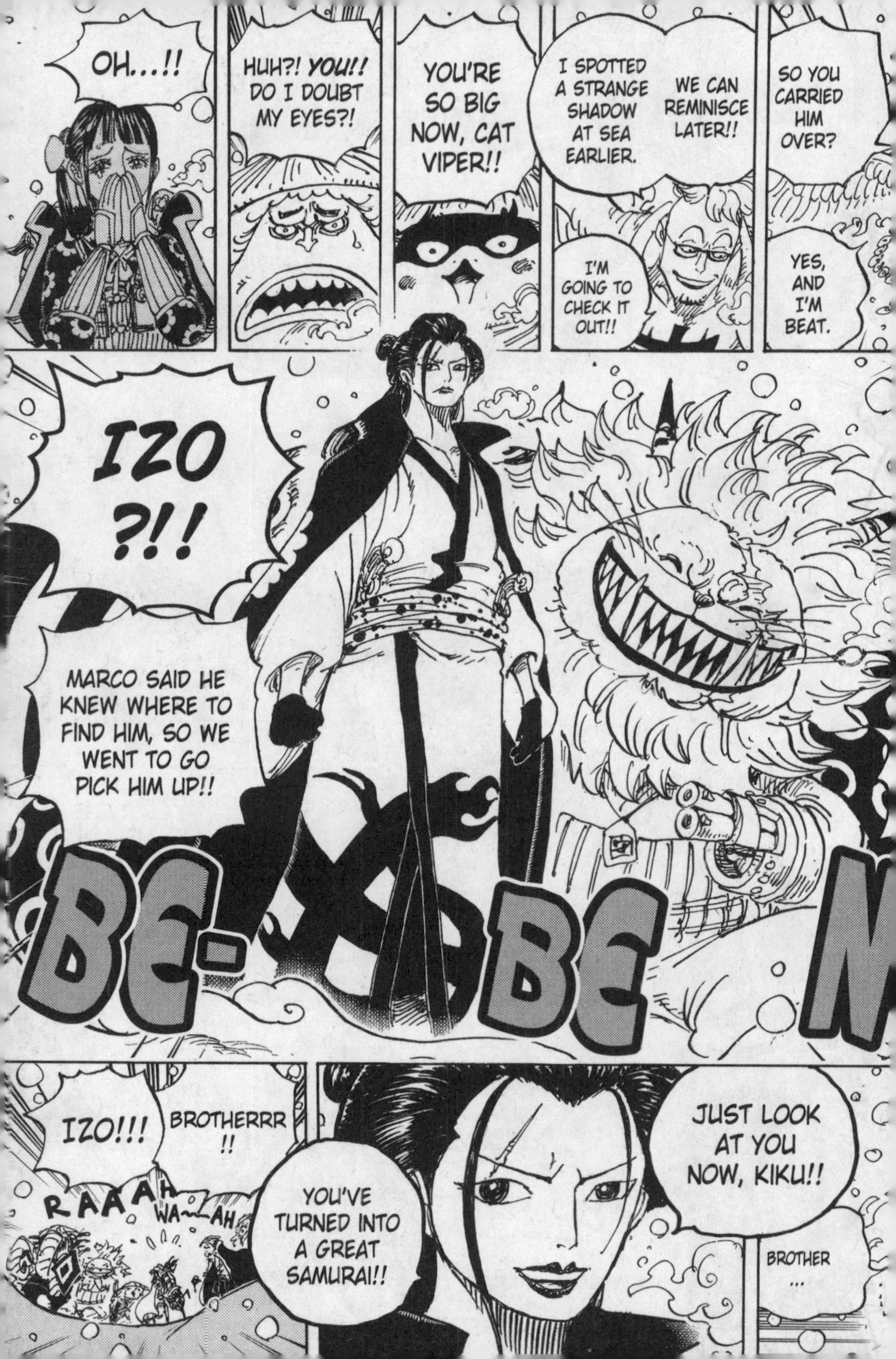
SO YOU CARRIED HIM OVER?
YES, AND I'M BEAT.
WE CAN REMINISCE LATER!!
I SPOTTED A STRANGE SHADOW AT SEA EARLIER.
I'M GOING TO CHECK IT OUT!!
YOU'RE SO BIG NOW, CAT VIPER!!
HUH?! YOU!! DO I DOUBT MY EYES?!
OH...!!
IZO ?!!
MARCO SAID HE KNEW WHERE TO FIND HIM, SO WE WENT TO GO PICK HIM UP!!
BE- BE N
JUST LOOK AT YOU NOW, KIKU!!
BROTHER ...
YOU'VE TURNED INTO A GREAT SAMURAI!!
BROTHERRR !!
IZO!!!
RAAAH
WA~AH

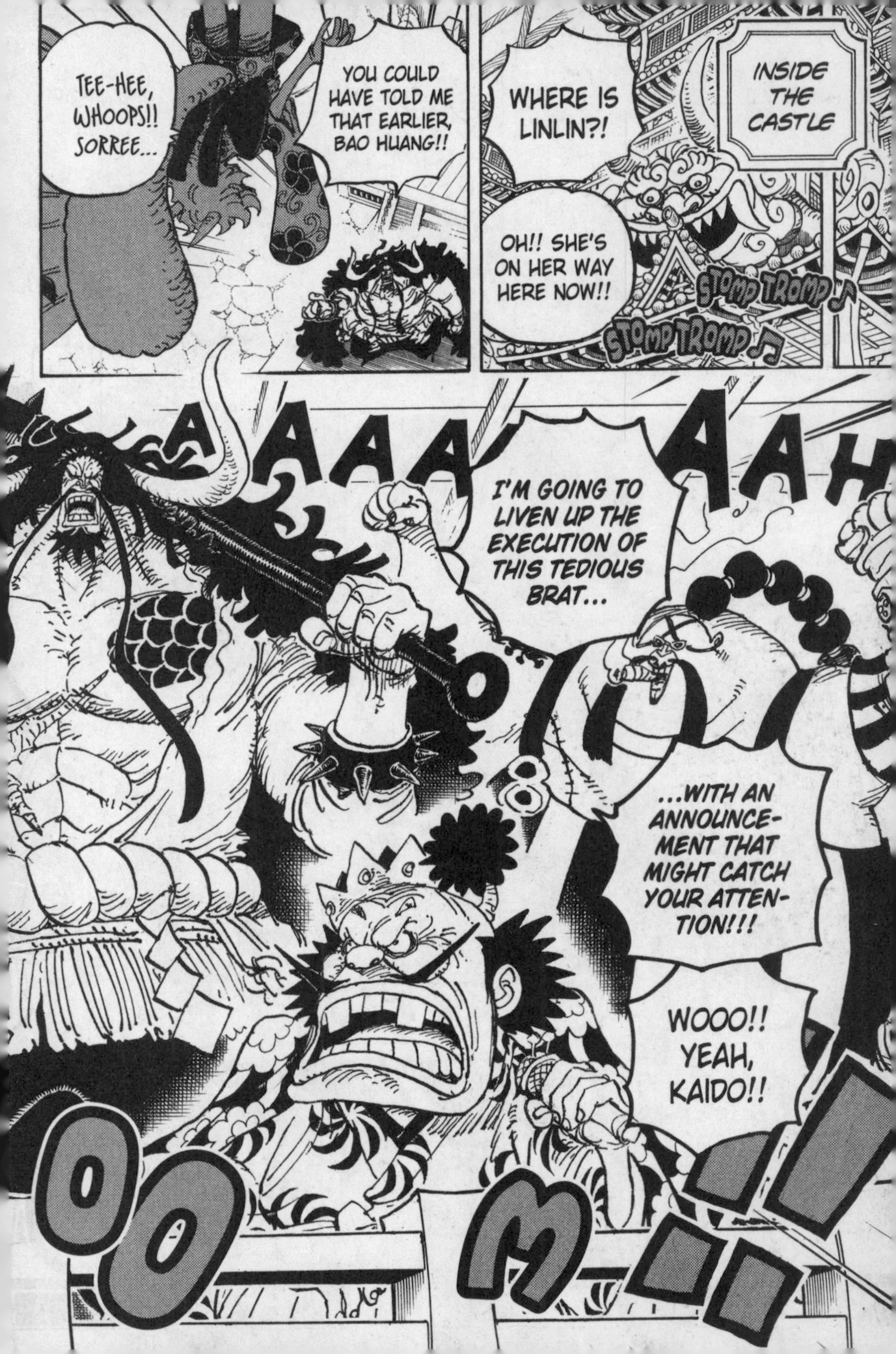
INSIDE THE CASTLE
WHERE IS LINLIN?!
OH!! SHE'S ON HER WAY HERE NOW!!
STOMP TROMP ♪
STOMP TROMP ♫
YOU COULD HAVE TOLD ME THAT EARLIER, BAO HUANG!!
TEE-HEE, WHOOPS!! SORREE...
AAAAAAH
I'M GOING TO LIVEN UP THE EXECUTION OF THIS TEDIOUS BRAT...
...WITH AN ANNOUNCEMENT THAT MIGHT CATCH YOUR ATTENTION!!!
WOOO!! YEAH, KAIDO!!
OOM!!

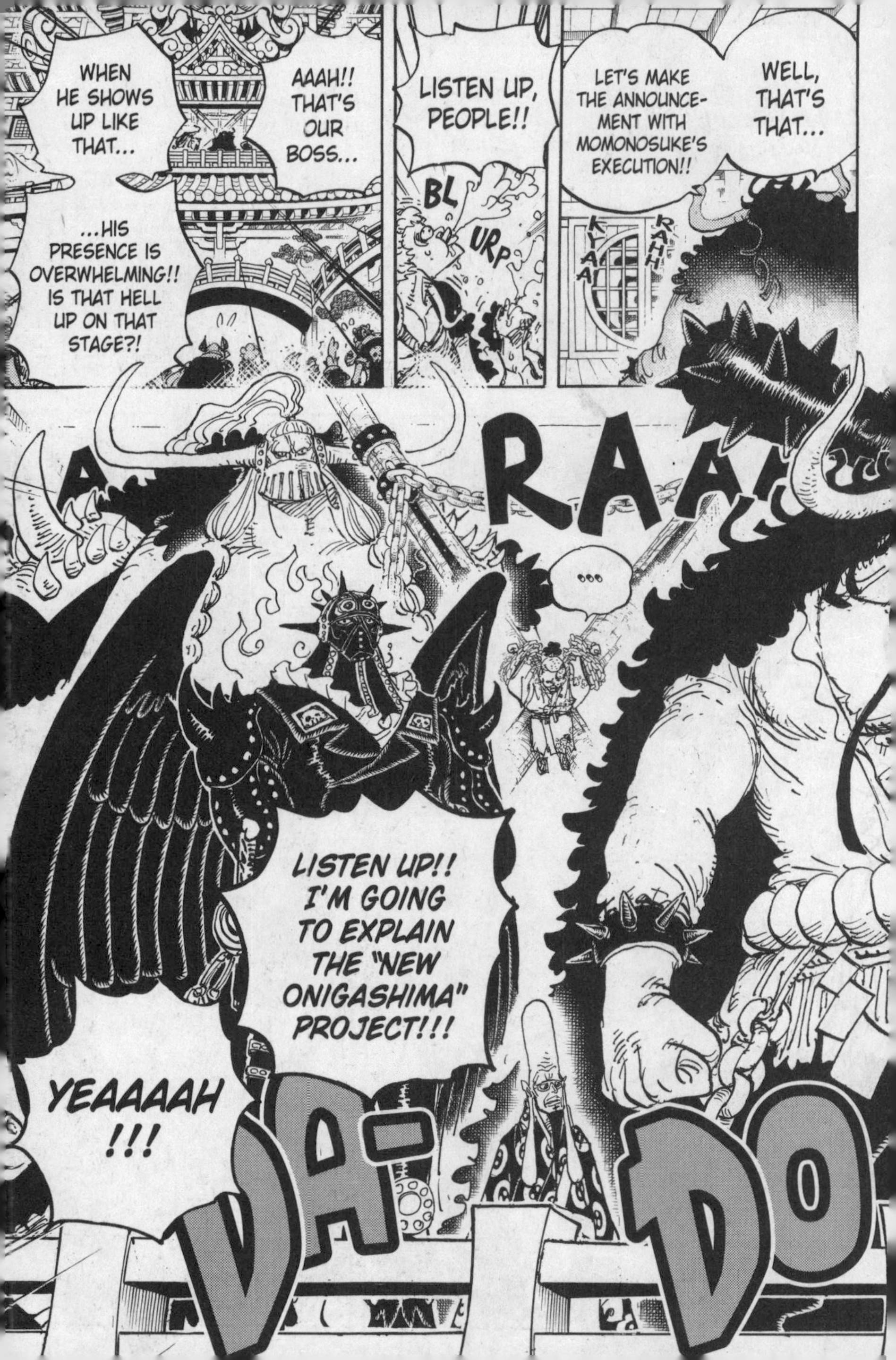
WELL, THAT'S THAT...
LET'S MAKE THE ANNOUNCEMENT WITH MOMONOSUKE'S EXECUTION!!
RAHH
KYAA
LISTEN UP, PEOPLE!!
BL
URP
AAAH!! THAT'S OUR BOSS...
WHEN HE SHOWS UP LIKE THAT...
...HIS PRESENCE IS OVERWHELMING!! IS THAT HELL UP ON THAT STAGE?!
RAA
A
...
LISTEN UP!! I'M GOING TO EXPLAIN THE "NEW ONIGASHIMA" PROJECT!!!
DO
DA-
YEAAAAH !!!

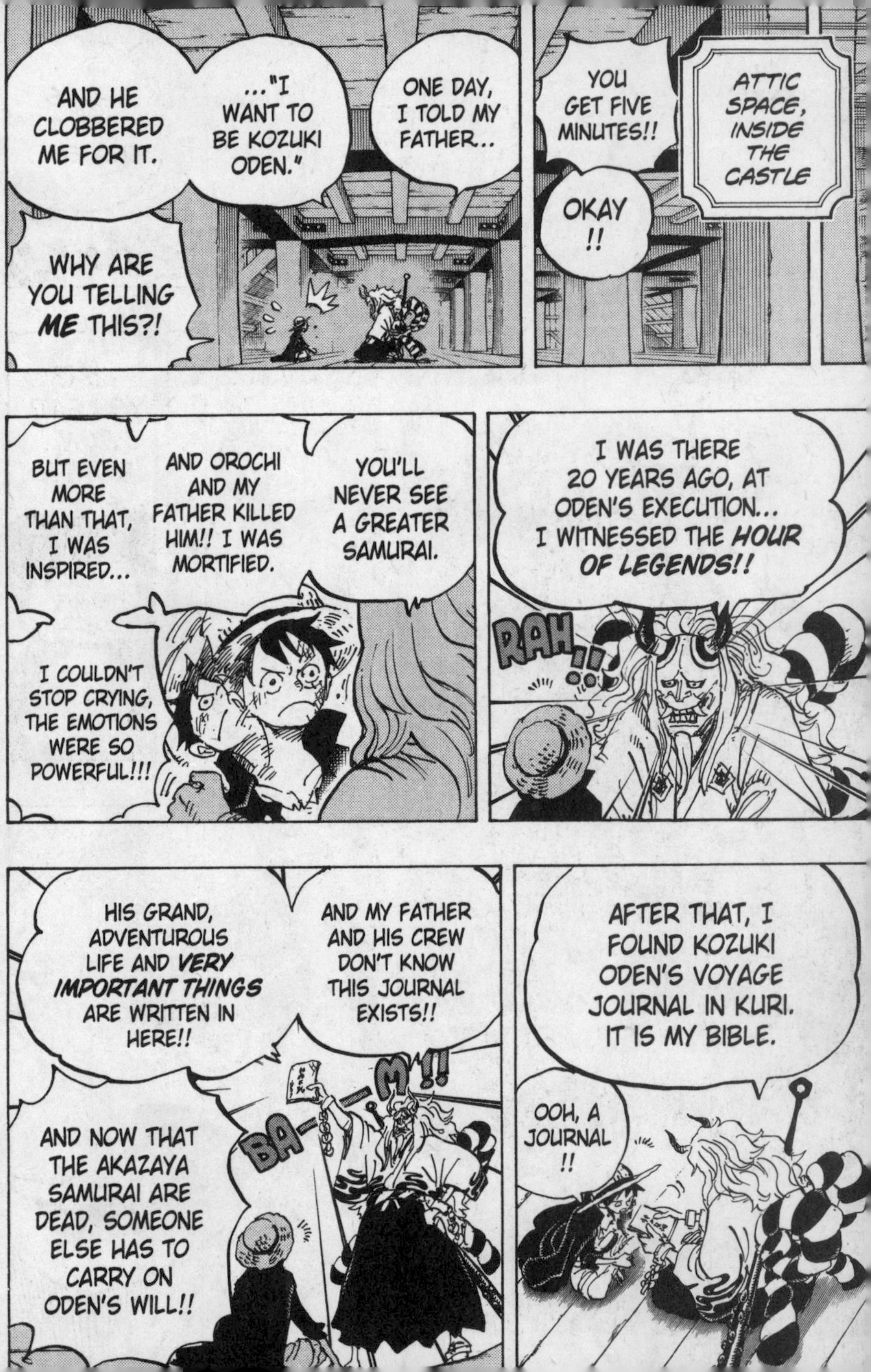
ATTIC SPACE, INSIDE THE CASTLE
YOU GET FIVE MINUTES!!
OKAY !!
ONE DAY, I TOLD MY FATHER...
..."I WANT TO BE KOZUKI ODEN."
AND HE CLOBBERED ME FOR IT.
WHY ARE YOU TELLING *ME* THIS?!
I WAS THERE 20 YEARS AGO, AT ODEN'S EXECUTION... I WITNESSED THE *HOUR OF LEGENDS!!*
RAH!!
YOU'LL NEVER SEE A GREATER SAMURAI.
AND OROCHI AND MY FATHER KILLED HIM!! I WAS MORTIFIED.
BUT EVEN MORE THAN THAT, I WAS INSPIRED...
I COULDN'T STOP CRYING, THE EMOTIONS WERE SO POWERFUL!!!
AFTER THAT, I FOUND KOZUKI ODEN'S VOYAGE JOURNAL IN KURI. IT IS MY BIBLE.
OOH, A JOURNAL !!
AND MY FATHER AND HIS CREW DON'T KNOW THIS JOURNAL EXISTS!!
HIS GRAND, ADVENTUROUS LIFE AND *VERY IMPORTANT THINGS* ARE WRITTEN IN HERE!!
BA--M!!
AND NOW THAT THE AKAZAYA SAMURAI ARE DEAD, SOMEONE ELSE HAS TO CARRY ON ODEN'S WILL!!

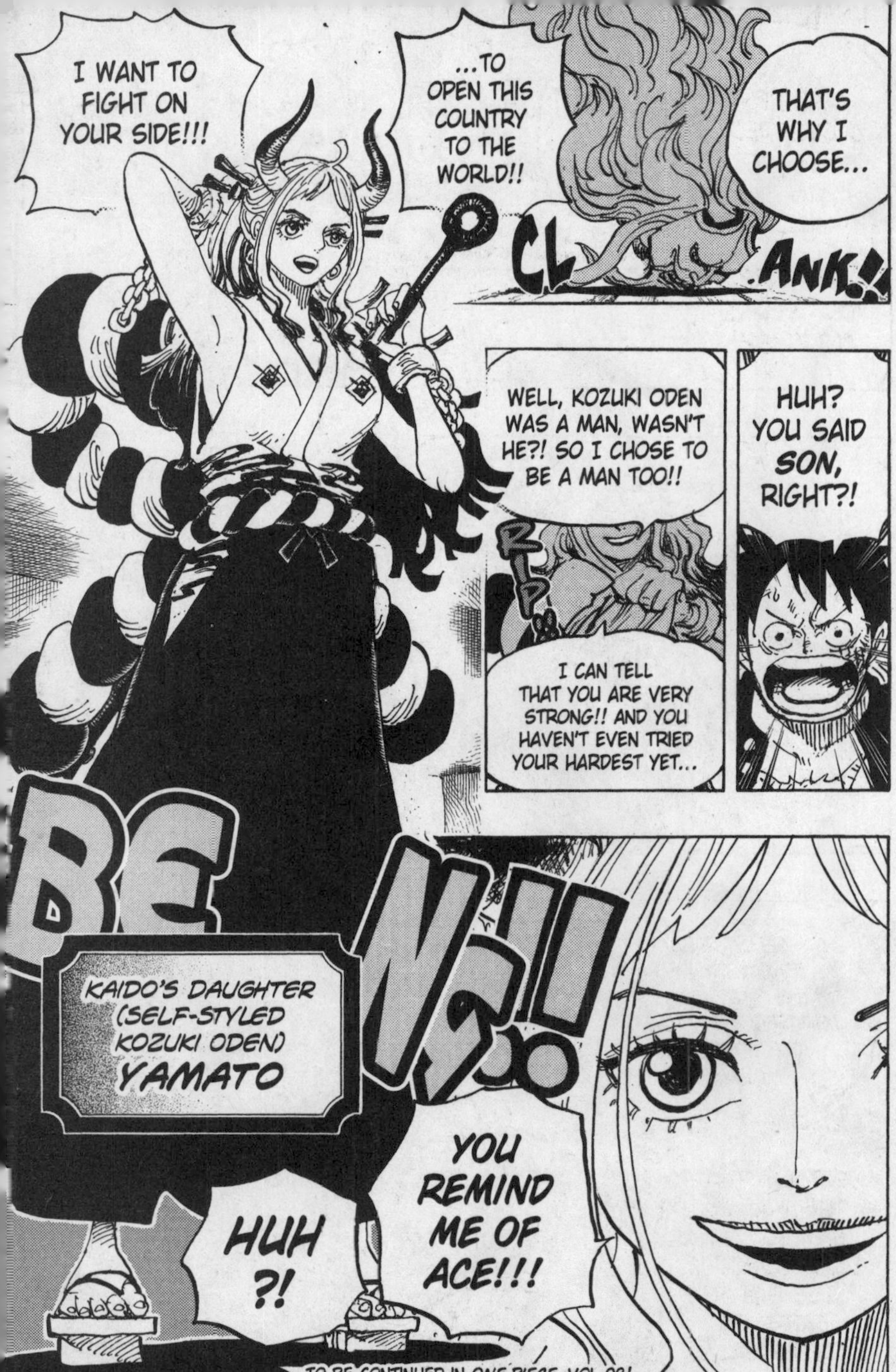
THAT'S WHY I CHOOSE...
CL...
...ANK!!
...TO OPEN THIS COUNTRY TO THE WORLD!!
I WANT TO FIGHT ON YOUR SIDE!!!
BEEN!!
KAIDO'S DAUGHTER (SELF-STYLED KOZUKI ODEN) YAMATO
HUH? YOU SAID SON, RIGHT?!
WELL, KOZUKI ODEN WAS A MAN, WASN'T HE?! SO I CHOSE TO BE A MAN TOO!!
RIP
I CAN TELL THAT YOU ARE VERY STRONG!! AND YOU HAVEN'T EVEN TRIED YOUR HARDEST YET...
YOU REMIND ME OF ACE!!!
HUH ?!

TO BE CONTINUED IN ONE PIECE, VOL 98!

COMING NEXT VOLUME:

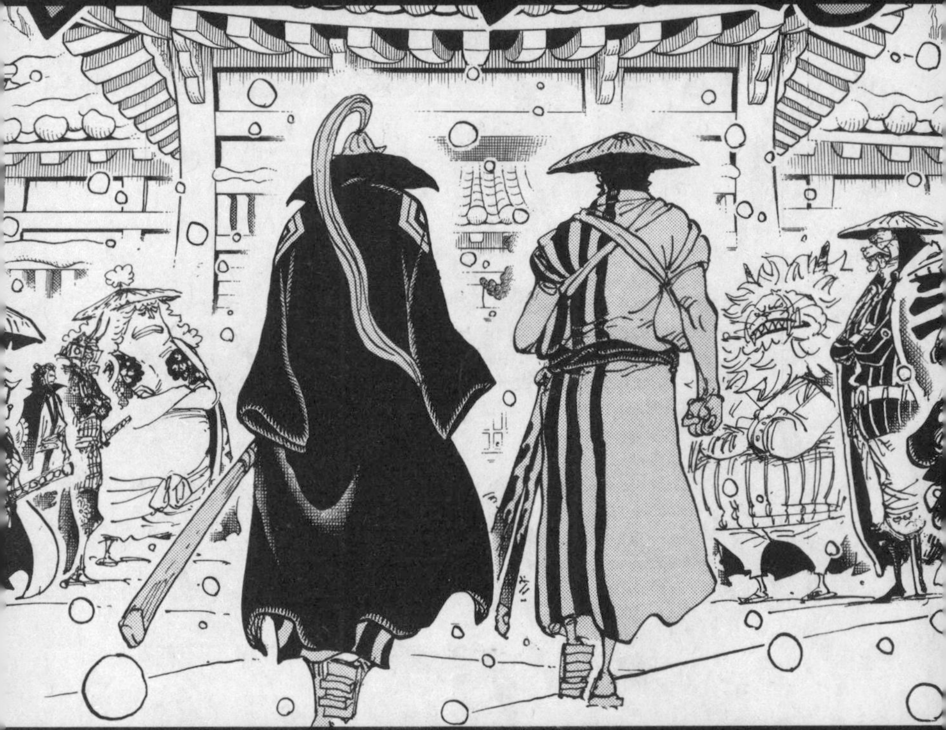

As the samurai face off against the one who betrayed them and Luffy makes a new ally, Kaido makes a move that threatens to upend everything! Get ready for the start of the greatest battle since the Paramount War!

ON SALE DECEMBER 2021!

尾田栄一郎

My eyesight is getting worse these days, and it's harder and harder to make out fine details, so if I don't put on my glasses before bed, I can't see what's happening in my dreams. Just kidding!! Hope you enjoyed volume 97!!

-Eiichiro Oda, 2020

E iichiro Oda began his manga career at the age of 17, when his one-shot cowboy manga **Wanted!** won second place in the coveted Tezuka manga awards. Oda went on to work as an assistant to some of the biggest manga artists in the industry, including Nobuhiro Watsuki, before winning the Hop Step Award for new artists. His pirate adventure **One Piece**, which debuted in **Weekly Shonen Jump** in 1997, quickly became one of the most popular manga in Japan.

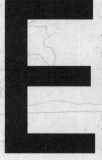

ONE PIECE VOL. 97
WANO PART 8

SHONEN JUMP Manga Edition

STORY AND ART BY EIICHIRO ODA

Translation/Stephen Paul
Touch-up Art & Lettering/Vanessa Satone
Design/Yukiko Whitley
Editor/Alexis Kirsch

Printed in Canada

Published by VIZ Media, LLC
P.O. Box 77010
San Francisco, CA 94107

10 9 8 7 6 5 4 3 2 1
First printing, August 2021

viz.com

DEMON SLAYER

KIMETSU NO YAIBA

Story and Art by
KOYOHARU GOTOUGE

In Taisho-era Japan, kindhearted Tanjiro Kamado makes a living selling charcoal. But his peaceful life is shattered when a demon slaughters his entire family. His little sister Nezuko is the only survivor, but she has been transformed into a demon herself! Tanjiro sets out on a dangerous journey to find a way to return his sister to normal and destroy the demon who ruined his life.

BORUTO
=NARUTO NEXT GENERATIONS=

CREATOR/SUPERVISOR **Masashi Kishimoto**
ART BY **Mikio Ikemoto** SCRIPT BY **Ukyo Kodachi**

A NEW GENERATION OF NINJA IS HERE!

Naruto was a young shinobi with an incorrigible
knack for mischief. He achieved his dream to
become the greatest ninja in his village, and
now his face sits atop the Hokage monument.
But this is not his story... A new generation
of ninja is ready to take the stage, led by
Naruto's own son, Boruto!

ASTRA
LOST IN SPACE

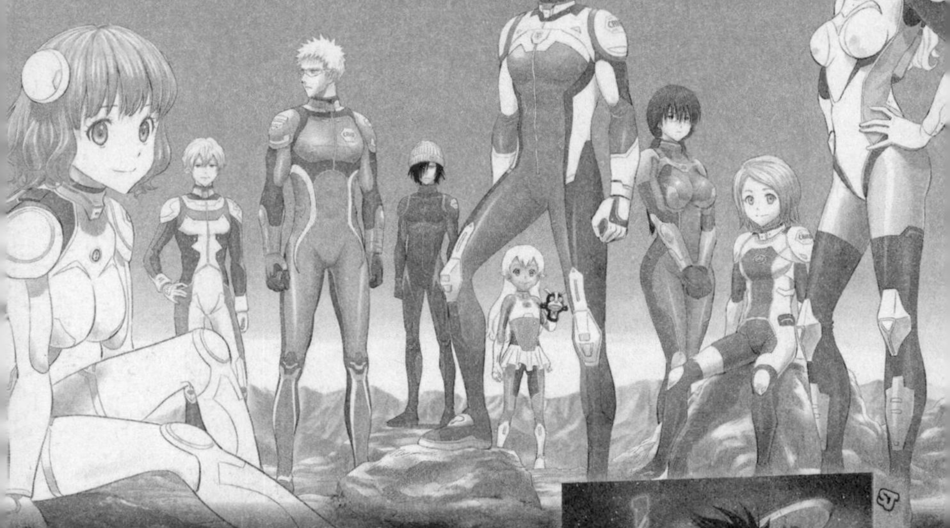

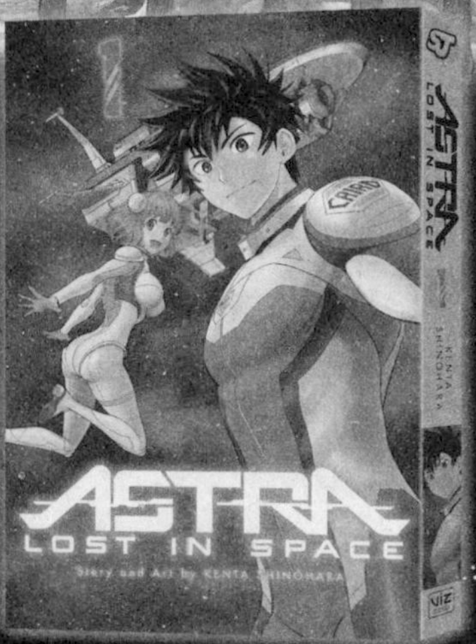
ASTRA
LOST IN SPACE
Story and Art by KENTA SHINOHARA
ASTRA LOST IN SPACE
KENTA SHINOHARA
VIZ

CAN EIGHT TEENAGERS FIND THEIR WAY HOME FROM 5,000 LIGHT-YEARS AWAY?

It's the year 2063, and interstellar space travel has become the norm. Eight students from Caird High School and one child set out on a routine planet camp excursion. While there, the students are mysteriously transported 5,000 light-years away to the middle of nowhere! Will they ever make it back home?!

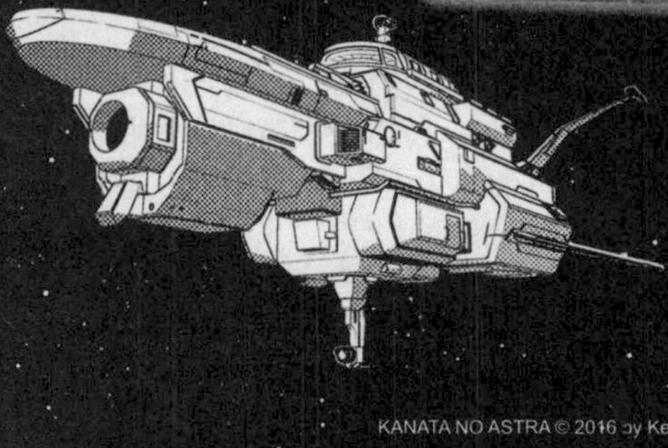

VIZ RATED T TEEN

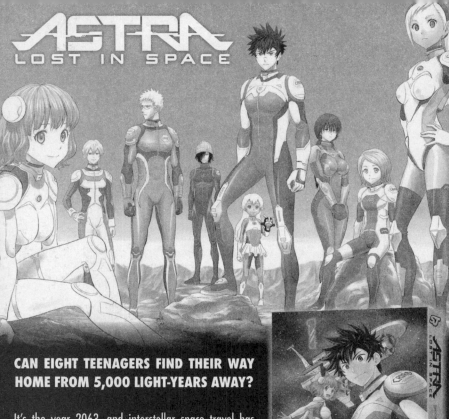

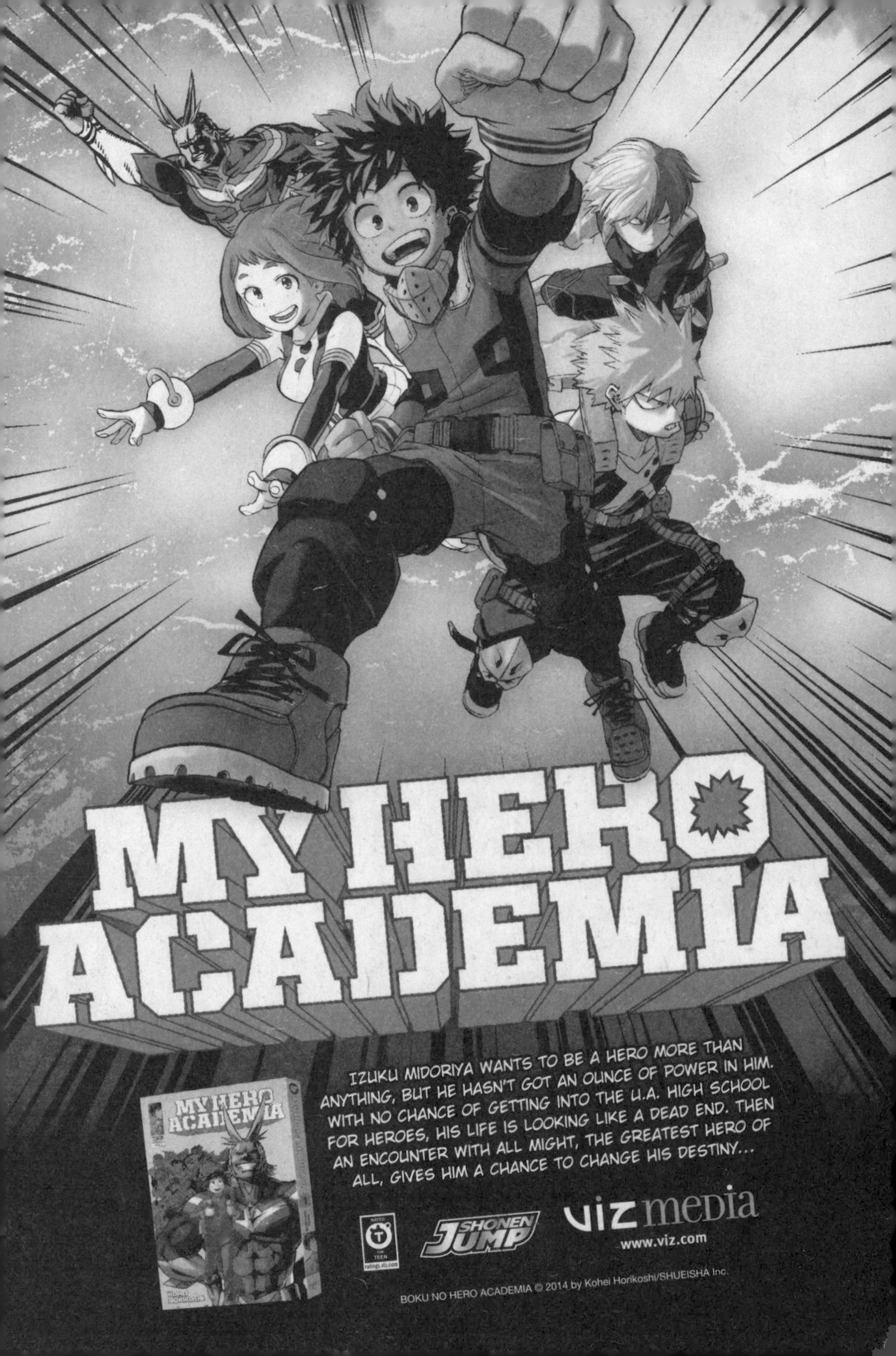
MY HERO ACADEMIA
IZUKU MIDORIYA WANTS TO BE A HERO MORE THAN ANYTHING, BUT HE HASN'T GOT AN OUNCE OF POWER IN HIM. WITH NO CHANCE OF GETTING INTO THE U.A. HIGH SCHOOL FOR HEROES, HIS LIFE IS LOOKING LIKE A DEAD END. THEN AN ENCOUNTER WITH ALL MIGHT, THE GREATEST HERO OF ALL, GIVES HIM A CHANCE TO CHANGE HIS DESTINY...
SHONEN JUMP
viz media
www.viz.com
BOKU NO HERO ACADEMIA © 2014 by Kohei Horikoshi/SHUEISHA Inc.

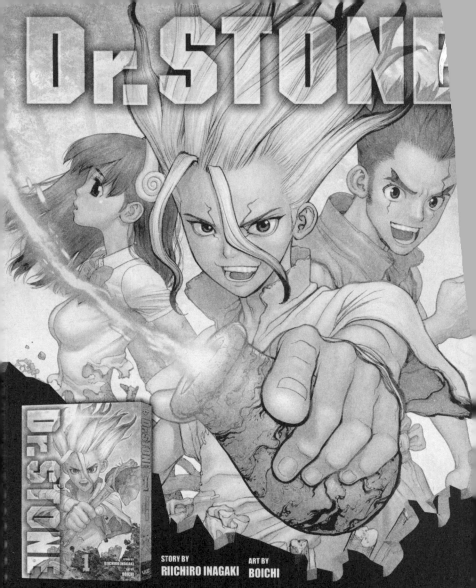

Dr. STONE

STORY BY
RIICHIRO INAGAKI

ART BY
BOICHI

One fateful day, all of humanity turned to stone. Many millennia later, Taiju frees himself from petrification and finds himself surrounded by statues. The situation looks grim—until he runs into his science-loving friend Senku! Together they plan to restart civilization with the power of science!

RATED
TEEN

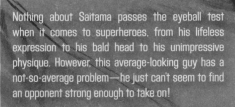

THE PROMISED NEVERLAND

STORY BY **KAIU SHIRAI**

ART BY **POSUKA DEMIZU**

Emma, Norman and Ray are the brightest
kids at the Grace Field House orphanage.
And under the care of the woman they refer
to as "Mom," all the kids have enjoyed a
comfortable life. Good food, clean clothes
and the perfect environment to learn—what
more could an orphan ask for? One day,
though, Emma and Norman uncover the
dark truth of the outside world they are
forbidden from seeing.

You're Reading in the Wrong Direction!!

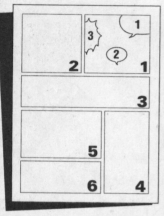

Whoops! Guess what? You're starting at the wrong end of the comic!

...It's true! In keeping with the original Japanese format, **One Piece** is meant to be read from right to left, starting in the upper-right corner.

Unlike English, which is read from left to right, Japanese is read from right to left, meaning that action, sound effects and word-balloon order are completely reversed...something which can make readers unfamiliar with Japanese feel pretty backwards themselves. For this reason, manga or Japanese comics published in the U.S. in English have sometimes been published "flopped"— that is, printed in exact reverse order, as though seen from the other side of a mirror.

By flopping pages, U.S. publishers can avoid confusing readers, but the compromise is not without its downside. For one thing, a character in a flopped manga series who once wore in the original Japanese version a T-shirt emblazoned with "M A Y" (as in "the merry month of") now wears one which reads "Y A M"! Additionally, many manga creators in Japan are themselves unhappy with the process, as some feel the mirror-imaging of their art skews their original intentions.

We are proud to bring you Eiichiro Oda's **One Piece** in the original unflopped format. For now, though, turn to the other side of the book and let the journey begin...!

—Editor